Bret Christian has been a newsman all his working life, beginning his career on the Perth *Daily News*, and working in Melbourne and Sydney before returning to Perth to write a daily newspaper column. He started his own suburban Post Newspapers group in 1977. His interest in police investigations gone wrong led him to unearthing many extraordinary injustices, some of which he helped put right. His successful book on the subject, *Presumed Guilty*, was published in 2013.

Bret lives by the sea at Cottesloe with his partner, Jane, where they have raised six children and more pets than they can count. He is still a reporter for his newspapers, and, compelled by his Viking roots, spends his spare time in and on the ocean.

Stalking Claremont

Bret Christian

ABC BOOKS

The ABC 'Wave' device is a trademark of the Australian Broadcasting Corporation and is used under licence by HarperCollins*Publishers* Australia.

HarperCollins*Publishers*
Australia • Brazil • Canada • France • Germany • Holland • India
Italy • Japan • Mexico • New Zealand • Poland • Spain • Sweden
Switzerland • United Kingdom • United States of America

HarperCollins acknowledges the Traditional Custodians of the land upon which we live and work, and pays respect to Elders past and present.

First published in Australia in 2021
This updated edition published in 2022
by HarperCollins*Publishers* Australia Pty Limited
Gadigal Country
Level 13, 201 Elizabeth Street, Sydney NSW 2000
ABN 36 009 913 517
harpercollins.com.au

A catalogue record for this book is available from the National Library of Australia.

ISBN 978 0 7333 4248 6 (paperback)
ISBN 978 1 4607 0902 3 (ebook)

Cover design by George Saad
Cover image: The Continental Hotel in the Perth suburb of Claremont, Western Australia by Tony McDonough/*The Sydney Morning Herald*
Map produced by flatEARTHmapping.com.au, contains data © Open Street Map contributors 2020
Typeset in Bembo Std by Kirby Jones
Printed and bound in Australia by McPherson's Printing Group

MIX
Paper from responsible sources
FSC www.fsc.org FSC® C001695

‘There is nothing more deceptive than
an obvious fact’

– Arthur Conan Doyle

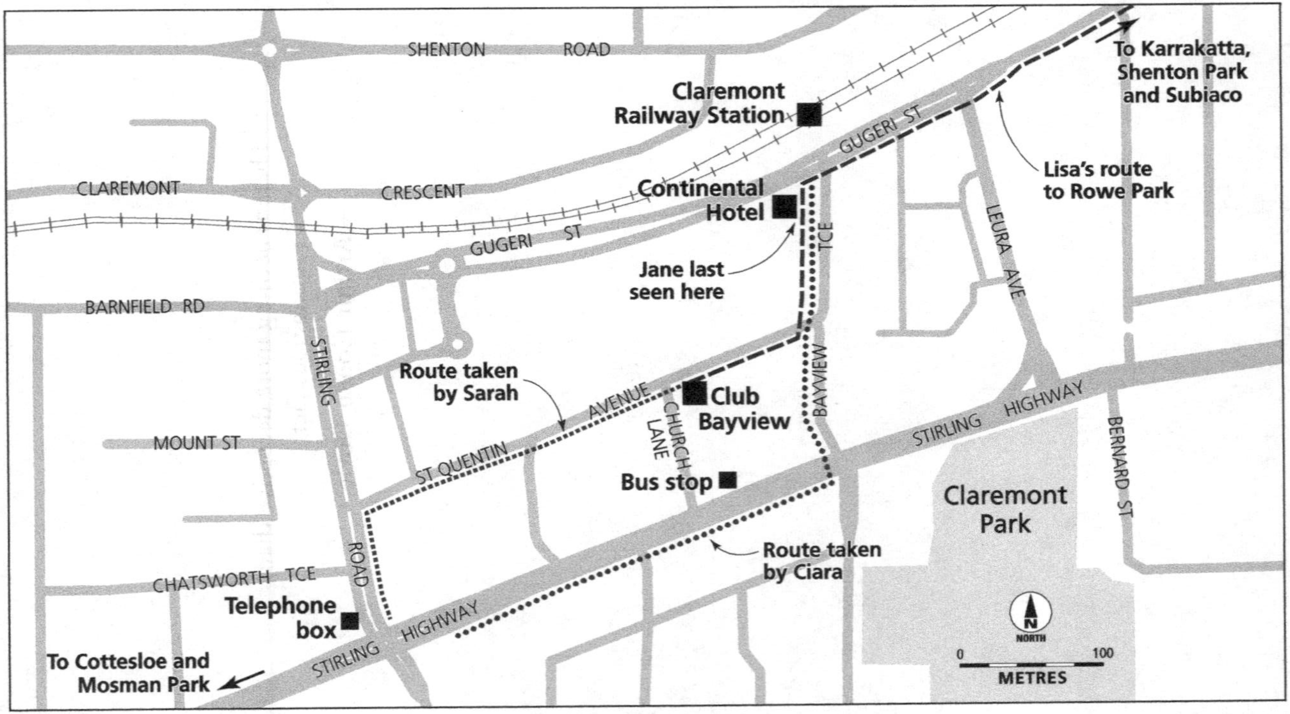
SHENTON ROAD
Claremont Railway Station
To Karrakatta, Shenton Park and Subiaco
CLAREMONT CRESCENT
GUGERI ST
Continental Hotel
Lisa's route to Rowe Park
Jane last seen here
TCE
LEURA AVE
BARNFIELD RD
STIRLING ROAD
Route taken by Sarah
AVENUE
Club Bayview
BAYVIEW
MOUNT ST
ST QUENTIN
CHURCH LANE
Bus stop
STIRLING HIGHWAY
BERNARD ST
Claremont Park
Route taken by Ciara
CHATSWORTH TCE
Telephone box
To Cottesloe and Mosman Park
NORTH
0
100
METRES

Contents

Preface

A bogeyman appeared to leap from the pages of our childhood storybooks in the late 1950s and early 1960s. Our family of seven discussed an all-too-real demon as we sat around the kitchen table in our home in Claremont. How could we protect ourselves?

As preteens, the prospect of sleeping with wooden clubs under beds was alien to our previously carefree childhoods in a safe suburb. Our nights were now haunted by a man who murdered strangers in their beds. Our parents drilled into us the importance of double-checking that all doors and windows were securely locked each night.

We breathed a sigh of relief with the rest of the community when the serial killer, Eric Edgar Cooke, a thirty-three-year-old truck driver and father of seven, was caught in 1963 and hanged in 1964 after committing eight murders. His trial judge called him a monster.

In coming decades, two more serial killers were to operate in the same areas Cooke had prowled.

At the age of twenty-eight, as the 1970s ended, I had left my job as a daily newspaper columnist to start a chain of suburban newspapers. At the centre of their circulation area was the then-sleepy urban village of Claremont, a short walk from our childhood home where we had shivered in fear. Claremont is an historic suburb situated halfway between Perth, the capital of Western Australia, and its Indian Ocean beaches.

The four editions of the *Post* newspapers serving Claremont and its surrounding suburbs thrived from their first print-runs. They reported the rhythm of local life, its people and its politics, its quirks and its crimes. On their pages in 1986, they recorded the evil work of a serial killer couple, David and Catherine Birnie. Some of their ghastly abductions of young women happened in the paper's catchment area, four of the couple's victims murdered. The Birnies eventually confessed to their crimes.

The smell of fear that Cooke and the Birnies engendered returned in the mid-1990s. Gradually, realisation was dawning that yet another serial killer was operating in Claremont.

The *Post*'s reporters documented each twist of what turned out to be an epic spanning decades, a saga both horrible and fascinating.

We lived and worked in the middle of it all, sharing the grief of those close to the murder victims alongside the fear of the great unknown. Someone was weaving a black, evil thread through the tapestry of our peaceful lives.

Was he a local, living among us, abducting and killing almost in plain sight?

After news spread of yet another abduction, with no news of the victim's fate, the *Post* reported on its front page on March 22, 1997: 'A businessman wept in public, his pain typical of our community's anguish. He does not know the victim. Men and women have lost sleep out of their concern for the young woman, her family and friends. They have felt unable to function properly, and talk of little else except the disappearance.'

Decades later, *Post* photographer Michelle Stanley reported: 'I can still see the faces of the police at the murder scene. They had failed to stop another murder. They looked mad, crazed. It was hideous.'

Nobody wanted to believe that such vile things could happen, but here they had. Someone was getting away with murder.

Could anyone ever rest easily again?

As a journalist who has told thousands of stories, the inside chronicle of the Claremont serial killings and their aftermath is like no other I have covered; it is crying out to be told. There is a public craving to know the truth about what really happened, in order to properly face the past and future.

In this strange story, what stands out is the culprit's incredible luck, the grief he caused, the bad luck of his innocent victims and that of the innocent men who fell under the gaze of police. Details that explain how someone got away with murder for so long have remained hidden until now.

What follows also is a letter of love to my community, which retains its pre-serial-killer, laid-back, carefree innocence, along with its charming *naïveté*, good humour, goodwill and trust, despite its bruised heart.

1

Graveyard

On a hot summer's Saturday night in February 1995, Lisa*, a lithe, athletic seventeen-year-old, borrowed her older sister's driver's licence for a night out that was to end, as usual, at a nighclub in the suburb of Claremont, close to where she lived. She had no qualms about being out alone late at night – Claremont was familiar turf, so benign during the day that even in the black of night young women felt sheltered, close to places where their mothers had taken them shopping. The village looked and felt safe, unlike the central-city nightclub strip of Northbridge, which had a reputation for alcohol- and drug-fuelled violence.

This protective ambience, tragically, provided a false sense of security.

In the early morning hours, Claremont's dark underbelly was exposed. More than twenty reports had been made to police in the late 1980s and early 1990s of young women in the vicinity of Claremont being followed and pounced on or groped indecently, of attempts made to rape them or drag them into cars.

In March 1990, a woman jogging in Kings Park was raped by a masked man – one of three almost identical attacks.

In one serious crime, a young woman walking home late at night had been stripped and almost raped in Rowe Park. Another who was orally raped in the same park in 1987

* Not her real name

had bitten hard into her attacker's penis, causing the rapist considerable blood loss and him to flee.

In 1992, two women were raped near Swanbourne railway station, one stop from Claremont, after walking home from central Claremont late at night.

In 1994, there had been two attempts to drag women from their cars at the traffic lights on Stirling Road near the railway subway.

On each occasion, the women fought back and escaped. Was this a series of unrelated perpetrators? Or, more chillingly, was it one person, honing his skills in the Claremont area, seeing what worked and what didn't?

As she made plans for her night out, Lisa was blissfully unaware of this spate of crimes. She knew her night would likely end at every young locals' favourite nightclub, Club Bayview. The club's allure was hypnotic and irresistible – pumping music, mirrorballs lighting the dancers, friends from local schools and neighbourhoods who socialised easily, and young men – all in the centre of a familiar neighbourhood just a long walk to her parents' upmarket home. Although underage, Lisa's model good looks and laminated card were green lights to the discriminating bouncers.

Lisa had already been to two parties that night – a work event, then a gathering at a friend's home in nearby Mosman Park – and to another nightclub in Northbridge. Her travelling party consisted of a group of friends in their teens and early twenties, all dancing and drinking.

Some time after 1 a.m., Lisa walked from Club Bayview with a male friend to wait outside the local hotel. The couple was trying to leapfrog other would-be taxi passengers to catch a lift to the young man's house in Gugeri Street.

The pair stood outside the hotel long after its midnight closing time. After a long, frustrating wait, and with no cab in sight, Lisa, fatefully, returned to the club, leaving her companion to walk home solo. At about 2 a.m., her other friends had left or were making their move home. Lisa later left Club Bayview alone on foot, heading towards her male friend's house. She had spent all her money and could not afford a taxi, even if she could find one.

She never reached his house.

Lisa's walk took her along well-lit Gugeri Street, which followed the railway line until the path veered through Rowe Park, the halfway point of her 700-metre journey. Overhead, the mature tree canopy fought back the street lighting.

Waiting unseen inside the gloom was a light-coloured van and its driver. Before Lisa knew it, someone much taller, heavier and stronger than her had jumped her from behind, pushing her flat on her front onto the grass. She froze. This lightning-quick attacker instantly rolled her over, sat on her stomach then shoved a cloth into her mouth. She had no chance to scream. The man again swiftly turned Lisa over and bound her hands very tightly behind her back. He lifted her 'like a baby' – as she would later recall – one hand behind her knees, the other in the middle of her back. His van, which Lisa could tell was a work van, was waiting in the park nearby, its cargo door open. Once in the back of the van, Lisa had her head shoved into a calico bag and her feet tied tightly together with the same cord that bound her wrists. She was hog-tied.

Lisa had glimpsed her attacker, a tall man with dark hair, wearing a light T-shirt and jeans, but mostly she kept her eyes shut, figuring she would have a better chance of survival if he thought he could not be described. He said very little the whole time – just 'shut up'.

Somehow, in the park, Lisa's sister's driver's licence had come out of the pocket of her denim vest – it either fell out or had been groped by alien fingers.

Lisa heard the driver put the van into gear and drive off. After what felt like an age, the van stopped. Lisa was dragged from it, the man holding her under her arms. Her black shoes came off. The attacker untied her feet, pulled the bag from her head and the gag from her mouth, groped her breasts, pulled down her shorts and underwear and twice raped her. She lay motionless during this life-changing ordeal, eyes tightly closed, playing dead or unconscious.

She believed the man would kill her when he was finished with her.

'I remember repeating, "Oh God, oh God, I can't believe this is happening,"' she later told police. 'It was very painful – I was trying to relax my body so it wouldn't hurt. I started to cry, but not loudly.'

She said the first rape lasted five to ten minutes. The man did not speak.

Her attacker picked Lisa up roughly then dumped her into bushes. He walked away, watched and waited, then seeing no movement, returned and retrieved her. He again lifted her, dumping her this time in the middle of much more dense scrub.

Terrified, she lay listening as the van started and drove away.

She waited five minutes then rolled to her knees. Seeing graves, she realised where she was: just a kilometre from Rowe Park, inside the even darker Karrakatta Cemetery, sentinel tombstones her only witnesses.

She had been left for dead, naked from the waist down, her hands still bound tightly together behind her back, barefoot and lonely among the dead, listening in fear for the van to come back.

With dawn about to break, the temperature had dropped to sixteen degrees Celsius. Summoning her considerable courage, tenacity and fitness honed from sports, Lisa struggled to her feet and started running barefoot in the early morning blackness, dodging tombstones.

'I just ran.'

She reached the boundary fence and kept running, embarrassment at her naked state preventing her from knocking on doors of the houses she passed. She shrugged her vest off her shoulders so it fell to her wrists, and pulled it low with her elbows.

Lisa headed towards the sole light she saw. It was the Salvation Army's aged-care unit, but when the automatic door opened, she saw nobody. Inside, she found a telephone and attempted to push its buttons with her chin. This valiant ploy appeared to have failed when the phone receiver fell. Amazingly, a nurse's voice came from the earpiece.

Lisa told her she had been raped but that she could not identify her location.

'Stay where you are and I'll call the police,' the voice said.

The call to police was recorded at 5:29 a.m., but by then Lisa had despaired, and kept moving.

Outside once again, the cord still cutting painfully into her wrists, Lisa spotted what she thought was her abductor's white van.

In terror, she ran across the road and hid behind a Range Rover. The van passed without slowing, but her heightened fear gave her extra strength. She managed to free one hand from its bindings.

Still in terror and shock, but thinking clearly, Lisa found a corner telephone booth and tried to call the phone of the house where she had been headed. No answer. She called her shocked father, reverse charges.

'Dad asked me if I was all right and I said no. I was crying – I said I'd been raped.'

Her father asked what she could see. She told him she could see the sign of the glamorously named Hollywood Hospital. He told her to head there and he would come.

Lisa crossed Monash Avenue, pulling her top low, her binding still flapping from her left wrist, presenting a distressing sight as she banged on the door.

'I became hysterical, crying out for help to get inside.'

A nurse let her in, wrapped her in her arms and then in hospital pants and a gown, cutting off the tight cord.

Police arrived, as did her parents, who found their teenage daughter 'extremely distressed and sobbing'.

Police from 79 Division, the overnight rapid-response squad, spoke with Lisa then drove her back to Rowe Park, and to the spot where she had been raped in the cemetery, calling forensic officers to bag samples. They recovered her shorts, underpants, shoes and the binding, as well as her hospital garments. Drag marks and disturbed ground in the sandy, leaf-littered graveyard were photographed.

Lisa was taken to 79 Division office in central Perth, where she told her story to specialist detective Theresa Kurtis, who noted that Lisa 'was visibly shaken and distressed'.

Detective Kurtis drove Lisa to the Sexual Assault Referral Centre (SARC) in nearby Subiaco. Twenty-five years later, the memory of that visit was still firmly imprinted on the examining physician, Dr Amanda Barnard.

'The things that make this particular case stick in my mind were the violent nature of assault by a stranger, the fact that she had been hooded and restrained, the extent and painfulness of her injuries and given the fact of her youth and that she was a virgin.'

Dr Barnard swabbed, carefully labelled and stored external and internal samples, noting plant matter tangled in Lisa's hair, and abrasions, tenderness and grazing to her breasts, arms and knees, plus painful marks to her wrists and ankles.

Removing sperm, sand and dust samples from Lisa, Dr Barnard noted that the examination was especially painful because of bruising, swelling and tenderness.

Lisa, traumatised, was driven home by Detective Kurtis to her distraught parents, who enveloped her with understanding and protection.

But the lost driver's licence added to her anguish. It showed her full home address and, as far as she knew, her attacker had it in his possession.

In a show of solidarity and support, her large group of

young friends, male and female, gathered at her home later that Sunday.

A wave of terror again hit the young woman, when a light-coloured van that she thought she recognised from the night before drove slowly past the property. Friends ran for their cars in hot pursuit, but failed to locate it.

*

At first, the scenario of abduction, binding, hooding and rape seemed to some Claremont detectives a fantasy, so far-fetched that some initially considered it a false report.

Her horrific tale and the results of tests on the exhibits recovered from the crime scenes were turned over to the suburban Claremont Criminal Investigation Branch and to a female officer, who took statements and organised more forensic tests.

Claremont detectives made public appeals for witnesses or for other information, interviewing people who had been at Club Bayview on the night, as well as taxi drivers, to check whether they had seen or heard anything unusual.

Suspicion landed on Lisa's male friends from her night out. The distraught young men agreed to be DNA swabbed, but scientists made no matches with the full samples left on Lisa by her attacker.

'No response to rape reports' read the headline in the *Post* newspapers nine days later.

Then, with no apparent leads after six weeks, at the end of the minimum write-off period, the local investigation was ended.

Lisa's case file was marked simply as 'Uncleared offence – no trace of offender'.

There were leads, however. Police had interviewed a security guard, Wayne Wookey, who had been on duty at Hollywood Hospital the night of the attack. At about the time the teenager had been driven to the cemetery, Wookey and a hospital cleaner had been smoking cigarettes at the front of the hospital, facing Monash Avenue.

Wookey had seen a technician's van, marked with the Telecom logo on the side, driving towards him with its headlights on high beam, coming from Williams Road, the location of the phone box Lisa had used to call her father. The two men saw the van turn in front of them and drive slowly past the hospital. Wookey described a distinctive cut-away design of the vehicle's front bodywork. This description matched that of the Mitsubishi L300 vans issued to Telecom technicians at the time.

When local detectives took statements from this guard and others at the hospital, they made one glaring error.

Doorknocks can be a rich mine for digging up witnesses and other information. Had someone been returning home from a night out and seen or heard something? Perhaps a baby had woken a parent, or an insomniac smoker had been having a late-night puff on a front veranda of one of the beautiful Federation-era homes facing Rowe Park.

The detectives never found out, because they neither visited nor knocked on the doors of any of the fifteen houses overlooking Rowe Park. Had they done so, they may have uncovered a vital clue.

*

Attacks on young women, as well as attempted abductions, during either the day or night, continued to plague Claremont and surrounding suburbs.

In March, just a month after Lisa's abduction and rape, terrified teenagers had been attacked by a man in a Subiaco street, while another teenage girl had been indecently assaulted at a nearby railway station.

'You're coming with me. You know you want me,' said

the predator. The girl broke free and ran, seeking safety at a crowded intersection.

In April, a woman named Ruth told *Post* reporters of being stranded late one night. A taxi she had called did not show, though the company had given her a priority number.

'Nightclub patron stalked' read the headline in the *Post* on April 18, 1995, the article recording the ordeal of the twenty-four-year-old woman who had hidden from a male driver who was persistently hounding her. He had followed her down a driveway near Eric Street, Cottesloe. She was rescued after running to a group of strangers walking on Stirling Highway. That report joined the dots with what had happened to Lisa at Karrakatta, and was one of many similar, worrying incidents reported that year.

In September 1995, a local mother sharing her bed with her four-year-old daughter was raped by an intruder who broke into the house at 3 a.m.

Two teenaged girls were attacked as they walked home from high school in October.

In December, a woman washing dishes looked up to see a flasher outside her kitchen window.

Early on a Sunday morning in early December 1995, nine months after the attack on Lisa, Katrina Jones was walking alone on Stirling Highway, upset after a fight with her boyfriend. At about 2:30 a.m., a driver did a U-turn and stopped to offer her a lift in his white van. The driver was described as good looking and aged in his early twenties. Jones accepted. The man said he was a technician with Telstra and that he was heading for Cottesloe beach looking for 'damsels in distress' like her. The polite driver duly drove her fifteen kilometres to where her car was parked in Perth's northern suburbs. When Jones got out, the driver followed, grabbing her and trying to kiss her.

'No, because I will drop you.' She told him she was a blue belt in taekwondo, and he backed off.

A resident of the next parallel street to Stirling Road, Davies Road, had called the *Post* after the attack on Lisa in 1995 to report that, in the early hours of a Sunday morning, a naked young woman had knocked on her door, frantically asking for help. The young woman said she had been driven to a dark secluded spot in nearby Claremont Golf Course in what she thought was a taxi. She had been stripped naked by the driver but escaped. The householder said police had attended when called, but the newspaper's attempts to confirm details with local police were unsuccessful.

Curious sightings of a telco vehicle were also made in Karrakatta Cemetery. Almost a year after Lisa's abduction, a Telecom or Telstra van was seen parked inside the cemetery four or five times, between 6 p.m. and 7 p.m., with a man sitting inside. It was near the intersection of Smythe Road and Monash Avenue, where Hollywood Hospital is located.

Another sighting was in Stirling Highway, near Stirling Road, on the fringe of Claremont's central business district.

Different descriptions of the driver were given, but despite the vagaries of vision in the early morning darkness, they were close enough to match one man.

2
Sarah

Two hours after midnight on January 26, 1996, two weeks short of the first anniversary of Lisa's abduction and rape, another young woman's fun night on the town took a sinister turn.

Country-born Sarah Spiers was bubbly and friendly, always up for a night out. She came from a close and loving family. Father Don was a tough businessman who ran a team of sheep shearers from Darkan, two and a half hours south of Perth, where Sarah had attended primary school. For high school, Don and Carol Spiers sent their elder daughter Amanda and then Sarah to board at a Catholic private school, Iona Presentation College in Mosman Park, near Claremont. At age eighteen, Sarah was an attractive, polite and popular young woman with a ready smile, straight blonde hair and green eyes. She attended business college after leaving school in Year 12 and quickly found a job as a receptionist with BSD Consultants in Subiaco. On weekends, Sarah loved to socialise at pubs and clubs, frequenting Cottesloe and Claremont, where she knew plenty of young women and men. She had no steady boyfriend.

Don Spiers was a cautious man, and felt he and Carol had done everything possible to ensure their daughters were safe in the city. He had looked around for a safe area to buy a home for them, before he settled on an apartment in South Perth, ensuring that Sarah had her own transport.

Amanda and Sarah were best friends who had shared everything. Almost daily, Sarah had spoken to her mother in Darkan.

Friday, January 26, 1996 was the Australia Day holiday. Sarah and some friends had prepared a picnic to enjoy the warm summer evening while they listened to a live performance in Kings Park by singer Wendy Matthews, but they arrived too late for the show. After their picnic, they caught a taxi to Cottesloe's Ocean Beach Hotel, arriving at about 8 p.m., enjoying the company and a few drinks. At midnight, Amanda had picked up Sarah and three friends, as arranged, and dropped them in Church Lane, next to Club Bayview, at 12:15 a.m. Sarah leaned into the car and gave her big sister a hug and a kiss, before the friends headed for the line of teens and twenty-somethings waiting to get into club. After a half-hour wait, they were inside, Sarah dancing, laughing with friends and enjoying a few more drinks.

At about 1:30 a.m., Sarah told Emma Wates, a close friend she had met at school, that she was leaving. Emma tried to persuade Sarah to stay on with her and her friends, but Sarah said she was going to get a taxi and walked alone down the stairs of the club. She politely chatted with two doormen whom she knew, then walked west.

As Sarah headed down the increasingly lonely end of St Quentin Avenue, turning left into Stirling Road, the bright lights quickly faded. Ahead in the distance, the fluoro light in the phone booth, around 500 metres from the club, cast only a small pool of light in the darkness.

Transport home from Claremont in the early hours of the morning was always a bugbear. From bitter experience of booked cabs that did not turn up, nightclubbers had learned that a taxi called by payphone to a location far from the club would be less likely to scoop up a rival hail while on its way to the phone booking. Experienced clubbers called this practice leap-frogging. Like many revellers who could not find rides home, Sarah figured that, the further she walked from the club, the more likely she was to get a cab.

At 2:06 a.m., Sarah picked up the handset, calling Swan Taxis. In the chilling call recording, her young voice can be heard giving her last name, Spiers, to the operator, and her destination, Mosman Park, although she lived in South Perth, in the opposite direction. Sarah's friends later speculated she had taken up an offer made by a girlfriend to sleep the night in Mosman Park, because it was a far cheaper cab ride than to South Perth.

The cab driver who responded to Sarah's taxi call, Jaroslav Krupnik, was in Stirling Highway, Cottesloe, only two minutes from her location. He continued along Stirling Highway straight towards Claremont but, when he reached the big traffic light-controlled intersection with Stirling Road, at 2:09 a.m., he did not see his fare waiting. He saw nobody. He decided to continue on, driving around the block to try his luck outside Club Bayview, where he quickly landed another fare, two young women and a man.

Claremont is an intimate place. One of the young women inside Krupnik's cab was Chelsea Palmer, who knew Sarah as a casual acquaintance. Though their journey out of central Claremont took them again past the phone box where Sarah had made her last call, those in the cab saw no sign of her. A witness who walked by at 2:15 a.m. also did not see another person.

Police appealed for information, and three young men who had been in a car travelling in Stirling Road towards Stirling Highway came forward. They told police that when their car was stopped at the red light, they had seen a young woman matching Sarah's description waiting outside a gym, BC The Body Club, at the intersection. The teen had crossed Stirling Road from the payphone and was leaning on a Telstra bollard.

Front-seat passenger Mark Laidman noticed that the young woman was very attractive, his description of her closely fitting that of Sarah. He had also noticed the headlights of a car behind theirs, which was also approaching the highway. It was a short distance behind them, and to their left in the kerbside lane next to Sarah. Laidman turned to look at the car but could provide police with only the vaguest description. He said that, viewed from the front, he thought the car looked like a Mazda 808, a car with square headlights.

After the traffic lights changed to green and the front car turned right into Stirling Highway, Laidman looked back again and noticed that the car behind had not followed theirs through the intersection. One of the men even suggested turning back to check that the girl was safe, but they did not follow up this idea.

From this account, it was very likely that in the few seconds after the traffic lights to Stirling Highway changed to green and the young men's car moved off, the car behind them remained stopped, and Sarah wound up inside that vehicle, abducted. All inside the two- to three-minute window of time before the taxi she called was due to arrive.

*

Amanda woke on Sunday morning and saw Sarah's bed had not been slept in. That was no great cause for alarm. But Sarah also did not turn up for a family function later that day.

Then the conscientious employee did not arrive at work on the Monday morning for her receptionist job at BSD. She was reliable and respectful, and would not have missed work without calling in. Sarah's bank account had not been touched since Friday night.

Amanda was particularly alarmed because she was about to turn twenty-one and Sarah had been excited for her, preparing for the party. Sarah simply would not have disappeared without saying a word or attempting contact. Amanda, her heart heavy with dread, walked into South Perth police station at 9:20 a.m. and reported her little sister missing. Before leaving home, she called her father, Don Spiers.

In response to Amanda's frantic call, Don and Carol Spiers made an emotional three-hour dash by car to Perth to start a search, talk to police and appeal to the public for help.

For those people closest to Sarah, an excruciating, agonising process began. They knew instantly that this was no routine missing person case.

'She is one of the most together and responsible people out of all of us,' said distraught nineteen-year-old friend Rebecca Giglia. 'None of us can quite believe this has happened.'

For for the rest of Sarah's community, the truth dawned even more slowly, many clinging to hope that she was just taking some time out or that she had met somebody and had neglected to call home.

Police treated Sarah as one of many missing persons reported, and began to build a profile of Sarah's movements before and after leaving the club, putting out a plea for witnesses. Detectives from the Major Crime Squad interviewed witnesses at the club – somebody must have seen Sarah after she had spent her time at the club drinking, dancing and chatting happily. They also talked to taxi drivers who might have picked her up.

Police circulated Sarah's description: 160 centimetres tall (5'4"), shoulder-length blonde hair, green eyes, medium build, fair complexion, wearing a light-coloured T-shirt, Portman's beige tailored shorts and beige suede shoes, and carrying a black denim jacket. A metal yellow key ring shaped like a sunflower held her house key.

Missing persons officers began knocking on doors in Claremont and Mosman Park, asking if anyone had seen Sarah. It was three weeks before police officers began to doorknock homes across the road from the point where Sarah had last been seen.

Her desperate friends wasted no time. They printed and distributed 8000 posters through Claremont and the surrounding suburbs, and in the city.

A flood of information, some very specific but much of it useless and time-consuming, poured into police from frantic members of the public.

Days passed and still no news. Don, Carol and Amanda took turns to sit by the phone at the sisters' apartment, willing the phone to ring with even a scrap of useful information.

'Every hour that passes creates more concern,' said police acting Detective Inspector Paul Ferguson, who was in charge of what he now feared was a homicide inquiry.

Chillingly, police had received calls from four people in Mosman Park, who reported being woken by a woman's desperate, blood-curdling, high-pitched screams between 2:30 a.m. and 3 a.m. on Saturday, about the time Sarah would have arrived there had she been picked up from Claremont about 2 a.m. It was only a short distance from Sarah's old school and where her friends lived.

One of those witnesses was motor mechanic Wayne Stewart. 'It was like a person in trouble – something hurting her or scared her,' he said. 'It was very distressing.'

He was able to give a partial description of a car parked facing the wrong way next to a phone box in Monument Street, about one hundred metres from his balcony. It was a light-coloured station wagon. The wagon was not a taxi. From its wrap-around tail-lights, Wayne believed the car was a Toyota Corolla. He thought there were two occupants. He heard a woman scream very loudly then two doors slam in quick succession. Wayne's fiancée saw the car drive off.

Judith Borrett, who lived further away, had her bedroom window open on the quiet, still night. At about 3 a.m., she heard 'desperate, blood-curdling, terrible, terrible, screams, something you would never forget'. She said they were three high-pitched female screams, very close together, stopping suddenly.

'Horrific' screams at identical intervals were also reported by Robyn Peters, a woman who lived a kilometre away from where the car was spotted. 'Then it went completely silent.' She said the screams woke her at about 2:30 a.m., and appeared to be coming from the park across the road, but the area was very 'echoey'.

Detectives recorded the information in a file that became known as the 'Scream Serials'. They decided not to share any of this information with the public, nor did they doorknock the houses that were closer to the car.

*

Even well before Lisa was abducted and Sarah disappeared, strange tales of after-midnight transport incidents around Claremont's party district had abounded, stories some thought were just folk tales, but which now took on a sinister significance, adding to a sense of both dread and intrigue.

Local lore spoke of hidden, random, chaotic and at times frightening encounters experienced by young women who could not find taxis. Reports had been made of different men cruising in cars through the streets of Claremont late at night, offering lifts to strangers: stranded clubbers, male and female, some alone and the worse for wear. Some accepted, some were attacked, and almost all attacks were unreported in the news media.

Most of the drivers had good intentions, but at least one was far from a good Samaritan. Police had some descriptions of drivers and their vehicles, acting Detective Inspector Paul Ferguson said, but these were being kept confidential to see if they could be eliminated from suspicion.

The shock of Sarah's disappearance now encouraged some young people who had been offered lifts to come forward with their stories.

'Club girl tells of crawler' was the *Post*'s headline three weeks after Sarah's last night out. A nineteen-year-old woman told the newspaper how she and her friends had twice been given lifts in a private car to the nearby suburb of Dalkeith, most recently at 3:30 a.m. On their second trip, the passengers recognised the same driver. Only then had they become frightened. The young woman said, 'I thought it was a bit creepy. I realised I was stupid to do it.' She said the driver had been quite pleasant. 'He doesn't talk much – he mumbles. It seems he is a bit of a loner and he has nothing better to do on a Saturday night than picking up hitch-hikers for a bit of conversation. He just asked how the night had been.'

She said she had seen him driving on Stirling Highway at different times of the night and in the early mornings. She and her friends had hidden in a side street and watched him drive past multiple times, leading them to report their sightings to police investigating Sarah's disappearance.

Police told the *Post* that they had details of not one but several drivers who had offered free lifts to girls who had left Club Bayview.

Then twenty-year-old Marnie McKenzie, from Cottesloe, told police that, ninety minutes before Sarah had disappeared, Marnie had been offered a lift while walking along that same street, Stirling Road.

Her male companion had been lagging behind, so she appeared to be alone. 'No, thanks,' she had said, tilting down her head as she kept walking.

Lore of another kind surfaced: stories of fake taxis – cars without taxi markings or with fake markings – that picked up passengers and charged unmetered fares. Clubbers had hailed these cars without a second thought, often in a haze of alcohol, unaware that they carried no cab company radios nor meters. Some of their passengers, interviewed by *Post* reporters, described these rides, their drivers and vehicles in convincing detail.

Among the most interesting of all the calls that poured into police was one from a young woman, Julie-Anne Johnson. She had been waiting for a taxi at a bus stop in Stirling Highway, in the early hours of Sunday morning, just twenty-five hours after Sarah vanished. A white 1992 to 1996 Toyota Camry, a car with square headlights, pulled into the bus bay. The driver leered at her through the open window without speaking. He was there for so long, more than ten minutes, that she walked off. The car abruptly left. She saw that the vehicle had a Telstra sticker on the door. Her report went into the file, where it remained, unheeded, for months.

Around this time, press reports and some more junior investigating officers occasionally linked Sarah Spiers' disappearance to the Karrakatta Cemetery abduction and sexual assault. But the focus on fake taxis had taken attention away from Lisa's abduction a year earlier. It was argued that women who disappeared after searching for taxis were a far cry from the case of the unsuspecting seventeen-year-old who had been snatched and grabbed by a prepared predator in a dark park, then gagged, tied up with a bag thrust over her head, and driven off in a commercial van. Rowe Park was a blitz attack. It was assumed that Sarah Spiers had willingly accepted a lift, with whatever belief she had held about the car she had entered.

But not all serial killers use the same methods, all the time.

*

On February 8, Club Bayview expressed 'deep concern', offering a $10,000 reward for information. Its management had earlier wished for Sarah's safe return and said that 'in an increasingly dangerous world the state government needs to reconsider their taxi control, drink driving and public transport policies in order that party-goers may find a safe route home'.

The club also announced a courtesy bus for patrons, and pointed out that the club had a free taxi phone. Perhaps they were concerned that Sarah's disappearance would discourage people from patronising the venue. They need not have worried. In central Claremont's clubland, the party rolled on.

Fast-fading memories, coupled with the drive for a fun-fuelled night out, may explain why Sarah's disappearance and Lisa's attack in the cemetery had not much registered with clubbers, or at least had not modified their behaviour.

'What missing girl?' one asked *Post* reporter Nelli Noakes, who was on a late-night assignment in Claremont, two weeks after Sarah vanished. Noakes was there because a re-enactment of Sarah's last walk was being filmed for television in an attempt to draw out witnesses.

Partying clubbers wolf-whistled and catcalled at Amanda and the amateur actors, as the producers asked for second and third takes.

'What sort of ad is this? Just get on with it,' one called out to Sarah's friend Jasmine Glatz, who had bravely dressed as Sarah to act out her missing friend's last known movements.

Just weeks after Sarah vanished, local stalwart Jim Larkin told the *Post* why he was alarmed at what he saw from his Steamin' Screamin' hot dog van, parked outside Club Bayview most nights and well into the mornings.

Along with dispensing sausages in buns to hungry clubbers, Larkin kept a paternal eye on his customers, many the worse for wear after a night out drinking.

He remembered Sarah, remarking that she was thin, despite her liking for his cheese and onion rolls.

On the night she disappeared, Larkin had closed up early because, by 2 a.m., the crowds had been too drunk for him to handle, he said.

'The girls around here just don't seem worried about what could happen to them. Most nights when I drive home, they were hitching lifts along the highway,' he said then. 'They still do.'

3
Taxi!

On Saturday, February 3, 1996, a week after Sarah Spiers vanished, a Swan Taxis driver drove the mayor of Claremont, Peter Weygers, in a wide circle through Perth's western suburbs, then across the Swan River to South Perth, to a point close to where Sarah had lived.

At the wheel was Steven Ross, aged thirty-eight, who was showing Weygers what he believed had been the route of Sarah Spiers' last ride. He believed he had picked up Sarah, and her killer, the night she vanished.

Both were very unusual men, in very different ways.

Weygers was then fifty-two, a tall, strongly built, fast-talking, highly intelligent man with a finely tuned sense of justice. In the pursuit of it, he was dogged, fearless and, some might say, reckless.

His father, Hans Weygers, was a strict Dutchman from colonial Indonesia. When he caught Peter stealing a penny, Hans heated the coin on the kitchen stove then clasped his son's hand around it.

Hans had married Linda Mews, who was from a Claremont boatbuilding family directly descended from the west coast's first-fleeters, free settlers from Great Britain. Hans was a boat person of a different kind. Caught by the invading Japanese in 1942, he escaped to Australia in a small open boat, returning to the Celebes, now Sulawesi, at the war's end in 1945.

In 1949, Hans and Peter, then five, were captured by angry local freedom fighters rising against their Dutch colonial masters. Father and son were made to stand against a wall while a firing squad prepared to execute them both.

In English, little Peter called out, 'What's happening, Daddy?'

Suddenly, a cry came from the shooters, 'They're English – don't shoot them!'

The family was deported to Australia.

Hans used his forestry and agricultural skills to establish a tropical fruit plantation in Carnarvon, on the northwest coast, where he gave young Peter a rifle and the keys to a farm truck at the age of ten.

'I was a boy from the bush – a free-range kid who had shot snakes and goannas, rabbits, ducks and kangaroos – even shot fish – for food,' said Weygers. 'Then I was sent to board at school in Claremont for years eleven and twelve – caged in a boarders' dormitory at Christ Church.'

The school's temporary marketing slogan, 'Building Good Men', was spelled out in huge letters on one of its buildings, overlooking the corner where Sarah Spiers was last seen.

By the time he reached Year 12 at Claremont's Christ Church Grammar School, Peter Weygers' stubbornness in clinging to principle was already in evidence.

Weygers remembers a clash with the school's headmaster: 'Once, during divinity, Peter Moyes made an assertion about a religious canon, and I asked, "How do you know that?" Instead of answering me, he said I had insolently questioned his authority and ordered me to his office to be caned.

'When we got there, I told him I had done nothing wrong. I said if he tried to cane me, "I will pull the cane off you and cane you."

'He walked around the office with the cane for what seemed like half an hour, then let me go without caning me. I have never forgotten it.'

After school, Peter Weygers qualified as a school psychologist, specialising in promoting the interests of gifted students.

A girlfriend filled in a form nominating him as a Claremont town councillor and, by the mid-1980s, he was both mayor of Claremont and president of the Council for Civil Liberties.

'My aim as mayor was to make Claremont the best place to live, work and play,' he recalls.

'My dream was to make it like Vancouver Island, known for its flowers, museums, history, culture, nice shopping and a great community spirit. I gave it my life, day and night.'

Peter Weygers was a popular mayor, elected for four terms. His willingness to get involved was legendary. Late one Saturday night in March 1990, a Claremont resident called him to complain that someone had caked human excrement on the seat, walls and ceiling of a bus shelter. Rather than wait for the council work crew to come on duty, Mayor Weygers armed himself with a bucket, disinfectant, detergent, brushes and his Swiss army knife.

He found the structure was almost covered in the stuff, but he scraped and scrubbed away in darkness on his hands and knees.

'My mother said if you start a job you finish it and do your best.' It took him more than an hour.

The front room of Killara, the Claremont house in Richardson Avenue that he and his siblings had inherited from their mother, was stacked with Civil Liberties paperwork – loose, and in boxes and binders – covering the floor and furniture to the point where it was almost impossible to thread a way through. When Weygers arrived home each night, his answering machine would be filled with twenty or so messages, and another round of voluntary work would begin.

A trawl through just a fraction of the complex crusades he took on hints at how much time and effort he devoted to them, all as a volunteer. He tackled dozens of problems head-on at once – family court disputes, a police shooting and an assault, plus national issues such as opposing compulsory ID papers, the Australia Card.

By 1996, he was juggling four careers, each of which would daunt a mere mortal – his day job as a full-time school psychologist, Claremont's busy and active mayor, unpaid president of the in-demand Council for Civil Liberties, and owner and micro-managing landlord of twenty houses.

Weyger's acquaintance, Steven Ross, on the other hand, was easy to dismiss. Most did. The two had met in 1989 when Weygers had helped Ross solve a bogus passenger complaint in his role as president of the Council for Civil Liberties.

Not many who met Ross would guess that his intelligence had been tested at slightly above average, and that he had a savant-like memory for dates, times and the street addresses of long-ago taxi passengers. In years to come, the media would come to revel in portraying him as a dim-witted cabbie, who was banished to a mining camp hut for eating food that caused farting and for 'pissing in his Esky instead of using the toilet'.

He sported a ludicrous mopish haircut, presented as almost illiterate, and displayed unusual social mannerisms, grinning and laughing inappropriately and dropping bad jokes into serious conversations, jokes at which only he laughed.

He had missed most of his schooling because he helped support his family by acting as assistant to his mother on her office-cleaning contracts. Having left school aged ten without a formal education, his slight ability to read and write was thanks to Peter Weygers, who taught him in adulthood.

Ross passed most of his time working, driving taxis and delivery trucks. When he wasn't working, he was entertaining a series of girlfriends on Sundays, avidly watching his collection of 10,000 videos and DVDs, surviving on a diet of meat pies and Big Macs, drinking Red Bull energy drinks and gobbling No-Doz tablets.

He was a hard-working if simple man, with what turned out to be a dangerous flaw.

'He wanted to be a hero,' says Weygers, adding that Ross reminded him of Forrest Gump, the simple movie character who accidentally found himself in the middle of great events that he influenced. Their trip on February 3 was to mark the beginning of a very strange saga.

*

Because Sarah had told friends she was going home by taxi, and had called one, suspicions quickly grew in the community that a rogue taxi driver was the culprit.

'Chaotic' was how young clubbers, keen to get home after a night out, described late-night transport from Claremont. The don't-drink-and-drive message had penetrated, but there was no public transport in the early hours of the morning. That left only taxis and walking, and taxis in the heavily regulated industry were rare and often unreliable.

Stories abounded of fights for rides home from Club Bayview. One young woman complained to the *Post* that she had been yanked from a cab outside the club by a man, who commandeered the car for himself while snarling, 'I hate women.'

The taxi driver and club bouncer did not intervene. The shocked twenty-two-year-old did not report the incident to police.

In the week Sarah disappeared, one of her work colleagues, Jenny Smithson, wrote a searing letter about the 'deplorable' taxi situation and the attitude of some drivers who stopped for hails on their way to booked calls.

'We all have stories of taxis that have been booked, taxi companies that are repeatedly telephoned, long delays on hold and taxis that never arrive. Everyone Sarah works with has a disturbingly familiar story to tell of being left waiting for a taxi.

'What is the real price we pay for a lack of taxis in our city and what are we doing about it?'

She advised young women to take their cars on nights out, even if planning to drink. 'Losing your licence is better than losing your life,' she wrote.

The failure of the after-club transport system was summed up by another young woman who, with her friends, made a practice of racing home barefoot: 'We take off our shoes and run, because getting a taxi is such a hassle. You carry your shoes and get holes in your stockings.'

She said taxi drivers had told her they often avoided Club Bayview because customers there were rude, drunk or on drugs, aggressive, and sometimes sick in the car – all in return for a $3 fare. Some taxi drivers avoided Claremont altogether, preferring to work the Northbridge nightclubs.

*

The focus on taxis after Sarah's abduction was very much in the minds of driver Steven Ross and mayor of Claremont Peter Weygers on February 3, the weekend after she disappeared, as they tried to retrace the route Ross believed was Sarah's last ride.

Ross was certain he had picked up Sarah and her killer on the night she vanished, he had told the mayor, just a few days after the teenager was reported missing.

As only he could, Ross recounted in excruciating detail how, outside Club Bayview, a young woman he called 'the drunk girl' opened his car door and climbed in beside him. She was unable to give her destination so Ross tried to get her out.

Then down the stairs from the club walked Sarah Spiers, he said. She got into his cab's back seat, then a male passenger, a stranger to her, had appeared on the other side and slid into the cab next to her.

'The drunk girl', still in the front seat, finally asked to be driven to Dalkeith, about seven minutes away. On arrival, the young man started to follow her out, but changed his mind.

After the Dalkeith detour, Ross showed Weygers the route he took back to Stirling Highway, across the Swan River via the Narrows Bridge, stopping outside South Perth's Windsor Hotel, a twenty-minute trip from Weyger's art deco mayor's office in Claremont.

The male passenger had followed Sarah out of Ross's cab when it arrived at the Windsor, in the same suburb as Sarah's home. She left her dark jacket in the cab, but he saw it and passed it to her. The man paid the $23 fare with a $2 tip.

On hearing this story, Weygers immediately phoned Don Spiers with a detailed account of what Ross had told him.

'I suppose I was naïve,' Weygers says today. 'I was well meaning – I felt compassion for a father frantic about his daughter. I treated him like I would any other human being in crisis.

'I said, if you believe, as a father, that she is a victim of foul play, I would do what I could to ask for public help. I would pay to print and distribute missing person posters.

'He told me he was not happy with the police response at that stage – they were treating Sarah as a missing person as there was no evidence of a crime.'

He invited Spiers to meet him in his mayor's parlour, but this meeting did not occur for more than a month.

Steven Ross wanted to go to the police but Weygers was very cautious.

'I said to him, "They think you're an idiot. If you do that, you are going to get yourself in the shit."'

Ross had again sought out the Council for Civil Liberties in 1990, when police had pressured him into admitting he had forged a document after a bogus complaint about racism from a would-be passenger.

'I told him that, if he insisted on talking to police, to be sure he had a lawyer present,' Weygers said. 'The way he talks, his disability, his mannerisms and his joking make him an easy target.'

Peter Weygers and Steven Ross later retraced the driver's other taxi jobs on the crucial night, knocking on the door of a man Ross had delivered in Mosman Park. There they discovered a mistake: the trip to the Windsor had taken place not on January 27, the early morning that Sarah disappeared, but on January 26, the day before. On the night Sarah vanished, Ross had been working a long way from Claremont, driving south of the river. His passengers to the Windsor on January 26 have never been identified.

Independently, police were following up reports from other cabbies about Sarah's late-night movements After some initial confusion, they established that what had looked to be a promising lead, a cab ride Sarah had taken to Mosman Park from Claremont, was not on the night she disappeared, as first thought, but earlier. How she had left Claremont on the fateful night remained a mystery.

That information should have ended Ross's involvement but, in his eagerness to help, he quickly developed another theory. It went like this: perhaps the pushy stranger who Ross believed had got into his cab with Sarah outside Club Bayview on January 26 was a predator in the habit of lurking outside the club in the shadows, pouncing on drunk girls catching cabs alone.

Perhaps he had come back the next night at exactly the same time and done the same thing to Sarah, in another cab, this time becoming her murderer.

Find Ross's male passenger and you would find out what had happened to Sarah, the taxi driver had reasoned.

At this time, police had not released any information about Sarah's call from the phone booth 500 metres from the club.

Without telling Weygers, Ross made an appointment to see Grant Milner, a jovial, dedicated lawyer with an office upstairs in St Quentin Avenue, next door to Club Bayview, on February 19, 1996. Milner arranged for detectives to interview Ross in his office, in his presence. Ross recalls that Milner's fee for these services was $780.

The detectives did not, Ross says, take a formal statement. 'The first thing they wanted to know was if I had a criminal record. I said I did but that I wasn't guilty. They lost interest in my theory after that.'

Ross said that detectives then accused *him* of picking up Sarah the night she disappeared. After explanations about the muddled nights, the detectives and Milner realised that Ross had no solid information to give them about the early morning of January 27. Milner phoned police afterwards to apologise for wasting their time.

'I reckon Grant thought I was crazy,' Ross said. 'He said maybe I had picked up a different girl on the twenty-sixth.'

Nobody took any more notice of Steven Ross at this time. But his name, and that of Claremont's mayor Peter Weygers, had gone into police files.

Those files would later be re-opened again and again, to devastating effect.

4

Party Town

Police continued to sift the mass of information pouring into the Major Crime Squad offices. In March 1996, the search went international, with Interpol asked to circulate Sarah's image worldwide. They had used the newly popular internet to try to contact people interstate and overseas, who might have seen something useful while visiting Claremont at the time Sarah Spiers vanished.

This drew three responses from clairvoyants, all useless.

On January 30, the family went public.

A heartbroken Don Spiers braved television cameras to grimly address his teenaged daughter's abductor: 'At least one person knows and I urge that person, if they have any feeling for the anxiety and suffering they have caused us and Sarah's friends, to please ease some of it. They only have to call us and tell us what has happened to Sarah, or where she is.

'We haven't given up hope.

'People ask us how we are coping, but we don't have any options. We just have to cope.'

With all eyes and camera lenses on Sarah's distraught father, a detective standing at the back of the media pack leaned towards John Townsend, a reporter for *The West Australian*, and whispered, 'Wait and see, but I bet we will find this is connected to Karrakatta.'

*

Four weeks after Sarah disappeared, Don, Carol and Amanda Spiers sat down at their daughters' South Perth apartment to talk to the *Post.* Their emotions were ragged, their mood despondent, as they pleaded for any information about their missing daughter and sister. Sarah's red BMW still sat in the driveway.

Don was adamant that Sarah would not have left voluntarily. 'She has no reason to run away from the lifestyle she has; she and her sister have their own home. She has her own car and she has a job. Why would she run away from it?'

Fears that lurk deep in the heart of every parent poured out: 'I have always worried that something like this would happen. We all know there are predators out there.

'I knew from the day my daughters left home, there would be times when they would be vulnerable. You do all you can to protect them, but you know there will still be those times.'

He revealed that the family had been bombarded with phone calls from as far away as Sydney. However far-fetched the tip, the desperate family followed up each possible lead. Some callers were blunt and cruel, one even accusing Don of killing his daughter.

Then there were the so-called clairvoyants, around 300 of them. Loss, grief and high-profile cases are fertile ground for them to plant their seeds of doubt. Don does not believe in fortune tellers or psychics, and the last thing he needed was to waste valuable time and emotional energy on wild goose chases but, sadly, he also felt he had to deal with the possibility that someone with genuine information was posing as a seer possessing psychic powers.

'I think everyone is a clairvoyant these days,' he said.

He was given descriptions of the houses where Sarah was supposedly being held, but no house numbers. Don drove the suburban streets for hours, looking, searching.

He went on a tear-streaked dash to swampy ground around the Canning River, and traversed the metropolitan area with a psychic in his car for two days, always on the promise that 'the house where Sarah is being held is just around the next corner'.

Another clairvoyant had him driving 250 kilometres to the gold-mining centre of Southern Cross, where a man in a pub fitting a certain description was said to hold the key. This stranger never materialised.

One time, he was parked for hours next to the Continental Hotel, waiting for a person who had promised to tell him where Sarah was. No one showed.

Don Spiers quickly worked out what every police force has concluded: clairvoyants' visions always lack specifics, such as a name, address or car registration number.

Despite the popularity of 'psychic detective' television programmes, there is no proof anywhere that a clairvoyant has ever solved a crime. But it is understandable that any parent in this situation would cling desperately to every last hope.

'Many of them mean well and seriously believe their visions mean something,' said Don. 'But you can imagine how it feels when someone rings to tell you details of gruesome things that they are certain have happened to your daughter. And then you get another call, saying she is definitely alive. It's almost unbearable.'

Not all callers were cranks. Some just offered comfort.

Seven months after her precious child had vanished, Carol Spiers wrote an open letter to the people of her daughter's city: 'Hardly a day goes by that I don't receive a phone call from a member of the public, saying, "You don't know me, but my family and I would just like to let you know that our hopes and prayers are with you for the return of your lovely Sarah".'

In their letterbox, piles of cards and letters were delivered with similar messages from concerned, thoughtful strangers, she said.

'We are still waiting for that one phone call, or that one note in the mail, that tells us where Sarah is. Don, Amanda and I physically ache with anticipation of news of Sarah – she is loved by us so much. We will never, ever give up hope of having our daughter returned to us and that is the only issue we are interested in. Please do not give up. Please help us find Sarah.

'We still have hopes of seeing Sarah alive or hearing from her, and will do so until we have evidence to the contrary.'

*

In the years before it became a place where young women disappeared, Claremont was a rundown shopping strip. Then in the 1980s, intoxicated by a cocktail of optimism and easily borrowed money, staid, down-at-heel old Claremont had lifted her skirts and gone dancing.

The riverfront location, surrounded by street after gridded street of charming Federation houses with an old-world town centre, had made Claremont a magnet for renovators, attracting a new wave of families with ambition.

Above the Federation-era Bay View Terrace shops, a fashion design and cottage clothing industry suddenly blossomed in the 1980s.

The shopping strip's barber, bootmaker, pie shop, butcher, milk bar, bicycle shop, charity store, hardware supplier and grocer, which had provided generations of local families with necessities, became mostly high-end fashion boutiques, gift shops and jewellers, attracting well-heeled customers and even busloads of shopping tourists.

By the 1980s, the upmarket Old Theatre Lane shopping arcade had replaced the old movie house, Claremont Pictures, a place where hundreds of local kids thrilled in the dark to the double-feature Saturday afternoon matinees.

The corner 1902 Claremont Hotel, at the top of the terrace opposite the restored Victorian-era railway station, was faithfully renovated, throwing off its image as a haven for sad old drunks and rowdy football fans. It rebadged itself first as Cagney's then the Continental. Sons and daughters of Claremont's renovators made it their own.

Across Bay View Terrace from Old Theatre Lane, super-trendy Kim's Bar transformed the old liquor store, which, with the re-invention of the Continental Hotel and opening of Club Bayview around the corner in St Quentin Avenue, made the old town throb far into the early hours. It attracted a whole new generation, with a whole new set of reasons to come to Claremont.

Club Bayview – or Clubba, as the locals called it – was the heart of Claremont's nightlife. Its patrons, initially drawn from neighbouring suburbs, had graduated from the same prestigious private schools that concentrated in Claremont and nearby.

'Even if you were not a big fan of Clubba, you knew that's where your night out would end,' said one club regular. 'If you'd been to a pub or dinner or a wedding or a ball or a sports club function, you didn't have to work out your next stop. You just gravitated to where there would be lots of people you knew.

'It gave a false sense of security, as things turned out. If you were out in Northbridge, there is no way you would leave your friend there alone. But at Clubba the friends you arrived with would not think twice about leaving with someone they had met, or just drift off, leaving you alone. Men and women. Everyone trusted everyone. They assumed you were among friends and secure.

'If you had spent all your money, you could always walk home or find a lift.'

A blunt sign on Club Bayview's door had explicit instructions for rejected, disappointed would-be clubbers who lacked 'the look': 'Please do not be offended, but rather fade away quietly only to return another night, dressed to kill and looking very, very mature.'

Pretty girls had a much easier ride than males, according to T.J., a female regular: 'A tight dress and a big bright smile for the bouncers will get you far in a place like Club Bayview,' T.J. told journalist Michael Edwards in his report for the *Post*. Female clubbers became convinced that the doormen, perched on Club Bayview's first-floor balcony, were spotters who surveyed the girls below on St Quentin Avenue and alerted their ground-floor colleagues to which young women could have the $8 door charge waived.

One bewildered teen, who had been denied entry, felt her rejection so keenly that she wrote to the *Post* to complain, listing the fashion labels she had been wearing.

Club owner Jon Sainken replied to her published letter: 'We expect letter writers and other complainers to exercise their freedom of choice and not return. Unfortunately, when the ruffled feathers settle and the wounded pride heals and especially when it suits their purpose, they usually do.'

To reinforce the owner's point, the club's sign listing conditions of entry said that being escorted down the steps onto St Quentin Avenue was a journey from social enlightenment to obscurity.

Outside, lines would form at about 11:30 p.m. Inside, as Michael Edwards wrote, paid-up members headed for their more genteel, exclusive area, while the rest cruised for social contact in the dark, cavernous tennis court–sized punters' zone, with its central circular bar and DJ pumping out dance music at high decibels.

'In a throwback to the 1970s, a scantily clad go-go dancer gyrated to the beat,' wrote Edwards.

As Claremont's reputation as a nightspot grew through the 1980s and 1990s, its reputation as a party town after dark began attracting customers from far-flung suburbs, country towns and other states. League football stars and their hangers-on would arrive en masse. Strangers blended in easily, so long as they had the undefined 'look'.

'If there were anywhere else in the area to go, we would,' Ernest, aged twenty-two, told Edwards. Ernest had been thrown out of the club twice, once for dropping a glass, once for 'inadvertently questioning the intelligence of the club's bouncing staff'.

'But Clubba's got the monopoly and we're forced to put up with all their crap. It's noisy, crowded, expensive and staff have an interesting range of manners,' he lamented.

Another customer said he had little choice but to obey the commands of the hefty bouncer: 'I can complain about the place as much as I want, but in the end, nobody forces me to go there and nobody will force me to go back – even though I will.'

Adrenaline rushed to the brains of spirited young men and women in party mode, nostrils twitching, anticipating the whiff of romance. Party and mating mode can easily overwhelm carping misgivings about personal safety out on the street. Club Bayview remained the focal point for post-midnight revellers in the Perth suburbs between the city, Swan River and Indian Ocean, even after one of its patrons vanished.

'A bomb would have to go off in the place to stop people from the western suburbs going there,' patron J.K. told Michael Edwards. After Lisa's abduction and Sarah's disappearance, many young women insisted on arriving and leaving with male friends. But not all. Police sergeant Terry Hollier said the events had not deterred some women from leaving the hotel or Club Bayview by themselves. He was part of a patrol group taking the names and addresses of young women as a precaution.

One young woman, who had been to the Continental Hotel, had to be helped home by an older couple who rescued her. 'She was fortunate that we found her,' wrote local resident Rodney Thiele, who lived a block away from the hotel, in a letter to the *Post* in July 1996. 'She was able to walk only one block before collapsing outside our home.'

The public was largely unaware that during nineteen days in March soon after Sarah went missing, the new police Sexual Assault Squad received reports of twelve sexual assaults and bashings state-wide, many occurring when the offenders tried to force their victims into cars.

One blatant Claremont attack did become public in March 1996, six weeks after Sarah Spiers disappeared. A fit, strong, twenty-one-year-old woman had just left Club Bayview after drinking heavily. She was terrifyingly blitz-attacked outside the club in the early hours of a Sunday morning.

Her attacker bashed her head against a wall about six times while the two struggled, the man almost ripping off his victim's skirt. She told 79 Division officers that she had left the club at about 2 a.m. because she felt ill, and had been pounced on in Church Lane, the side street that runs beside Club Bayview.

She had believed she was going to be raped or killed, and had fought back hard. Club bouncers saw the struggle, came to her rescue and took her inside the club, where she was consoled by friends. The attacker ran away.

The police description and photofit image portrayed a dark-haired man aged about twenty-five, just under six feet tall with full, dark features, black hair and bushy eyebrows. No offender was identified.

As the crimes mounted, people did not want to believe that such shocking events could happen at random. If so, we were all in peril. We were all vulnerable. It is human to look for reasons, and many looked in the wrong places, focusing on the victims. Had they been drinking? Were their skirts too tight? This judgmental language was painful for victims' families. Only the perpetrators – or perpetrator – were to blame.

5
Downward Spiral

As waves of fear and panic swept through Claremont in the months after Sarah's disappearance, police were swamped with investigative leads from the public, especially what detectives call 'nominations'. These were names of men – men who people suspected were likely offenders.

Checking out each nomination left no time to trawl through the old, scattered and often difficult-to-locate files on precursor attacks, especially those committed far from Claremont and thought unlikely to be linked.

General distrust of police was also holding back the flow of valuable information about precursor crimes. Large numbers of women did not feel safe reporting attempted abductions or sexual assaults, or felt they would not be believed. They withheld this information, sometimes telling only their closest friends.

Fear of having every intimate aspect of their lives publicly exposed under cross-examination in court – or embarrassment, shame or family sanction – meant that details of many attacks on women did not make it to the police files. To add to this problem, files on some incidents that were reported were infuriatingly lost, disregarded or dismissed without proper forensic evidence being collected.

Don Spiers was upset to gain first-hand knowledge of this reluctance to report. One of the most important things he had learned from his family's heartbreaking resolve to listen to every telephone caller, he told the *Post*, was the lack of trust many in the community had in communicating with police.

'It's sad that people feel they can't come forward with information. Many of the people who have rung me have said they will tell me, but not the police.

'I feel so sorry for the detectives who have worked very hard to get a result in this case, that part of the community has decided not to talk to police.'

Dr Carol Deller set up the Sexual Assault Referral Centre (SARC) in 1975 with a roster of six doctors who, between them, examined on average one rape victim a day, including Lisa. They were usually the first point of medical contact for rape victims. Dr Deller said it took a lot of courage for women to report rape.

'Women were extremely frightened,' she said. 'Fewer than fifty per cent of victims would report the attacks to police.'

All was not lost. After a serial rapist was thought to be at large, even those rape victims who would not talk to detectives had forensic samples left by their rapists filed at SARC, just in case they changed their minds. But reluctance to report meant that hundreds of potential descriptions of 'stranger rapists' – a quarter of the total – were never entered in police files.

Somewhere, among the evidence of those shocking assaults, there might have been a vital clue to help police solve the Claremont crimes to date and prevent others.

*

Don Spiers prided himself in his bushman's self-reliance but his search for Sarah left his life almost overcome with a sense of helplessness. The tough shearer later said that he cried himself to sleep every night for a year after Sarah vanished.

He had energy only for following up information; motivation for nothing but finding clues about how and why Sarah had disappeared. He had not worked in his lucrative shearing business since that first sickening call from Amanda. His shearers and a committee of his clients ran his business.

Don's emotional pain and anguish were obvious. He said his frustration left him feeling sick and empty, with his insides carrying a constant physical ache.

He had spoken up for better nightlife security measures while a twelve-man team from the Major Crime Squad continued to work full-time on his daughter's disappearance.

In May 1996, he pleaded for a compulsory video library of surveillance tapes from premises such as Club Bayview, noting that footage, which had been taped over the next night, might have shown his daughter leaving the club. Had police received the tape, they may have known which direction she had walked and whether she had left the club alone.

He still held out hope.

'She knows her family loves her so much and her love just glows out of her,' he said. 'We still hope she's alive somewhere and being held against her will.'

Her employer, BSD Consultants, was holding Sarah's job open for her.

By that time, many members of the public began to feel that the missing teenager would simply join the ranks of the disappeared, in excess of twenty women citywide who had vanished since the 1980s, permanently and tragically, without trace or clue.

In April, five weeks after the attack on the young woman in Church Lane, next to Club Bayview, police inspector Con Calameri had told Claremont's new Night Safety Committee meeting that Claremont was safe.

Local police sergeant Phil Sutton weighed in: 'Claremont is still one of the safest places in Perth. Claremont has a very low crime rate. But because of Sarah Spiers' disappearance, whenever anything happens here now, it makes headlines.'

While police sought to reassure the public, Jim Larkin, the proprietor of the hot dog van, continued to be concerned. The streets of Claremont after dark were not as safe as police thought, he said. 'The night that there isn't something dramatic happening outside Club Bayview is pretty unusual.'

Out in the municipal and business world of local shop, boutique and restaurant owners, nerves were fraying. Customers were associating Claremont, even during daylight hours, with sinister happenings. Foot traffic and sales dwindled.

Around Claremont, suspicions grew, based on little or no evidence. Fractures were opening in the local business and civic communities. In the search for answers, people were pointing fingers. This meant that, in addition to the intense efforts of the by now sixteen detectives to find out what had happened to Sarah Spiers, two more battlefronts began to open up in Claremont.

*

In May 1996, a bailiff had gatecrashed the Claremont Council chambers, interrupting its Night Safety Committee meeting , which had been convened to address local crime in the wake of Sarah Spiers' disappearance that January. The committee included district police chief Con Calameri and local police, local residents, business leaders and council rangers, as well as Dr Jon Sainken (the owner of Club Bayview) and Peter Weygers. Its priorities were the installation of more public phones and a secure taxi rank, with a concierge to take the names of young women entering cabs. These were troubled times.

The bailiff served a writ for defamation on Weygers on behalf of Dr Sainken. The meeting abruptly ended, as Weygers and all his council members stood up and left. It was to be a long time before the group reconvened.

Claremont's mayor, Peter Weygers, and Jon Sainken had a bitter history. 'Club urged to help end assaults' read a headline in *The West Australian* shortly after the Church Lane attack in March. The report said that Weygers had blamed club patrons for trouble in the locality, and that he had called on club management to increase security patrols in the surrounding streets.

Although eleven police officers had been assigned to Claremont, Weygers had called for more post-midnight patrols and for a stronger presence of liquor and gaming officers, a barb apparently aimed at local premises licensed to sell alcohol. Liquor outlets should pay for the extra police, he said.

Police retorted that young people were not taking their own safety seriously in an area perceived to be well lit, but with dark alleys where nobody knew who might be lurking.

Then early in April, 1996, Dr Sainken hit back. He publicly refuted suggestions that his club could have done more to prevent the disappearance of Sarah Spiers. 'I think the Mayor's behaviour in this whole thing has been bizarre – the girl didn't disappear from Club Bayview. We've been made the scapegoat.'

Running parallel to all this unwanted attention was a separate issue of great interest to Club Bayview.

Dr Sainken's nightclub was in an expensive legal dispute with its local council, led by Peter Weygers. The council was disputing that it had ever approved the Club Bayview premises for use as a nightclub, only for 'a sophisticated après-theatre, piano bar and coffee house, where young adults and their parents might happen upon one another as the witching hour approaches', according to the original application. The club argued that the council had known all along that it *was* a nightclub.

A long list of social problems outside the club and hotel, alleging noise, vandalism, drug-use implements, broken glass and intimidation of council rangers was provided by Mayor Weygers in a press release issued in the name of Claremont Council.

In April 1996, local resident Jo Woods told the annual meeting of electors the club was the worst thing that had ever happened to the area and that it had contributed to the recent downturn in Claremont's image. 'I used to be proud of the fact that I lived in Claremont,' she said. The meeting opposed extensions to the club and voted unanimously for the council to encourage Club Bayview to operate according to its original modest application.

To this blizzard of legal cases, a third was added that was also occupying Dr Sainken.

Cottesloe's two beachfront hotels plus Claremont's Continental Hotel, today called The Claremont, were the main feeders of young after-midnight clubbers into Club Bayview. In a neat deal of vertical integration, which captured Claremont's youth market both before and after midnight, Dr Sainken had bought into the trust that owned the Continental, 200 metres away from his nightclub. The Continental was also booming.

Late in May 1996, the Continental Hotel was due in court to fight a formal council complaint, which included allegations that nearby residents' amenity was 'unduly disturbed' by hotel noise, amplified music and disorderly conduct by patrons leaving the hotel.

'Unfortunately, Mr Weygers has made a number of very negative statements to the media regarding Club Bayview which we feel have been inaccurate, unfair and defamatory … we have been forced into this unwelcome legal action to clear our name,' Dr Sainken said in a letter to the *Post* on May 28, 1996.

Dr Sainken's writ against the mayor was not popular, drawing negative comments from some *Post* readers.

'Hasn't there already been enough pain and suffering over this issue?' wrote Pip Buxton, who praised Weygers' efforts to improve safety and security. 'Come on guys, let us have a bit of peace,' she wrote, adding her congratulations to Club Bayview for providing a bus for patrons.

Peter Dunk, from neighbouring Swanbourne, asked whether Australia was too closely following the USA in its readiness to take legal action: 'Does this mean we are not allowed to be critical of anyone or anything?'

Dr Sainken replied: 'We accept that by its very nature Club Bayview will always be a favourite whipping post for some, but I would still like to see your paper present only the facts and reasonable comment,' lambasting 'wild and hysterical speculation that sometimes masquerades as opinion'.

Dr Sainken lobbied the Local Government Minister to refuse Claremont Council permission to cover the costs of Weygers' lawyers to defend the writ he had issued. He said he had searched the lands register and found Weygers was 'a man of considerable means', owning sixteen separate properties. 'I am confident that he has the intelligence and the means to either broker a peace or defend himself at law,' Dr Sainken wrote to the minister.

The council, however, with ministerial permission, voted to cover its mayor's legal costs, so Dr Sainken decided not to proceed with his writ because, he said, he was reluctant to put ratepayers' funds in jeopardy. In the elevated temperature of the times, much was at stake.

On Saturday night, June 11, 1996, the *Post*'s presses rolled with an edition carrying prickly opinions from prominent local people about their local paper's coverage of the tensions tearing Claremont apart. Had the newspaper bagged Club Bayview and blamed it for all the ills of Claremont? So wrote prominent local real estate agent Mack Hall in a letter to the editor.

'Parents should be delighted that such amenities exist and that their kids socialise locally. It certainly fills a big need for the young folk of today. I say hats off to the owners of Club Bayview and the Continental Hotel.'

In that same edition, Dr Sainken had placed a full-page advertisement with the eye-catching headline 'Hex, Jibes and Red Tape', addressed to 'the Club-Conti *Post*'.

It defended the nightclub's expansion plans and its permit to operate, adding: 'All we have ever wanted to do is to entertain a few local people as harmlessly as possible and make a living from a vocation we enjoy. As we do not play this game of local politics well nor with any enthusiasm, it is especially easy to make us look bad … with self-certain morality.'

The club's legendary allure was slipped into the text: 'Be there or miss out,' the advertisement added.

The very next day arrived the shock news of another young woman's disappearance.

6

Jane

Blonde, vivacious childcare worker Jane Rimmer, aged twenty-three, was well and truly a local. She, her elder sister, Lee, and her elder brother, Adam, had grown up in the family home in Keightley Road, Shenton Park, neighbouring the *Post* newspaper. Jane had attended the local Rosalie Primary and Hollywood High schools.

Their father Trevor worked in Perth city as an administration manager for an investment company. Mother Jenni worked as a secretary before finding a job at the Shenton Park Hotel, a short walk from their home.

Jane worked in a series of casual jobs while at high school, then held various positions before finding work she loved at Carrington Day Care Centre in nearby Nedlands, where she was regarded as reliable and popular with the children and their parents. She was friendly and had many friends, male and female, in her age group. She could sometimes be a little reckless; some acquaintances worried about her habit of walking home alone after she had been drinking, and said she had accepted lifts from strangers. In 1996, she was single and lived alone in a comfortable flat in the suburb of Wembley.

On June 9, 1996, Jane started her Saturday with a morning haircut and blow-dry at Deja Vu salon in Onslow Road near her home. At 6:50 p.m., Trevor drove her to the Shenton Park Hotel to meet Jenni for a drink. It was to be her last contact with her parents.

A taxi took Jane to a friend's house then to the Ocean Beach Hotel, where Sarah Spiers had also gone on the night she vanished. Another cab delivered her and some girlfriends at 7:43 p.m. to the Continental Hotel at the top of the terrace in Claremont.

Upstairs at the Conti, Jane became upset. Her friend Lynda Donovan walked her to the footpath, where Jane made disparaging comments about her own appearance.

'She was well on the way – she was affected by alcohol,' Lynda said. Another friend noticed she had been crying. 'Jane was very drunk by the end of the evening,' said Sian Chapman. They all left after 11:30 p.m. to walk as a group to Club Bayview, before deciding the line was too long to wait. They elected to head home.

The club's security footage shows Jane outside the club chatting to men and women, laughing and evidently enjoying herself.

The friends invited Jane to share a taxi home with them, but while waiting at the taxi rank outside Claremont train station, she changed her mind, recrossing the road to the hotel.

Outside the Conti, which closed at midnight, a security camera picked up Jane a minute into Sunday, June 9. In the video, she appears to be waiting for someone, checking her watch, looking north towards Claremont station. Then after a few minutes, a broad-shouldered man approaches her as she leans on a post, still outside the hotel. Jane throws her head back and laughs as the man walks up to her, but he has his back to the camera during their entire encounter. The man then walks south down Bay View Terrace before disappearing out of camera range. Jane's elder sister, Lee, later said that it was clear to her from the video that Jane was acquainted with the man, and that Jane had been drinking.

The footage and accounts from those in the cab then record Jane's friends having one more shot at enticing Jane into their cab when it arrives after a ten-minute wait. Although their destination is in the opposite direction, they direct the driver down Bay View Terrace, and tell him to slow down.

Jane is waiting, standing on the kerb, leaning on a pole, looking expectantly at the street. Lynda calls out to her but Jane waves the car off, shaking her head. Her friends never see her again.

The camera recording some of this was on rotation with others located around the hotel, so that it missed recording thirty-two seconds of the action on Bay View Terrace every minute. One rotation shows Jane at her station at the pole. She is wearing denim jeans and a long-sleeved, loose-fitting T-shirt, carrying a dark corduroy jacket with a small imitation leather handbag slung across her left shoulder, the bag resting on her right hip. She is wearing black leather boots and some jewellery, including a silver Guess watch. The next rotation shows a bare pole and empty road. Missed from the recording is how Jane had left – on foot, alone or in company, or picked up by a car – and in which direction.

*

Later that Sunday morning, in a semi-rural, isolated section of Wellard, a 45-kilometre drive south of Claremont, darkness had closed in eerily. It was a cool, still night, where loud sounds could travel for kilometres across the flat farmland. There were few landmarks of note – Greenacres Riding School, farmlets, plus a drug-rehabilitation centre two kilometres along the road. Two kilometres in the other direction was Casuarina, the city's near-new maximum-security prison.

Several hours after midnight, silence was split by screams.

The screams were enough to awake Kenneth and Judith Mitchell, who were sleeping as usual with their front bedroom windows open at their farmhouse.

'I was awoken by a very high-pitched and traumatic voice of a woman,' said Kenneth Mitchell. 'It went on for a while – I can only recall one lot of words: "Leave me alone. Let me out of here".'

The episode went on for more than five minutes, he said.

'It was very plain, very clear and very traumatic. After that it stopped, dead silence,' he continued. 'It was quite frightening, honestly.'

He heard a 'quiet' vehicle start up and saw lights reflecting off trees, heading towards Millar Road, which intersects with Woolcoot Road.

Judith Mitchell saw more, after she sat up in bed then went to the window – the shadow of a car 150 metres away, plus a light. She thought she saw someone walk behind a bush across the road at the end of their long driveway. 'A person hid. The noise seemed to get louder, like someone, a female, arguing. A car door slammed shut and it went off.'

Cheryl Sturcke and her husband, Ian, were sleeping when she heard a blood-curdling scream that stopped mid-cry followed by total silence.

'It woke us both up. I said, "That's a really serious domestic." It lasted five seconds, maybe longer. That's a long time. Never in my life have I heard a scream like that and I never want to hear it again.'

The Sturckes lived several kilometres from the Mitchells.

Ian Sturcke said, 'I've never heard a scream of that magnitude in my life. Never. It was female. Really high pitched, shrill.'

Both couples said the area is extremely quiet and nothing ever disturbed the peace there. Nobody went outside or called police. They all went back to bed.

Cheryl said that, two or three weeks later, there was a noticeable smell coming from beside Woolcoot Road where it met Millar Road.

*

The Sunday afternoon on the day Jane vanished, twenty-year-old Navy man Paul Langenbach and his friend, Tiffany Hughes, were riding horses along a deserted, unsealed stretch of Woolcoot Road in Wellard. At 2 p.m., Langenbach met with a spot of trouble. As the pair rode between roadsides thick with bush, something spooked his horse. His mount shied and threw him to the road.

Dusting himself off, he saw something glinting on the crushed-limestone road at his feet. It was a silver Guess watch.

He picked it up, showed his find to Hughes and later gave it to his girlfriend, Kathryne Owen, who worked at Greenacres Riding School on the other side of the fence that lined this road. She took the watch home.

Langenbach's horse being spooked right at that very spot is unlikely to be a coincidence. According to medical studies, horses recognise the smell of death.

*

At about the time Jane's watch was being picked up by Paul Langenbach, her father Trevor was phoning her flat to see why she had not arrived at her family home for Sunday lunch as arranged.

Alarmed when there was no answer, he drove to Wembley, his anxiety rising when he saw Jane's silver Mazda coupé parked in front of her building. The knot in his stomach twisted further as he let himself inside her flat with a spare key, gazing blankly at her neatly made bed. To his horror, he also saw Jane's untouched address and cheque books, the interior of her flat with its face-brick walls looking lived-in but undisturbed. Her car keys were on the table, her bed neatly made with the twenty-three-year-old's teddy bear snuggly on her pillow, while unframed wall posters of a sneering Elvis Presley and pouting Marilyn Monroe looked down at the scene, dread-laden in its normality.

After a frantic ring-around of friends, and with the spectre of the still-missing Sarah Spiers dominating everyone's minds, Jenni Rimmer reported her daughter missing to the Subiaco police that night. Close to midnight, the local cops officially listed her as a person missing from outside the Continental Hotel.

After the missing person report, the police immediately searched the railway line for one and a half kilometres from the Continental; checked back alleys and bins; 'emu-picked' large areas; interviewed staff in cafés, restaurants, bars and shops; and set up a mobile police station plastered with photos of Jane. Nobody had seen her.

Fears intensified when Jane did not arrive for work at the Carrington Day Care Centre in Nedlands, her workplace for five years.

The Homicide Squad swung into action. There was no 'missing person' delay.

Just thirty-three hours after Jenni Rimmer had reported Jane missing, Jenni and Trevor Rimmer braved television cameras. 'Please come home, or at least give us a call,' Trevor Rimmer pleaded to his daughter.

Asked about her relationships, Trevor said Jane had a steady group of friends but no boyfriend.

'Obviously, we thought the sun shone out of her,' he said.

As the fog of dread fell again on Claremont, the distraught owners of the Continental Hotel issued a statement discouraging people from going home alone late at night. The hotel, they said, was 'deeply distressed by the possibilities arising from Jane's disappearance from Claremont after leaving the hotel'.

Police released Jane's description – 167 centimetres tall, medium build, shoulder-length blonde hair and blue eyes. To imprint her image on the public mind, they dressed a model in clothes identical to those she had been wearing when she was last seen. Jane's brother and sister, Adam and Lee, mobilised a small army of friends to distribute 250,000 posters throughout Australia. They featured Jane's smiling face in colour under a headline that pleaded: 'Have you seen Jane Rimmer?'

'There has to be someone – or a group – who knows what has happened and where she has gone,' said Adam. 'We have to keep it out there, fresh in everyone's mind.'

The posters had been printed free of charge, among the many offers of help that poured into the family, including meals, groceries and poster distribution.

The posters, a media frenzy and a police information van parked outside the Continental prompted more than a thousand reports to police in that first week.

Detectives quickly noted similarities between Jane and Sarah Spiers: they were of similar age and appearance, both blonde and attractive, both had been alone after partying in central Claremont, and both had vanished without witnesses.

A serial killer who preyed on Claremont was now a distinct possibility.

*

The day after Jane vanished, senior officers mustered a dedicated group of detectives into a new squad named Macro Task Force, including Detective Inspector David Caporn. The overall investigation was headed by acting Detective Inspector Paul Ferguson, who was no stranger to serial killers.

Ferguson, studious-looking in glasses and moustache, had leapt to public prominence in the 1980s over the shocking series of abductions and killings of four women in suburban Perth, carried out by the couple David and Catherine Birnie. The detective remained deeply affected by what he had to hear and see as a result of those sadistic, sexually driven killings.

Caporn was considered a star investigator after he led the investigation into the brutal 1994 murder of jeweller Pamela Lawrence at her shop in Mosman Park. That investigation resulted in an arrest and conviction but was destined to end badly many years later. Caporn was personable, articulate, popular, clever, hard-working, tough and tactical – qualities that had propelled him through the ranks successfully and would continue to do so.

Macro dropped a lead blanket of secrecy on the Claremont cases from day one. Officers seconded from the Homicide Squad and others were required to sign confidentiality agreements, and banned from making any comment to the public or press, an unprecedented rule.

Being cast out of this elite squad was the penalty for any breaches, and some offenders were in fact banished for speaking too openly about the inner workings of the investigation.

Paul Ferguson became a favourite for newspaper, television and radio reporters hungry for any new snippets that advanced the biggest crime story for many years. His availability and readiness with a quick quote helped satisfy the craving for updates. In reality, he gave little away, cleverly sticking to generalisations. At the time, what sparse detail was released was thought to have been carefully crafted to help catch the killer.

Enlisting the help of a willing public when memories were fresh was always an alternative to impenetrable secrecy. Hard facts, when entrusted to a traumatised community eager to help, can produce high-quality clues. As a consequence of police secrecy, however, much of the information police received from the well-meaning public was useless and time-wasting.

Under these trying constraints, Macro members worked hard and long hours, barely seeing their families.

Immediately after Jane was reported missing, eighteen officers were assigned to walk Claremont's streets late at night, taking names, addresses and phone numbers of women going into Club Bayview and the Continental Hotel, then interviewing them later about their movements on the relevant nights.

Police on the job noticed that news of the disappearances had not deterred some lone young women from leaving the two local bars, although most were now seen in pairs or small groups, often with arms linked.

Conversation in Claremont and surrounding suburbs was about little else. Claremont's once-humming streets were all but deserted, with lines of taxis again waiting for fares.

7

Unstoppable

Lisa, now aged nineteen, was again gripped with terror. Just a day after Jane Rimmer was reported missing, she went public with her fears that Sarah and Jane had fallen victim to the same brutal predator from whom she had escaped at Karrakatta Cemetery. Her worst fear was that this man would be caught and stopped only if he offended again.

Lisa's clear-eyed reaction made her the most perceptive and prescient of all public commentators on the case. She was distressed and sickened by the disappearances of Sarah and Jane.

'This person is unstoppable,' Lisa concluded from her most bitter of experiences.

It was well known that Claremont was an easy target, she told *The West Australian* reporter Ingrid Mansell. Since her attack fifteen months earlier, she had lived with the fear that other young women would suffer a similar fate. 'I could not bear the thought of that happening to someone else.'

Her attacker had stolen her feeling of safety and security, and her natural tendency to trust people. She realised she was lucky to survive.

That same week, Macro also joined the obvious dots with the Karrakatta abduction and rape. Detectives were recalled to duty and worked non-stop on this earlier rape case.

Lisa, their living witness, had also been to a Claremont nightspot, and, on checking the files, detectives found there had been five other known attacks on young women in the Claremont precinct since 1992.

Their thinking agreed with Lisa's: catch the cemetery rapist and, quite likely, you would catch whoever abducted Sarah and Jane.

Macro now re-opened Lisa's file and handed it to Detective Betty Francis, on June 10, 1996, a mammoth challenge on her first day with the newly formed Sexual Assault Squad.

In Francis's words, the rape was 'a possible connection at this stage to at least two possible homicides'.

She traced the sealed brown-and-green evidence bags containing Lisa's shorts, T-shirt, underwear, shoes and denim vest; the hospital trousers and gown Lisa was dressed in at Hollywood Hospital; and the white washing line that had so painfully bound Lisa hand and foot.

Detective Francis'svisits to hardware stores and warehouses, looking for who manufactured and sold the line, revealed that the binding was an imported mass-market cord originating in Melbourne – a forensic dead end.

The brief police statements taken from Lisa on the Sunday morning of her ordeal on February 12, 1995, were broad outlines of the abduction, rape and rescue. Seventeen months later, at 9 a.m. on June 17, 1996, Francis picked up Lisa and drove her to the locations at Claremont, Karrakatta and Hollywood, then to her office. At her first in-depth interview, the stoic victim relived her ordeal in excruciating detail in a thirty-five-page statement. Betty Francis handed the file back to Macro.

The potential value of Lisa's sister's lost driver's licence was now recognised. Macro detectives doorknocked houses overlooking Claremont's Rowe Park, just 350 metres from central Claremont. Detectives at one front door were handed the missing driver's licence, seventeen months after it went missing. A child had found it near basketball courts soon after the attack, well inside Rowe Park, a long distance from the path Lisa had originally taken.

After so much time, any chance that the rapist's fingerprints could be lifted and matched to an offender arrested for another crime had been smudged away.

Like Macro, the police Bureau of Criminal Intelligence (BCI) was keen to pursue the clear similarities between Sarah's and Jane's disappearances, and Lisa's abduction and graveyard rape. They revisited statements from hospital security guard Wayne Wookey, who had spotted a telco van in the early hours after Lisa's attack, in Monash Avenue. Independently, Lisa had reported seeing a similar vehicle cruising the street, which she had hidden from in terror. That was on February 12, 1995.

Wookey had seen the logo on the side of the van. In various statements to police, he used the names Telecom and Telstra interchangeably to describe the logo. In mid-1995, Telecom had changed its name to Telstra, at the same time beginning an upgrade of its vast, Australia-wide fleet of technicians' vehicles. Changeover in the field was not instant and the logos, each featuring a red stylised T, were confused by laymen for many years afterwards.

BCI had also unearthed the report by Julie-Anne Johnson, who was leered at by a man driving alone in a Telstra vehicle in Claremont in an early January morning, 1996, the day after Sarah Spiers disappeared. Here was a possible red-hot witness link between the crimes against Lisa and Sarah.

BCI wrote to Telstra, asking for records of vehicles with Telstra stickers in February 1995, and the names of their drivers. Newly minted Telstra was by mid-1995 taking delivery of white family-type Holden Commodore station wagons, built by General Motors-Holden to its specifications, and branding them with new Telstra stickers. They had ladder racks and metal grills to separate the cargo area from the passengers. Telstra's pool of technicians' vehicles still included older vans and Toyota Camry station wagons, which had rectangular headlights.

Employees were allowed, under an agreement with their union and at a cost of twenty dollars a week, to drive Telstra vehicles home for private use after hours – it saved garaging and was thought to improve security. Vehicles included in the 'part-private' agreements were identified by an orange frame around number plates. In early 1995, however, the telco's vehicles were all branded with Telecom stickers. BCI had asked for Telstra drivers, and that is what it received.

A scientific attempt to trace the graveyard rapist was made just a month after Sarah's disappearance. Sperm recovered from Lisa's medical examination, labelled Unknown Male 4, was amplified and tested against male DNA profiles stored on the local database. No result.

Did Lisa's attacker really have anything to do with the other two missing women? Among Macro detectives, it had become an article of faith that both Sarah and Jane had been searching for taxis when they disappeared. As sensible young women, Sarah and Jane would not have got into strangers' cars. The culprit must be a taxi driver, their thinking went. Their vanishing acts were therefore in no way similar to Lisa's case. Lisa's had been a classic blitz attack, a snatch-and-grab carried out with military precision following a high level of planning, with equipment well prepared for the perpetrator's disgusting enterprise. The modus operandi (MO) was too different to be connected.

A fault line ran through this MO logic – when Lisa's abduction was thought to be irrelevant to the other Claremont cases, neither Sarah's nor Jane's bodies had been found. Police, therefore, had no actual evidence of the MO in their cases. They had made only assumptions, a dangerous way to investigate.

For the second time, the investigation into Lisa's rape was shelved, and the investigators' mindset hardened.

*

While Macro was working around the clock and wrestling with its various theories, the community was in uproar.

How could a second young woman vanish? From a safe place like Claremont? Who was doing this? What sort of monster was he? Was he clever or just completely mad and brazen? Why hadn't the police caught someone? Somebody must know something. The abductor must have made a mistake that would lead to a quick arrest.

More young people volunteered stories of fake taxis, cars with no radios or meters, and sometimes with bogus taxi markings on the doors. After Jane disappeared, one couple told of a 2 a.m. ride in a white Holden car they thought was a taxi, its driver possibly believing he was picking up a lone woman.

'I was in a short black mini and black top walking behind my boyfriend in the lit area near the club,' the young woman said. 'It could be that he didn't see my boyfriend.'

When her boyfriend appeared, the driver carried through with the trip, driving both to nearby Swanbourne. He charged five dollars for the short journey, though during the ride the couple noticed the car had no taxi meter.

Among the first people police interviewed after Jane's disappearance was taxi driver Steven Ross, who, four months earlier, had told police he had driven Sarah Spiers to South Perth the night before she disappeared.

'The cops asked me where I was that night that Jane went,' Ross said. 'I was working. They told me I had picked up Jane in my taxi and killed her.'

For the rest of his life, he mused that, if he had not had an alibi for the nights of two of the murders, he would have been jailed for them.

Claremont mayor, Peter Weygers, tried to get on the front foot a week after Jane Rimmer vanished, becoming even more active in the community, starting with a town centre security audit, which he called the Mayor's Night Walks.

He paced Claremont's streets with local business leaders and the boss of a private security company, assessing the hazard levels in the darker corners of Claremont's central business district, logging broken lights, unlit lanes and the need for more payphones.

He could not have imagined what was about to befall him in the following weeks.

8

Liberties

As a civil libertarian, Peter Weygers had a long history of rubbing up against bureaucracy and authority, especially police.

'All you seem to care about are the civil liberties of the criminal element and sexual deviants,' says one vicious letter on his files.

It ends with this threat: 'I PROMISE you that I will start a campaign to discredit you and all other Sunday Christians (do-gooders).' It was dated May 22, 1996, three weeks before Jane Rimmer vanished.

'I upset a lot of people – they said I defend criminals,' said Weygers. 'But that's the point of civil liberties. We advocate for the falsely accused, who are not criminals.'

This work did not endear him to police. In 1990, he launched a high-profile campaign against random stop-and-search powers for police, publicly berating them for what he called unjustified search warrants.

Fraud Squad detectives had arrived at his home one day at 7:30 a.m., armed with a search warrant seeking the origin of a political pamphlet. Weygers recognised one of the detectives from a long-ago classroom. In his typically blunt fashion, guaranteed not to impress, he blurted out: 'I know you. I failed you in Year Eleven.' He was not charged. Eventually, the legislation was quietly dropped.

That same year, he took photos of what he considered to be an unjustified police assault on an Aboriginal woman. For his trouble, he was threatened with arrest for assault and forced to hand over his undeveloped film. He was later to recount this episode in public under privilege at the Deaths in Custody Royal Commission.

He publicly criticised police for what he called 'cradle to grave' discrimination against Aboriginal Australians. Tom Clews, Assistant Commissioner of Police Operations, labelled his accusations ill-informed, outlandish, destructive and absolute rubbish. It took the police force decades to fess up, with Police Commissioner Chris Dawson publicly apologising to the state's Aboriginal people for their treatment by police, calling for an end to a history of racism and 'unconscious bias'.

In 1991, Weygers called for a royal commission into the police force after hearing many allegations that suspects had been bashed or otherwise coerced into making confessions. He publicly cited a string of perceived injustices, including deaths in custody, and called for bad cops to be weeded out of the force.

Peter Weygers did not hesitate to make his criticisms of police public, apparently oblivious to tight police mateship.

He was genuinely surprised to be told about centuries of tribal police self-preservation instinct. Criticism of even a single officer was taken to mean Weygers was anti-police. Criticise one officer and you criticised them all, the thinking went. The sting was also keenly felt by the officer's family and their colleagues' families.

'Police said they hated his [Weygers'] guts,' are the words in a sworn statement by taxi driver Steven Ross.

'I had to criticise police, it came with the job of president of the Council for Civil Liberties,' Weygers said.

He was about to feel, very personally, the sting of concentrated police attention.

*

With stark clarity, Peter Weygers remembers the life-changing moment he arrived home after a day at an education seminar on Thursday, July 4, 1996, four weeks after Jane had been snatched from Claremont, with still no sign of where she was. On his front door was a business card from 'detective sergeant Paul Greenshaw, Homicide Squad'.

On the blank side was a handwritten message: 'Mr Weygers. Please contact d/s Greenshaw or Det Weskin.'

Weygers recalls his reaction: 'I was very wary of police. As Civil Liberties president, I had listened to many stories of mistreatment at their hands – coerced confessions, unjustified charges.'

He asked his lawyer, Grant Milner, to deal with the request. Detectives delivered two explosive questionnaires to Milner's office.

The cover of each document, titled 'INSTRUCTIONS', stated that every word was important, that it might be checked later and that no corrections could be made to answers.

It asked for an alibi, an opinion on how police should conduct their investigation, and the five most important causes 'that created the situation'.

It then asked for detailed written answers to sixteen questions – among the most confronting:

Do you know who abducted or murdered Sarah Spiers?
Did you abduct or murder Sarah Spiers?
Did you take part in the abduction or murder of Sarah Spiers?
Should we believe your answers?
If your answer to the last question is yes, give one reason why.
What would you say if it was later determined that you lied on this form?
While filling out this form, what were your emotions?
Were you afraid while completing this form?
Did you ever discuss the possibility and reasons for the abduction of Sarah Spiers?

How do you feel now that you have completed this form?
If you were asked to pay for counselling for the parents, how much would you pay?

A second, almost identical questionnaire substituted the name Jane Rimmer for Sarah Spiers.

'Grant Milner answered the police,' Weygers said. 'He told detectives I could not help them – that I did not know any of the girls, had not seen them and did not kill them, so their questionnaire was irrelevant to me. He told them I would not be filling it out.'

The next day, July 6, 1996, he picked up that day's copy of *The West Australian* newspaper. It was a Saturday, the day when the paper sold about twice as many copies as it did on weekdays.

'I don't trust probe police' blared a headline. That headline had been toned down from the previous edition, where the even more emotive banner read: 'Mayor refuses to help Rimmer police'.

The newspaper said Weygers had refused to be interviewed by homicide detectives investigating the disappearances of nightclubbers Sarah Spiers and Jane Rimmer, and to fill in the questionnaires he had been presented by police. It quoted Detective Sergeant Paul Greenshaw as declining to say whether Weygers was a suspect or not, adding that the mayor could have information of value to the inquiry.

Greenshaw told the paper that he could not understand why Weygers would not co-operate, the report went on. 'For the Mayor of Claremont to refuse to assist police in an enquiry like this is unusual. I would have thought a person in his position would have been eager to assist. But any person can refuse to answer questions if they so wish.'

'Police asked a hundred people to fill in the questionnaire – four refused on principle,' said Weygers. 'I was the only one named publicly of all those even given the form.'

Weygers' side of the story was also printed. He had denied any involvement in the women's disappearances to the newspaper, but said he did not trust police. He had said he was happy to assist as mayor, or as president of the Council for Civil Liberties, 'but if they want to interview me personally, then I am a suspect and I will only do so with my lawyer present,' he told the paper. The Wood Royal Commission into NSW police had deterred him. 'On the advice of my lawyer, there is no way I would go alone.'

Peter Weygers said afterwards he could scarcely believe what was happening to him. Such public accusations were so alien that he was in a daze. 'To this day, I don't know who told the reporter about the police visit,' he said later. 'To me it was obvious – I am a civil libertarian and a psychologist. That questionnaire was arrant nonsense. All over the world, anyone with the slightest knowledge of civil liberties knows it is foolish to be interviewed by police without a solicitor present.'

It was ironic that one of the worst local breaches in civil liberties in recent times had been suffered by the president of the Council for Civil Liberties, he said.

Police had compiled and used the questionnaire after a visiting Israeli code-breaker, Avinoam Sapir, schooled them on the theory that guilty respondents might hint at their own responsibility for crimes when confronted. Police said that the people who were given the questionnaires were suspects.But in the immediate wake of the article, lawyers pointed out the legal and investigative traps.

In another *West Australian* report published a day later, John Prior, secretary of the Criminal Lawyers' Association, said that the technique could alienate the community, that it was legally dangerous because it denied basic legal rights.

He noted there was no formal warning that people were obliged to provide no more than their names and addresses to police, and that the questionnaire contained no disclaimer that people's answers could be used against them.

A few weeks later, Professor Don Thomson, head of forensic psychology at Edith Cowan University, echoed Peter Weygers' words that the questionnaire was nonsense, in the same category as calling in a clairvoyant. The form had grave consequences for a respondent, because any answers could be misinterpreted, he said. To the irritation of police commissioner Robert Falconer, he said Macro was clutching at straws.

Criticism intensified when it emerged that the questionnaire contained factual errors, such as quoting the wrong day of the week for Sarah Spiers' disappearance, thus asking people to provide alibis for the wrong day.

'The story, when it was published, implied I had something to hide,' Weygers said. I thought that common-sense, educated people would see that it was rubbish too.'

Police quietly dropped the idea of confronting potential suspects with the 'Did you abduct or murder Sarah Spiers/Jane Rimmer?' questionnaires because, they said, the intense public criticism had wiped out any chance of public co-operation.

Weygers hoped readers of the newspaper wouldn't give the article much credence. He is tall, ruddy-faced and instantly recognisable. He never went to bars or nightclubs. 'I'm too old and too visible and too well known – if I had been lurking alone around the streets of Claremont late at night, someone would have come up to me and said, "What are you doing here, Peter?" It was too ridiculous for me to take seriously.'

But readers did take it seriously. It soon became clear that many readers of *The West Australian*, the state's only daily newspaper, had formed the view from the report that the mayor was a suspect for two murders, or that at the very least he knew something about the two disappearances. Otherwise, why would police be pursuing him, and why would news of that pursuit end up on the pages of a serious newspaper?

'Readers believed there was no smoke without fire. What we had was just a smoke machine making smoke,' he said. 'If you protest loudly, you must be guilty. If you don't protest loudly, you must be guilty.

'It's probably the worst thing you can publish about someone, to imply that they are under investigation for murder, and are refusing to co-operate. Trial by innuendo, and it found me guilty.'

Acting Detective Inspector Paul Ferguson soon said publicly that Peter Weygers was not a suspect but a person of interest, who police felt could add something to the inquiry. He could not understand why anyone should have a problem answering the questionnaire.

'Ordinary people don't distinguish between a person of interest and a suspect,' said the mayor. 'I was even called a suspect in a headline in *The Australian* newspaper. The whole thing is some sort of grotesque nightmare to a law-abiding citizen.'

Characteristically, Weygers went on the attack, publicly ridiculing the questionnaire in print and on radio. Acting Assistant Police Commissioner Bob Kucera visited the mayor's office, informing Weygers that he was not a suspect, and asking him to stop publicly criticising police tactics. He also released a statement in August 1996, declaring Claremont to be 'fairly crime-free'. But Kucera's statement received minuscule publicity, having little effect in the wider world.

Many years later, police stopped using the label 'person of interest'. Only the term 'suspect' remained.

There is no doubt the newspaper report both unnerved many members of the public and, perversely, gave them some comfort. Here was a respected, professional, high-profile figure living among us in Claremont, readers believed, familiar with and with easy access to the local streets at night, who the police thought could be the murderer. At last, the cops were onto somebody.

'After that story was published, people felt they had permission to point a finger at me as the scapegoat for all the misery that was happening in Claremont,' Weygers said.

He was not exaggerating. Strangers in passing cars would slow down and literally point to him in the street and shout out one word: 'Murderer.'

'Look at the size of him – those poor girls,' was one remark a companion walking a few metres behind Weygers overheard from strangers. The daughter of a friend told him that all her friends were saying to her, 'That mayor killed those girls in Claremont.'

Peter Weygers' social subtlety filter did not always function well. Personal rumours circulated, evidently fed by gossip about Weygers' character and the police attention in the wake of the murders. He was a single man, given to making awkward flirtatious approaches to younger women in social and business situations, not registering that his blunt manner and mixed signals were, at times, interpreted as unwelcome advances. These stories expanded to take on a life of their own, once the world believed he was refusing to answer police questions about the Claremont murders. Some even reached the ears of police.

The original newspaper report so horrified three members of the Claremont Town Council, they forced an urgent special meeting on March 24, a week after the article was published, in an attempt to censure their mayor. Weygers countered that he had suffered a gross invasion of his civil liberties. He told councillors that the report had been inaccurate: 'I have spent ten years fighting corruption and crime in this community.' His argument was convincing. His council passed a vote of confidence in its mayor.

The publicity's effects really hit home when parents at a school where he worked as a child psychologist told the education department that they no longer wanted him to counsel their children.

'I continued to receive bullying, intimidation and harassment on a huge scale. With a few exceptions, people felt they could not support me.'

'People craved an answer to what was happening in Claremont, any answer, and the newspaper gave them an answer,' he said. 'People clung to it like a lifebuoy, overcoming all logic that told them it could not possibly be right.'

Weygers was urged to sue the newspaper for defamation, but logic initially deterred him. Lawyers advised Weygers that taking legal action would give the allegations more currency. Peter Weygers demanded a full public apology from police for linking his name to the murder of Jane Rimmer, but contrition came there none.

*

Talk in Claremont was about nothing else but the disappearance of Jane Rimmer. One missing girl might be a runaway, but two were far too much of a coincidence. Numbers were down at Club Bayview and the Continental, there were fewer single women and proportionally more men out and about. Some even commented that there were more police on the streets than clubbers.

9

Rooster

On the afternoon of Saturday, August 3, 1996, a couple was driving their two children and a dog along deserted, unsealed Woolcoot Road, Wellard, when they spotted a rooster crossing the road. The children asked if they could chase it.

When the car stopped, the youngsters' mother, Tammy van Raalte, took the opportunity to pick some of the spectacular arum lilies growing in abundance, in full bloom after winter rain. Imported and declared pests because of their toxicity to stock, the beautiful lilies appear suddenly and grow rapidly in the wet months, then die off quickly in southwestern Australia's parched summers.

A giant specimen a few metres from the road, inside a 'cavern' in the undergrowth, caught van Raalte's eye. She walked a little along the tea-tree scrub line.

What she saw in the next moment was to remain etched in her mind forever. She spotted what seemed to be a log. Moving closer, something touched the back of her leg. It was a small human foot. Van Raalte's gaze travelled up from the foot, disbelief causing her to take some time to register what she was looking at.

She saw Jane's naked body, lying face down and partly on its side, partly concealed within the new growth of weeds, plus bare twigs and sticks. Leaves from branches that had concealed much of the body had long since died. No attempt had been made to bury this unfortunate young woman. Huge white lilies had grown up between the female's limbs, covering her face and tangled hair.

For fifty-five days, Jane Rimmer had lain undiscovered beside Woolcoot Road, four metres from the riding school fence, her feet a metre from the road.

Van Raalte yelled for her husband to call the police. As he drove to Greenacres Riding School next door with the children, his wife insisted she would stay with Jane, refusing to leave her alone for another second. She kept Jane company for the twenty minutes it took for police to arrive.

As van Raalte waited for the first responders, she was approached by two horse riders, who had found a wooden-handled clasp knife further along the road next to a real estate sign, its blade exposed. The knife was the type issued to Telstra technicians, 4200 of them issued in Western Australia since 1992.

As horrible as the discovery of Jane's body was, it was a breakthrough police had been awaiting. Uniformed officers from Kwinana police station then two detectives from the same office were soon on the scene, satisfying their superiors that, indeed, it was a naked human body that lay in the bushes. They blocked the road and, within hours, more than twenty officers swarmed the once-quiet dirt road – local police recalled to duty, followed by their superiors, then the Homicide Squad led by Paul Ferguson and David Caporn. A scene-of-crime unit of the police video section, plus forensic officers and pathologists soon arrived.

Now they had a crime scene rich in forensic opportunities, as police say.

Detectives took pathologist Dr Karin Margolius to the scene, followed by two other pathologists. Dr Margolius examined Jane's body where it lay, before gently removing the vegetation and further examining the marks it now carried.

There was a massive diamond-shaped opening at the throat, joining both collar bones and meeting towards her centre. Because after-death changes had occurred in the open environment, it was not possible to determine the size of the original wound, but clearly somebody had cut Jane's throat.

Jane had been dragged by the arms to her resting place, causing some joint dislocation.

She had evidently put up a fight in her last moments. Her left wrist was found 'flopped' in an unusual attitude, with a V-shaped cut, severing the tendon. She had been stabbed as she held up her forearm in a boxer's fighting stance, either to hit her attacker or push him away, or both.

Dr Margolius and police noted the thin branches that had been placed on her body had been torn from the trees directly above, while scrub and low vegetation had also been torn out to partly conceal her. Although all Jane's clothing was missing, her jewellery, apart from her watch, was all present.

Jane was gently lifted onto a sheet and taken to the road, where the physical examination continued. Each twig, each weed, each piece of soil over, under and surrounding the body was packaged and labelled. The hope was that somewhere among all those samples may later be discovered a forensic link to Jane's brutal and callous killer – a hair, a fibre, perhaps internal DNA.

Jane was taken to the mortuary where the post-mortem continued, including X-rays to check bone breaks and locate any bullet or other implement left behind. No trace of a weapon was found.

Jane was positively identified from her dental records and navel ring.

In a bizarre episode that appears to have broken forensic rules, after the autopsy, Dr Margolius cut a clump of tangled, matted hair from Jane's head and washed it in a trough. She handed it to detective Vicky Smith, who shampooed, washed and brushed it, and took it home. She tied it with an elastic band and placed it in a gift box to give to Jane's family. 'It was a keepsake, an act of kindness and compassion to the family,' the detective said.

The police video of this episode horrified an international fibre trace expert when he viewed it many years later. No attempt had been made to filter the washing water to capture fibres from the sample. Other debris from Jane's hair was simply tipped onto the floor.

*

A realist, Trevor Rimmer had been preparing himself for bad news, but still it came as a gut-wrenching shock. He was at home, preparing dinner for his wife and family, when came the dreaded knock on the door.

'I'd hoped it would end differently from this. I suppose from the very first night I was preparing myself for the worst,' he said afterwards. 'I just want to remember Jane the way she was, a bubbly little girl. I no longer wish for vengeance; I just have sympathy for them. How could they do this?'

When the news broke, Jane's mother, Jenni, was not at home, but a couple of blocks away having drinks with friends at her workplace, the Shenton Park Hotel.

Detectives offered to take her home first, but the moment she recognised the Macro officers entering the bar, she knew why they had come. They walked her outside and confirmed the worst. Jenni was inconsolable.

After the first devastating shock, Trevor was to say later that, in some ways, the discovery of Jane's body had been a relief to his family. Jane's parents were told there had been no sexual assault.

'At least we know now and can put Jane's body at rest. We are thankful for the twenty-three years we had with Jane. Whoever did this cannot take that away.'

His feelings flew immediately to the Spiers family, whom police had also notified about the discovery of a body. Carol

Spiers hoped that the disappearances were not connected, that the same killer had not abducted her daughter. Her family had not given up hope of finding Sarah alive. Sympathy cards, letters and phone calls had continued to pour into the Spiers household.

'We will never, ever give up hope of having our daughter returned to us and that is the only issue we are interested in,' said Carol. She and her family hoped that the fact both girls were last seen in Claremont was a coincidence. 'Please do not give up. Please help us find Sarah.'

*

Hardly a scrap of information escaped into the public domain, neither the state of the body, nor the cause, time and place of death. Waves of speculation swirled through the community. Persistent rumours were passed on as truth – that Jane had been held prisoner and tortured for days or weeks – and these untruths spreading like wildfire. Even when proof to the contrary emerged, police kept this information tightly held.

Months after the freak moment he had discovered Jane's watch, Paul Langenbach, while driving along Woolcoot Road, spotted a heartbreaking memorial to Jane on the verge. It was a makeshift cross, fashioned by detectives from local wood and police crime scene tape. The cross was right beside the spot where Langenbach had been thrown from his horse.

Suddenly realising the significance of the silver Guess watch he had found, he called the police. The timeline proved that Jane had been killed the morning she was abducted and that her body had been left in Wellard the same morning.

Was Sarah Spiers here at Wellard as well, somewhere close to where Jane was found? Police and criminologists are familiar with serial killers who use the same disposal areas for multiple victims, referred to as 'dump sites' in raw police parlance.

Police divers probed several square kilometres of Wellard's swampy winter lakes, while teams picked over the muddy, scrubby flatlands, examining every old beer can, piece of paper, or bit of flotsam that might help, but it was decided nothing useful was collected. Puzzlingly, none of these seized items was forensically examined.

It does not take a criminal profiler to work out that the murderer had picked his disposal site carefully – it was less than an hour's drive from Claremont, dark and remote.

Clearly, the murderer had been down that limestone track before, in daylight, and scoped out his surroundings. He knew that the spot would be deserted late at night, his evil deeds staying hidden from any houses, where a car could be driven without being scratched or leaving tell-tale damage to the local growth.

Like Lisa's Karrakatta rapist, Jane's killer had come prepared, this time armed with a knife and some kind of binding material. He was cool, confident and practised, with ice running in his veins.

Paul Ferguson told the public that the killer was someone who was comfortable operating in Claremont. He did not mention the untested Telstra knife.

The discovery of Jane's body sent the media into meltdown. It became a national sensation. Jane's murder pointed to a vicious maniac preying on Claremont, wrote *The West Australian.* Television channels set up cameras in Claremont for live crosses to their news bulletins as each tiny snippet was unveiled.

To help prompt possible witnesses' memories, a video appeal for information was broadcast in June, starring singer Kate Ceberano and John Wood, a TV police drama star. This drew more than 2000 new pieces of information, 1500 of which were passed on to the Macro Task Force, though no promising leads were found.

Alongside their televised plea for information, police distributed 10,000 leaflets and posters, warning young women not to relapse when it came to being vigilant, and cautioning them to avoid car parks and other isolated places unless they were accompanied. The posters also appealed for information about anyone whose behaviour had changed. This was to prove to be another massive time-waster, because it focused even more negative attention on Claremont and taxis.

Taxi drivers' income plummeted. People using cabs had halved since Sarah Spiers disappeared, and numbers had only just returned to normal. They plunged again as all drivers came under suspicion. Some drivers were even spat upon.

'We lost millions of dollars in fares,' said Taxi Council member Hugh McLennan. 'For a couple of years, drivers at night almost starved. Passengers didn't want to get into cabs. They were terrified.'

Police made a sweep of 5500 taxi drivers' criminal records, paying special attention to prior convictions for violence and sex offences, with more than thirty-five drivers sacked in the months after Jane Rimmer's disappearance. The remaining drivers said they wanted DNA tests to exclude them from suspicion. Oddly, drivers working on the night of the Karrakatta abduction were not included in this sweep, such was the hardening mindset among senior officers that the MOs were too dissimilar.

Detectives had a fair question for taxi driver Steven Ross when they visited his home in Embleton: Ross had inserted himself into the Spiers investigation, so maybe he really *was* involved. Where had he been in the early hours of the morning of Jane's disappearance, June 9? Police traced his passengers and another witness. They seemed satisfied that Ross was not the culprit – at least for the time being.

*

Jane Rimmer was cremated at Karrakatta Cemetery. Her 500 shocked and traumatised mourners, including the state's premier, Richard Court, filled the chapel to overflowing.

Jane was sometimes the life of the party, sometimes the reflective poet writing of friendship, and she enjoyed a special relationship with the children at the Carrington Day Care Centre, Reverend Robert Anderson told the mourners. He said he knew Jennifer and Trevor Rimmer wished it was all an awful dream and that, somehow, they would wake and find the hurt had gone.

'We feel both outraged and helpless in the face of such distorted humanity that is capable of inflicting such wounds,' the reverend said. He hoped the justice system would apprehend those responsible and protect society from its enemies.

'Essentially, though, this will not return Jane to us.'

10
Ciara

News that Jane's death had been so starkly confirmed threatened to spin Claremont's social unrest out of control.

Only four weeks had passed since the publication of the mayor's refusal to answer a police questionnaire had caused his reputation irreparable damage. The torrent of publicity that followed the discovery of Jane's body again turned an adverse public focus on Claremont's mayor, and brought a swift reaction from Jon Sainken.

Sainken's lawyers wrote to Weygers, stating that Club Bayview had in no way been responsible for reporting Weygers to the Macro Task Force, adding that the club's owners sympathised with the mayor's exposure in the press. Dr Sainken described the suggestion that Weygers had had anything to do with the disappearances as having 'hideous implications.'

But this letter did not mark a lull in hostilities.

In November 1996, the club won its appeal to increase its capacity to 385 people, but was required to agree to a raft of conditions. These included employing two security guards with dogs to patrol the streets, installing more phones, supervising taxi ranks, and employing street cleaners. The club appealed to the Supreme Court against some of these conditions.

Ever provocative, Weygers, who had worried that Claremont's nightspots were attracting crime to his town, went public on another front. The club was about to face court for its tenth charge of overcrowding in its ten years of operation, having already paid $13,435 in fines for exceeding its permitted numbers.

The mayor urged the state government to begin a strike-out rule for liquor licence holders – if convicted ten times for offences such as overcrowding, venues should automatically have their lucrative liquor licences suspended or cancelled. Weygers said crowd restrictions were a public safety issue, in light of a fire at the club where arson squad officers said an accelerant had been employed. Three apparently deliberately lit fires broke out at or close to the club in the mid-1990s, all of them unsolved. Gang turf wars were suspected. His idea attracted support from a government minister.

*

As the summer of 1996–97 reached peak temperature, the hunt for the Claremont killer was still at full pace. Police forensic officers returned to Jane's bush grave at Wellard in February, after the baking sun had sucked the last drop of moisture out of the soil.

Twenty officers again combed the now-dry paddocks for any sign of Sarah Spiers, or any clues left by Jane's killer while the ground had been waterlogged in winter.

Still prominent, just off the road, was the simple cross now hung with rosary beads, marking the spot where Jane had been found. Police teams searched dried-out swamps and wells, but picked up nothing of note. The debris they did collect was again not even tested.

Detectives hoped, desperately, that it would not take another murder before the killer was to leave evidence for a breakthrough.

*

During 1995 and 1996, various telco vehicles, driven by lone males offering lifts to women in the early hours of the morning, were noticed on the otherwise deserted streets of Cottesloe and Claremont.

In 1997, police asked for 'living witnesses' to come forward – women who had been offered lifts but refused, or who had got into vehicles and become concerned, or who had been dropped at the locations they requested.

Astonishingly, after these public police pleas, a parade of witnesses reported to police a series of incidents involving a lone man in a telco car doing just those things.

Not long after Jane's murder, a telco car with a ladder on the roof was seen driving five times up and down Eric Street, the main route to Cottesloe beach, near the Ocean Beach Hotel.

From the bar that overlooks the ocean, Natalie Young saw the same white station wagon with a Telstra logo on the door making a turn for the second time.

After leaving for the hotel with friends, the twenty-four-year-old flagged down a Holden station wagon she thought was a taxi, but it was the Telstra vehicle. She refused a ride and it drove away, but circled the block twice more. She told police its number plate was framed in orange.

In the summer of 1996–97, Jane Ouvaroff, aged twenty-two, had been drinking on a night out in Claremont and was walking home with two male friends. She also flagged down a white station wagon that was driving past Rowe Park after midnight.

This isn't a taxi, she thought as she climbed into the front seat. Thinking quickly as the vehicle drove off, she told the driver she had left her shoes in the park. He stopped to let her retrieve them, and she roused her two male friends lying out of sight. They saw the wagon carried a Telstra logo and had tools in the back. The driver took all three to nearby Shenton Park without incident.

In December 1996, two other young women walking along Eric Street from the Ocean Beach Hotel were picked up by a man in a white station wagon with a Telstra logo on the bonnet. When the car reached Claremont, Annabelle Bushell, then aged twenty-two, 'felt a strong instinct to get out'. She looked up and saw a red traffic light. When the car stopped, she jumped out, opened the back door and dragged her friend, Trilby Smith, aged eighteen, out of the car.

Another tragedy was to motivate police to seek out these unreported stories in July 1997. But in mid-March 1997, just four months after that last-known encounter between a young woman and a telco vehicle on the streets of Claremont and Cottesloe, another woman would not have such a lucky escape, and another family would stare into the abyss.

*

Ciara Glennon, a popular, slightly built twenty-seven-year-old lawyer who lived with her parents in Mosman Park, had recently returned to Perth from her year-long backpacking trip to be bridesmaid at the wedding of her younger sister Denise, a doctor. Ciara was born in a bush hospital in Zambia in 1969 where her parents, Denis and Una, a proudly Irish Catholic couple, worked as missionaries. The family came to Australia when Ciara was aged five. In high school, like Sarah Spiers, she attended the Iona Presentation College near her parents' home. After leaving school, she studied law at the University of Western Australia, then started work at the law firm Blake Dawson Waldron in Perth city. She had left Australia in April 1996, two months after Sarah disappeared but before Jane Rimmer was abducted, and missed the intense publicity surrounding the terrible crime. She had previous boyfriends but was single. She loved the beach and parties, and maintained a wide circle of friends from school, university, work and beyond, socialising mainly in Perth's western suburbs. Ciara dressed smartly for work but off-duty was known for her downmarket attire. Her petite, slim build at 152 centimetres (5') tall belied her independent, feisty, strong-willed and at times fierce nature.

Staying with her parents on her return, Ciara had spent a week catching up with friends and family, then the following week she resumed working at her old law firm. On her return, the big impression she had previously made as an accomplished lawyer was rewarded by being handed an important case.

About 7:45 a.m. on Friday, March 14, 1997, her mother, Una, drove Ciara to a bus stop outside the Hungry Jack's fast food outlet on Stirling Highway, in the heart of Claremont, where Ciara got the bus to work. It was the last time her mother was to see her.

Unbeknownst to Ciara, that bus stop was a viper's vortex. A man in a Telstra vehicle had stared creepily at Julie-Anne Johnson there, the night after Sarah disappeared.

After work that day, Friday night drinks were served in the Blake Dawson Waldron's sixteenth-floor boardroom, from 5:30 p.m. until 11 p.m. The night marked the end of Ciara's first week back at work. She was in boisterous good spirits, her colleagues said, drinking champagne then wine.

A colleague suggested they head to the Continental Hotel for an early St Patrick's Day drink. Ciara was in two minds about partying on. 'Very unfortunately, she decided to come,' said workmate and friend Abigail Davies.

Five people packed into a tiny Holden Barina car owned by Neil Fearis, the law firm's senior partner, Ciara's boss, and family friend of the Glennons. He drove Ciara and three workmates to the Continental.

Arriving about 11:30 p.m., Ciara and Davies walked hand in hand into the busy bar. Davies later told a court that Ciara was not unsteady on her feet. 'She was drunk, but she was very much in control of everything about her person,' she said. They separated, Ciara moving around the ground floor of the

Continental, having little if anything more to drink. At one stage, she threw her black jacket on the floor near a table. A male friend picked it up and tied it around his waist for safekeeping. Ciara retrieved it and headed for the corner door exit alone, just before midnight, pausing to chat with friends at tables on the platform outside.

A confirmed sighting placed her outside the Bellissimo café in Bay View Terrace, next door to the Continental. This corner was where Jane Rimmer was last seen, and where Lisa and a male companion had vainly waited for a taxi the night she was abducted. Ciara was en route to Stirling Highway, still alone, perhaps in search of a taxi.

She was still wearing her work-day outfit: white T-shirt with a faint pink flower pattern, short black skirt, black single-breasted jacket with a white metal Claddagh brooch – two hands clasping a crowned heart – pinned to it, black shoes with two-inch heels and black bag with a shoulder strap.

Several women said they saw Ciara walking downhill, crossing and recrossing Bay View Terrace as she meandered towards Stirling Highway, then turning right on reaching the main artery. In all, twelve people reported sighting her on foot. Passers-by placed her outside a computer shop on the highway, close to the Bay View Terrace intersection.

One report had her standing on the footpath with arms folded. Another witness saw her reach the south side of Stirling Highway, head back in the direction of the Continental, then change direction on reaching the median strip, returning to the south side of the road. At that point, a passing motorist saw her raise her right hand above her head as if trying to hail a cab. Logs from a mobile phone being used in another passing car were used by police to pinpoint that time at close to 12:15 a.m.

Across the road was the bus-stop shelter and seat where Una Glennon had dropped Ciara that morning, and where a man in a Telstra car had leered at a young woman twenty-five hours after Sarah vanished from the next intersection. Sitting on the seat outside the well-lit Hungry Jack's, munching hamburgers, were three men in their early twenties, who had a grandstand seat to what happened next. They had been drinking at the Continental, but did not miss much. Each of the men, who police would label the Burger Boys, remembered a different aspect of the scene that played out in front of them.

First, they saw Ciara Glennon on the opposite side of Stirling Highway, walking along the footpath outside a computer shop. She was alone and 'maybe intoxicated', said one of the men, Brandon Gray.

Alert to Claremont's dangers, Gray yelled out a warning. His friend Troy Bond said Brandon had called to Ciara that 'it was stupid of her to hitch-hike'.

'She stuck her finger up,' Bond said.

His attention was then taken by a white Holden Commodore station wagon across the highway on the same side as Ciara, driving very slowly towards Mosman Park, with Ciara walking some distance ahead of the vehicle.

Ciara kept walking. Then Troy Bond saw her approach the station wagon that had now pulled up at the kerb beside her, not far from the traffic lights at Stirling Road. That spot was almost in line of sight of the phone box where Sarah Spiers had made her last taxi call, thirteen months earlier.

The young men watched Ciara's slight figure as she stood on the footpath, interacting with someone in the car. They saw her bending over, hands on her knees, apparently conversing through the front passenger window. Then was a moment when none of the Burger Boys were watching. When they turned to look again, both Ciara and the car had gone.

Gray was a Holden enthusiast and able to give a good description of the car. He described a white, very recent model Holden station wagon, model designation VN, a Series 1. The men were definite that the vehicle carried no taxi lights, taxi signs or markings, at least not in their line of vision on the driver's side.

Gray later told police that he noted unusual teardrop shaped cut-outs in the car's distinctive wheel trims. Later, police discovered that these were the wrong Holden hubcaps for that model car.

The Burger Boys were among the last to see Ciara alive. Two other witnesses, one forced to pass the slowly moving station wagon, and another travelling in the opposite direction, described a similar interaction between Ciara and an occupant of the vehicle.

*

At 3 a.m. on Saturday, 15 March, Una Glennon had checked on her daughter, and discovered her bed was empty. She consoled herself that Ciara was an adult, had just returned from travelling the world alone and did not have to account to her parents.

Later that morning, when Ciara failed to turn up for a hairdressing appointment in preparation for her sister's pre-wedding party that night, Una became alarmed. She called her husband, Denis, who was sailing with friends to Rottnest Island. Denis cut short his trip and raced home. Una then called around Ciara's friends, who in turn phoned more of her friends and acquaintances. Nobody had seen Ciara or heard a thing from her.

Hearts heavy with dread, Ciara's family made a missing person report at Cottesloe Police Station at 4:30 p.m. that Saturday. The Macro Task Force, still working feverishly on the first two abductions, was devastated to now have a third on its hands.

The next day, news of Ciara's disappearance hit Claremont and the wider public with cyclonic force. The similarities with the other crimes were all too obvious. The sense of dread was palpable.

State crime squad commander Bob Ibbotson announced that police feared a serial killer was on the loose. This official confirmation knocked an already jittery population sideways.

'Mad with fear' was the description of the mood in the early 1960s, when serial killer Eric Edgar Cooke broke into homes in Claremont and surrounding suburbs, stealing money, attacking young women, and murdering eight men and women.

Numb with fear was the initial reaction when Ciara disappeared, the massive trauma magnified by the close sense of community.

Initially, Ciara's distraught parents could find only a year-old photo of their missing daughter, an image that was emblazoned on every newspaper and television bulletin in the country. Unfortunately, it was not until the following Tuesday that a more up-to-date image of her was found among Ciara's stored holiday clothing. Taken at the end of her travels, it showed a young woman strikingly different from the first photo. Now her skin was tanned and her dark brown hair, which tumbled and curled below her shoulders, was sun-bleached with prominent blonde streaks. She had let her hair out as her Friday night had worn on. If a sighting of her the night she disappeared was compared with the right image, she was hard to miss.

'There is a very distinct difference, and that's an unfortunate thing,' Commander Ibbotson said.

Forensic officers went into Ciara's bedroom to examine and photograph each personal item, strewn about a room by a traveller still in backpacker mode. They seized Ciara's toothbrush, two hairbrushes, a razor and some clothes, delivering them to PathWest laboratories to produce a reference DNA sample, in case the worst had happened.

Ciara Eilish Glennon was no pushover, despite her diminutive height and weight of just 45 kilograms. Her friends said that, if under threat, she would take every opportunity to fight back, verbally and physically, and make every effort to escape.

'We're confident that the way she's been brought up, she will fight on and we're hopeful she will be found at this stage,' said Denis Glennon, through tears, a few days after his daughter had reported her missing. 'We are a strong family and I don't cry easily, but Ciara's alive, we believe that.'

He said he did not believe she would get into a stranger's car. 'It would have to be somebody she knew or possibly she just called a cab and got into that.'

Desperately, Una called into radio station 6PR on March 29, expressing the same sentiment. She said she believed her daughter was being held captive, possibly in an outer suburb. She implored listeners to be on the alert for any screams or cries for help, and to observe any unusual behaviour in their neighbourhoods.

'This is the third time this terrible thing has happened. I would not want any mother or any family to go through the pain and anguish and sheer heartbreak that Denis, Denise and I are experiencing.

'A piece of us is dying every day. Please help us with any information and keep praying that we will find Ciara. People just cannot disappear off the face of the Earth. Someone must be coming into contact every day with the person or persons responsible. I still believe Ciara is alive somewhere in Perth or in nearby areas.

'Ciara is strong and she is a fighter and I think she will fight on as long as she can.'

11
Siege

Claremont was on fire, just as surely as if an incendiary bomb had been dropped on the village. So much public terror, grief, fear and dread threatened to overwhelm the community that Police Commissioner Bob Falconer felt compelled to issue a call for calm.

'We're into a mixture of panic and paranoia, fear and distrust and the blaming stage,' he said, warning the community not to get swallowed up in mistrust. Pointing the finger at someone and bouncing theories around could lead to the community becoming dysfunctional and self-destructing, he said.

But people were frightened, really frightened. Everyone could identify with the victims. They were vulnerable. They had a human face. They were just like us. They could have been any one of us, walking home or looking for a taxi. Calls to report unusual behaviour had made ordinary citizens suspicious of each other.

With the fate of his daughter unknown, Denis Glennon blasted the Claremont Town Council at a news conference. He said it had been 'obvious to anybody for a year now' what needed to be done about security in Claremont, but installation of a secure taxi rank and cameras had only started since his daughter had disappeared.

Information began to emerge about the way Ciara's Friday had unfolded. But some of the most crucial information that was passed to police by a populace eager to help, such as a good description of the car that her abductor drove, was clutched tightly by police as closely guarded secrets.

During this eternity of fading hope, church leaders had combined to ask their congregations to pray for all three Claremont women. Denis Glennon said he could now fully understand the trauma that the parents of Sarah Spiers and Jane Rimmer had gone through.

Politicians were as deeply affected as the general population. 'There is a sense of depression across the whole area,' said Colin Barnett, the district's local member of parliament. The man who would later become state premier said, 'People are talking about it all the time. They are worried about their own children and those of their friends.'

Police Minister John Day and two other government ministers visited Denis Glennon the Monday morning after his daughter was reported missing. The same day, Day and premier Richard Court fronted the microphones to announce the state's biggest-ever reward – $250,000 – in exchange for information from the public to solve the crime.

The speed of announcing the record reward, however well intended, drew accusations that the government was showing favouritism towards an affluent, well-connected friend of the Liberal government, Denis Glennon, whose successful business had recently been granted $22 million in government funds for a recycling project in partnership with a government agency.

Many asked, where was the reward for the other two women?

Joining this chorus came the voice of another grieving mother, Margaret Dodd, who lived in a low socio-economic part of Mandurah, south of Perth. Her daughter, seventeen-year-old Hayley Dodd, vanished in 1999. She was last seen alone on a lonely country road north of Perth. Margaret Dodd received no ministerial visit, and slammed the police investigation as being less than diligent. One of the officers involved agreed.

Dodd complained that, unlike people living near high-end Claremont, she had had to beg the government to offer a $50,000 reward for information.

'Hayley was put on the backburner,' Dodd said. 'We were nobody. Hayley didn't matter. We were not important enough to get the resources.'

At the top of the Terrace, the Continental's owners instantly draped a huge banner above the hotel's main entrance, its script boldly headlined 'The Spirit of Claremont'. It read: 'We have no other choice but to carry on. Join us if you choose ... we'll help get you home.' It offered a supervised taxi rank, courtesy bus and beefed-up video surveillance.

'Claremont has been picked on in some way,' Club Bayview and hotel part-owner Jon Sainken told a meeting of Claremont's Safety and Security Committee a few days after Ciara disappeared. 'We are in a state of siege. We can go back to normal again when this menace is eradicated.'

Though the killer was still out there, Sainken emphasised that his club's courtesy bus had taken up to 250 patrons to their front doors in one night, the driver waiting until each passenger was inside the house. But some young women still insisted on walking alone to their cars, even arguing with security escorts to leave them alone.

With police confirming the possibility of a serial killer, the *Post* asked former Federal Bureau of Investigation (FBI) expert on serial killers, Dick Ault, to weigh in on the recent crimes. The article, published on March 22, 1997, pointed out that, if this was indeed the work of a serial killer, it would be the third time in living memory that a serial killer had stalked Claremont and surrounding suburbs.

Ault said that police would be examining similar prior crimes in the Claremont area. 'Main common characteristics are sexual flaws in their make-up and craving for power,' the *Post* reported. 'Their adult lives of crime usually start in a relatively minor way, such as peeping Toms, progressing to assault, rape and finally murder.'

'You will find there would have been rehearsals,' said Ault. 'To them, abducting and killing women is a passion. They view the world in terms of opportunities to commit these crimes. It's their art work.'

He said the killer's ability to disable an abducted woman in a car was a puzzle to many people, but this had been easily perfected by genius-level Californian serial killer Edmund Kemper. Kemper, 'the co-ed killer' of the 1970s, murdered ten people, including his own mother. He picked up hitch-hiking university students, drove them to isolated locations, then used his sheer size and weight to overwhelm all resistance. Ault said stressors in the killers' lives were likely to lead them to hunt for more victims. Job loss, relationship breakdowns, births, deaths and family crises were likely triggers. His analysis was to prove uncannily accurate.

*

In the weeks after Ciara's disappearance, police enlisted the help of two profilers trained by the USA's FBI. They told the police that offenders frequently took intense interest in reported details of their crimes, even inserting themselves into the fringes of the investigation. When finally caught, they were often found to be keeping souvenirs of their victims and newspaper cuttings describing the cases, revisiting the details over and over in their minds, while relishing the knowledge that they had outfoxed the police, believing they were impervious to capture.

Armed with what was known about these quirks of serial murderers, police and profilers decided to set a trap for the Claremont killer.

On Wednesday, April 2, 1997, the two profilers announced that they would hold a public conference outside the Continental Hotel at 1:30 p.m. on Friday. With Ciara's whereabouts still unknown, captain David Caldwell, a criminal behaviour consultant and crime scene investigator from South Carolina, USA, and FBI-trained criminal profiler Claude Minisini from Melbourne, reported they had examined the streets and lanes of Claremont and, the next day, they would release more details about their approach during their street corner exposition.

Their tactic was obvious – curiosity can get the better of killers, and there was a chance that this one would turn up to discover what the police knew. Plainclothes officers would mix with the crowd and no doubt arrange for photographs to be taken.

Late on the Thursday morning, before television and newspaper crews prepared to descend on Claremont for this bizarre event the next day, Denis Glennon, who was at a business meeting in a Perth boardroom, received a police phone call. A detective strongly advised him to return home.

Macro members arrived there to tell Denis and Una devastating news. At about 9:30 a.m., Thursday, April 3, 1997, the body of a compact five-foot tall woman had been found in coastal scrub country at Eglinton, 51 kilometres north of Perth – further north of the city than Jane Rimmer's body had been found to the south. It was Ciara Glennon.

Twenty-three-year-old plasterer Jason Atkinson had made the shocking discovery. He was walking on a track in dense scrub, coastal saltbush and grass trees, looking for cannabis plants. In this semi-rural fringe of the metropolitan area, he had noticed a smell and looked into a valley-like contour, expecting to find a dead kangaroo.

This young man was permanently scarred by what he saw next: Ciara's body lay between two big grass trees, almost entirely covered with browning vegetation.

Atkinson raced to call police from the nearby tomato-packing shed where, that morning, he had dropped his girlfriend at work. When he led them to the scene, he was so traumatised that he refused to go near Ciara's body, instead gesturing in the direction from a distance.

'He was distressed, he was in shock,' said Charlie Carver, the senior officer of Joondalup detectives, who had been directed to the body by Atkinson.

Like Jane, Ciara was face down. She was lying slightly to her right side, almost a mirror image of how Jane Rimmer was found. Her body was almost fully covered with tree branches plus grass and scrub ripped from close by, and from above. As was the case with Jane Rimmer, Ciara's killer had made no attempt to bury her. She was about 50 metres off Pipidinny Road, and a short distance from a limestone track that connected with the sealed road.

Ciara was wearing her black skirt, hitched up, and her now almost-completely blood-stained white top and underwear, but her shoes were missing. Also absent was her shoulder bag and its contents, including her sunglasses and risqué novelty toys she had bought on the Friday for her sister's hen's party on the Saturday her parents reported her missing. Ciara's Claddagh brooch was gone, along with her jacket.

Ciara's parents' and friends' description of her as a fighter, strong-willed, resourceful, resilient, tenacious and feisty proved to be heartbreakingly accurate.

Examination of her body showed she had indeed fought fiercely for her life, trying to fend off a frontal attack by a person wielding a blade. Classic self-defence wounds were obvious, with a large twenty-centimetre long gash recorded, cutting tendons on her right arm, which was underneath her. Her right forearm was stabbed to the bone, twice. In what was evidently the cause of her death, her throat had been horribly cut with a sharp knife in a long, sweeping motion that passed from the left side of her throat, across her vital neck arteries and airways to her right shoulder, then continued deep to her spine to above her left shoulder, leaving only seven centimetres of her neck uncut. A second sweeping gash joined the first above her spine and continued over her head, down the right side of her face and ended at her lower jaw.

The wound to her forearm showed that, as Jane had done, Ciara had held up her forearm like a boxer, a featherweight versus a heavyweight. Two tell-tale cuts to the bone, about three centimetres apart, were found on her lower right arm.

Blood-staining showed she was killed where she was found, or very close by.

An extraordinary, poignant find was a clump of Ciara's auburn curls, sitting on her shoulder, cut at both ends. Two passes of the killer's sharp knife had apparently lopped it off while cutting Ciara's throat.

Again, it was obvious that Ciara's murderer had scoped out this makeshift grave site in advance, in daylight. He had evidently driven off the main highway, Wanneroo Road, into Pipidinny Road, then driven exactly two kilometres before turning left, then driven about 40 metres along a track. The nearest house was 500 metres away, surrounded by vegetable market gardens. The killer had parked his vehicle on the track. Ciara's body lay about 30 metres into the scrub.

For some weeks, Telstra crews had been working on phone lines along this stretch of road. After Ciara went missing, some of these telco workers remarked that they could smell a dead kangaroo.

Police rushed in numbers to the scene to confirm the shattering find. The Continental corner conference was quickly cancelled and detectives, forensic officers, a pathologist, the two profilers and the media descended on Pipidinny Road.

Television and newspaper camera operators were kept at the Wanneroo Road intersection, well back from the scene; some were caught trying to sneak through the sandhills, while others used helicopters to photograph the forensic work being performed around the gruesome discovery. The camera crews hovered over Paul Ferguson, plus Dr Karin

Margolius, two other forensic pathologists, doctors Clive Cooke and Gerard Cadden, plus police forensic and scene-of-crime officers. Profilers David Caldwell and Claude Minisini were also there, along with two police photographers and Macro Task Force men. This team and others worked all day, photographing the forensic examination of Ciara, where she lay and again when she was moved onto a white sheet, the processes captured on a one-hour video.

The team carefully sifted sand around the body, took damp soil samples from underneath her and closely examined the tracks that spread in all directions, the team sweating in the thirty-five-degree autumn heat.

They measured the height of nearby trees and photographed scars on them, where an evidently tall person had ripped down the branches used to conceal Ciara's body.

Ciara's long hair was tangled in vegetation. Sergeant Robert Hemelaar, head of forensics, placed the lopped-off hank of Ciara's hair in a sealed sterile jar.

Though her Claddagh brooch was missing, the rest of Ciara's jewellery, including a navel ring, bracelet and watch, were intact.

Dr Margolius's examination at the site, and later at the morgue in Nedlands, confirmed that, along with defence wounds on her arm and forehead, there were much smaller but very significant defects. The ring fingernail on her right hand was shorter than its well-manicured companions, while her left thumbnail was freshly torn, evidence of close-quarter defence wounds. Ciara had ripped the nail as she had desperately clawed at her far bigger, taller, stronger murderer.

At the morgue, a technician wielding a huge pair of scissors clipped off her nails, while forensic police officer Adam James McCulloch held a fresh yellow-top jar under each nail as it was snipped.

When the technician reached Ciara's left thumb with its torn thumbnail, he remarked on how difficult it was to find some nail to cut. He scraped 'gunk' from the nail bed into its jar held by McCulloch, who screwed shut the yellow lid. McCulloch lent his initials to the sample number: AJM 40.

Six days after Ciara's body was found, the most likely of her fingernail samples were chosen for DNA testing, but they did not test her left-thumbnail sample. A PathWest forensic scientist looked through the clear Perspex of the jar marked AJM 40, noted the small size of the sample and wrote that it was not suitable for DNA testing. Negative results came from the other nails, which had been deemed suitable for testing.

Martin Blooms, the forensic scientist who had also analysed samples recovered from Jane Rimmer, could detect no physical or chemical sign of sexual assault. But, as he had found with Jane, Ciara's body had lain in the open too long for him to tell. 'A negative result does not mean one thing or another,' he said.

Meanwhile, Dr Margolius had reached a dramatic conclusion: the back of Ciara's skull had been fractured in a twelve-centimetre long line, consistent with having been hit by a long, heavy object. The forensic specialist concluded the killer's hit had been hard enough to stun his victim temporarily. Later, a London pathologist from the Royal College of Surgeons was more specific, speculating that the weapon used was something like a heavy screwdriver.

Dr Margolius was present when a hank of Ciara's hair was clipped and cleaned, to be presented to her parents a few days before what would have been her twenty-eighth birthday, on November 20, 1997.

This touching act of compassion was perhaps meant to make up in some small way for refusing to allow Ciara's family members to view her body, so gruesome were her injuries. The gesture was later criticised as extremely risky, given the importance of Ciara's hair as a catcher of incriminating hairs and fibres. Tests on just one fibre caught in the hair could change the course of the investigation.

Within Macro, Ciara's confirmed death sparked another examination of the abduction of Lisa and the terrible crimes against her. The samples of Unknown Male 4 were taken out of storage at the PathWest lab for further tests, two weeks after scientists had tried unsuccessfully to retrieve an offender's DNA profile from under Ciara's fingernails. Significantly, the scientists also recovered scores of fibres and some strands of hair from Ciara that did not match her own hair or clothing.

Forensic scientists have a saying: 'Every contact leaves a trace.' Microscopic examination of fibres can be vital in placing an offender at the scene of a crime, just as DNA analysis can. Each fibre was carefully preserved and labelled.

Had some of these fibres come from the killer, or his clothes, or his car? Fibres had also been recovered from Lisa after her ordeals in Rowe Park and Karrakatta, and from Jane Rimmer. If matches were to be found with any of the hundreds of fibres from these three crime scenes, or with fibres found on the clothing of someone arrested for the murders, such evidence would be extremely valuable in court.

*

Back in Mosman Park, the Glennon family was devastated. After police had left Ciara's family home, Denis Glennon experienced a crisis in his Catholic faith. 'I got so angry with God. I remained angry for a long time,' he later told students at his daughters' old school, Iona Presentation College, where his wife, Una, still taught.

'All the prayers! Why did he not answer them? How could he be so cruel to us? How can he be a good God? If he is all-powerful, how did he let this happen? He let me down. Why did he not stop this? Why should I believe in God anymore? Some person did an evil thing to Ciara and my family.' Denis Glennon later reconciled, saying: 'We cannot have it both ways. We either have free will or we are only puppets of God.

'You reach a point where you realise there are no answers as to why it happened to our particular family.'

Word that Ciara's body had been discovered flashed around the country. Don Spiers, shearing sheep on a farm, was crushed when he heard on his radio that an unidentified body had been found. Carol was told by a friend. Was it Sarah? For well over a year, Don and Carol had clung to hope that their daughter was still alive. They had to endure an excruciating wait until well after nightfall before they found out it was not her.

12
Tiny Dancer

Paul Ferguson from the Macro Task Force gave a frank overview of three alternative scenarios police were examining, now that Ciara's body had been found.

Ciara, a smart, sensible, well-travelled young woman, had apparently not been drinking after arriving at the Continental. After she left, she had either voluntarily got into a car she believed to be a taxi, police car or some other official vehicle she would trust; or she was an acquaintance, however casually, of the driver, perhaps a man she had met the same night. Or she had been forcibly abducted in a blitz attack. This was the most unlikely method of abduction as it would be difficult to remain unnoticed.

On April 3, Ferguson asked for help from the public, saying that the murderer could be anyone's friend or colleague, and appear to be a normal and pleasant person.

'As terrible as this discovery is, it is a major breakthrough for the investigators. The discovery will have a significant impact on the person responsible and will result in his being preoccupied and distracted.

'In the workplace, people should be alert for a workmate who took time off after news spread of the discovery of the body, of workmates who can't concentrate and who suddenly change plans.'

He appealed to employers to check their records for men who had taken time off work after the bodies had been found.

The worker might develop headaches, appear anxious at work, and their work performance might have suffered.

*

That same week, Dr Sainken issued another statement saying 'our heartfelt sympathies are with her family and friends'.

He said the events must have greatly intensified the anguish to Sarah Spiers' and Jane Rimmer's families.

Five weeks later, his business partner, Barry Jones, said trade at the hotel had been badly affected, despite spending thousands on security and installing ten cameras. A catastrophic fall in takings, to a quarter of previous levels, forced the hotel to lay off half its bar staff, with losses mounting as they pumped thousands of dollars a week into free drinks. Even the daytime trade of high-street hairdressers and previously thriving boutiques had been hit hard. Fear was contagious. Claremont felt creepy.

'It was an extremely traumatic time for everyone involved in the hotel – the customers, partners and staff,' Jones recalled later. 'The trauma was felt especially by the young women on the staff. They were frightened. Security had to escort them to their cars.'

The defiant 'Spirit of Claremont' sign was not enough. Business went through the floor. 'There was no-one in the hotel – we had to round up friends to come and drink for free in the bar to make it look busy. Even they were afraid.

'The hotel had been so popular – it was a friendly place, the village pub. Ninety per cent would come in from a five-kilometre radius. They would know or be acquainted with twenty or thirty people in the bar – people they went to school with, neighbours, sportspeople. The West Coast Eagles came in regularly.'

The *Post*'s Nelli Noakes noted that the once-overflowing venue now had many tables to spare, the dancing had stopped and the men now far outnumbered women. Women could not help looking at the men around the bar and wondering if one of them was the killer, she wrote.

Hot-dog seller Jim Larkin was not optimistic that being extra streetwise was going to last: 'The people around here have very short memories,' he said.

*

Few clubbers trusted taxi drivers anymore, and drivers returned the sentiment, making it almost impossible to find a cab in Claremont. Because of Denis Glennon's insistence that streetwise Ciara would never get into a car she did not know and, therefore, had most likely climbed into a taxi, her disappearance continued to throw the focus back onto cabs, with a retired forensic scientist suggesting in late March that all taxis should be impounded and tested for evidence. Police Commissioner Bob Falconer advised people not to take unnecessary risks and to take precautions when hailing taxis, saying that security staff needed to note cab numbers.

Within four days of Ciara's death being confirmed, police began checking booking records and compiling dossiers on all taxi drivers who had been working on the nights the women disappeared, especially those drivers working all three nights. Booked jobs were traceable but hails were impossible to track in the days before GPS and digital taxi meters.

Cabbies reported that takings had dropped by forty per cent, even before Ciara Glennon had disappeared. They said passengers blamed taxis for the murders. In bitter terms, one driver recounted tales of the abuse and income loss he had endured for years after the Claremont abductions.

Another told the *Post* that, in the late 1990s, he had regularly picked up the same single woman in Claremont. He was intensely annoyed that, each time, a companion would walk to the car with his passenger and inspect the floor and cargo area to make sure there was no predator hiding, as well as noting the driver's name and number.

'The feedback from drivers is that very few taxis will service Claremont in future,' said Rod Leicester, taxi unit manager for the Department of Transport, in late March 1997. 'They really feel quite vulnerable. They will go anywhere but Claremont at the moment.'

The taxi industry agreed to unprecedented scrutiny, believing it would help restore the plunging confidence in drivers. Taxi drivers volunteered to provide DNA samples to eliminate them from suspicion. Police called in 3500 metropolitan cabbies, taking saliva swabs from 700 to test their DNA. They set up an underground car park and required cabbies to drive their cars in for forensic testing. Cops checked the criminal records of all drivers, cancelling seventy-eight taxi drivers' licences because of prior offences, some quite minor. A further 168 were sent warning letters.

Supervised taxi ranks were installed outside Club Bayview and the Continental Hotel, where the names and addresses of passengers were recorded before they got into cabs. But security men failed to prevent young women, bored with waiting, from wandering off to Stirling Highway to leapfrog for cabs – just as the three missing women had apparently done. Just ten days after Ciara's body was discovered, two pizza delivery drivers said that they frequently saw young women in the streets of the western suburbs, apparently drunk, trying to wave down cars late at night to beg lifts. On some occasions, they walked recklessly into the paths of cars to stop them.

Once again, police turned their attention to taxi driver Steven Ross.

Within days of Ciara's death being confirmed, detectives returned to his home in Irwin Road, Embleton, asking him where he had been when Ciara vanished.

They were especially interested in a device called a power-zapper that they knew Ross had, a $200 Taser-like stun-gun that he and many other taxi drivers had bought from an importer for protection. Ross told them he had tested his on a cat, but the poor startled animal had just run away.

The device had stopped working after Ross dropped it in water, and he was able to tell police where it was – he had given it to a friend. They recovered the stun-gun and kept it as evidence.

Ross also assured Macro that he had an alibi for the night of Ciara's abduction: four schoolgirls he had picked up at a school in Riverton, on the opposite side of the Swan River from Claremont. Detectives checked and seemed satisfied with his alibi.

Claremont's turmoil roiled on, with local conversation about little else. The Macro Task Force swelled to scores of detectives and support specialists, the biggest and most expensive task force ever assembled in the state. Their job was to check out, as best they could, 34,000 pieces of information received in the first seven weeks since Ciara vanished, sparked by the sheer outpouring of emotion, desire to help catch the fiend, and reward money.

The cops established that 1500 people had been in Claremont in the half hour before Ciara was abducted. They traced and interviewed them all, but found no promising leads.

*

Ciara's family had decided that her funeral, held on April 10, should be an ecumenical event, a bringing together of the community 'to preserve decency and the Australian way of life', said Denis Glennon. Father Kevin Long, a family friend, presided, accompanied by archbishops, priests and a rabbi, with the state premier and his cabinet ministers among the mourners.

Two weeks earlier, Father Long had blessed the marriage of Ciara's younger sister, Denise, at a church in inner-city

Leederville. The family had decided to go ahead with the wedding while Ciara was still missing. Life must go on, Denis Glennon had said.

Here was an entirely different service. St Mary's Cathedral was crowded with well in excess of a thousand mourners. Many did not know Ciara, or her family, but felt drawn to her funeral to say goodbye.

When Ciara's body was discovered, said Father Long, the community was united. 'It had to choose one of two ways to go – the way of madness or the way of hope.'

Fighting to retain his composure, Denis Glennon, at his feet his daughter's coffin with her pink ballet shoes atop, addressed her directly: 'When I am at my lowest, and feel that I can't continue, I think of you in your bridesmaid's dress made by mamma, but you never wore.

'You were our first daughter, our pride and joy, part of our grand family plan.'

Ciara, said her father, had excelled at school and at law school; she was a free spirit, a ballerina who always jumped from the highest diving board and swam the furthest out to sea. But she was still fragile and vulnerable. 'You were a bright, vital young person with a sunny outlook on the world. We are lucky to be able to say you were our daughter. Farewell, my little friend. God bless you.'

After the hearse had gone, little knots of girls from Iona Presentation College, the Catholic school in Mosman Park that Ciara had attended, gathered near the gates of St Mary's Cathedral, wearing their familiar light blue uniforms and panama hats. Their cheeks were streaked with tears, their faces ashen. They hugged each other for comfort, wrote the *Post*'s George Williams.

Ciara's violent death had hit the tight school community of Iona with horrible force. Iona was also the school where Sarah Spiers and her sister Amanda had boarded, and where Ciara's mother taught. The Iona links spooked some people, with occasional callers to police naming male staff members, all of whom were cleared by police inquiries. But that was not enough for some. Amid this miasma of fear, a blonde ex-Iona student took protective action. She dyed her hair dark.

'Around ten years ago Ciara Glennon wore one of those uniforms and one of those hats,' wrote Williams. 'Now her body was in the black car with the flowers, disappearing down the street, another car full of grieving relatives following.'

The next day, on the front page of the *Post* was an image of the Glennon family at Ciara's funeral service, where Father Long had said, 'It was as if our city had stopped still, convulsed as if gripped with grief and revulsion'.

13
Incendiary

Almost unbelievably, another layer of angst had been added to the hothouse atmosphere of violent death, grief, terror and anger that now pervaded Claremont's once-peaceful urban village.

It was council election time, usually a period of mundane, genteel smalltown politics. With Ciara's remains only just interred at Karrakatta Cemetery, however, her abduction from Claremont and her death were overwhelming the campaign.

The central cast of this new drama comprised Jon Sainken, vocal owner of the local nightclub with an interest in its hotel; Ciara's father, Denis Glennon; and the local mayor and person of interest, Peter Weygers.

In 1997, Weygers had been Claremont's mayor for twelve years. From February 1997 until election day, he walked the streets, doorknocking every resident of Claremont in this, his fifth campaign, hoping to be elected for another three years. He had applied for six months' leave from work to knock on 4500 doors, stressing the need for people to keep safe in this murderous climate. By the time of Ciara's funeral in April, he had worn out two pairs of shoes. But the hapless mayor was about to catch murder blowback from two different directions.

Soon after the funeral, Denis Glennon visited his daughter's grave alone at Karrakatta. He made her a personal promise. 'I told her I would do all in my power to find the person, or persons, responsible for killing her, or I would die trying,' he later recalled.

Despite the anguish he was suffering, Denis Glennon had bounded into action days after Ciara was reported missing. A former deputy mayor of another district and a man familiar with the inner working of town councils, he visited Claremont's CEO Rob Stewart just a few days after his daughter vanished to appeal for more closed-circuit television (CCTV) cameras on the streets of Claremont. 'He's very interested in security in Claremont,' Stewart said. The council's Safety and Security Committee met the next night to discuss the issue. It had not met since May 1996, after it was interrupted by Dr Sainken's writ served on Peter Weygers. With no hope of meeting the $250,000 cost, the council decided to appeal to the state government to fund the installation of CCTV cameras in central Claremont.

Meanwhile, with the fate of his daughter still unknown, Denis Glennon kept himself busy. Rob Stewart gave the distraught father the use of a desk in the Claremont Council chamber, plus access to council meeting minutes and records of the police, council and local businesses' Safety and Security Committee.

Throughout late March, Peter Weygers saw Denis Glennon sitting alone for days in the Claremont Council offices, busily writing notes. 'It was very, very unusual,' he said.

On April 18, sixteen days after his daughter's body was discovered, Glennon wrote to the council, criticising Weygers and Stewart. In a long letter, he questioned the council's handling of safety issues; the delays in installing lights, payphones and security cameras in the town; and the absence of meetings of the Safety and Security Committee.

'In what ways did the mayor's personal views on the use of video cameras ... his views on the operation of Club Bayview and Hotel Continental and his focus on the defamation case ... influence staff in the ... measures required to upgrade safety and security in the Town of Claremont?' Glennon asked. 'My review of the minutes and information has revealed some very disturbing issues. They also raise very serious questions about the decisions and actions of the mayor and/or chief executive officer … during the period July 1996 to March 15, 1997.'

These were the dates after the abductions of Jane and Ciara.

Glennon wrote that he would continue to pursue both the mayor and CEO until he received satisfactory answers.

Weygers later stated that he had always been careful not to reply to Glennon's attacks because of the tragedy his family had endured, adding that in view of the extreme grief Glennon and his family were suffering, Glennon might not have considered his criticisms with customary care. 'I'm a psychologist; I understand grief and the ways it can manifest,' he said.

But the mayor had responded to Denis Glennon's general safety questions – a bank of payphones existed at the post office opposite the Continental and he was all for cameras given the circumstances, provided they were effective and did not provide a sense of false security, he had told a council meeting on March 24.

Unmonitored cameras and their poor visual quality at that time made their usefulness very limited, he said. Months later, he provided a list of examples of crimes in the town centre that cameras had not deterred, and cameras that had also missed seeing the crimes occurring.

The poor quality of the last image of Jane Rimmer outside the Continental Hotel was also a maddening source of frustration to police. The monochrome pictures distorted the colour and shade of her hair and clothes, and missed vital seconds of the action. So unhappy was Glennon with the answers provided by Claremont that he had called Rob Stewart at home and threatened to launch a ministerial inquiry into the council's administration.

Although so far unopposed in his quest for a fifth term as Claremont's mayor, Peter Weygers continued doorknocking, with the emphasis on advising residents how to keep safe. On the day nominations closed for the job of mayor, Thursday, March 27, Peter Olson also threw his hat in the ring.

Olson had retired from the council in 1979. His family owned the local newsagent's property in Bay View Terrace, opposite the Continental. Olson cited safety as the major element of his campaign. 'I am very concerned about things like the inaction of the safety committee,' he said. 'The mayor has a conflict of interest with his involvement in civil liberties.'

With the elections looming, Weygers said Glennon had made it plain to him, in a call on the day Olson had nominated for mayor, that Glennon wanted to see Weygers ousted from the mayor's office.

At Claremont Council, a decision was made to outsource the prickly problem of how to respond to Denis Glennon's now-public letter of complaint. The job landed with a respected Claremont resident, Professor Patrick O'Brien, who let fly: 'I repudiate absolutely Mr Denis Glennon's insinuations that the Town of Claremont has been in some way responsible for the disappearance and death of his daughter,' he wrote in a letter tabled at the next council meeting on April 28. 'His allegations and suggestions are cruel, hurtful and insulting.'

He alleged that Glennon had 'entered the political realm by turning the brutal murder of his daughter into a political and electoral issue' and called his letter to the council 'a political document … damaging the reputations and careers of entirely innocent persons, notwithstanding the deep sympathy all felt for him'.

In a series of incendiary passages, Professor O'Brien alleged blame-shifting and asked whether Ciara had been adequately warned by her family and workmates about the dangers of walking the streets of Claremont alone at night. He did not hold back, his attack also embracing police and owners of Claremont's 'night-spots and drinking houses'.

Glennon said his lawyers had advised him not to read the letter.

Peter Weygers said that he in no way publicly supported Professor O'Brien's statements, nor would he repeat them.

On April 26, the *Post* published on its front page the fact that Weygers had separately lodged two sworn 'undue influence' complaints with the department of local government, alleging that Glennon had pressured him not to re-stand for the position of mayor, allegations that Glennon denied. Weygers' complaint went nowhere.

As the mayoral election loomed, Denis Glennon's well-connected friends began calling their contacts, urging them to vote for Peter Olson as mayor.

In the last days before the election on Saturday, May 3, Dr Sainken weighed in. He signed a letter delivered to all Claremont households, urging electors to vote for the alternative candidate, Peter Olson, misspelled 'Olsen'.

From his large semi-circular home office dominated by a grand piano and overlooking the Swan River, Dr Sainken launched a blast directed squarely at an embattled Mayor Weygers. The club owner versus his town's mayor. The psychiatrist versus the psychologist.

It was addressed 'Dear Fellow Resident' with the headline: 'Mr Weygers' attack on Ciara Glennon's dad – the last straw?' It said: 'unfeeling attacks by the mayor and his cohort Paddy O'Brien [were] deliberately adding to the suffering of the Glennon family … suggesting a complete absence of sympathy and understanding of family values … and deficiency of wisdom and judgment' as well as 'an alarming absence of vitally important character elements required to properly fulfil that public office'.

It went on: 'This unnecessary criticism of Ciara's father is apparently designed to save the mayoral skin.'

Peter Olson was bemused by this wave of unexpected support from Dr Sainken. He said he knew of Dr Sainken but did not know him personally, and had not asked for his help. 'It certainly had nothing to do with me. It was between him and Mr Weygers,' he said.

Another, unsigned flyer of unknown origin said: 'If you're young or young at heart, have children or grandchildren who go out and about … vote for improvement, vote Peter Olsen.'

The Weygers camp launched a last-minute counter-attack, with an army of volunteers hand-delivering flyers headed 'Who is Dr Jon Sainken?' the day before and on election day, saying that Club Bayview and the Continental Hotel, controlled by Dr Sainken, had been the last drinking spots of the three girls who had gone missing.

'Dr Sainken has been continuously trying to expand these drinking spots and has been in dispute with the council and Mr Weygers, who had opposed their unlimited and uncontrolled expansion.'

But that was not the end of the damaging paper war.

Evidently out of nowhere, on the day of the election, under the inflammatory heading 'Weygers "put off" Glennon queries', *The West Australian* newspaper, quoting unnamed local sources, published trenchant criticism of Weygers for allegedly delaying replies to Denis Glennon's written questions about safety and security. Invoking the name Glennon ensured the headline attracted maximum sympathetic attention.

That report was the last nail in the coffin of the Weygers campaign, though the paper's unnamed sources had it wrong, according to Weygers. He was not at the meeting cited.

To add to his woes, things had changed in Claremont, not just by the murders but the district's demographic. Older residents had been moving out of their Federation-era houses to be displaced by renovators – affluent baby-boomer couples with children. As these children grew into teenagers, their rite of passage was through the gilded doors of Club Bayview, the social hub of Perth's western suburbs. By age eighteen, they became eligible to vote in federal, state and council elections.

A vigorous recruiting campaign urged them to enrol and to vote locally for a new mayor in order to protect Claremont's nightspots. A strong belief took hold that Mayor Peter Weygers wanted to shut down 'their' nightclub.

Not without reason – Weygers had asked the club to take more responsibility for security outside its doors, and said the club's presence had attracted crime to Claremont. He had referred to Claremont's becoming a 'mini-Northbridge', while his council had spent $100,000 in legal fees opposing the expansions of the club and hotel.

'Weygers seemed to put blame on the hotel,' said Barry Jones, Dr Sainken's Continental partner. 'He said we gave girls too much to drink and didn't look after them.'

To add fuel to this fire, the mayor's argument for a ten-strike liquor ban had attracted some government support at a time when the club was on its tenth strike.

On polling day, club and hotel staff phoned their young patrons urging them to get out and vote for Olson.

Neil Fearis, Ciara Glennon's boss who had dropped her and other staff at the Continental the night she disappeared, was one of the friends who had rung around his contacts in Claremont, at Denis Glennon's request, to help vote Mayor Weygers out.

Remarkably, when the votes were counted, Peter Weygers had attracted about as many votes as he had at the election three years earlier. They were from his friends, the legion of people he had helped, and his committed elderly supporters. But this time, a lot of fresh voters had turned out to vote in the optional poll.

On the Saturday night, when news reached the young crowds at the Continental and Club Bayview that Peter Olson had beaten Peter Weygers 1377 votes to 1015, it was party time.

'Young people dance as mayor is ousted', was the *Post* headline on May 10 that described the action.

Craig Hutchinson, Club Bayview's manager, told the paper's reporter Nelli Noakes that the result was a victory for the youth of Claremont, who had turned out in unprecedented numbers to tip out Weygers, an assertion confirmed by the official count.

'The results show that Claremont's relatively recent nightlife scene has become a potent political force in the town,' Noakes wrote.

'Young people were very voter-aware this year,' Hutchinson said. 'The ones I rang about it were definitely a lot more aware. Saturday was a big night at the club in general, but there were extra celebrations there and a bit of a party up at the Conti.'

Weygers also blamed his defeat on the campaign waged among young voters, plus the newspaper report a year earlier that named him as having refused to answer a questionnaire about the disappearances of Sarah and Jane. His 'person of interest' label was still uppermost in many minds, despite police denials that Weygers was a suspect. The mud had stuck, he said after the election.

Then, his run-in with Denis Glennon and the nightspots' campaign against him, and Sainken's letter in particular, had finished his chances. Dr Sainken's letter to electors had succeeded in attracting sympathy for Glennon, he said. It looked as though the mayor was attacking Glennon, leading voters to turn to Olson. Weygers pointed out that Dr Sainken's letter was on his psychiatrist's letterhead and made no mention of the writer's nightclub and hotel interests in Claremont. On May 5, he lodged a complaint with the medical authorities, and was to allege that the election flyer posed as an analysis of the mayor's mental state. He asked the Medical Board to investigate whether any breach of ethics of the profession had been committed. The board replied that it appeared Dr Sainken had not breached the Medical Act and that the Board would take no further action.

Weygers was devastated that ratepayers had kicked him out of his mayor's chair. He clearly felt a deep injustice, but said he did not want to appear a sad and bitter loser. He reaffirmed his respect for democracy and vowed to fight on. In this mind, what happened next confirmed that forces were arraigned against him.

While he was fighting to retain office, Macro police had been checking Weygers' alibi for the night Ciara Glennon disappeared.

He had had no independent alibi for the first two disappearances, as he lived alone and had been asleep in the early hours of those mornings. On the night Ciara was abducted, at about 12:15 a.m., he had been at a council function at far-away Morley, with a photo and an indelible interaction with two other guests to prove it.

Another guest, Jean Mulder, a fellow Claremont councillor to whom he had given a lift home, swore Weygers could not have been at home before 1:30 a.m. Detectives interviewed other people at the function and confirmed his alibi.

Then in the immediate aftermath of his election defeat, two more shocking indignities were to be visited upon the ex-mayor, still punch-drunk from severe blows to his personal and public persona.

On May 6, a menacing death threat was left on his answering machine by a man with a deep, deliberate voice.

The next day, at the front fence line of Killara, his house in Richardson Avenue, Claremont, somebody delivered a freshly severed cat's head into his old metal letterbox. It had been sawn from a ginger cat and was carefully placed, unwrapped.

There was no note and Weygers could offer no explanation, other than the death threat and gruesome delivery must have been connected with each other and with the council election, or with the public suspicion that had been cast upon him for murder. He took the severed head as a mafia-style warning, similar to the one portrayed in the 1972 movie *The Godfather*, in which the protagonist awakes to find planted in his bed a severed horse's head.

'I can only assume it's part of a campaign to shut me up,' a stunned Peter Weygers said at the time. 'At the moment I'm praying that I'm not the next one to lose his head.'

Police took the head away but found no clues to the perpetrator.

14
Unconventional

Determined to do whatever possible to find his daughter's killer, Denis Glennon started a fund to help pay for additional police resources with his wealthy and influential business friends, including Neil Fearis, his close friend and Ciara's boss; Michael Chaney, the boss of the national conglomerate Wesfarmers and future National Bank and Woodside chairman; and Julie Bishop, who would become Australia's Foreign Minister.

Bishop had known Ciara Glennon when she worked as a summer clerk at the law firm Clayton Utz. Ciara had many friends at the firm. 'The young women in particular were devastated when they heard the news and I found myself counselling them,' Bishop said.

Called the Secure Communities Foundation, the fund kicked off with $250,000 during the electric, grief-soaked atmosphere of fear and helplessness in the aftermath of Ciara's murder being confirmed. This unheard-of external funding was to tempt officers into exploring techniques they had not used before, including a criminal-tracking computer system from England, and importing profilers and psychiatrists to Western Australia from interstate and the USA. From San Francisco, they also imported a lie detector operator and his machine, despite the fact that lie detector results are not recognised in any Australian court. The foundation also paid for upgrading the local forensic laboratory, PathWest, enabling it to buy two genetic analysers to cope with the flood of mouth swabs taken from taxi drivers and others. These analysers, called Profiler Plus, were a huge leap in automated DNA analysis.

Contributions rapidly rose to $850,000, with the extra money slated to supplement the local police budget, including sending officers to the USA.

Behind the scenes and with the help of these extra funds, Macro was ramping up its fight against the phantom killer. The police tactics were based on the assumption that he was still prowling Claremont in a car, searching for victims. The number of police and specialists working on the case now pushed close to a hundred. Macro had grown even larger than the team that had probed the notorious backpacker serial murders in NSW between 1989 and 1993, which arrested the culprit, Ivan Milat, eight months after an appeal to the public for information. He had been identified via a precursor abduction, which was non-fatal but shared many details with the murders.

Macro reopened the file of the unsolved Church Lane attack on the twenty-one-year-old woman whose head was bashed repeatedly against the wall outside Club Bayview six weeks after Sarah Spiers vanished. Result: nil.

The squad continued to trace and interview everyone who had been enjoying the local nightlife on the night Ciara vanished. By May 1997, the total had risen to 1800 people who had visited Claremont that night. Each was identified, logged and mapped. All that work put police no closer to identifying a killer.

The night after Ciara Glennon's murder, and unknown to the council, club or community, the Macro Task Force had installed a secret video camera inside Picnic Boutique, a shop in central Bay View Terrace. From Thursdays to Sundays, the camera was trained on cars turning from Bay View Terrace into St Quentin Avenue, where Club Bayview is located, intended to record details of hundreds of number plates that police then entered into a computer system.

Despite police having access to the best camera technology, its unblinking eye missed more than half of the licence plates. Poor camera quality in the day, poor lighting at night, a poorly mounted camera and people walking past blocking its line of sight were later given as reasons why it had not picked up the killer's number plate. The black-and-white results were smudgy and primitive – sometimes just black.

After Ciara's disappearance, the Macro squad also commandeered roadside Multinova speed cameras from the traffic branch, yanked out their single-shot cameras and replaced them with video cameras.

They were installed along Stirling Highway and operated in the early hours of the mornings to record plate numbers of all passing cars. These were as ineffective as the Picnic Boutique camera. There was no way to correlate the name of each registered owner with details of who was driving each of the 70,000 cars photographed. No useful matches could be made using the ever-changing Department of Transport computer systems, not to mention the ponderous software operating at the time.

As private resources continued to be poured into the investigation, Macro tried another ploy, utilising the profilers it had imported, paid with funds raised by the Secure Communities Foundation. The supposed near-magical powers of profilers, immortalised in movies such as *The Silence of the Lambs*, dazzled many detectives. But did profilers really lock up the bad guys? By the mid-1990s, overseas sceptics were questioning the effectiveness of psychological profilers in identifying actual offenders before they were caught.

But Macro was all ears. They wanted a list of personal characteristics owned by serial offenders, compiled by forensic psychologists and psychiatrists who had interviewed such offenders in jails. The plan was then to broadcast this list of characteristics to the public via television, to inspire citizens to report suspicious friends, neighbours and work colleagues.

David Caldwell and Claude Minisini, the two profilers who had planned to hold a press conference to draw out the killer on the day after Ciara's body was discovered, advised acting Detective Inspector Paul Ferguson that they were looking for an organised killer, a controlled man who might be showing signs of guilt after his victims' bodies had been discovered.

They compiled a list of likely characteristics:

- is a white male, born between 1960 and 1971, probably living alone
- has access to vehicle less than ten years old
- is likely an acquaintance of all three victims, or a 'charmer'
- is regularly employed, earning $30,000 to $100,000
- is self-oriented
- has short-term or tumultuous relationships with women
- is insincere, but could present a façade of sincerity
- has episodes of immaturity
- has a high degree of self-control, discipline and patience
- has a high regard to personal presentation
- generally displays a pleasant disposition and is non-threatening
- would not be described as a 'career criminal'
- is likely to demonstrate tidiness, organisation and planning
- is likely the oldest child in the family.

*

The profilers said it was likely the killer would blend into the community, be able to win the trust and confidence of young women, be intelligent and socially adept, be in a relationship, have a steady job and either live or work in the area. Another common factor, as surmised by the profilers, was that the serial killer would also use the services of prostitutes.

Many such profiles were enlisted by Macro as the years went on but, unfortunately, the description of an offender who led an apparently mundane life obviously embraced thousands and thousands of men.

Armed with this profile, Paul Ferguson called a press conference and advised an eager public to watch for changes in the behaviour of workmates or other people they knew. He added that the killer would have a job and drive a late-model car – and be meticulous about cleaning it. The message was reinforced in a blitz of paid television advertising repeating the same messages. For extra impact, stations broadcast a re-enactment film of Ciara's last walk, featuring national stars, recorded at a cost of $20,000, again paid for by the Secure Communities Foundation.

In the five months after Ciara Glennon disappeared, fired up by the profilers' versions of suspicious behaviour, the calls to Crime Stoppers grew to 43,500. Police were inundated with tips about suspicious acquaintances, colleagues and neighbours taking days off work or washing their cars. A very large number of the tips were useless, given the scattergun nature of the 'profile'. The time and resources it took to filter all these tips for anything useful, plus follow up investigations, made it unsurprising that calls by Dick Ault, the FBI profiler contacted by the *Post*, to review prior crimes in the district with sexual overtones remained on the backburner.

At a frenzied pace, Macro officers continued to interview hundreds of men whom citizens had nominated as suspects, plus men identified by Macro's own inquiries. Those who could not be eliminated by alibis remained on their list.

Detectives continued to kick down the doors, as they put it, often with devastating consequences for innocent suspects. The *Post* received many calls from traumatised families, most of them unwilling to go on the record in case they attracted more police attention. Several men did identify themselves and told their stories on the record.

'One grudge and three calls to Crime Stoppers was all that was needed,' one devastated man told the *Post* in August 1997. 'For every one person they do catch, they probably ruin at least one hundred lives for a couple of weeks.'

Four Macro Task Force detectives had arrived at the Claremont house of the young family man while his partner and two children were at home, the full-on police presence greatly upsetting his two children. The father had been identified on Club Bayview's security video on the night Sarah Spiers disappeared but had not come forward to police.

Detectives took him outside and questioned him for more than an hour.

'I was quite happy to answer their questions, but they didn't have to come when the kids were here.'

Later, with the help of friends, he was able to establish an alibi for each of the relevant nights, but not before detectives had thoroughly searched his house and quizzed him about a frayed rope tied to a piece of wood they found in his yard – a broken child's swing.

Police also quizzed his partner – they had phoned her at work and ordered her not to talk about the conversation. She was questioned about whether her partner liked to 'strangle' her while making love.

The man's father and five of his friends were also questioned, asked about the suspect's movements, his bank accounts and his relationship with his partner.

The self-employed man needed two weeks off work to reassure his family and put his house back in order after the search. He said he felt as if he had been treated as guilty until proved innocent.

Darryl Lane, who believed he had been identified by locals as he delivered pamphlets at night, became so sick from police visits, questioning and searches of his Daglish flat that he could not work. 'They told me I am the chief suspect for this,' he said.

Four detectives came knocking after Sarah Spiers vanished, and two more turned him over after Jane Rimmer failed to return home. 'Police said they had a lot of complaints about me.'

One reason Macro police were searching houses was killer trophies. Serial killers often hoard souvenirs taken from their victims, using them to relive their fantasies, as Ivan Milat had done. If found, the items provide direct links between the killer and his victim – pure gold in terms of court evidence.

Some serial killers also give items of their victims' jewellery to wives, girlfriends and even their mothers, saying they had found these trophies.

Other serial killers exhibit different weird behaviour, as had David Berkowitz, the New York City killer 'Son of Sam'. He relived his fantasies through revisiting the sites of his random street shootings, attempting to find the graves of his victims, and also collecting clippings from newspapers that reported details of the outrages. Macro officers conducting house searches also kept a lookout for collections of clippings.

The innocent men whose homes were raided and searched, whose family lives and relationships were thrown into turmoil, were collateral damage in a desperate war. They were by no means the only severe casualties.

15
Kerb-crawler

Macro Task Force deployed undercover surveillance squad officers, also known as UCOs or Dogs. They trailed men in cars who were kerb-crawling the streets of Claremont after midnight.

In about September 1997, their interest was piqued by one driver who was taking a great interest in young women walking out of Claremont. Startled and concerned, the covert cops watched this driver slow down as he passed one particular young woman on a Claremont street, then do circuits of the block to pass her thirty times more.

This man was Lance Williams, a shy forty-year-old public servant who lived in Cottesloe.

Police learned he worked as a clerk for the Department of Main Roads in Redcliffe, near Perth Airport, processing heavy haulage permits. They became alarmed when they found his job gave him access to personal information from vehicle registration files.

After consulting with a forensic psychiatrist and delving further into Williams' background, some Macro officers became convinced they had their man.

He had lost his driver's licence for twelve years following a drink-driving conviction. Just before he regained it, he had bought a new car, days before Sarah Spiers was abducted.

He had made several suicide bids that same year, 1996 – the year both Sarah Spiers and Jane Rimmer disappeared. Suffering from depression after a friend died of cancer, he had tried to hang himself, cut his wrists and walk into the surf. When he told his father of these episodes, his family admitted him to hospital. Police knew they were dealing with an unusual and vulnerable man.

In September 1997, police placed Williams under surveillance. Their technicians crept into his office and home and installed bugging devices. Covert video and audio surveillance showed this man manifested signs of obsessive-compulsive disorder (OCD). He constantly arranged and rearranged documents and objects, tidying them then minutely changing their positions to make sure they lined up.

Reporters who later interviewed Williams said he exhibited some signs of being at the high-functioning end of the autism spectrum.

UCOs followed him to work and were waiting for him when he left work at exactly the same time each day. They were still on his tail as he almost inevitably drove straight home. Sometimes, at night, he would drive along the beaches and parks overlooking the ocean near his home. Occasionally, he would make closing-time forays past the two beachfront hotels in Cottesloe, showing interest in minimally dressed, tipsy young women. Surveillance cops secretly filmed his every move, at times becoming alarmed at his personal behaviour, although he interfered with nobody. He did not try to interact with any of the women, or try to lure them into his car.

After several months, Williams became aware cops were watching him. If he had any doubt, it evaporated when a microphone they had installed above his office workstation fell through the ceiling and was left dangling by wires.

Lance Williams all but stopped going out. He was a virtual prisoner in his parents' home and at work, when he was not on stress leave or in hospital. He had stopped attending his social club and even stopped his regular visits to the local library.

'It just doesn't feel comfortable,' he said after being tailed by police as he returned a book.

Macro decided it was time to set another trap.

*

In March 1998, detectives scoured the police force for bait: young, blonde female police officers. Recruited from both local and interstate police stations, they were dressed up, wired for sound and set loose on the streets of Claremont late at night.

Lance Williams did not offer lifts to any of the decoys – in fact, he had already worked out that police were setting traps for the killer. He later told detectives that, on six occasions, he had noticed women he thought were policewomen trying to entice drivers to pick them up.

One undercover female officer had walked through Claremont Park behind the council chamber, her safety protected by armed but invisible Tactical Response Group (TRG) officers disguised in black outfits. Lance Williams stopped his car beside the park and watched the woman progress through its dark shadows. Police, hearts in mouths, waited for their prey to make his move. He made no attempt to follow.

A good Samaritan act was to be his downfall later the same year. At 3 a.m. on Sunday, April 5, 1998, a year after Ciara's murder, Lance Williams stopped his car at a red traffic light on Stirling Highway, where it meets Stirling Road, very close to where both Sarah Spiers and Ciara Glennon had last been seen.

A blonde policewoman dressed for a night out approached the passenger's side of Williams' car, leaned into the window and asked him where to find a bus stop. Williams knew all about local buses and their timetables. In the years after he had lost his driver's licence, he had often caught the last bus home from his visits to Crown casino.

'You won't find a bus at this time of night,' he told the decoy.

She said she wanted to go to Glyde Street, in Mosman Park, about eight minutes along the highway. Not waiting to be asked, she opened the passenger side door and climbed into the front passenger seat.

The adrenaline pumped in the TRG officers who were watching every movement from unmarked cars, as well as listening in to audio from their colleague's hidden microphone. All they heard were her innocuous conversations with Williams.

The TRG kept the car under intense observation, ready to swoop should they detect any danger to the courageous policewoman. For all she and they knew, she was about to be abducted by the Claremont serial killer.

Williams noticed that the woman was nervous but the trip passed without drama. When the pair reached Glyde Street, his passenger opened the door and left.

Police immediately pulled over the driver, searched Williams and his car and seized a knife. Williams maintained it was a small pocketknife on his key ring. Police apparently disagreed. Having found him with a weapon, they detained him.

As he sat in a police car, an officer told him it was routine for arrested suspects to provide a swab for DNA. He meekly submitted, allowing the officer to scrape inside his mouth with a cottonwool ball on a stick, which was then placed into a sterile jar. Officers also plucked and saved three strands of his hair. Back at the station, they seized his clothes.

They impounded his car. Searching it, they found a receipt for detailing the vehicle shortly after Sarah Spiers's disappearance. Williams explained that this was a free service, part of a deal when he bought the car, the sale registered by the dealer just before Sarah vanished.

Williams explained that he had not picked up the car until a few days after Sarah's Australia Day abduction, having had to wait for his driver's licence to be restored.

For hours, they questioned him intently. Williams freely admitted to driving around Claremont late at night, watching girls, making sure they were safe. He said he had agreed to drive the covert policewoman to her destination out of concern for her safety, because he knew there was a serial killer at large.

He told detectives that when he had earlier driven past a girl in Claremont thirty times, it was because he thought she should not have been out alone at night, after what had happened to other women in the town. It upset him when something looked out of place, such as a girl walking the streets at night. He said he was very particular about things and liked to see everything in its correct place. He wanted to see where she went. He admitted he had overreacted on that occasion.

'They have nothing to fear from me,' he said.

He explained that his suicide attempts and hospitalisation in 1996 were caused by his inability to handle pressure at work after he had been promoted.

Police asked him where he had been on the nights of the three murders. At the time of the abduction of Sarah Spiers, Williams, like Peter Weygers, had been living alone in his flat. Because of his mental struggles, afterwards, he had moved in with his parents, who confirmed his alibi for the dates and times of the second and third abductions. His mother, a very light sleeper, would have heard his car if he had tried to drive away while she slept, she said. Lance's move to their home only heightened the suspicions of police.

After thirteen hours of questioning, police released Williams without charge. Detectives had no evidence to hold him.

When news leaked on April 8 that police had detained an unnamed driver and questioned him about the Claremont serial killings, it caused a sensation. Were we now about to see, at last, the arrest of the state's most feared man?

One woman, who had formed a professional relationship with Williams, visited his flat regularly. 'He didn't seem dangerous at all,' she said. 'He was cautious but talked fondly of his family.'

She received a shock when Macro called and grilled her for hours, probing her for every detail of what happened inside the flat. 'You'd think they were writing a novel about it,' she quipped.

Police swarmed over Lance Williams' seaside flat. They found nothing incriminating, although they seized more clothes and six knives. At his parents' home in Eric Street, a main route to Cottesloe beach, they dug up the backyard, thoroughly searched the house, took yet more clothing and snapped extensive photographs inside and outside both properties. Searchers failed to turn up any missing items belonging to a Claremont victim, or anything else to link their man to the crimes. Yet they continued to surveil him around the clock.

*

On May 22, 1998, six weeks after they had detained Lance Williams, Macro unplugged another torrent of information from the public. On the advice of profilers, Macro released photographs of replicas of the missing items. One was the gold sunflower key ring carried by Sarah Spiers on the night she vanished. The other was the silver Claddagh brooch Ciara Glennon had pinned to her jacket.

Despite a flurry of interest and over thirty more calls to police nominating possible suspects, this publicity drew no 'shining light' of information at the time, according to a Macro spokesman.

By now, the number of pieces of information collected by police had reached 80,000. Macro was working as hard as ever, overtly and covertly.

For many months, police had managed to keep secret their around-the-clock covert surveillance of Lance Williams. Inevitably, its intensity would lead to it hitting the headlines. The first hint came from a headline in the *Post* on July 4, 1998: 'Police stakeout puzzle'. The paper noted that Cottesloe residents had become worried after seeing a series of cars parked off Eric Street for two months. One local discovered the cars were registered to the police force, which refused to discuss whether the cars were linked to Macro.

The newspaper's interest was further piqued when local Scouts publicly complained that police who parked outside their meeting hall, watching the house opposite around the clock, had been using their toilets. A *Post* journalist reported on September 5, 1998, that Scout leader John Andrewartha asked his local ratepayers' association meeting if police could contribute to the Scouts' $500 water rates.

Neighbours now told reporters of the earlier raid on the Williams' family home involving four police cars, after which the watching resumed as normal. Local people said they were puzzled because the surveillance was becoming so blatant. When Williams was home, police watched the house from the front and from a laneway at the back.

So far, all attempts to extract a confession from Lance Williams had failed. A confession would give the case against him a huge boost, but how to get their suspect to cough? Lance Williams himself offered a solution.

Until the Claremont case, local police had never used a polygraph – their normal budget could not justify the expense of a process whose results were inadmissible in court. But these were desperate times. A year earlier, polygraph operator and ex-FBI special agent Ronald R. Homer had made the long trip from the USA to wire up sixty-one Claremont subjects who had no alibis, mostly taxi drivers. Six had refused to take the test, six had 'shown indications of deception', while the results of another twelve were described as inconclusive.

Thirty-eight were telling the truth, according to the Homer results. When Lance Williams came under intense scrutiny, he too asked to be tested, in the hope it would clear him.

Perth's business community was footing the $40,000 bill, people whose own families shopped in Claremont, who knew young people who had partied at its nightspots and knew the Glennons. The Secure Communities Foundation paid for Homer to fly from the USA a second time with his lie-detector machine, this time targeting only one test subject – Lance Williams. Although results would be useless as evidence in court, police felt the pressure could be enough to make Williams crack.

It was only after asking for the test that Williams consulted a lawyer for the first time. The advice was to refuse to submit to this unproven device. He went ahead anyway, sure he would be cleared. It was a decision that backfired badly.

There are good reasons why Australian courts will not admit lie-detector evidence, not least because evidence about general credibility or propensity to tell the truth is not admitted.

The machines themselves measure anxiety levels – in theory, anxiety rises when people are lying. No matter how hard they train themselves, they cannot regulate their blood pressure and heart rate, the machine recording variations to these on a graph.

There are exceptions. To become anxious, a lying person would need to feel guilt. Psychopaths – serial killers – lack feelings of guilt and empathy for others. People accustomed to lying can trick the machines, and they do.

The reverse is also true. Some people become over-anxious in test conditions – those who may be clinically depressed or who blame themselves for things over which they have no control can fail the test, even when telling the truth, as the University of NSW's senior lecturer in psychology, Dr Peter Birrell, told ABC Radio at the time.

Finally, websites and books give instructions on how to defeat the polygraph, such as placing a sharp pebble inside one's shoe, pressing on it so as to cause pain, thus tricking the brain to project a reaction that masks guilt.

Williams knew none of this. It was the last weekend in August 1998, almost a year after he had first come to police attention. Homer set up his controversial machine and prepared his questions. Williams failed the test, his answers showing deception, according to Homer.

Five months after he was first detained in Claremont, Lance Williams' name became common knowledge. Word leaked to the media that he had failed the test. The next day, he was interviewed by media workers outside his workplace. To the reinvigorated media scrum, waiting to question him on the test results, Lance Williams answered all questions patiently.

Asked if he was the serial killer, he replied: 'No, I'm not. I went voluntarily to do a test at the police station. I mean, I was under no obligation to. I just wanted to, because police were parked over across from my parents' house on weekends and, you know, sort of waiting for me at work and that. I just thought, *Well, I'll go in there, do the test*, because I had nothing to hide, you know?'

After that interview, his name became public knowledge for the first time via a television news broadcast.

On September 1, 1998, a massive headline dominated the front page of *The West Australian* above a photograph of Williams in his car. Its report began: 'The chief suspect in the Claremont serial killings publicly protested his innocence.'

The same day the article was published, David Caporn, by then promoted to superintendent and head of Macro by Police Commissioner Bob Falconer, upgraded Lance Williams' status from person of interest to suspect at a press conference.

Civil libertarians railed against police for releasing 'dubious' test results as a pressure tactic to get the subject to confess. Police denied they had deliberately leaked the result.

Horrified lawyers lined up to warn that the public focus on Williams would taint his jury and put justice in jeopardy, were he to be charged and tried for the murders. Although the results would be inadmissible in court, a future jury could be influenced by publicity that Williams had failed the test, said John McKechnie, Director of Public Prosecutions. The media seemed to heed these critiques, and for years afterwards, Williams was referred to as 'a Cottesloe public servant' in most media reports.

One familiar voice was making itself heard in support of Lance Williams, at least through the pages of the *Post.* It was Peter Weygers, still president of the Council for Civil Liberties, though his credibility was now enfeebled.

By late 1998, a poisoned media was largely avoiding asking Weygers for his views on civil rights. Publicity about his involvement in the 'Did you kill Sarah/Jane?' questionnaire fiasco had led many reporters to discount him. Courageously, and to the fury of some officers, he continued to get under the skin of police, this time saying Williams had suffered many breaches of his civil liberties. He added that police, media and public scrutiny could drive an innocent suspect to suicide.

Weygers publicly made an obvious point: Williams had provided samples of his DNA but had not been charged with the murders, nor had he been cleared.

'This can only mean the police do not have DNA samples to compare with those of suspects,' Weygers said. 'What, then, was the point in pressuring hundreds of taxi drivers and other suspects into providing saliva samples? Are we to assume it was simply a pressure tactic to bully people in order to see how they would react to being asked to provide samples?'

Williams said he was far from alone in failing Macro's lie-detector tests. He thought he knew why he had failed. He had found it easy to answer five of the six questions he was asked – name, place of work, did you kill the girls? No. Attempting to be truthful, however, he was hesitant when asked if he had ever intentionally hurt anyone. He was not sure. This was because, he later told reporter Alison Fan, he had had the usual childhood fights with his brothers and sister, and could not be certain whether he had intentionally hurt any of them.

An agog populace, craving information and scapegoats, could feel even more comforted: police were on the right track. It was only a matter of time.

Just two weeks later, according to a report in *The Bulletin* magazine on September 15, 1998, it was revealed that some journalists were told in a confidential briefing that police were ninety-eight per cent sure they had the right man.

*

Once the six-month covert stakeout of Lance Williams' parents' home was outed, the situation became even weirder. Media crews wandered down to Cottesloe at will to photograph unmarked police cars with two officers inside watching from beside the scout hall.

As Williams ventured out for his very limited outings to work and to the shops, library or video store, he was quite obviously followed by police. So bizarre did this charade become that, when their prey planned changes to his routine, such as attending a meeting, appointment, or work function, he or his parents phoned detectives to tell them in advance of the anticipated changes.

Detectives and forensic officers called at the car park of his government workplace while he worked in the building above, secretly searching his car for any forensic traces that might connect it to the murder victims. They stripped his car's front and rear floor carpet as well as the boot lining, took them away for testing, and replaced them with new carpets, all without the car owner noticing.

The result of this intense police work was nil. Not one shred of physical, witness or confession evidence was found against him, just odd behaviour that drew suspicion.

16 Primal Person

Macro was pinning a lot of hope on its search for physical evidence. With cash from the unconventional Secure Communities Foundation, they had been able to set up a direct link with the FBI in the USA.

Police in Western Australia had made only cursory examinations of Ciara Glennon's clothes. Now, in late January 1999, they sent them to the FBI, along with tree branches that had been found laid over the remains of Jane and Ciara, and Ciara's matted hair.

Police told Williams that his clothes, plus exhibits seized from his and his parents' homes and cars, would also be sent to the USA for tests.

'A detective said to me, "That will put you in the picture or out of the picture." That was four months ago. It's dragging on a bit,' he said.

The privately raised money also paid for David Caporn to visit the FBI's Behavioural Science Unit in Virginia, the home of serial-killer profilers, and access its laboratories. He publicly praised the Americans' use of lie detectors.

There was still a mysterious Telstra driver lurking in the background of the investigation around this time. In December 1998, detectives had a crack at tracking the driver of the elusive Toyota Camry with Telstra markings, like the one spotted at the bus stop in the early morning after Sarah Spiers had disappeared. The driver had been behaving oddly, leering at a young woman who was alone and waiting for a taxi.

Police sent Telstra a fax, asking for a list of all its active vehicles from January 25–28, 1996. Although it was registered and operational by Telstra in January 1996, the Camry station wagon driven on the night Sarah had been abducted had reached the end of its service life in May 1996 and was sent to auction. Because it was no longer registered to the telco in December 1998, it did not appear on the list that Telstra provided to the police.

Police shared no information about a possible Telstra vehicle or Holden station wagon with the public, nor did they make a public plea for tips about Telstra, despite knowing of other women being offered lifts in Telstra vehicles. Even Tim Atherton, the Assistant Police Commissioner in charge of crime from April 1998 to September 2002, was not told of the Telstra connections during regular briefings from Macro detectives.

'I was never, ever told,' he said in 2020. 'I can't understand why there was never any mention of a man in Telstra vehicles. The investigators said Lance Williams was a pervert and that he'd done it.'

In the autumn of 1998, Paul Ferguson went on leave, battling a Corruption and Crime Commission complaint about a historical matter unrelated to the Claremont murders. He was replaced as head of Macro by David Caporn, promoted to the rank of superintendent. At age thirty-eight, Caporn was the youngest officer in the history of the force to attain that rank. His already-powerful influence in the force increased, as did his grip on the Claremont investigation. He was to remain intensely focused on Lance Williams.

Detectives asked Williams if he would submit to a psychiatric examination. He readily agreed – anything to clear him and get the police permanently off his back, and to leave his parents alone.

Macro imported yet another profiler from the USA, a well-credentialled FBI-trained forensic psychiatrist called

Dr Gregory Saathoff, paying his fee and expenses with money from the Secure Communities Foundation. Dr Saathoff was an associate professor of clinical psychiatric medicine. He was a former US Army psychiatrist who served in many roles, including as the chief psychiatric consultant for the FBI's Behavioural Analysis Unit. He hugely impressed local detectives.

Over two days at a clinic in West Perth, Dr Saathoff subjected Lance Williams to intense questioning about every aspect of his life – his relationships, friends, girlfriends, habits, health, work, leisure. Williams later complained that, during this high-stakes scrutiny, he felt food- and sleep-deprived. His denials were constantly disbelieved. 'I said, "Just go and look somewhere else" – they were putting the picking up of girls on me, trying to humiliate me.'

Profilers love to tie together the common threads that constantly appear in the backgrounds of convicted serial killers who have been interviewed in jails. They believe that, inevitably, the killers had childhoods where they did not receive unconditional love, were given no opportunity to learn empathy for others nor that other people were valuable. These damaged kids grew up thinking that only their own status was important, and that other peoples' status could be disregarded.

In Lance Williams' sessions, the interviewer searched for childhood clues, his relationships with his parents, siblings and friends, as well as behaviour that might provide pointers to his having committed the horrible deeds that were traumatising his neighbourhood, and his entire city.

The profiler told Macro it was highly significant that Williams still lived with his parents in his fifth decade, that his mother was a tough, powerful matriarch who ruled his life, seen as another characteristic of the backgrounds of serial killers.

Whatever the psychiatrist's conclusion, this was untrue.

Williams' father, Jim, an imposing country-bred man who owned and ran a petrol station in Mosman Park, was a traditional head of his household. Jim and Norma Williams had brought their son up in a loving atmosphere to respect others and never hurt anyone. Williams was asked by the well-briefed forensic psychiatrist where he had seen a girl hitch-hiking in Claremont and whether he had cut the victims' throats. 'I said I didn't know what happened to them.'

Williams again pointed out that, though he had previously suffered problems with depression and had attempted suicide, been on medication and had been in hospital, he would still be living in his own home were it not for the unprecedented police and public pressure.

Dr Saathoff advised police that, in his opinion, Lance Williams was a primal person who had a fantasy life and was angry and reckless, a dangerous mix. He was emotionally and psychologically capable of serial murder, he said.

The unpublished psychiatric reports greatly elevated the police views that Lance Williams was their man.

Macro detectives continued to consult Dr Saathoff in the ensuing years, right up until August 2007.

Williams said later that he had never received the results of his two-day grilling, and had been told only that he had failed the character test. 'How do you fail a character test?' he asked.

Claude Minisini, the original profiler brought from Melbourne, also confirmed that Lance Williams fitted the profile he had assembled, most of which had not been released to the public.

In reality, this technique's usefulness in catching murderers was extremely limited. Some sceptics pointed out that 1980s FBI-style profiling had quickly dated because it had never identified a serial killer nor led to one's capture. Profiles provided only 'I told you so' moments *after* the killer had been caught in the act, or captured by other means, such as good, conventional detective work, forensic science and lateral thinking.

Again, and again, Williams publicly declared his innocence: 'Everyone would love someone to be caught.' But he realised that opinion against him had only hardened. 'They will be following me for the rest of my life,' he said. He was not far wrong.

*

The pressure that police continued to put on the Williams family was relentless. It led Norma, out of weariness and frustration, to make what some saw as odd and revealing public statements, such as 'if they think he did it, just get on with it and charge him'.

This, naturally, caused another wave of excited speculation among police and the media.

'The mother of a *man police believe is Perth's serial killer* [author's emphasis] yesterday called on police to end her family's nightmare,' was the first paragraph in a January 31, 1999, report in Perth's *Sunday Times.* While it did not name the Williams family, by then it was well known.

The *Irish Times* sent a reporter to Western Australia to investigate, its interest sparked by Ciara Glennon's strong Irish roots. Her parents hailed from counties Mayo and Monaghan, the report said. On February 6, 1999, the paper informed its readers that a Macro officer had said police believed with 99.9 per cent certainty that a quiet, introverted, insignificant civil servant who lived a short drive from the Glennon's home was the Claremont serial killer.

The public belief that Lance was the culprit, once lodged firmly in its consciousness, proved almost impossible to shift, as it had for many police.

The millions that police were spending on the murder investigation, and in the pursuit of Lance Williams, were rapidly multiplying, soon adding up to become the most expensive in Australian history. Nobody begrudged the expense – the killer was a menace and had to be taken off the streets. But the focus on Williams inevitably affected the intensity with which other suspects were pursued.

Reports of other men trying to entice young women into cars were often not followed up, nor written statements obtained. One Macro detective recalls that Macro was unofficially split into two camps – the A team and B team.

The much larger A team, chasing Lance Williams, was the team everyone wanted to be on, because when he was eventually charged, the glory would reside with them.

The B team followed up the other leads still being called into Crime Stoppers, a task some detectives saw as just going through the motions. This work was necessary to eliminate other men nominated by an ignorant public, who did not know what police thought they really knew about the internal workings of Lance Williams' mind.

Gary Adshead, a police reporter for *The West Australian* newspaper, revealed many years later: 'Crime reporters knew Williams was the prime suspect. Police made sure of it.'

He quoted his notes of conversations with a Macro detective from the era: 'If you knew what we know about this person it would blow your mind. Don't underestimate this guy. Most of the media are operating with about five per cent of the information. You're dealing with a very unique individual.'

Adshead concluded: 'Williams had abnormal interests in the disappearances. He was guilty of being weird'.

The publicity machine rolled on. What reporters had been told about him, off the record, gave most media outlets supreme confidence to publicly push suspicions about Lance Williams to the limit, and sometimes past it. Over the next few years, many media outlets felt free to pillory Lance Williams further, if not by name then with photographs of the back of his head, his parents' house and his beachside home unit. Several published this extremely loaded assertion by unnamed police: ever since their ‘prime suspect’ had been kept under constant observation, there had been no more murders.

Every ‘known’ detail of the murders and the twists and turns of the investigation were still being reported Australia-wide and internationally, in television news bulletins, newspaper reports and feature articles, magazine covers and on radio, with Williams the suspect.

The Australian newspaper and *The Bulletin* magazine pushed back. In a blistering editorial published on September 7, 1998, *The Australian* excoriated an apparent police campaign that it said was evidently designed to put so much pressure on Williams that he cracked and confessed. Such tactics, with the connivance of some ‘hysterical’ media, might prejudice the integrity of a future trial, the paper said, or destroy the life of an innocent person. ‘The tactics are misguided and unintelligent.’

‘Rush to judgment’ is what *The Bulletin* labelled ‘the police and the media stretching the definition of prime suspect’.

Two important facts were being kept from the public. Had they been released, they might have made the ordinary person far less inclined to believe Lance Williams was the Claremont serial killer. A minority of detectives felt these details should have turned Macro’s attention away from Lance Williams. Most, however, remained rigid in belief of his guilt.

The first uncomfortable evidence was the undeniable, detailed observations by the Burger Boys, who had described Ciara Glennon’s interaction with the occupant of a late-model white Holden Commodore station wagon – a vehicle very distinct from the much smaller, light-coloured Hyundai Sonata sedan Lance Williams owned. Police knew his car well from following it around the streets of Claremont with Lance at the wheel.

Macro had halted the work of a police ‘Commodore’ squad set up after they interviewed the Burger Boys, visiting used car yards and contacting owners. This team had concentrated on tracing a Holden Commodore station wagon sporting the wrong hubcaps with unusual teardrop-shaped cut-outs, apparently designed for the next model Holden and fitted to an earlier car at the factory as a tryout. Once Lance Williams arrived so dramatically on the scene, those in charge disbanded the Commodore squad before it had completed its work.

The Burger Boys' sighting was a discrepancy that had to be rationalised away, in order to accept all the other 'evidence' that maintained Lance Williams as the police prime suspect. Internally, police pointed out that other witnesses had mentioned different vehicles present on Stirling Highway when Ciara disappeared, even one waiting up a side street on the opposite side of the highway. So, perhaps the Burger Boys had got it wrong. After all, they had been drinking.

The other massive clue that pointed away from Lance Williams also had to be buried, if Lance was to be the man. There were obvious, undeniable victim similarities between Lisa's abduction from Rowe Park and rape in Karrakatta Cemetery, a year before Sarah Spiers disappeared. The Claremont serial killer had stalked similar young women who also enjoyed Claremont's nightlife. The cemetery rapist had left behind his full DNA profile, one that did not match Williams' DNA.

If Lance Williams was truly the serial killer, that non-fatal cemetery crime could not possibly have been connected to 'the Claremont series'. In that event, the eerily similar elements of all four cases must have been incredible coincidences.

Thus, the Macro train continued to career down tracks leading in the wrong direction, coming perilously close to derailing.

17
Shoot Me

Right at the head of the police service, as Police Commissioner Bob Falconer prepared to retire in mid-1999, to be replaced by a New Zealander, Barry Matthews, the Claremont series remained top of mind. Falconer denied reports in April 1999 that the Macro Task Force had recently been downgraded, although by the turn of the century, only eight officers were working on Macro full time.

'We used tactics and strategies that are not commonly used,' Commissioner Falconer said, in reference to the lie detector tests, FBI-trained profilers and forensic psychiatrists. 'We make no apologies for that. His [Lance Williams'] behaviour has dictated that he continues to be the main focus of the investigation.'

When he retired in June 1999, Commissioner Falconer singled out his force's failure to solve the Claremont killings as one of his greatest regrets. 'Murders have us stumped: Falconer' was the large black headline in *The West Australian* that day.

Falconer said the crimes would not be solved unless there was an unforeseen breakthrough, such as a glaring mistake by the murderer, or completely fresh information from the public.

'Squeeze him until he pops' was the technique the FBI had told Macro to employ against its chief suspect.

Such were the fears for their daughters and sisters that very few raised their voices in objection. Nobody wanted to be responsible for seeing the serial killer get away with killing, and killing again.

By the year 2000, Lance Williams had been off work for eighteen months with depression. Police should 'just shoot me,' he remarked to ABC reporter Gerald Tooth in June.

As Weygers had pointed out in September 1998, police still had no physical evidence linking Williams to the crime, despite having collected DNA evidence from him. Macro chief David Caporn said police would not comment on what they had found at the crime scenes, nor whether they had samples of the offender's DNA.

He said later that DNA samples collected during the mass screenings could be compared with DNA obtained sometime in the future, presumably if the serial killer struck again and DNA was recovered from that later crime scene.

So where was the investigation, still the subject of intense public interest, now headed? The years ticked over into the twenty-first century, with no result and with no let-up in the intense surveillance of Lance Williams. Police still awaited the results of forensic tests from the USA, and conceived some more of their own.

When not in hospital, Lance Williams' sole human contact consisted of his parents, family and workmates. His main 'company' was his police shadow.

In an awkward, yet at some level comical, moment, he had even sat down for coffee with two so-called covert officers, detectives whom he had unexpectedly walked right into and recognised while leaving a shop in central Claremont.

Back home in Eric Street, police were still parked next to the scout hall opposite the Williams family home at peak danger times. During the early morning hours of one surveillance shift, bored cops had spotted a burglar going from house to house along the street, checking for security weaknesses, including scoping the Williams' home.

Unable to leave their post, the detectives called uniformed police to pick up the man who, it transpired, had for weeks been catching the last train from his home in the southern suburbs, methodically burgling Cottesloe houses, then catching the first commuter train home, his backpack stuffed with loot.

Lance Williams' mother begged the police to leave her family alone, noting that police watchers had dropped off and were only apparent on weekends and at night.

Police denied surveillance had been scaled back.

Then Lance Williams and his family began to notice that their shadows failed to turn up on schedule. Lance believed police were at last leaving him in peace.

But the UCOs had not been called off. Covert surveillance continued to dog the Williams family. Police had bugged Lance's car so they could listen to all conversations inside, and had fitted it with a GPS tracking device so they knew its location at every second. Initially, the hidden tracker had been hardwired secretly into the car's electrical system, meaning that Williams had frequent inexplicable problems with flat batteries. Royal Automobile Club roadside assistance vans were frequent visitors to the Williams household.

The tracker was covertly replaced with a battery-powered one, but its batteries had to be regularly changed by police who would steal up to Lance's car, usually at night.

Many officers remained so convinced that the killer was Lance Williams that they had refused to stop watching him. If there was to be another murder and they had missed their quarry going out on that same night, there would be hell to pay.

Police technicians installed a hidden video camera in the Eric Street scout hall, powered by the mains electricity supply and trained on the Williams' home.

It sent a continuous signal via a dedicated phone line to Macro headquarters. Every image of every boring suburban moment was recorded: the time Williams left for work, when he arrived, when he returned – almost identical every day, though sometimes Lance would drive along the beach and park overlooking the ocean.

On one occasion, police became very interested when Lance's car, tracked by its slap-on GPS device, was seen driving southeast of the city in a long loop. Officers held their breath when it headed roughly in the direction of where Jane Rimmer's body had been found. They exhaled when the car did not stop.

Excitement again rose when the car again suddenly headed in that same general direction and began haunting the Rockingham area, well south of Perth. But it turned out that Williams had sold his car and bought another one. The GPS had to be secretly retrieved and attached to the new car.

Police had installed another video camera in a private house, trained on Williams' flat in Little Marine Parade, where its owner stayed occasionally, interspersed with periods in hospital.

*

By 2000, young women were returning to Claremont's nightspots, complacency setting in once more, due largely to the belief that police knew the identity of the Claremont serial killer and had him under surveillance.

'They are walking the streets alone late at night,' the town's mayor, Peter Olson, said in April 2000, after he had come under fire for failing to deliver his election promise of high security. He said the council constantly monitored security measures: street lighting and tree pruning to cut down on shadowed areas.

'It seems that it is another generation of young kids who have graduated and may be too young to have been affected by the disappearances in the same way,' Olson said.

David Caporn said girls were at risk of predators anywhere if they walked in quiet areas alone or accepted lifts from strangers. 'We can't scare the life out of people – all that we ask is that they take common-sense precautions.'

Young women who had encountered the type of predators referred to by Caporn and had lived to tell the tale saw no connection between their experiences and the serial killings. They believed police knew who the killer was and were watching him. As a result, some failed to report their suspicions to police, reports that could have led directly to the killer. Among those who did report, some became alarmed that police were reluctant to explore a possible connection, another unexpected result of the focus on Lance Williams.

In March 2000, with the Williams family's overt surveillance a bad memory, police announced another line of investigation. This was to look back on old crimes against women in Claremont, which may provide a link to the Claremont killer.

'The case is solvable without there being another murder,' Caporn announced. The plan evidently involved a trawl of previous, less serious or 'precursor' crimes along the lines suggested by Dick Ault. But the idea was not pursued.

Then, out of the blue, came a startling, possibly game-changing discovery at an all-too-familiar location: Karrakatta Cemetery.

A top-secret police operation swung into action among the tombstones in early morning darkness in late November 2000. It centered around a grave not far from where Lisa had twice been raped after being abducted from Rowe Park almost six years earlier.

This covert Macro activity had been prompted by the discovery of a pair of black women's underpants on Ciara Glennon's gravestone about two weeks earlier, the underwear found by a female relative of Ciara's who had reported her find to superintendent Caporn. Alarmingly, Ciara's initials were on the garment's tag, in her handwriting. Police theorised that, before her overseas travels, Ciara had bought and labelled the underwear, and that this item was in the shoulder bag she had been carrying when she was abducted. The bag was among the items missing when her body was located off Pippidiny Road. Police were unable to confirm with Ciara's friends whether she had a habit of packing spare underpants.

Macro launched Operation Wintergreen.

The briefs were taken for forensic testing while police hid a surveillance camera to watch Ciara's grave, day and night.

The camera twice captured images of a couple, a tall man and young woman, one carrying a torch, visiting the grave late at night, reading inscriptions. The first visit was recorded exactly one month after the garment was found, the second exactly one month later.

Police then hid in the cemetery to conduct live surveillance, but the mysterious couple did not reappear. Nothing more was left there.

Specialist DNA tests later showed the garment had been in contact with at least two people. One was Ciara Glennon. Another was possibly a male. Naturally, possible DNA matches were sought against the swab taken from top suspect Lance Williams, but there was no link. The male sample remained unidentified.

Startlingly, these tests revealed that unusual, foreign microscopic fragments and rare chemical traces were the same as those that had been found on a mysterious 'fibrous mass' that had been recovered with Ciara's body.

Groups of fibres common to some of those found on Jane Rimmer and Lisa were also identified on the underwear.

Macro was still covertly tracking Lance Williams; he had not been to the cemetery at the recorded times. The man recorded by the camera did not look like Williams. Wintergreen fizzled without result.

Another year clicked over, still with no resolution. With signs that the police were backing off from their full-throttle Claremont investigation, a January 2001 newspaper report about Caporn's Australian Police Medal ceremony, the award given in recognition of outstanding police service, noted that the 'middle-aged Cottesloe public servant' was still the prime suspect. Remarkably, in a pointed statement, Caporn said that, while Macro might not have made an arrest, it had saved lives by preventing further murders. He and a band of investigators were piecing together the case against the serial killer, the report said. The public could relax. The cops had their man.

*

In 2003, a Macro detective uncovered what he thought was forensic dynamite. He re-examined old photos taken by a police photographer inside the lounge room of Lance Williams' beachside flat in 1998, and noticed that a heavy fire poker, plus the accompanying fireside brush and shovel, were missing from the rack of tools. Could the poker be the weapon that had stunned Ciara Glennon and fractured the back of her skull? The wound had been identified by pathologist Dr Karin Margolius when she performed the autopsy on Ciara in 1997.

Detectives bought three identical Fireside branded pokers and compared them with a mould of the defects on Ciara's skull. They believed they had a good enough match to explore further, so a detective packed a poker in his luggage for a flight to London, where a Royal College of Surgeons pathologist – who had earlier said it was likely the depression in the skull had been caused by a heavy object, such as a large screwdriver – confirmed the poker fitted the wound. Here was confirmation that, not only was Macro on the right track about Lance Williams, but it had almost reached Central Station.

*

Out in citizen-land, where none of this was known, public criticism was mounting at the lack of progress in finding the Claremont killer. Mayor Peter Olson had observed the complacency of local youth as well as the deep effect on residents and the drop in retail business, with many shoppers scared to go to Claremont even during the day – though the nightlife in Claremont remained vibrant. He was mortified that the killer had made his town infamous. Wherever he travelled in Australia, as Claremont's civic leader, people mentioned the Claremont serial killings and wanted to discuss them.

This was not helped by the extraordinary secrecy still surrounding the Macro investigation, with all police and civilians involved required to sign confidentiality agreements. As *Post* reporter Paige Taylor wrote of the murders on January 25, 2003: 'To this day, the public does not know the causes of death, other injuries, weapons used, any defence wounds, any clues found, the interval between abduction and death, whether death occurred at the sites the bodies were found, the state of clothing or evidence of any other related assaults.'

Senior police responded by ordering a forensic review of the material they held, run by Ken Sanderson, a forensic senior sergeant. Skewed towards seeking a forensic link with Lance Williams, the review concentrated on the hair, fibre, soil, torn-off branches and DNA collected from the crime scenes where Jane's and Ciara's bodies had been discovered, as well as the six knives seized from Lance Williams' home. These had been sent, in 1999, to the FBI labs in Virginia, USA, along with Lance's reference DNA samples, fibres from his car's boot and debris vacuumed from his and his parents' homes. The FBI was taking an inordinate time to deal with the evidence from Australia – four years so far. No incriminating blood, DNA or fibre matches were detected in 1999 or 2003 in labs in either country.

Had Ciara Glennon managed to gouge some DNA from her murderer? Macro detectives held a series of meetings during 2003 to urge PathWest to prioritise more DNA testing of the eleven samples collected from Ciara Glennon's fingernails.

There was a strong expectation that any DNA detected would show a link to Lance Williams. PathWest increased the amplification of its Profiler Plus technology beyond the lab's accredited limit, in tests called low-copy-number, or LCN.

Any results would be useless for court purposes. But even a faint, unaccredited result would be very useful in informing a suspect being interrogated that his DNA had been found under a murder victim's nails.

The cops ordered testing of every sample, from each of Ciara's digits plus a double from one of them. Scientist Aleksander Bagdonavicius had again retrieved AJM 40 from the PathWest fridge and peered through the Perspex. But he could see no nail and no cotton bud tip. He said he could not identify the tiny quantity of material, writing on his worksheet: 'Debris only. Not suitable for analysis.' He put it back in the fridge, unopened, along with several separate jars also containing poor-looking samples from other fingers. The yellow-top jar labelled AJM 40 that contained 'gunk' from Ciara's left thumbnail bed went untested, again. The rest of the nails yielded no result, even with extremely high-sensitivity LCN testing.

The hunt for the killer became an expensive waiting game, in money and manpower. Without a confession or hard forensic evidence, there was no way to build a case in court against Lance Williams. Macro felt it had no option but to keep monitoring their man until, once again, he was overcome with what they believed to be his irresistible urge to kill. But this time, police would be tracking him by GPS and so would know where he went. Macro had to continually return to a Supreme Court judge to renew warrants, each time forced to justify why it wanted to clamp tracking devices outside and listening devices inside Lance Williams' car, and one belonging to his parents.

By May 2003, Williams was on indefinite sick leave, being treated in a mental health unit. His anxiety was caused, his parents said, by police harassment. Cops followed him to hospital. They took fresh hair and DNA samples, on the back of the strong fire-poker link.

Jane Rimmer's father, Trevor, was having doubts about the continuing police focus on Lance Williams. As with all the parents, police had provided Trevor with far more information about the deaths and details of the investigation than was known to the public. Jane's dad expressed disquiet.

'It would be less worrying if the investigative team didn't appear to have all their eggs in one basket,' Trevor said on January 29, 2003. 'I'd like to see a more open approach.'

Emphasising the strong police belief in the likely guilt of Williams, who he did not name, Superintendent David Caporn's response was that it was 'somewhat amazing' that, after almost six years, Williams continued to rank as the number one suspect. 'He has no alibi.'

Still, signs were emerging that the police hierarchy was tiring of throwing enormous resources – tens of millions of dollars – at Macro, with no result in sight.

By the end of 2003, the squad was down to half a dozen detectives from its 1990s peak of one hundred, with published news reports saying that Macro was being wound down in the absence of new evidence.

Ten internal and external reviews of Macro's work had been conducted since 1996, police said, and all had concluded that everything that could be done was being done. News reports of a slowdown were not welcomed by those most affected.

Denis Glennon was well known in police circles to make full use of his direct line to the top Macro detectives, also making frequent contact with the Commissioner of Police, Barry Matthews, and to senior cabinet ministers if he thought it necessary. Such was his pull and the community's empathy for his terrible situation that he could always arrange a meeting with the state's most senior police at short notice, and state ministers never said no to his approaches.

Glennon was a powerful personality, influential in politics and business, a forceful and formidable figure, in no mood to allow the death of his precious daughter to go unresolved and unpunished. He had made good use of his access several times in previous years, when the media had reported that Macro had done all it could and may be dismantled. His intervention was always followed by backflips and strong denials. This time was no different – the case was still live and open, the police were eager to now publicly point out, and the 'Cottesloe public servant', whom they did not identify, was still clearly in their sights.

'All indications are strongest in that direction – still,' said Mel Hay, Assistant Commissioner for Crime Investigation and Intelligence Service, in November 2003.

18

Napper

Eight years had now elapsed since Karrakatta and still no salve came for the stricken families of the abducted, murdered and missing young women. All they had to cling to was assurances that the man some Macro officers freely referred to as 'the offender' was under surveillance and thus unable to murder again. For the police to move on from this mindset would take massive change. Change was coming, driven not by Macro but from within the red-brick walls of an old, modest, single-level office that squatted on the banks of the Swan River, on the campus fringes of the University of Western Australia (UWA).

This change, glacial though it was, began with Robin Napper, an energetic, youthful-looking retired detective superintendent from Britain, who retained a *Monty Python*-esque sense of humour despite the horrors he had encountered at the sharpest end of a police career.

Napper had been a forensic consultant and former British detective superintendent, who specialised in sexually motivated crimes and unsolved cold cases. In the UK, he had worked on serious crime investigations, including stalking, arson, terrorist and sex crimes, specialising in harnessing the vast opportunities for crime-solving opened up by rapid advances in DNA technology.

He was part of the successful new British approach to cold cases that embraced teamwork from all disciplines, alongside the latest forensic technology. As head of operations at the

National Crime and Operations Faculty, he had advised on complex homicide cases where the investigations had gone cold. By drawing on outside expertise, the team's efforts had solved most of the cold cases thrown at it, often in the most unexpected ways.

From 1998 to 2000, as detective superintendent with NSW Police, he advised the NSW government on forensically driven policing, introducing the use of DNA evidence in that state and steering DNA legislation. In one ground-breaking case, Napper tackled a horrific and baffling rural mystery, helping to trap the elusive culprit who had savagely bashed and sexually assaulted ninety-one-year-old Rita Knight on New Year's Eve, 1998, in the NSW country town of Wee Waa. In April 2000, he initiated the mass voluntary DNA screening of 500 men, which led to Knight's rapist, her forty-four-year-old lawnmower man Stephen James Boney, going to the local police station to give himself up, even before his DNA sample was tested.

Surprisingly, this success helped add to the unpopularity of Napper among a faction of old-school NSW detectives. They did not appreciate a newcomer with these newfangled scientific ideas solving a case they had been unable to crack.

'In Sydney, I was this smart Pom talking about science,' Napper said.

Senior police compiled a list of twenty-two NSW rapes and four murders, cold cases they thought would be solvable by revisiting them and retrieving crime-scene material from the exhibit store and testing it for DNA.

If he had harboured any doubts about where he stood with some of his colleagues, these evaporated after he put out a call, prior to the Wee Waa arrest in April 2000: What was Sydney's highest profile unsolved murder mystery?

The reply was instant: The Wanda Beach murders of 1965 – schoolgirl killings that had horrified Australia. The two teens were found dead, buried in the sand after a day enjoying the beach.

In 1999, Napper discovered that the bathing costumes of the fifteen-year-olds, school friends Marianne Schmidt and Christine Sharrock, were still held in a police store. The clothing had never been DNA-tested, but a semen sample had been recovered and placed on a microscope slide.

The day before Napper was to retrieve the exhibits, a Sydney Sunday newspaper published a report that the case was being reopened with a search for the offender's DNA. Then Napper received news that shocked him. He was told on the Monday morning that he was off the case; he would no longer have anything to do with it, and the exhibits were unavailable for testing. The families of the murdered teens have yet to see a culprit identified.

In Sydney, cold-case investigations were being shelved in favour of security work for the October 2000 Olympic Games. Robin Napper headed to Perth with his family for a job with the University of Western Australia, where he helped to start its Centre for Forensic Science and establish a forensic science course, attended by graduate students, lawyers and police eager to improve their knowledge.

Despite the headwinds he had faced in Sydney, the newcomer's expertise was temporarily embraced by local police and prosecutors. He was a novelty in Perth. Though he had transitioned into the academic world, the cop always lurked within. Invited to Perth's police headquarters and the office of Director of Public Prosecutions, he made presentations to their personnel on the collection, analysis and use in court of DNA evidence.

As the Claremont cases dragged on without result, there were rumblings that here on Macro's doorstep had landed a man who had helped drive Britain's successful Enigma cold-case review process. He had a stellar track record and could perhaps provide a new gateway to solving the baffling Claremont mysteries, the public was told in newspaper reports in 2002 and 2003. He also approached officers on the case in person.

In May 2003, Assistant Commissioner for Crime Investigation and Intelligence Service Mel Hay approached Napper for a discussion about Macro. Hay had been an assistant commissioner since 1994. He had been awarded the Australian Police Medal for distinguished service in January 2000. He was unenthusiastic when the ex-copper outlined the overseas approach that had worked so spectacularly. The most effective strategy, Napper said, was to follow the UK and USA review practice – to assemble in one room an independent, outside team of investigators and experts in all forensic fields, with the team briefed by Macro. The local investigators would then temporarily step back while this fresh set of eyes examined every detail of the case.

In Britain, such collegiate cold-case reviews were standard after serious crimes remained unsolved. Often it was the scientists, in some cases the technicians, who noticed crucial anomalies that had been missed by the initial investigators.

Hay insisted that a series of independent reviews had already happened, or were under way. He rejected the approach that would see Macro stand aside, saying Macro was still conducting external reviews. Everything that could be done had been, or was being done, Hay said. The talks led nowhere.

The secret LCN testing for DNA conducted that same month on most of Ciara Glennon's fingernail samples had showed no result. Macro was still awaiting test results on other crime scene samples from the FBI. Their focus was trying to prove Lance Williams was the culprit. There was no result.

Frustrated, Robin Napper waited, then went public. A series of follow-up newspaper reports in late 2003, quoting Napper's views, infuriated Macro. He was now looked upon as an unwelcome interloper, with some detectives interpreting his public comments to mean that he was saying local cops didn't have a clue.

Napper retorted that this was not so. The faculty review processes always relied on information provided by the local police. They would set out the evidence then step aside while the new team reviewed the case. This rule prevented firmly held but possibly wrong beliefs of the original team from influencing the review team's work.

'What I'm suggesting is a supportive move to help catch the killer, not something to embarrass Macro,' Napper said in November 2003. 'I was a police officer for thirty-one years. I am one of them. I don't underestimate the difficulties they have with this case.' But, he added, 'They certainly have to modernise and be more forensically driven. They jealously guard their way of doing things but they can't see that there are people that want to help. They have to be bold. These reviews do work and are standard in the UK and the United States.'

Napper emphasised that Macro would not lose control of the case. That team would decide afterwards where to take any new information uncovered.

Mel Hay responded publicly that he did not agree with the UK review model. Napper's job was to expand the university's Centre for Forensic Science. 'But let it not be at our expense,' Hay said.

In an interview, Napper endorsed profiler Dick Ault's call for a thorough investigation of all possible precursor crimes. Experience had taught police worldwide that this was extraordinarily effective. When committing the earlier crimes, the serial rapist or murderer is likely to be far more careless, leaving behind the type of forensic and witness evidence that they become obsessive about concealing as their crimes escalate.

Serious offenders almost always commit less serious crimes before the big ones, gaining confidence and practising their craft before moving on, often in parallel with a continuation of their earlier careers.

'A man doesn't just walk out his front door one day and become a serial killer,' said Napper, a few years after the

Claremont murders. 'I call it the apprenticeship. Serial killers learn their trade on the job. Among the most common precursor crimes to serial killings are domestic burglary and minor sexual offences – flashers, peepers, stealers of underwear from washing lines.'

The more they get away with it, he said, the more confidence they gain in committing more serious sexually related crimes. They operate in particular geographical areas with which they are familiar, and are also known to put some distance between their homes and where they prowl.

'In England, it is fundamental to the investigation that you look at precursor crimes. It is standard practice and has been for a long time. It's the first thing you look at.'

Once started on the rising escalator of sex crimes, how could future serial killers be stopped before it really was too late, the *Post* asked Dr Thomas Müller, an international forensic psychologist speaking at a conference in Perth in March 2003. His answer was that prevention lay in hard work by dedicated police.

Opportunistic home invaders may also be opportunistic rapists at the same time, Dr Müller said. They enter houses looking for property to steal. While there, they get the idea of invading the homeowner's space – an idea that can lead to thoughts of rape if they unexpectedly find a woman alone at home.

According to Dr Müller, the scene of each home invasion, from a simple domestic burglary upwards, should be visited as soon as possible by a police team that includes an officer scientifically trained to swab surfaces for traces of DNA.

By building up a database of DNA taken from all 'minor' crime scenes, including car theft, police had a far better chance of identifying offenders and preventing much more serious crimes such as rape, murder and even serial killings.

*

The clash of ideas on how to progress the Claremont case was not Robin Napper's first run-in with Perth police, nor was it to be the last. Once he had started working as an independent academic, defence lawyers in criminal cases had begun asking him for advice in other high-profile local cases.

He had never before worked for the defence. His introduction was a complex and sensational murder trial, in which Canadian national Rory Christie was convicted then eventually acquitted after appeal of the murder of his estranged wife, Susan, whose body was never discovered. Mrs Christie, aged forty-two, was last seen outside her flat in Daglish on November 15, 2001. Rory Kirk Christie, thirty-five, had custody of their young son. He was charged with his wife's murder, convicted by a jury and sentenced to life imprisonment in 2003. Napper had worked with a volunteer team to gather evidence presented at the trial, some of which was ultimately accepted by the Court of Appeal. Mr Christie was still in jail when he went on trial again for the murder in 2005, after the appeal court ordered a retrial. The defence submitted that there was no evidence Mrs Christie had been murdered inside her flat as the prosecution had said, that a spot of blood on his tie was not the result of Rory Christie committing the murder, and that he had not had the opportunity to dispose of her body. Mr Christie's prosecution had been based on flawed physical and circumstantial evidence.

It was partly Napper's advice that had unearthed the forensic evidence that destroyed the police case. The judge halted the second trial without hearing the defence case and released Mr Christie, who returned to Canada with his son.

Napper began to be portrayed in some local press reports as a 'new chum', a know-it-all from overseas who got things wrong, did not know the facts and did not know the local scene. A complaint had been made about Napper to the judge, but it was resolved satisfactorily. Napper had done nothing wrong.

Napper said that he had never criticised Macro, offering only to help. One response to this offer stood out, starkly ironic on a number of levels.

'A group of detectives came to the university in 2001 to talk about forensics,' Napper recalls. 'I said, "Perhaps I could be useful in the Claremont case." I will never forget the reply: "That's sorted. It's just a matter of time."' Lance Williams was their man, and that attitude was to not change for many years.

19

He Who Waits

If some local police saw Robin Napper as a threat to their reputations, even more alarming for them was the appearance in Perth of Sydney-based journalist Wendy Page, a mild-mannered and experienced producer for the ABC's long-running television series, *Australian Story*, in late 2003.

A Perth native, Wendy Page was bringing with her a formidable record, winning accolades for her detailed examinations of injustices, including those that had occurred in her home state. Her 2002 Walkley Award-winning series on John Button, who had been wrongfully convicted for a murder committed by serial killer Eric Edgar Cooke, provoked Australia-wide shock, fascination and admiration.

Now she was back in Perth to compile a comprehensive episode on the Claremont cases, a very touchy local subject, especially among police.

Page lined up numerous interviewees, including sergeant Paul Coombes, Macro's operations manager, and superintendent David Caporn, Macro's leader.

She was able to confirm that Lance Williams had been under twenty-four-hour surveillance for six years, yet police still lacked the evidence to charge him. She said the officers she interviewed were extremely displeased when she put to them the view of some of her other interviewees: that Macro might be suffering from tunnel vision and was focusing most resources on that one suspect.

The strongest reaction came when she put Robin Napper's suggestion to Caporn and Coombes, that there was a strong case for a full external, independent 'whole case' review as run in the UK.

'Invoking Napper's name was like throwing an incendiary device bang in the centre of Macro headquarters,' Page said later. It was clear to her that a cold-case review by outsiders was seen as an in-your-face insult.

The animosity towards Robin Napper seemed an impassable roadblock. For many local police, Napper was a no-go zone, although during his long police careers in Britain and afterwards in Sydney, he had always worked for the prosecution side.

Wendy Page felt the thumbscrews tighten as she produced her film towards the end of 2003. By January 2004, Macro officers were becoming more desperate. Paul Coombes phoned her, in what she described as a pressure call to exclude Robin Napper from her film. Coombes was critical of Napper, saying 'he doesn't know anything about Macro. It's not a cold case – there's still a full team on it.'

In parts of Coombes' interview with Page that were not broadcast, the detective was clear in expressing the prevailing police line: 'We are very aware that the offender has been under tremendous pressure and stress, and his family also would have been under tremendous pressure as well.'

It was clear to Page that the offender the officer was referring to was Lance Williams.

After Coombes failed to steer Page away from Robin Napper, David Caporn called her. She said Caporn was clearly anxious and uncomfortable about Napper appearing in the *Australian Story* episode. 'It was a fairly unpleasant call,' she recalls. 'He sounded furious. But I was not about to be bullied into dropping the angle about the need for a full external review – which was only part of our story anyway.'

She had been especially careful with her due diligence regarding Robin Napper, checking his comments about the way the UK conducted whole-case reviews and his suggestion that Macro should follow suit. Her calls to a wide range of police, investigators and academics in the USA, Canada and the UK convinced her she was on safe ground.

'Then I got the call – from Denis Glennon.'

Page was convinced David Caporn was behind the call. Glennon was close to Macro and Caporn in particular. His Secure Communities Foundation had funded Macro's unconventional investigations.

'Poor Mr Glennon, Ciara's grief-stricken father, was so distressed about my forthcoming programme that he'd called the managing director of the ABC's Perth branch, Geoff Duncan. Duncan had suggested he call me direct.

'He began by telling me the word around town was that my story was going to be very unbalanced.

'I knew, because of all the calls I'd had from Coombes and Caporn, his comments could have come only from the police, and most likely Caporn, and I told him so. He'd vested and invested so much into this murder investigation and he was beside himself.

'He was vehemently opposed to the story from day one. He had declined to participate in it because, he said, absolutely no good could come from it, other than to cause immense further grief to the families of the murdered girls.

'Now the police were telling him that my story was going to be unbalanced,' Page said. 'He said he'd heard also that my story was to be very critical of Macro, which was absolutely not the case, and that I was taking the *Post* newspaper's biased view of the Macro investigation.

'Inevitably, Robin Napper's name came up. Napper was definitely persona non grata. I explained how police had constantly tried to discredit Napper to me and that they seemed incensed that I had interviewed UK police.

'I explained that I had spoken to the UK National Crime Faculty and New Scotland Yard to verify the comments that Napper had made to me on camera about their methods. I also told him that everything Napper had said to me about the merits of a whole-case review had been borne out in my extensive research. These murders were still unsolved. It seemed reasonable to investigate how such cold cases were handled elsewhere in the world.'

Napper had put Wendy Page in touch with Professor David Barclay, his much-admired former boss, who was head of physical evidence at the National Crime and Operations Faculty in the UK.

In his interview with *Australian Story*, Professor Barclay said that Macro, seeking help in the Claremont case, had sent some information to England. But he said they had not made an effective contribution to Macro because they just didn't have enough information.

Whole-case reviews by a completely new team of investigators were necessary, Barclay added, because it was 'impossible to pick up a case and start it again if you were originally involved in it, because you've got preconceptions. A complete fresh start is absolutely essential.'

Page spoke with many of the experts from interstate and overseas who had already conducted the ten external reviews for Macro.

They confirmed that they had seen only pieces of the case. No new team had sat down all together, UK-style, at the same time to examine the entire body of work. Lauded NSW detective superintendent Mike Hagan, who had headed the successful police probe into the infamous 'Granny killer case' in Sydney, had come to Perth for two weeks to look over the Claremont cases. He praised Macro's work but was also supportive of the *Australian Story* episode, saying it had the potential to flush out new information.

'I think Denis Glennon was fairly shocked to hear how far and wide I had consulted,' Page said.

'We ended up having a long "off the record", very amicable conversation, which … I felt it was very productive. He seemed pleased that whatever criticisms we might broadcast about Macro at least we were offering some solutions.

'In the end, I said, "Why don't you just go and meet Napper and see for yourself that he is a very decent man?"

'He called me very shortly after our conversation to say he'd be meeting Napper at UWA the next day at nine a.m.

'My next conversation was with Don Spiers. It was clear that Coombes had warned him, too, about my story. Spiers also invoked Napper's name, telling me that he'd almost caused a murder trial to go off the rails.' This was a reference to the Christie trial, which Page understood, having sat through it.

'I felt very sad about that, and worried that Spiers' trust in me may have been eroded. He didn't need that extra stress. Coombes was his family liaison officer and they had become very close over the eight years since Sarah went missing. But I felt very sorry for Coombes, too.

'I assured Don Spiers we were not criticising Macro at all, and nor was that ever the intention. We were simply canvassing options for a new way of looking at this long-running case.'

Denis Glennon drove his Jaguar to the university on January 16, 2004, where he and Robin Napper held the first of two meetings. Napper outlined in detail how cold-case reviews worked. He told Glennon that the UK had learned a painful lesson from the Yorkshire Ripper serial killer case. Detectives had interviewed the killer, Peter Sutcliffe, several times, but had released him after missing some clues, only for Sutcliffe to keep on killing. 'Because of information overload, they'd been chasing other leads down the wrong path and they had missed him, and lives could have been saved,' Napper said. Sutcliffe was not arrested until a patrolling police officer caught him in the act of preying on yet another potential victim. In 1981, Peter Sutcliffe was convicted of murdering thirteen women and attempting to murder seven others.

As a direct result of these blunders, the British Home Office established the National Crime and Operations Faculty, where Napper had worked, which quickly had success with its full-case, 'outside sets of eyes' reviews. Glennon asked Napper to explain the review process in writing, which he did in an eighteen-page report, outlining how cold-case reviews had solved serious British crimes. It included examples of how the process had succeeded in identifying culprits in other cases, as well as a list of suggested experts. The list included the names David Barclay and Malcolm Boots.

Glennon wielded considerable political clout, and police dared not dismiss him. He was a grieving father who maintained close relationships with senior police, a driving force for the Secure Communities Foundation that had raised close to a million dollars to enable police to throw extra resources at the Claremont cases.

He had intimate access to the police and their investigation, 'a deep personal involvement', Glennon said later. 'They permitted me to enter their world.'

He said Macro had shared secret information with him, no matter how hard to bear, and allowed him to assist. His push for a full review of the case was felt forcefully by Caporn – 'anything to get the case reviewed', Caporn told the author. He said that Ciara's father was ferocious and vocal, providing a lot of input and money through the foundation.

The *Australian Story* interviews were recorded largely in 2003, to be broadcast in early 2004.

Before that episode was put to air, however, local police tried a pre-emptive strike. Mel Hay had written an email to each of the state's 5000 police officers to say that there had been ten independent major reviews of the Claremont murder investigation since 1996, including one conducted in the UK and four in the USA. Claims that Macro had not been subjected to satisfactory independent reviews were wrong and needed to be corrected, he wrote.

Hay did not reveal that the USA inquiries had targeted one suspect only – Lance Williams.

Superintendent Caporn weighed in, too, adding publicly that a review was already underway by a local forensic sergeant, Ken Sanderson, who had had no prior involvement in the Macro inquiry.

*

Wendy Page's documentary, 'He Who Waits', was the first *Australian Story* episode to go to air after the holiday break, on February 9, 2004. Its impact Australia-wide was immediate and dramatic.

The programme was introduced as examining Australia's longest-running and most expensive murder investigation. Paul Coombes, David Caporn, David Barclay, Robin Napper, Don Spiers, and Trevor and Jenni Rimmer were among the subjects Page had interviewed.

Implied criticism of Macro came from an unexpected source – Jane Rimmer's mother, Jenni. Families of the victims had solidly backed the police line, but Mrs Rimmer now joined her husband Trevor in publicly expressing doubts about the intense focus on Lance Williams.

'If he had nothing to do with it, I feel really sorry for him. If they're so confident, I can't understand why he hasn't been charged. There's obviously something lacking after seven years. They should have caught the person by now. I don't think it'll be solved.'

In the episode, David Caporn retorted that the media had led the community to believe police were interested in only one person. 'I can assure you that we've looked far and wide, and that, as every year goes by, several people have been looked at very closely.'

He added that Macro was well positioned to solve the crimes, especially with advances in technology.

Robin Napper began his interview by accurately warning that serial killers look and act in the community like ordinary people, presenting as normal and non-dangerous, like your neighbour. 'They don't walk round with horns sticking out of their heads.'

He contradicted the police assertion that its methods in the Claremont case had been completely reviewed ten times.

'It's how you look at the word "review". A complex investigation is like a huge jigsaw puzzle, and you cannot solve that by sending one piece of the jigsaw puzzle off to an expert overseas and asking him to tell you what the picture is.' He said this case was crying out for a giant workshop; a full, comprehensive case review using experts from around the world. 'This Claremont case has now remained unsolved for eight years. An independent case review will bring in experts from all the different fields – geographic profilers, forensic profilers, different pathologists and different investigators. And the host force gives them the material, then they literally stand back and leave them to it to do the whole review.'

Wendy Page attempted to interview Mel Hay for her programme but he declined. However, she broadcast his written promise that, later in the year, if the latest forensic review still had not identified the killer, WA Police would ask overseas experts to conduct another 'comprehensive review'.

That broadcast brought two significant reactions.

First, Denis Glennon sent Wendy Page an email, saying that he and his wife Una had watched the episode and that it had been 'fair and balanced. Thank you.'

Second, the morning after 'He Who Waits' went to air, Mel Hay was further pinned down by presenter Liam Bartlett in a follow-up interview on ABC radio. Bartlett declared that there was a sense of urgency because 'there is a person loose out there who is going around killing people'.

Hay locked in the police's commitment for a whole-of-case independent review of the Macro investigation in the form suggested in *Australian Story*. Denis Glennon's application of pressure in high places, and the court of public opinion, had clearly worked. Fresh experts in a range of disciplines were already being contacted to conduct the review, he said, examining evidence collected by Macro over the previous eight years.

'He Who Waits' and the response to it marked the beginning of a long, slow, looping U-turn, which would eventually enable the Claremont investigation to reach its dramatic destination.

20
Fuming

Before the Claremont serial killer could be arrested, however, entrenched prejudices first needed to be shifted.

In his interview with ABC radio's Liam Bartlett the day after 'He Who Waits' was aired, Assistant Commissioner Mel Hay demonstrated just how ingrained these fixed ideas were. On air, he made it clear that a Cottesloe civil servant remained Macro's main focus, somewhat spoiling the effect of his announcement of an open-minded, independent review.

Although police were looking at other people, if Macro was right about its prime suspect, Hay said, there had been no more murders of the same type as those in Claremont.

'There is no one else who matches the profile,' he said. He was clearly referring to forty-six-year-old Lance Williams.

The day after Page's programme was broadcast, the *Post* received a call from a reader about a tip that he had tried to pass on to Macro. This caller said he had phoned police because he had overheard a man boasting about being the Claremont killer and how he had picked up the women.

The caller, who provided his name and address, said a Crime Stoppers operator had told him 'not to worry, they knew who had done it and we're just waiting for him to make a mistake'.

The caller told the paper: 'I was so disgusted, I never called [the police] again.'

Meanwhile, the police's concession to adopt Robin Napper's suggestions for a whole-of-case review did not end resentment of him, nor did it mean they were finished with him – not by a long shot.

After 'He Who Waits' aired, many more people were inclined to listen to Napper's views. He was happy to expand on them: Serial killers were very rare, so it was not surprising that most police forces had little experience in dealing with them, he said.

'Many of the old methods of policing approached crime-solving the wrong way around. The focus has been on getting a confession from a likely-looking suspect. Investigators can develop tunnel vision by focusing on one or two aspects of an inquiry.

'Instead, the science needs to be done from the very beginning,' said Napper. 'Forensic science is just as important as traditional police investigation. The full-case review is a fantastic process and very stressful, but can be very successful.'

He said the host force needed to commit to making every single item of material available to the visiting experts, including the contents of all historic files of murder, rape and indecent exposure, dating back years before the first known Claremont murder.

Some local officers were in no mood to listen. Local detectives were fuming, *The West Australian* newspaper reported on February 14, 2004. Police repeated that there had already been ten reviews.

'The problem with airing these types of unjustified criticisms is that they can cloud the issues and only seem to boost the offender's confidence,' Mel Hay was quoted in the article.

Soon after the *Australian Story* episode was broadcast, local officers looking for dirt on Robin Napper had made enquiries among anti-Napper officers in NSW, who gleefully fed the Perth daily newspaper twisted accounts of some of Napper's work in Sydney. Napper was puzzled to then be contacted by old police colleagues from across Australia and overseas, asking him why they had been receiving phone calls from Western Australian police wanting to know about his police career. Napper suggested that the energy being put into checking his unblemished background should be put into solving the murders.

Within a week of the ABC broadcast, *The West Australian* published a long report, quoting florid opinions from Napper's old enemies among NSW detectives.

Macro sergeant Tony Potts weighed in, saying that criticism from outside experts such as Napper could damage the Macro inquiry and possibly have a significant emotional impact on the victims' families.

The Sunday newspaper of that same weekend took the opposite view: 'It is a shame that the new review took such prodding,' John Flint wrote in the *Sunday Times*.

'Misleading messages from Mr Hay have done the police service no favours. They helped cultivate a perception that the WA service was precious and didn't like outsiders – albeit well-meaning ones like Mr Napper – interfering in its affairs.'

In parallel with the cold case and Napper controversies, an explosive policing crisis was looming. Unknown to the public, at the moment 'He Who Waits' was being broadcast and digested, senior police and politicians were sweating their way through preview copies of a devastating judicial critique of police corruption in Western Australia.

*

'Corrupt West Australian police the nation's most inept' was the front-page banner headline in *The Australian* newspaper on March 3, 2004.

For more than a month, Western Australia's senior police and politicians had been poring over some grim reading material. Advance copies of a long report by Commissioner Geoffrey Kennedy, ponderously titled 'Royal Commission

Into Whether There Has Been Corrupt or Criminal Conduct By Any Western Australian Police Officer', contained stunning and damning conclusions.

When it was finally released publicly, after the two-year inquisition, most of the population, who regarded all police as the good guys, were agog.

Premier Geoff Gallop said the police behaviour revealed in the former Supreme Court judge's report was 'utterly unacceptable'.

Most explosive was the evidence Commissioner Kennedy heard from 'rollover cops': detectives who had broken the rigid police code of silence in exchange for immunity from prosecution. These officers had turned state's evidence after being caught in phone taps.

The *Post* concentrated its coverage on the behaviour of some local officers under the headline 'Police lied in court'. 'The police royal commission has confirmed that the Claremont CIB in Stirling Highway was a centre of corruption,' the newspaper's report said. 'Detectives tortured suspects and stole money and belongings of local victims of crime.'

In a grim coincidence, all this had been happening right under the nose of the president of the Council for Civil Liberties, though he had been unaware of it. Peter Weygers' first-floor mayoral office overlooked the Claremont CIB through the trees of Claremont Park.

Two rollover detectives from Claremont, whose evidence was believed by Commissioner Kennedy, revealed that senior detectives had passed on illegal trade secrets to junior detectives, techniques that had been used to concoct evidence in order to frame suspects when they appeared in court – suspects police had believed to be guilty.

Methods included faking statements and verballing suspects. 'Verballing' is a term for the police practice of inventing incriminating conversations, and then police committing perjury in court to swear that these invented conversations actually took place. The practice had diminished since 1995, when interview statements started to be recorded on video, but some loopholes remained.

'It should not be assumed that the practice has passed into history,' Commissioner Kennedy said.

One rollover witness, a detective, said he had verballed suspects between twenty and seventy times, and had lied at trials to support this evidence.

Commissioner Kennedy also buried the notion of 'one rotten apple', often repeated by police unions and the police hierarchy. This idea asserted that there had been only isolated incidents of corrupt behaviour in an otherwise clean police force, and that, anyway, it had all been in the past.

Commissioner Kennedy said rollover witnesses had implicated more than fifty serving or former officers. Not all officers had given evidence but all had denied the allegations. These denials had been false when assessing the weight of the evidence. 'This state of denial, including as it does a number of officers who are still in the police service, is a matter of serious concern.'

The *Post* reported: 'Significant, sustained corruption has infected the West Australian police service for the past 20 years.' The inquiry had implicated about 500 officers and called for a complete transformation of a 'mediocre' force that lacked leadership and internal scrutiny of corrupt officers.

The man at the top of the tree now had to grapple with and digest this tsunami of sludge, as well as recruit panel members for the promised review of the Claremont murder investigation.

Initially, this job fell to Barry Matthews, the police commissioner who had been appointed from New Zealand and who had steered his force through the morale-sapping royal commission process. But his term was ending in mid-2004. In a departing statement in April, he conceded that the Claremont investigation would need be wound up unless new evidence was found.

His replacement, Karl O'Callaghan, at forty-seven, was the state's second-youngest police commissioner ever, and the best-educated. He arrived with a PhD, a qualification he had attained in his spare time after joining the force as a teenager. He also stood out because he had never been a detective. At every opportunity, he continued to ride his traffic patrol motorcycle. The commissioner was also a guitarist who still fronted his band The Filth, and adorned his new office with relics from another obsession, *Doctor Who*.

Dr O'Callaghan set about doing what the royal commission recommended he needed to do: clean up the force. He also said it was his fervent hope that the Claremont serial killings would be solved on his watch.

He had also inherited the whole-of-case Claremont review process, whose panel members had just been announced. Among the list of names was one that would become very familiar to local major crime detectives: David Barclay, head of physical evidence at the national Crime and Operations Faculty in the UK. Wendy Page had interviewed him for her *Australian Story* episode. His input, with that of his colleague, fellow scientist Malcolm Boots, was to play a key role in the Claremont case.

The panel would convene in Perth in November but, before it did, Macro launched an eleventh-hour blitz on some of its recycled targets.

In the midst of this confusing fog of corruption findings and a new direction for the Claremont probe, the new commissioner settled into his chair in June 2004. His and Macro's every action for the next six months would be keenly observed and broadcast in minute detail in a national media frenzy.

21
Raids

Half an hour before midnight on a Wednesday in April, 2004, eight weeks after 'He Who Waits' was broadcast nationally, journalists and photographers stood next to big steel pots that contained smelly chemicals. The location was the rear car park of a low-rise block of 1960s flats in Little Marine Parade, Cottesloe.

More foul smells wafted in from the west, borne by a gentle sea breeze from the Indian Ocean across the road. The poisonous, acrid stink issued from one of the top-floor flats, where luminol, a chemical compound that police use to detect traces of blood, was being sprayed inside by police forensic officers. Luminol needs to be applied at night because it glows in the dark when exposed to traces of iron found in blood residue. But blood, even what remains of cleaned-up blood, is not the only substance to which luminol obligingly responds. Luminol is also sensitive to watermelon and citrus juices and to bleach, among other things. So, if luminol glows when applied to a mark on a wall or carpet, further testing needs to be carried out to determine whether the stain, visible or not, is indeed blood.

The flat belonged to Lance Williams, who had lived there at the time one of the three women went missing from Claremont. His father Jim sat on a couch in his son's flat as the nominated observer.

This night, the luminol illuminated nothing of interest and everybody went home.

Macro's head, Detective Sergeant Martin Crane, led two raids that night. He had taken over the previous August, although Superintendent David Caporn was still a consultant to the squad.

Earlier that same night, the same cops had made a thorough search of the nearby home in Eric Street of Lance Williams' parents, Jim and Norma. It had taken place under the gaze of a huge contingent of reporters and cameras.

Norma Williams pleaded for the police to leave her family alone, having endured seven years of police and media attention. She said police had told her it was their last chance to get vital evidence for the crimes and that they would not be back.

It had been a long day for the hounded couple. In daylight, police had swarmed through their modest home, bagging samples and taking them away. Forensic officers had probed the backyard with a long metal bar and swept it with a metal detector, waiting until dark to spray the interior of the house with their poisonous chemicals.

Police said they were revisiting some of the scientific investigation carried out earlier, a final foray in light of advances in scientific techniques. What new science was deployed went unexplained – luminol was invented in 1937. As at Little Marine Parade, police conducting new forensic searches at Eric Street also found nothing incriminating.

The chief suspect himself was sanguine. 'I have no bitterness towards police because they obviously have a job to do,' he told reporters. 'But I have had two long periods off work over this. The longer it takes, the more the stress builds up.'

*

That same month, Peter Weygers was again drawing attention to himself. A year earlier, he had taken another public swipe at police over the 'organised culture of corruption and cover-up, torture, theft, verballing and false confessions' revealed in evidence heard at the royal commission.

Now the extremely negative headlines he was attracting were not in connection with the Claremont murders but with his Civil Liberties support for Gary Narkle, a man with an outrageously long rap sheet for a range of serious crimes, including home invasions and sexual assault. Narkle was facing court on a rape charge, which he denied.

In Narkle's words: 'I did a lotta bad shit, but I didn't do that.'

The Council for Civil Liberties expressed serious concerns about the justice of this latest charge, whatever Narkle's record. Weygers predicted that Narkle would not be convicted at a retrial, and he was right.

Narkle was soon released from prison on appeal, after the victim felt unable to give evidence in court for a fourth time.

According to his sentencing judge in 2002, however, Gary Narkle was a notorious criminal, a diagnosed psychopath and sexual predator who targeted young women. In State Parliament in 2004, he was branded a serial sex monster.

Politicians tore into Weygers through the pages of *The West Australian*, which pilloried one of that newspaper's old targets in an editorial. A senior politician accused Weygers of victim-blaming and asked if it was appropriate to employ him as a psychologist counselling school-aged children, he said in a letter to the Director General of Education.

Weygers was carpeted for an hour and a half in front of his head of department. Four women at his workplace, a local primary school, had complained about some remarks he allegedly made in a staff room. He was convinced the complaints were influenced by negative headlines. The department suspended him from contact with children and from going onto any schoolgrounds during school hours, restricting him to 'office duties', and moving him to an empty office in a disused school on the fringes of the metropolitan area, still on full pay. This sanction again attracted disparaging headlines. For the next fifteen years, he was given very little meaningful work to do.

After a legal process lasting eight years, Weygers was cleared of the complaints but continued in his isolated, demoralising desk job, unable to do the work he loved. Some might be happy to pull a salary of $120,000 for a non-job, but Peter Weygers was far from happy. From the day he was carpeted, he never again counselled children.

'Crim-lovers' are low on the police list of favourites. Any effect of the red-hot public scrutiny of one of its old persons of interest on Macro is not known. What is known is that, with the independent review panel into the murders yet to begin its work, and without explanation, Macro turned its attention back onto Weygers and taxi driver Steven Ross. Police began surveillance of both men.

Its climax came on Wednesday, August 25, 2004. On that morning, Weygers was working alone as usual at the Swan Education District Office. He and his partner, Vicki, had been staying at the house Weygers owned nearby in Irwin Road, Embleton, along with Vicki's university student son, Matthyas, then aged twenty-two. Weygers, then aged sixty-two, had bought the house from Steven Ross when the taxi driver had got into financial difficulties caused by his poor literacy. Ross had moved into a transportable mining-camp unit dropped into the backyard.

That Wednesday morning, Matthyas had seen heads, which turned out to belong to police officers peering over neighbours' fences, as detectives in plain clothes surrounded the Irwin Road house. Then the cops began jumping the fences. The occupants had no idea who they were or what to expect. Even when they shouted, 'Police!', Matthyas's mother Vicki feared they were actually gang members impersonating cops. She was on the phone, calling for help.

'The police knew I was at work,' Weygers said. 'They had been following me for a long time. Vicki had seen the same people in shopping centres and in other remote and unlikely places.

'Vicki at first called me and said there was someone outside taking photos,' he recalls. 'I left and headed for the house. Men in plain clothes had started banging on the door, and Vicki had called [lawyer] Tom Percy. He said that as it was not her house, she did not have to answer the door.

'She didn't. They started yelling at her that if she didn't answer they would smash their way in. Poor Vicki's legs were like jelly. She just sat there paralysed with fear. She has been traumatised ever since.'

Weygers called local police at the Morley station to say someone was breaking into his house. Uniformed officers attended but said the people in plain clothes were police.

They handed over a search warrant, which said they had reasonable suspicion that somewhere in the Irwin Road house there were specific items of clothing, jewellery and other possessions that had belonged to each of the missing and murdered Claremont women. They were also searching for documents relating to the women plus 'fibre, blood and soil samples'. The search warrant contained detailed descriptions of missing clothing, a sunflower key ring belonging to Sarah Spiers, and novelty sex toys Ciara had bought as a joke for her sister's hen's night.

'We had no idea why they were there. I didn't own the house at the time of the murders and I had had it completely stripped and repainted after I bought it,' said Weygers. 'The police said their search warrant was for the house, not for us.'

Steven Ross watched as officers surveyed the mess inside his transportable home. 'Have you reported a burglary?' one asked.

'No, I always live like this,' he told them with a grin, noting that they gave only a cursory look at his messy quarters and a storage shed crammed with household goods before shutting the door.

Forensic officers and detectives stayed for the rest of the day and into the night, spraying the house interior with luminol.

Police required Matthyas to remain in the house to observe their operation through the night. He was young, frightened and traumatised, but he had the presence of mind to video what he could of the search, stating afterwards that the detectives' main focus had been on personal papers, including Weygers' tax returns and Civil Liberties documents.

Police seized a laptop computer containing all Matthyas's university work, a second computer containing the records of the Council for Civil Liberties, discs, videotapes and back-ups. With their steel spike, they probed the gardens.

'They tore apart the cushions on my mother's favourite sofa,' said Matthyas. 'The goldfish were all dead the next day, I assume poisoned by the luminol.'

Television news crews had set up outside-broadcast vans to beam reporters' dramatic live-crosses into the evening news bulletins, their backdrop the house and police searchers. It was a big story, with massive national and international coverage. Any development in the Claremont serial killer saga was a sure-fire ratings winner.

Instantly, the Irwin Road house became notorious. Had police at last identified the man who had brought so much grief to so many people? They were 'armed with new information', according to a report in *The West Australian*, with that report also linking the house to Peter Weygers. It quoted Macro leader Martin Crane as saying that the raid did not involve Weygers 'in any shape or form'.

Ross's white station wagon was of obvious interest to police, given that the secret Burger Boys' statements had described Ciara Glennon interacting with the driver of a white Holden station wagon at the time she was last seen alive. But the station wagon that Ross had been driving in 1996 and 1997 was not the vehicle described by the Burger Boys. 'My taxi was a Ford

Falcon EA station wagon, white with lights and all the Swan Taxi signs,' Ross said.

The Burger Boys knew their cars, and were definite that the vehicle they saw was not a Ford but a Holden Commodore wagon, model VS Series 1, with no visible taxi markings.

When the Falcon was deregistered at the end of its taxi life in 1998, after the murders, then re-registered as a private car, Ross bought it cheaply from its owner. Peter Weygers occasionally drove it when his own car was off the road.

Police towed away the Falcon for forensic testing. Detective sergeant Crane announced that tests on this car and on Ross's Toyota taxi truck had yielded items of interest. In fact, forensic officers had found a suspicious-looking stain in the cargo area of the wagon.

Crane had raised public expectations when he said he hoped tests would produce a lead in the eight-year investigation. But further forensic tests showed the stains were not human and police returned the vehicles after two weeks. Crane continued to assert that there were items of interest that required further examination 'and could be the breakthrough that we are seeking'. Loaded reports such as these caused many in the community to believe that an arrest was only a matter of time.

Less than a week afterwards, a car full of women stopped outside the Irwin Road house. One woman emerged from the back seat and shouted to the first man she saw: 'The guy who is the murderer lives here, doesn't he?' She was addressing Peter Weygers, who said later he and his tenant now lived in fear of being attacked by vigilantes. He had been living between this house and Killara in Claremont, but moved into Irwin Road permanently to protect a traumatised Matthyas, now startled by every noise.

Matthyas felt a justified paranoia, as more cars slowly drove past the house, the vehicle occupants staring, sometimes shouting.

'I just didn't feel safe. I was afraid to go home after this,' Matthyas said. He began sleeping in his university's computer laboratory, showering in the engineering department and sneaking home in darkness to retrieve clothes.

Peter Weygers publicly criticised the raid, saying it had been politically motivated. Detective Sergeant Crane said Ross had been identified as a person of interest several years ago and continued to be a person of interest.

Police Commissioner Karl O'Callaghan went further, his remarks reported far and wide suggesting that police had a new lead for the Claremont serial killings.

He said the information the police were working on was new intelligence, but dismissed the notion that Macro was moving away from its previous focus, meaning Lance Williams, of Cottesloe.

He said: 'I would describe it as an important development, but it is just a response to intelligence.'

22

Circus

Early on the morning of Tuesday, September 14, 2004, Steven Ross, then aged forty-seven, had been driving a cab through the night before turning to his day job, making deliveries in his taxi truck. He describes what happened next:

'The cops were watching from across the road in Maylands when I dropped off the cab to its day driver and picked up my ute. They followed me and pulled me over down the road. They got me when I was half-asleep and groggy from driving all night.

'They impounded my ute at Maylands police station and took me to Curtin House [Macro headquarters in central Perth].

'That's when they said I was picking up young girls for Peter and taking them to Peter's place at Richardson Avenue in Claremont. They said I was dropping them at Peter's then going back to work.

'They said Peter and I … were bum-buddies and gay. They said Peter had power over me and I did everything he said, that he controlled me. That's rubbish.

'They said Peter walked around his garden in his underwear. They must have been watching him for months.

'They'd been following me for months as well – they knew everywhere I'd been, everything I'd done. They said I had been really busy. They had nothing on me because I hadn't done anything wrong.

'They held a big photo of Sarah right in front of my face and said, "Where is she?" They shoved it in my face. One cop said, "Where is she? Come on, tell me, what the fuck did you do to her?"

'I said nothing. I wasn't there. I was still half-asleep.'

He said detectives had produced the defunct power-zapper that they had retrieved from the woman Ross had given it to years earlier. He alleged an officer said the public wanted a taxi driver to be charged over the murders.

'I said I hadn't had breakfast and was thirsty. They gave me a country meat pie and a can of Diet Coke.

'They tried to put the murders on Peter. They had checked my alibis and realised I had an alibi, so they said I must have delivered girls to Peter to murder. The cops said I had ten minutes to go to Claremont and back, pick up Jane Rimmer. But I didn't have time to kill her. I had taken her to Peter's and he killed her, is what they said.'

What they did not say was how Ross and Weygers could have abducted and murdered Ciara Glennon. Detectives had checked and confirmed Ross's ironclad alibi for the time of Ciara's abduction, 12:15 a.m. That same night, the mayor had been photographed at a far-away municipal function and arrived home, having given a lift to a fellow Claremont Council member, sometime after 1:30 a.m.

And why had Steven Ross originally come forward via his lawyer to help the police with the story that Sarah had caught his cab the night before she disappeared? Perhaps it was insurance, to explain away Sarah's DNA or other forensic traces that might later be found in his taxi.

Ross had refused to make any statement implicating Weygers. 'None of that is true. None of it happened.' Ross also refused to provide a DNA sample. He said he had not trusted police since his experience in 1990, when police accused him of murdering his partner, Erica Muller, who had died of natural causes.

'They stitch people up. They put people in jail for nothing,' he said in an assertion that echoed some of the findings of the royal commission, released earlier the same year.

Steven Ross swore a statutory declaration with the help of lawyers about the content of the interview, which had finished at 2 p.m.

It said police had forced him to provide a DNA sample by plucking hairs from his leg.

*

By this time, two camps had pitched their tents within Macro. One faction strongly believed Lance Williams was the serial killer. The other was just as firmly convinced it was Peter Weygers. Nobody but Williams and Weygers were realistically on Macro's radar.

Both police factions relied heavily on profilers' theories. It was possible to make bits of the profiles fit both men, just as it was possible to make the same bits fit thousands of other men in the community. The entrenched rival beliefs were bolstered by other factors – Williams' obsessive nighttime driving through Claremont, and Weygers' knowledge of and access to his town, as well as the dozens of calls about him to Crime Stoppers whenever his name was publicised in relation to the murders, in finger-pointing 'nominations'.

The day after police detained Steven Ross, questioned him and forcibly removed DNA samples from him, detectives had gone to Weygers' office in Midland, telling his boss that they wanted to talk to him. Weygers refused to come out. He had contacted his lawyer, Grant Milner, who arranged for police to interview Weygers in Milner's office in Claremont.

'Detective Sergeant Martin Crane was there,' Milner said later. 'Weygers said nothing at all except he got Crane's back up by calling the officer a liar. He said, "I am not going to do any speaking – you are going to stitch me up like Button and Beamish and the Mickelbergs."' (John Button and Darryl Beamish were in the early 1960s both wrongfully convicted of killing young women, women who were in fact victims of notorious serial killer Eric Edgar Cooke. The three Mickelberg brothers were convicted and jailed for swindling the Perth Mint out of gold bars in the 1980s. A former detective on the case later admitted that evidence had been falsified to secure the convictions. All three brothers were exonerated.)

'Crane said the police wanted Weygers' DNA. Weygers initially consented, then refused. Crane said he would be forced,' said Milner.

Weygers recalls the exchange differently. He says that, after initially agreeing to provide a sample for DNA testing, he set three conditions. These were that he required police to state that they had DNA from the crimes scenes to compare with his own DNA; that if there was no match, they would destroy the sample he had provided; and that they would then publicly announce Weygers had been cleared.

Milner confirmed to Weygers that the police had the power to forcibly take DNA following a change in the law in 2002. Both men said their impression was that the sample would be taken with Milner present.

'Next day, Crane rang and said he had exercised his right to do it another way,' Milner said. That day, September 16, was to be long and stricken for the former mayor.

Weygers was at his alternative home in Irwin Road, absent from work with a bad dose of flu and laryngitis. All that morning, Vicki had noticed a dark blue, late-model car parked in a side street.

Mid-morning, Weygers was driving along Irwin Road with Vicki, heading for a doctor's surgery. Suddenly, an old-model car drove in front, cutting them off. Behind, a blue unmarked police car briefly sounded its siren.

The two cars containing four detectives sandbagged Weygers' Toyota. He was told to get out, and was spread-eagled against his car, his legs kicked apart. At the roadside, police searched his body, including between his legs, he said. He was made to get into the back of a police car while Vicki was left sitting in the passenger seat of the Toyota.

'One of them looked in the car and saw Vicki [who was born in the Philippines], turned to me and said, "We're going to enjoy your little black slut while you're in prison."

'She was terrified. They just left her sitting there, not enquiring whether or not she could drive.'

The police car with Weygers inside left at high speed. Vicki, who did have a licence, tried to follow but was soon left behind.

At Curtin House, Weygers was taken to an interview room where he told police, 'I am not going to give you a sample with consent.'

Martin Crane had assembled the paperwork under the new law to enable him to obtain DNA forcibly from a suspect.

Below is Weygers' account of what happened next. Martin Crane said he had no comment to make on Weygers' version, other than that the procedure had been carried out according to law. He later told the ABC that Weygers was a person of interest in the Macro investigation and that the DNA test had been conducted under identification laws. 'Mr Weygers has been in our custody today,' he said.

'One of the officers was especially aggressive,' Weygers said. 'He said to me, "You're pretty good at complaining." I had made an official complaint to the Premier, Geoff Gallop, about the police attitude during the Embleton raid, and about non-return of property, including the computers seized in that raid. Matthyas was studying for his university exams and police had taken his study materials.'

An officer, he said, had told him he was going to obtain his DNA 'his way'.

'"We are arresting you now," he told me.' Weygers said he

had replied that he would give the sample voluntarily if police showed him reasonable grounds.

'They refused to give me a reason as to why they thought I was the killer. They could not because I'm not.

'I asked to see the warrant. They showed me a piece of paper, which said that reasonable cause was set out in an internal police memo dated 16/9. They pulled it away before I could finish reading it. The memo was not attached.'

A police officer had then pulled hairs from Weygers' arm.

'This is pure body banditry,' Weygers said.

'After they had put the hairs in a bag, I said, "Am I still under arrest?" They said no. So, I got up to leave.

'[An officer] jumped up and blocked my way. The only way I could get out would be to assault him, then I would be on an assault charge. Someone shouted, "Video off." I don't know if the video was running. I was never asked for consent to be videoed.'

Martin Crane said later it was normal to videotape a DNA procedure if tape equipment was available.

'A cop said, "You can sit down. You are a wanker. We've met people like you. We're going to get you. You're a fucking murderer."

'They just wouldn't let me go, even though I was not under arrest.

'[Another detective] forearmed me in the chest. In all, three of them assaulted me.'

As Crane escorted Weygers from the building, the officer re-arrested him. 'I believe I was re-arrested three times – four in total,' Weygers said.

Weygers said Crane told him he had a warrant from a magistrate to search his Claremont home.

Waiting outside Curtin House there was another surprise – a bank of media cameras. Someone had tipped off television and newspaper reporters. Detectives drove Weygers to Killara, his home in Richardson Avenue, Claremont.

There, officers wearing overalls emblazoned with the words 'Police Forensic' were swarming over his California-style bungalow, its gardens and roof, lifting tiles. They searched the roof cavity and looked in the shed, and bagged clothing and other items from the house. Their haul included fifty of Weygers' ties, presumably to check for a match with a thread of green silk found at the Eglinton bush site where Ciara Glennon's body had been found. They rolled up carpet and took it away, then dug up the ground in the narrow space between the back of the garage and the rear fence.

Police took one look inside Killara's garage, which was crammed with household goods from Weygers' rentals, then promptly shut the door.

In the middle of such an unfunny afternoon, one light moment amused one of Weygers' neighbours watching through the fence. A police officer who had been shovelling for the remains of Sarah Spiers behind the Weygers garage emerged from the narrow space, triumphantly clutching a bone. A knot of other officers excitedly gathered around. Gloom rapidly descended when someone pointed out that what the cop's gloved hand held was a chicken bone. This paltry poultry exhumation was the only suspicious item seized in the highly publicised, high-profile search.

Weygers said detectives told him they were leaving no stone unturned because the external review of the Claremont serial killings was soon due.

Martin Crane said he did not want this raid to become a circus, but it did, in the full gaze of the country's media.

When Weygers had emerged from Killara with Martin Crane, police still searching, Channel Seven reporter Alison Fan shouted from behind police tape that, if Weygers was not under arrest, he could talk to the media. He walked up to reporters wearing rubber gloves, a suit and trademark tie featuring the Australian flag. Sniffling from severe flu, his voice croaking, he let fly.

'Steven Ross is making a statement that the police offered him a deal – they said that if he confesses that he sleeps with me and brings girls to me to kill, they won't charge him,' said Peter Weygers as he felt his world falling apart.

He was being persecuted and publicly vilified, he said. 'This is an outrageous breach of my civil liberties. This is a gross invasion of privacy. This is a gross invasion of rights. I have no idea what their excuse is for this absolutely disgraceful conduct.'

He said the raids were politically motivated – that police had an agenda to discredit the Council for Civil Liberties. He later reasoned that the raid might have been related to a tip-off to Civil Liberties, leaked to a politician, which said prison officials had been accused of smuggling drugs into jails.

'They thought we knew more than we did,' Weygers said. Years later, an anti-corruption investigation proved that a network of corrupt prison guards, prisoners and organised crime syndicates were systematically smuggling drugs into the state's jails, a longstanding problem.

Martin Crane told the media that a significant development was closely linked to the Embleton operation.

Police stayed late into the night, pumping their foul-smelling luminol over the walls and floor of Killara. The house was roped off at the footpath with police tape. Behind it, the search was filmed by a phalanx of television and newspaper camera operators, about thirty media men and women in total – local, state and national. The guaranteed saturation coverage on that night's news and in the next day's newspapers, nationally and internationally, left nobody in doubt that an important development was afoot in the search for the Claremont serial killer.

It's extremely difficult to look innocent of serial killings when you're shown on national television being escorted from Macro headquarters by Macro detectives, then the media reveals that police have forcibly sampled your DNA, and raided and searched your house.

23
Psychic

The home of the president of the Council for Civil Liberties and a Justice of the Peace raided by the police squad investigating serial killings? Horrible murders of pretty young blonde women in Claremont, from the upmarket town where Peter Weygers was mayor at the time? The suspect the now-wealthy son of a proud pioneering family? A school psychologist who, just a few months earlier, had been forcibly put out to pasture? The media loved all levels of ironies in this story. It had everything, and their audiences lapped it up.

Again, television news crews set up live feeds into the nationwide evening news bulletins. That night and into the following days, a blizzard of publicity tracked every aspect of the raid and its aftermath. Error-ridden feature articles probing the minutiae of Weygers' life were published, locally and nationally. The strong implication was that Weygers had done something terribly wrong to attract such intense police attention.

'Claremont killer task force raids home of civil libertarian', 'Weygers forced to give DNA' were the headlines dominating the front page of the next day's *West Australian* newspaper.

The *Post* compiled its decade of interactions with Weygers into a profile: 'Friends say he is passionate, courageous and committed and has great stamina and integrity. Critics say he is obsessive and dreary.'

'Closing in on a killer' was the nationally circulated *Sydney*

Morning Herald headline above a purported profile of the Civil Liberties president, published September 25, 2004.

'The shameless public crucifixion of WA Council of Civil Liberties president Peter Weygers, to stir up a lynch mob to sell more papers' is how Detlef Ullrich, a Civil Liberties member, saw it.

People who had doubted Weygers' guilt after police had targeted Lance Williams now thought of the former mayor as guilty. In fact, Lance Williams welcomed the switch in public attention from himself, saying that perhaps now police had realised he was not the killer. That, too, was wishful thinking.

Three days after the raid, *The West Australian* published a false rumour that Weygers had gone overseas. He had not, but the perception that he had fled to escape justice inspired further damaging headlines across the country.

Ironically, Macro veterans who were no longer involved in the day-to-day running of the squad were also furious – at least those in the faction that believed Lance Williams was the killer. The Richardson Avenue circus was taking the heat off their main man.

Its subject was devastated. If Weygers had felt socially shunned and vilified and had had fingers pointed at him eight years earlier, when the 'Did you abduct or murder Sarah Spiers?' questionnaire had become public, his social isolation was now absolute.

'I was subjected to huge suffering, both physical and psychological,' he said. 'I was terrorised and traumatised, and the trauma has never left me.'

Relatives overseas who made internet searches for his name were horrified to see him branded a serial killer.

He later said he developed a heart condition related to the stress, which he believed had shortened his life. He told of severe sleep loss, and would shake and sweat, his eyes darting, close to tears. To the untrained observer, he seemed to display symptoms of severe post-traumatic stress disorder (PTSD).

From all accounts, his partner Vicki and her son Matthyas were equally affected.

'That day and night was a singular horror, born of bias and nurtured in prejudice,' was his description.

He said he often felt suicidal, at one point blurting that he was still alive because he didn't have the guts to take his own life. In the weeks after his arrests and the raids on his houses, he had become convinced that police were trying to drive him to suicide.

'If that happened, the public would take it as an admission of guilt. The police would consider the case solved. That would have coloured the entire expert review that followed,' Weygers said.

Most searing for him was his offended sense of morality. What was it that had led police to believe Peter Weygers was a person so bad that he was a serial murderer? What was the 'new intelligence' and 'important development' that the police commissioner said justified such drastic renewed attention?

'But the police refused to show me their search warrant. A reasonable suspicion is no more than a hunch. You can't ruin somebody's life on a hunch.'

A signed email to the *Post* on September 2, 2004, from a woman who urged the newspaper to 'keep up the articles connecting Peter Weygers and the taxi driver with the Claremont serial killings' is telling. It arrived weeks prior to Weygers' arrest, his forced DNA test and the raid on his house.

The writer offered names and details to verify her claims that 'he's been allowed to get away with murder. The public should be aware of the animal he is. Someone has to stop him before there are more victims.'

The *Post* verified the writer's identity, a woman in her forties, who, while now denying that she was a psychic or clairvoyant, had advertised herself as a psychic in 1996, the year Sarah Spiers and Jane Rimmer had disappeared.

Over the next months and years until 2008, the *Post* had a

series of sporadic conversations and email exchanges with her. She was happy to later claim possession of psychic powers, in 2005 and 2008.

In 2004, she claimed to have nominated Peter Weygers to detectives as a murderer many years earlier, just after the disappearance of Jane Rimmer but before Jane's body was found. She said she passed her 'information' to police shortly before news of the 'Did you murder Jane Rimmer?' questionnaire became public. That episode wreaked devastation on Weygers' reputation and life. She claimed she had provided police with hard evidence.

'I have never claimed to be a psychic or medium … I actually take credit for being the one who first drew police attention to Weygers … to link his name to all of this. I contacted Crime Stoppers about both matters before Ciara was murdered and again the day she disappeared. I had hoped that if he [Weygers] was charged he would be off the streets.'

She also claimed to be the first to come up with the delivery-man scenario – a taxi driver who caught young women and took them to Weygers. She identified this catcher as Steven Ross.

She circulated these complaints to targeted recipients, Macro and other police squads.

'I believe that what I told the child abuse detective resulted in the raids on the Embleton and Claremont houses,' she said.

Macro's policy towards the many psychics who offered 'information' was to toss them into a box in one corner of their operations room. But, in her own words, this woman had never claimed to police to be a clairvoyant. She said she had offered police and the Education Department 'good, solid information'. Then, on the phone to the *Post*, she stated: 'Jane Rimmer is appearing in my dreams and giving information to me.'

She said she was entitled to her opinions about Weygers, whom she bluntly accused of being a killer. 'I have no grudge against him other than to want a mass murderer off the streets,' she wrote.

She had met Weygers in the mid-1970s while a student at Hollywood High School, where he had an office. He has confirmed this.

Her closest friend, whom she gave the pseudonym Sally, formed a relationship with Weygers while at university, aged twenty-three. The couple split up in the mid-1980s. She said that Sally would know all about 'Weygers' murders'. The psychic woman listed six, including the three women abducted from Claremont.

She had made numerous calls about him to Crime Stoppers, and had sent damning written statements to the police commissioner, Macro, senior politicians and the Education Department. Some emails directly accused Weygers of murder.

Macro tracked down Sally, then also aged in her forties, who said she had no complaint to make about Weygers and had no other useful information to offer.

The psychic claimed regular contact with Macro, including receiving a phone call the day before the raid at Embleton to say her information was being followed up.

Analyst and Civil Liberties member Tom Lawson traced the woman's address and collected twenty different pseudonyms the woman had used when blogging, including her married name.

'Many of her postings are highly defamatory, and not exclusively of Mr Weygers,' Lawson wrote. 'She professes to possess detailed information about the Claremont serial killings, information never made public.'

This begs the question: Did those twenty different names also surface in calls to police?

Macro head Martin Crane said the information used to obtain the search warrant on the Embleton house had not come from the woman. 'Everybody and anybody that's of interest to this investigation, we need to eliminate,' he said.

Ciara Glennon was murdered nine months after the psychic claimed to have first contacted police about Weygers. She said Ciara's death was a result of police failing to act decisively on her warnings.

'Explain that to the Glennon family when Weygers is finally convicted,' the woman wrote.

Among all the oddballs blogging ceaselessly about the Claremont serial murders, this woman stood out. She purported to have intimate knowledge of the inner life of Peter Weygers. She was skilled at weaving her own thoughts, 'information' and guesswork through the publicly known facts. She was authoritative and articulate, adept at directly reaching politicians and the police. She was hard to ignore.

In September 2004, before the raid on Killara, she claimed to have seen in psychic visions that Sarah Spiers was buried behind Peter Weygers' garage. She claimed to be the informant of fact for the police raid on Killara.

Again, it may or may not be coincidence, but when Macro raided Killara on September 16, 2004, armed with probes and shovels, they dug up only one spot in his large backyard: behind his garage.

With the spotlight's full glare turned on Peter Weygers, not every member of the public swallowed the police line. One astute punter, who had clearly followed the case closely, wrote to the *Post* pointing out that police had spent upwards of $20 million chasing possibly the wrong people. The writer said the media was all too eager to point the finger at suspects favoured by police, quoting Dr Christopher Waddell, from Carleton University in Ottawa, Canada, on the dangers that can arise when police and the media work too closely together.

'That compromises, and in some cases eliminates, the media's ability to fulfil its role of holding public institutions up for scrutiny and accountability.'

The *Post*'s publication of his detailed and thoughtful observations failed to endear the newspaper to Macro.

*

A few days after the raid on Killara, on September 19, detectives took Steven Ross out of his taxi again. They all went back to Macro headquarters where Ross was told one of his alibis did not stack up. He said detectives had again offered him a deal.

He provided the names and addresses of his fares on the night in question and said he was saying nothing more until police brought him another pie and a can of Coke. They let him go.

'I'm being framed for murder,' he announced, saying he had been threatened with media exposure and relentless police scrutiny. He said police tried to coerce him into making a deal conditional on a confession implicating Weygers. 'If they can't find the killer, they are trying to put someone away.'

He said police had told him the Western Australian public wanted a taxi driver to be charged.

Police continued to watch Steven Ross, and to follow him. They pulled him in again and said he had been seen taking rides alone at a fun park, Adventure World. Ross cheerfully owned up, saying he enjoyed day passes there but had done nothing wrong, and the management had not complained.

Then police closed down the Bayswater rubbish tip to search through tonnes of rubbish, after Ross dumped some junk he had picked up from one of Peter Weygers' rental houses. On another day, two unmarked police cars had followed him to Bayswater Waves swimming pool where a friend's son went swimming. Police accused him of 'perving on young boys', he said.

Eventually, his police shadows made no attempt at concealment. They kept up the pressure, taking him in again and offering him a lighter sentence if he would implicate Peter Weygers. He refused.

Then, in the beginning of October, Macro detectives raided the Claremont Council offices armed with a search warrant, demanding that the council produce certain documents. They seized the minutes of the safety and security meetings held soon after Jane Rimmer disappeared, the meetings attended by Weygers as mayor, along with local business people and police. The seized papers turned out to be the police's own documents.

Peter Weygers claimed to know the raid had been directed at pressuring him. 'They continue to traumatise, terrorise and criminally defame me,' he said.

But the cavalry was soon arriving – at least, that is how many members of the public anticipated the arrival of the out-of-town cold case team members about to review Macro's work. Others were defensive, including some police. Our cops are as good as anyone's, some were saying. And anyway, we know who did this – we just need a breakthrough so we can nail them.

For the parents and siblings of the abducted women, the fly-in experts were knights in shining jets.

24
Fresh Eyes

In early November 2004, the visitors from across the seas and the Nullarbor Plain were greeted warmly, and with high hopes. They met the families of the three Claremont murder victims, promising to do their utmost.

'The last roll of the dice in the hunt for serial killer' is how *The Australian* newspaper's headline described the review. That report bore a pessimistic tone, quoting senior police as saying that the murders might never be solved.

Macro was down to about six officers. David Caporn, now an assistant commissioner of police, and Inspector Paul Coombes were in charge of providing information to the panel.

The visiting team members were keen to learn as much as possible about the characters and backgrounds of the young women: What were they like? How would they have acted on a night out, and reacted to a threat? Would they have responded with fight or flight? Or the third F: Freeze.

In their turn, the distraught families quizzed team members for details of what exactly had happened to their daughters.

Parents and siblings of the victims were on a rollercoaster ride of expectation and disappointment, said panel chairman, Detective Superintendent Paul Schramm. Personable and quietly spoken, Schramm was careful to explain that the team did not possess magical powers. He was a South Australian veteran of more than a hundred homicide investigations solved by solid police work. The hopes of the families and of the entire community now rested on his expert team.

'They are being cautioned by the team that there may not be the development they are looking for,' Schramm said.

The team went straight to Claremont's compact business district late at night, 'a critical place to start'. They trod the last known walks of the missing women, pacing out the steps and measuring the times, attempting to see and feel, as closely as possible, what those three young women had experienced.

Sarah Spiers and Ciara Glennon had different starting points and had walked different routes, but they were abducted at almost the same end point, the intersection of Stirling Highway and Stirling Road. These two crimes were committed fourteen months apart.

Jane Rimmer's last confirmed sighting was from the eye of the Continental's revolving camera.

'These are predatory crimes – it's likely the offender has sought out women on their own walking around alone in various degrees of intoxication,' said Schramm. 'How and why the women got into the killer's car was still a mystery. We will work out what deception was used against the girls.'

The team also visited the sites where the two bodies were found, piecing together the young women's last terrified moments.

The panel would look beyond the eight names of suspects provided by local police, and would examine cases of missing women before and after the Claremont series. Other than the three suspects, who were well known to the public via their public statements, the police gave no clue to the identity of the others, or how seriously police regarded them. Twenty-four women were still listed as missing.

Schramm was quick to pass on the compliments of the parents for the police work done so far. That the team felt the need to say this was pushback against waves of disquiet now rippling through the community, questioning the work of Macro. The sentiment summed up by the sceptical *Post* reader after the public raids on the homes of Williams, Weygers and

Ross was now being shared more widely, along with the awful thought that police might have been concentrating on entirely the wrong suspects for eight years, overlooking the real culprit.

Review team members examined a cache of police documents that would fill a tea chest – a fraction of the paperwork local police had collected, representing 120,000 pieces of information, 70,000 calls and the results of 10,000 interviews.

Criminal profiling again beguiled the reporters, as it does reporters everywhere who are desperate for a quick, almost magical solution from exotic experts. These experts are seen to have an ability to reach by remote control deep into the minds of unidentified criminals.

Review team member Joël Kohout, an FBI-trained profiler and sexual homicide expert, mirrored the observations of other profilers. Most pertinently, she began by cautioning that profiling can cause investigators to overlook the real culprit who, when found, would lack power in his own life.

'Killing gives him a sense of control, a huge sense of real power … [they kill] when they are very angry and feel powerless.'

She said that, when caught, the killer will very likely be the oldest child in the family, with a domineering mother and an absent or useless father.

The community was dealing with an organised, methodical offender, not one who killed in a frenzy, thus leaving behind lots of evidence. There was no overkill. He was someone likely to blend into the community, an apparently normal man with a steady job, often fitting easily into different situations – a chameleon, even charismatic, but a 'moral flat-liner' with no conscience.

A selected victim will be one of opportunity and have fulfilled the predator's fantasy criteria, such as age, hair and stature. Nothing is random. The killer will have a death kit ready – weapons, ropes, masking tape.

This one had acted alone; he was intelligent and well organised, carefully planning his murders.

Their man would live within a five-kilometre radius of Claremont, be familiar with its streets and the geography of the disposal sites. He had killed his victims before dumping their bodies.

Even if the profile was accurate, Kohout was describing huge numbers of potential offenders. But her conclusions should have set alarm bells clanging. If she *was* right, it was clear that the local police were still targeting the wrong person, or persons.

Little, if anything, she described in her profile matched the lonely, socially awkward figure of Lance Williams – nor, for that matter, did it match the studious, eccentric, overachieving Peter Weygers, nor the freewheeling Steven Ross.

After the panel had finished its work, the members expressed disappointment that they had not fingered the killer. They enumerated the problems law enforcement had faced in looking for clues: no body in the case of Sarah Spiers; no kill site nor vehicle nor witnesses to any of the murders.

Somehow, the young women had ended up in their murderer's car and been quickly subdued. Perhaps, the panel speculated in a confidential report to Macro, the women had been duped by the vehicle of someone with status in the community, such as a security guard or police officer.

This secret Schramm report specifically mentioned 'a Telstra employee'. The team speculated that a direct clue to the culprit may eventually be found in his choice of a non-threatening vehicle – such a taxi, fake taxi, police car or commercial vehicle, which might provide some comfort to young women looking for a ride home.

The list of twenty-four other missing women was ruled out as low priority, apart from two: twenty-two-year-old Julie Cutler, whose car had been found in the surf at Cottesloe beach in 1988, within easy walking distance of Lance Williams' home. Julie's body was never found.

The other case that needed to be reinvestigated for links to the Claremont series was the murder of Hayley Dodd, the seventeen-year-old who had disappeared from a rural road north of Perth in 1999. This was the unsolved case that had so enraged Hayley's mother Margaret as she attempted to secure a reward to match the $250,000 offered on behalf of Ciara Glennon. 'I had to scream to get a $20,000 reward,' she had said.

Peter Weygers and Steven Ross were still on the list. This list was still topped by Lance Williams, partly because of his stalking behaviour and the bad impression he had made on USA forensic psychiatrist Greg Saathoff. He had provided the opinion that Williams was capable of being a serial killer.

Secretly, the Schramm team made thirty-three recommendations for further action by Macro, including pursuing neglected testing of forensic trace evidence recovered from the victims.

The team was also especially interested in Telstra vehicles observed on the weekend Sarah disappeared, the sighting of a Telecom van near Hollywood Hospital the night Lisa was raped, and the 'near-misses' by women who were offered late-night lifts in the Claremont-Cottesloe areas by drivers of Telstra vehicles.

*

While all media eyes and ears were on the review team leader and its profiler, two quiet, reserved British scientists in the five-person review squad discovered the keys that would eventually help unlock the door to the baffling Claremont case.

David Barclay and Malcolm Boots were both experts in physical evidence, which they knew would solve the riddle. By 2004, scientific advances had proved that, while witness and confession evidence can be vital, it can also have serious drawbacks. Stark evidence of this is clear from disastrous courtroom verdicts, and the hundreds of wrongful convictions overturned by the discovery of the real culprits' DNA profiles, years after mistaken witness evidence or malpractice by police and prosecutors convicted the wrong person.

Both British scientists had vast experience in homicide reviews. Professor Barclay was the head of physical evidence at Britain's National Crime and Operations Faculty; Boots was a DNA expert, a senior forensic scientist with the British Home Office. Their crime-solving talents far exceeded their specialist qualifications. Barclay said the Claremont crimes were sexually motivated, but that sexually motivated murders do not necessarily mean sexual contact.

The pair trawled through all the forensic records from the Claremont cases they could track down. In the last days of the four-week review, they made an interesting, and alarming, discovery. None of this startling information was shared with the public, except in an oblique way.

The two scientists found records of 4000 fibres, hairs and possible DNA samples that had been recovered from the sites where Jane Rimmer's and Ciara Glennon's bodies had been found. When they tracked the progress of the samples through the testing laboratories, however, they discovered that many had either not been tested, or not tested against each other. Such comparisons could prove whether body hair or fibres came from the body or clothing of one murderer, or from different murderers.

Obvious Macro prejudices jumped out at them. Thick green silk recovered from Ciara's bush gravesite had been tested only against clothing Lance Williams had owned and against the ties seized from Peter Weygers' wardrobe. Foreign hairs recovered from Ciara Glennon had been tested only against those found in Lance Williams' car and his parents' car, with negative results. They had been compared with nobody else's. It appeared that Macro was interested only in comparisons that put Lance Williams or Peter Weygers in the frame.

The same applied to multiple 'foreign' pollen samples recovered from Lance Williams' car.

Similarly, DNA of two unknown males recovered from Ciara's underpants found on her grave were compared with Lance Williams' DNA but nobody else's. There was no match.

Much more work needed to be done on these largely neglected samples to see if they matched vehicles or samples from other crimes thought to be unrelated, the pair said.

'These comparisons could hold the key to solving the baffling murders,' the *Post* reported in December 2004.

The fibres, along with a trove of material recovered from the crime scenes, were still available for comparisons. Find them, test them and compare them with the other crimes, the panel recommended.

As Barclay explained: 'Every contact is an opportunity to transfer saliva, hair, fibres and other material. If we get a match and we know who that person is, through a vehicle, or an address, or by some other means, the Claremont case has been solved. We haven't anywhere near reached the end of the process in the Claremont investigation. This work has not even been started.'

The task force recommended that the investigation should not be scaled back or closed. But in the public domain at least, Macro seized this opportunity to mark its own homework.

Most media coverage of the review of local police work was obligingly favourable, in the absence of any published findings by the panel seen as critical of Macro. 'Serial killer inquiry gets thumbs up by reviewers' headlined *The West Australian*, which reported that the Macro investigation had been found to be thorough and comprehensive. It said the report found no fault with the attention given to Lance Williams, Peter Weygers and Steven Ross.

Only the *Post* revealed the startling hair and fibre news, its reports published some days after the high-profile press briefings and glowing praise for Macro.

Behind the scenes, the review panel had recommended revisiting the circumstances of how Lance Williams had come to be a suspect. The Schramm experts had been very taken with the significance of the snug fit, the match between the skull fracture identified at the back of Ciara's skull and the fire poker missing from the fireside of Lance Williams' beachfront flat, a 'fact' unknown to the public.

Because the experts concluded that the killer had acted alone, some media interpreted this as eliminating the so-called Steven Ross and Peter Weygers team. But the panel did not eliminate the pair. The news reports about a lone murderer had no discernible effect on lifting public esteem of Weygers and Ross from the low point it had reached.

Also unknown to the public, the panel put together a full report on the crimes against Lisa, recommending a reinvestigation of the obvious similarities between the murders and Lisa's abduction from Rowe Park and rape at Karrakatta Cemetery.

They noted that Karrakatta, too, had featured witness reports by Hollywood Hospital security guard, Wayne Wookey, of his sighting of a vehicle carrying a telco's logo.

In fact, a Telstra 'person of interest' had already been hauled in by police, creating a giant distraction. He was a former interstate police officer who had joined the telco, did not have alibis for the nights of the murders and had failed a lie-detector test.

All incidents involving Telstra vehicles were collated – during the years women were being abducted from Claremont, drivers of a Holden or other vehicle had been involved in at least six other interactions with young women late at night in the Claremont and Cottesloe areas, each report mentioning a Telecom or Telstra connection. But it appears investigating officers were sidetracked by the innocent ex-cop, who was kept under surveillance and deemed worthy of a further probe. He was later eliminated by forensic evidence.

In all, twenty-three Telstra employees had been investigated. The panel recommended a much wider investigation of any Telstra link.

Schramm had given local police a lot to chew on in their main report, including the possibility suggested by Professor Barclay that the murders may have stopped because his last victim, Ciara Glennon, had fought back and scared him, not because the murderer was being watched.

Nobody 'out there' was to get a hint of any of these details, clasped tightly to the police bosom.

*

Even more secret was the fact that the main Schramm study was not the only startling report to emerge from the fly-in review.

Behind the scenes, David Barclay and Malcolm Boots did not regurgitate the public accolades handed out to the Western Australian police. As they prepared to depart, they presented their second secret report, called the Secret Annexure, to Commissioner Karl O'Callaghan in person. It expressed serious concerns about how the local forensic systems had fallen down badly, and they were not shy about saying so. Their forthright denunciation was to have far-reaching effects. In old movies and television cop shows, science had seemed boring when compared with tough, intuitive detectives who just 'knew' when a crook was lying. This gut-feeling identification of culprits would be followed by bullying and threatening of suspects, often at gunpoint, *Dirty Harry*-style. High-speed car chases were usually thrown in for extra effect. Then dramas such as *CSI* came along with their sexy, glamorous and witty scientists who cracked complex cases before dinner on the first day. Crime fiction changed, creating hero scientists.

On our screens were men and women with PhDs working alongside tough, smart detectives, cross-pollinating logical, critical thinking to all parts of the investigation. Television's *CSI* scientists held control of crime scenes, their work entwined with that of detectives, the whole team interpreting and cross-referencing information.

'Most scientists are very intelligent, bright people who are interested in detecting crime,' says Professor Barclay, himself renowned for his lateral thinking in crime solving.

Such highly productive crime-scene interactions between scientists and police was not working in Western Australia, the two scientists told the police commissioner. The police sent crime-scene samples to be tested, then returned the results to police for interpretation – a disaster waiting to happen. The two British scientists discovered that local police not only worked in separate silos from the scientists and rarely spoke with them, but the state's scientists were themselves separated into two different buildings in different suburbs.

'Throughout the time of the Claremont case, individual scientists, however competent, tended to be doing their tests in isolation in the laboratories,' he said.

The scientists doing the analysis worked in a vacuum. They had no context for their work and did not know the overall crime-scene picture, let alone had the opportunity to discuss forensic opportunities with detectives, with whom they rarely spoke. They simply sent in test results.

Detectives almost invariably communicated with them through unqualified police in the forensic division, with little opportunity for discussion or follow-up questions.

David Barclay and Malcolm Boots informed the commissioner that the local forensic system was as far from the *CSI* television image as could be imagined. The lab set-up was extremely wasteful. The two laboratories did not fit the definition of forensic laboratories, because the scientists were not given the information necessary to interpret results.

However competent, local cops with 'Police Forensic' written on their overalls were not scientists but police officers, who had come up through the ranks with no tertiary qualifications or high levels of specialist training. They were far down the police pecking order, way below police royalty, the homicide detectives.

In addition, the property tracing system was a nightmare, the review panel had found.

'The worst ever forensic records. The worst IT [information technology] system anywhere, ever,' the report said. In fact, they wrote, it was worse than no system at all.

In one excruciating example, the Schramm panel had asked local police to retrieve some trace samples. What should have been a simple task took the local police team four days.

It was now apparent to those who had access to the secret report that accusations of tunnel vision, although hotly denied by Macro, appeared to be valid.

For Macro to digest and act fully on these fresh lines of enquiry meant a mind-shift away from the usual suspects to a far more macro approach.

25

Special Crime

Macro was, by the end of 2004, well past being the longest and most expensive murder investigation in Australia. It still had a long way to run when Dr O'Callaghan, at the urging of his underlings armed with the Barclay and Boots secret report, eventually decreed that things must change, with a new cold-case homicide squad operating in a much-improved way. O'Callaghan's response to the Everest of criticism from the two British scientists would come to transform the Claremont investigation.

Despite the exciting new 'forensic opportunities' the Schramm team had mapped out, Macro continued to focus on its three main suspects, by now nervous wrecks from years and years of intense attention.

Astoundingly, just weeks after the Schramm team's measured identification of vast new leads that required following, Macro pulled Steven Ross from the cab of his delivery truck in Seventh Avenue, Maylands, on December 16, 2004.

The cops took him to Macro headquarters where they again accused him of playing a part in the murders. Again, they seized his Ford Falcon station wagon, then drove him around Claremont pointing out various landmarks, saying they had taxi company records that showed he had picked up Sarah Spiers the night she had vanished. He had taken her to the Windsor Hotel in South Perth, where Peter Weygers was waiting, they said. Previously, they had accused Ross of driving Sarah to the Weygers house, Killara, in Claremont.

'That is all bullshit,' Ross told the *Post*. 'They won't show me the taxi records. How could anyone have known I was driving passengers to the Windsor? I didn't know it myself. I didn't have a mobile phone in those days.'

They told him Peter Weygers kept newspaper clippings of the murders and had refused to give his DNA voluntarily. They had again shown Ross the power-zapper. 'They said I used the zapper to stun people in my taxi.'

Police produced photos Ross had taken of his girlfriend in bed after she had died of an illness in the early 1990s, and also pictures of her funeral, he said.

'They called me a sick person.'

Ross said he fully expected to be charged with the murders. Police told him he would remain a suspect until they could verify the information that he had given them.

Lance Williams was also still on the hook, significant Macro figures firmly believing that the circumstantial case against him was compelling. By now, however, the Supreme Court had refused to renew the warrants that enabled police to bug conversations in his car.

Nervous Macro detectives remained fearful that if Lance Williams committed a serious crime that Macro missed, heads would roll.

Although they had stopped tailing their prey, for four more years they continued to follow his movements via the GPS tracker they had legally attached to his car. They also maintained the secret fixed video camera in the scout hall in Eric Street, Cottesloe. It was trained on the front of Williams' parents' house and hardwired back to a recorder at the squad's headquarters. Just how this would have prevented another woman being abducted is a mystery. In the event of another abduction, police coming on duty after a weekend would be able to see whether Lance Williams had left home, but that is all. It would be far too late for an unfortunate victim. Macro called it risk management.

The third suspect, Peter Weygers, had become hyper-vigilant. 'I was always on edge,' he said. 'They never left me alone.'

One evening, he and Vicki were driving on Stevenson Avenue, a parkway in Claremont, when a police car approaching from the opposite direction did a sudden U-turn, chased their car and stopped them, blue lights flashing.

'The officer said the Toyota Camry I was driving was low at the back – there must be a body in the boot,' Weygers said.

By now, he would sweat and have an anxiety attack whenever he saw a police car.

The surveillance continued until at least 2007, with Peter Weygers documenting seven instances of being pulled over by police for no reason related to his driving.

'We've got you this time,' an officer told him one evening in Mounts Bay Road, Perth. He had been in the passenger seat, with Vicki driving, but police breath-tested him anyway, and he returned a zero reading.

At least Macro returned the fifty ties they had seized from his home.

In May 2005, Weygers decided to run again for mayor. 'I've done nothing wrong. People may think I'm the serial killer but I'm not,' he said before the poll.

That was hardly an election-winning slogan. Reputational damage had done its work. Unlike the former mayor's glory days, he finished a distant last, with 385 votes, while his two opponents together polled 2609.

*

Although Schramm had said the Claremont cases were still capable of being solved, Macro Task Force was disbanded in October 2005, two years after Wendy Page began recording interviews with Robin Napper for *Australian Story*.

'This is the most important criminal investigation that WA has ever had, and it doesn't get much more serious than that,' said Deputy Police Commissioner Chris Dawson, after Macro was dissolved.

Macro's replacement was the stand-alone Special Crime Squad, then unique in Australian law enforcement. It was housed in an anonymous office block in central Perth's Adelaide Terrace, remote from the old Macro office. It mirrored the composition of the Schramm team and the British approach, first outlined by Robin Napper on Wendy Page's ABC programme, 'He Who Waits'. Its handpicked Special Crime detectives worked alongside intelligence analysts, technicians and forensic experts in the one office, which was physically separated from the rest of the force.

Its brief was to focus on all cold cases while taking to heart the criticisms and suggestions of David Barclay and Malcolm Boots, including the thirty-three lines of inquiry that had not been completed in the Claremont cases.

The new squad was headed by Detective Sergeant Anthony Lee.

'Do I have expectations that Special Crime Squad will see something that ten reviews and 250 previous investigations didn't see? It's possible, but unlikely,' he said.

Unresolved questions and avenues of inquiry still needed to be followed, said Chris Dawson.

Special Crime's squad of thirteen officers from a wide range of disciplines was well down in numbers from Macro's peak of more than one hundred in the 1990s. It set out to review the Claremont 'forensic opportunities' missed the first time around and to test links to other crimes involving missing women. It also looked at lead-up or precursor offences of lesser severity that may have led to rapes and murders.

Seized with new enthusiasm, Special Crime began the massive job of organising and cataloguing vast files accumulated over ten years. It was watched over by David Barclay, who had twice returned, quietly, to Perth after the Schramm team wrapped up in December 2004. He was now attached as an advisor to Special Crime, working in the same room with detectives, crime analysts and scientific support staff.

'It's exactly the sort of integrated approach that I would recommend and that we now use in the UK,' he said.

One month after the squad had been formed, another giant cold-case problem landed in its lap, which took most of Special Crime's attention. It was a challenge tailor-made for the brand-new unit. But solving this unrelated cold case would stall the Claremont investigation and caused reverberations that were to shake the local police service to its core.

In November 2005, the High Court of Australia had ordered a retrial of Andrew Mallard, a drifter who had then been in jail for almost twelve years for the 1994 violent murder of Mosman Park jeweller Pamela Lawrence. Her head had been bashed thirteen times with a sharpish object while she was alone in her shop at closing time.

The cornering and charging of Mallard had been a classic case of detectives jumping to conclusions, based on their gut feelings about a suspect. They followed this up with a severe case of tunnel vision. Andrew Mallard had been doubly unlucky, a victim of coincidence, the phenomenon that infects every big investigation – and every homicide inquiry is huge. Some of those coincidences now seem almost beyond belief. Mallard had just been released from police custody, questioned for prowling and stealing from a church and convent in the area, and dropped back in Mosman Park by taxi. He was in the area close to the time of the murder, and familiar with Lawrence's shop. Police, led by David Caporn, later found Mallard at a psychiatric unit and asked him to theorise about how the murder had occurred. A video of his rambling regurgitation of information fed to him by police was produced in court as a confession to murder. Mallard had unluckily been at the wrong place, at almost, but not quite, the wrong time, as the evidence eventually revealed.

Following the High Court's order for a retrial, a series of media reports cast further doubt on Mallard's guilt. Director of Public Prosecutions Robert Cock dropped the charges and the retrial was abandoned, with Andrew Mallard immediately released from jail in 2006.

Special Crime Squad was landed with the job of reinvestigating the crime, with the help of David Barclay. In the process, Barclay taught this new cold-case squad valuable lessons: go back to basics with the physical evidence, track each exhibit, retrieve each item for retesting if necessary, make sure it had been matched correctly with evidence collected from other crime scenes, and log the results properly.

Special Crime now discovered that some files about the Pamela Lawrence murder had been mislaid, shunted down a cul-de-sac. They had been sent to the police internal affairs unit because of questions raised about the conduct of some officers, and there they had stayed.

In one file, the squad found a plaque – the photograph of a palm print that forensic officers had originally located on the front of a display case in Pamela Lawrence's shop. Detective Mal Shervill, by 2006 an assistant police commissioner, had noted that the palm print had originally been tested against that of the charged man, Andrew Mallard. But because it had not matched Mallard's hand, it had been discounted as having no importance. Detectives had been so fixated on Mallard that they had looked no further.

A decade after Andrew Mallard was convicted of wilful murder, Special Crime ran the palm plaque through the police print database. By now, old palm print records had been scanned in, and the result was momentous – a hit. The palm print belonged to a British man named Simon Rochford.

In July 1994, Rochford, aged thirty-eight, was grilled by homicide detectives for the murder of his Australian girlfriend, Brigitta Dickens. Some of the same police who grilled Rochford had grilled Mallard, in the same interview room, just seven weeks earlier.

Rochford, who had entered Australia from Britain in 1993 on a false passport, had beaten Dickens to death in the beachside suburb of Scarborough after she had uncovered his lies and false identity. The unusual weapon Rochford wielded on Dickens was a home-made club, the same weapon that had killed Pamela Lawrence, as was much later proved.

Upon this discovery, a wave, not of jubilation but of consternation, crashed over the Special Crime's office.

'Everyone was shitting themselves that day,' one officer said.

Leaping to the top of every mind was the formidable name of David Caporn. By then, this charismatic leader of men and women was Assistant Commissioner and head of counter-terrorism and state protection. The popular and powerful detective had not only been the top man and spokesman for Macro, but also the officer in charge of the investigation that locked up Andrew Mallard for life back in the mid-1990s. David Caporn's reputation for solving that shocking murder mystery saw his rising star shoot into the stratosphere. Soon after, he was appointed front and centre of the high-profile Claremont cases.

When Special Crime made the breakthrough that finally pointed the finger at Rochford in 2006, Caporn was a senior and influential member of the police executive, the star investigator who many insiders believed was destined for the police commissioner's chair. He would have been a popular choice.

The palm plaque that now placed Simon Rochford inside Pamela Lawrence's jewellery shop provided a hot alternative murderer. During his twelve years locked behind bars after his arrest, Andrew Mallard had continued to deny that he had any knowledge of the killing.

Monster questions now loomed. If the print put Rochford in the frame, how come so much evidence presented against

Andrew Mallard at his murder trial had pointed to him, and to him alone? Rochford, serving a fifteen-year sentence in Albany Regional Prison for the murder of Brigitta Dickens, suicided in his cell hours after the news broke that he was suspected of the murder of Pamela Lawrence.

What had gone so badly wrong? A public inquiry to get to the bottom of it brought a long, excruciating parade in front of retired NSW Supreme Court Judge John Dunford, tasked with probing 'the alleged misconduct of public officers'. The witnesses gave evidence at hearings of the Corruption and Crime Commission (CCC) over four months in 2007. Justice Dunford concluded David Caporn and Mal Shervill had engaged in misconduct when they brought about alterations to the statements of four witnesses, these alterations describing a man who could have been Mallard, after the witnesses had originally described a man who could not have been Mallard. This could not have been coincidence, the commissioner said.

He also made recommendations about the interviewing of suspects who were mentally unfit.

Caporn had been in charge of the investigation, and with interrogating Mallard. The police commissioner should consider taking disciplinary action against Caporn and Shevill, wrote Mr Dunford.

David Barclay was scathing when called to the public CCC hearings. Police had jumped to conclusions, notes of vital forensic tests had not been kept and evidence had been selectively presented to court, he said in evidence. Police had thought Mallard was probably guilty.

'My impression is that the police picked out the things that looked to them as if they supported his involvement and ignored the rest,' he said in evidence. 'Witness and confessional evidence should always be backed up by physical evidence.'

The weakness of the prosecution case should have been brought to the attention of Mallard's lawyers, he added.

Caporn and Shervill resigned from the force in February 2009, after being told their assistant commissioner contracts would not be renewed.

Disciplinary action was brought against Ken Bates, the prosecutor in the case. He was fined $10,000 for failing to disclose to the court a written police report.

So, it came to pass that the first high-profile notch in the belt of Special Crime, the new, super cold-case squad now in charge of the Claremont murders, was David Caporn, whose long carriage of the Macro investigation had covered crucial periods.

In a graphic and unforgettable way, the unpleasant Mallard episode demonstrated to local detectives the sledgehammer effect a painstaking forensic review can have on a baffling murder mystery. This lesson was not lost on the few officers still toiling away with that new focus in the Claremont investigation, as the CCC presented its bombshell Mallard report to Parliament on October 7, 2008.

26

Smear

Murder mystery was everywhere. As if the scandal of the Pamela Lawrence murder and the continuing probe into the Claremont serial killings were not enough for one medium-sized city, yet another sensational homicide was occupying vast police and forensic assets from August 2007. This, too, would intersect with the Claremont investigation.

That August, police had dug up the body of Supreme Court registrar Corryn Rayney, the mother of two schoolgirls, after someone buried her a week earlier in the sandy soil under a she-oak copse in inner-city Kings Park. By early 2008, the populace was still agog at the discovery.

Tips and information had poured into Task Force Dargan, the code name for the squad set up to investigate. The result of one such tip headlined the bulletin of top-rating Channel Seven's six o'clock news on January 11, 2008.

News footage showed the front door of Killara, Peter Weygers' home in Richardson Avenue, Claremont. The bulletin said Major Crime Squad detectives were questioning him about Corryn Rayney's murder.

The West Australian's newspaper's headline the next day announced: 'Civil liberties chief interviewed as part of Rayney murder inquiry.'

The report was accompanied by large photos of Rayney's husband, Lloyd, and of Weygers, plus a caption that said both were under investigation.

'The detectives came to my door and asked me if I was going to confess to murdering Corryn Rayney,' Weygers said afterwards. Police had told him they had received 3000 calls from members of the public, nominating possible culprits.

'They had been given the job of investigating me because I was high profile,' he said.

Weygers said he looked over one detective's shoulder to a sheet of notes – and read the address of a house Weygers owned in the suburb of Belmont. The house was rented by a delinquent tenant who Weygers was trying to evict over a debt of $8000 for damage, theft and overdue rent. During an acrimonious legal process, the tenant had threatened to 'make my life hell', Weygers said. 'She said: "I am really going to fix you up."'

A short time later, detectives had appeared on Weygers' doorstep. They said later they had received a tip-off but would not disclose the tipster.

Weygers learned that the tenant had told police Weygers owned a house in Bentley, very close to where Mrs Rayney was last positively seen.

'Even if the police are obliged to follow up every anonymous tip, I can't think of anything more damaging than those inquiries being published by an unquestioning media,' said Weygers. 'What about the other 2999 people nominated? Are they to be defamed and vilified, as I was?

'Next I'll be blamed for daylight saving. It's the Claremont serial killer debacle all over again. People don't remember the fine details. All they remember are the key words: Major Crime Squad, murder, Rayney, Weygers.'

Stress causing sweating and shaking reactions returned with force. He and Vicki felt traumatised, nauseated and overcome with anxiety all over again.

*

The Special Crime Squad worked separately from Major Crime and was not involved with the Rayney investigation. It treated the Claremont murders as a cold case, closely examining possible links to other cases, such as Lisa's summer-of-1995 abduction and cemetery attack, following up one of the Schramm team's recommendations.

By March 2007, new sets of eyes had moved Lisa's case to the top of Special Crime's list. Detectives re-interviewed the witnesses and conducted more DNA tests with suspects.

Some at Special Crime firmly believed Lisa's shocking blitz attack was a precursor offence by the same man responsible for the three Claremont murders. But entrenched belief still persisted among the old hands, who clung firmly to the Lance Williams or Peter Weygers theories. There could be no connection, they believed. The Williams and Weygers DNA samples did not match DNA gathered from Lisa's attack. Therefore, that logic went, the cases were not connected.

The squad then revisited the case of Sarah Spiers, the case where no body was found, in microscopic detail. Again, further avenues of investigation were listed.

Country-born detective sergeant Jim Stanbury, who had been recruited from the Australian Crime Commission in 2006, took over as head of the Special Crime Squad in early 2008. Stanbury had been one of thirty officers who, in their spare time and with police sponsorship, had obtained university forensic science degrees, specialising in DNA techniques. Re-educating willing officers had been an initiative of Karl O'Callaghan's, which had been inspired by David Barclay's withering criticism of the lack of scientific expertise in police ranks and liaison between detectives and scientists.

That year, again acting on David Barclay's recommendations, two forensic officers – senior sergeants Ken Sanderson and George Paton – had set about the massive task of tracking, recording and cataloguing each physical evidence sample recovered from the Claremont cases. They had to completely review the forensic filing system, so scathingly described by David Barclay as worse than no system at all. The pair spent 1600 hours locating, reordering and assessing all physical evidence. Despite this intensive work, they found nothing they could see that would lead to the cases being solved. By mid-2008, the conclusion was reached that there were no leads left to chase.

A dejected Special Crime Squad met the victims' devastated parents, with no alternative but to break the news that their daughters' crime scenes were 'forensically barren'. The crushed families were doubly disappointed because their hopes had been raised by the Schramm review and again by the formation of the Special Crime Squad.

Then followed a loss of brainpower, perhaps prompted by the pessimistic prognosis. Under pressure to solve new murders, the Major Crime Squad had been 'borrowing' officers from Special Crime and not returning them. By mid-2008, the Special Crime squad was depleted to a few officers.

Fresh talk took hold that the Claremont probe had reached an investigative dead end and would soon have to be shelved. The enormous time and resources devoted to it would have been wasted.

*

If the police hierarchy was losing interest at this point, the outside world was not. The saga was once again about to explode into the public arena, demonstrating how hot the public outrage at the Claremont homicide series still burned.

A decision to release blurry black-and-white closed-circuit television footage of Jane Rimmer at the Continental Hotel, her last confirmed sighting, showed that the murders had not receded one millimetre from the front of the public's mind.

A television company, Graham McNeice Productions, had approached Special Crime to make a documentary. Officers had correctly guessed that, without the squad's input, the film would focus on the publicly available material, specifically about Lance Williams, Peter Weygers and Steven Ross.

Seizing the opportunity, the squad's leaders decided that, from a cold-case perspective, the footage of Jane Rimmer needed to be released at last. Twelve years after it was recorded, they gave the company a copy of the tape, which it enhanced. Jane is seen interacting and laughing with a mystery man on the footpath in Bay View Terrace, outside the hotel. Detectives figured that, even after this long delay, a friend or family member might recognise the stance of Mystery Man, photographed from behind.

As the documentary went to air in August 2008, it detonated an explosion of interest. Even after so many years and tears, the images dominated news bulletins, websites and newspapers for days. Asked why they had waited so long to release it, police replied that the video had been shown in the 1990s to 700 people who had been in Claremont on the night Jane vanished, but not one had recognised the man. Who was he?

Failure this time, too. Despite hundreds of tips that poured into police, nobody came forward with a name for Mystery Man. Either he was not a local, memories had faded or someone who might have recognised him had by now joined the thousands of other educated locals who were living and working in far corners of the globe.

Detectives had also advised the filmmakers on a re-enactment of what the Burger Boys had seen of Ciara Glennon on the footpath in Stirling Highway. It was Ciara interacting through the passenger window with someone in a light-coloured station wagon.

The Burger Boys had described the vehicle as a white, late-model Holden station wagon, with no visible taxi lights or markings. One of the three had called out to Ciara that it was stupid to hitch-hike. She waved him off, a *Post* report said. In reporting this information, the paper added that one of the

Burger Boys could distinguish Holden makes and models with precision.

A police spokesman told the questioning media that they were unsure whether or not the car had been a taxi. They also did not want to restrict public information to one vehicle only, a tactic that had narrowed the scope of a much earlier, unrelated murder investigation in the mining town of Collie. In the Claremont re-enactment, senior police had ordered the vehicle's make and model to be blurred. In the public mind, this left open the possibility that the car could have been the white Ford Falcon station wagon driven by Steven Ross. But in March 1997, the time Ciara disappeared, Ross's car had carried full taxi lights and signs.

Despite a drought of new evidence, amid the torrent of renewed public interest, the few police and scientific specialists left in the depleted Special Crime office were not in the mood to give up on the Claremont families.

27
Breakthrough

The flimsy cases against the usual suspects had been advanced not one millimetre by the forensic review, nor the Mystery Man tape. They had implicated no offender.

So who was the Claremont serial killer?

This basic puzzle confronted two police sergeants as they sat in front of a blank piece of paper in the Special Crime Squad office in mid-winter, July 2008, a month after Ken Sanderson and George Paton had delivered their long review. These two cops knew that most recommendations of David Barclay and Malcom Boots had been carried out, and some results analysed. But not all thirty-three recommendations of the Schramm review had been completed.

The few remaining hair- and fibre-analysis tasks, when completed, were thought to lead nowhere. It was the firm belief among many police that the only hope of finding new evidence was the chance discovery of a secondary murder site, such as a vehicle or 'safe house', where the murderer may have taken victims before disposing of bodies. But no such goldmines were on the horizon.

With Corryn Rayney's murder investigation and other new crimes sucking in all available police resources, the Special Crime Squad offices were almost empty, its badly depleted remnants grasping for a way forward. The chances of solving Claremont were looking grim.

Two men left in the room that winter's day were the head

of Special Crime, detective sergeant Jim Stanbury, and forensic officer sergeant George Paton.

As they gazed on the vast volume of material collected around the Claremont case, they made a decision to start again from scratch. They would set a new course, ignoring any of the unsubstantiated conclusions so far reached about suspects, and assumptions about sources of trace evidence.

They began by writing a list of what they now *really* knew and what they did not know about the trace material collected from the various crime scenes, and began to enter this data into the police computer system.

They made another crucial decision – to elevate crime-scene samples recovered from the Karrakatta Cemetery abduction and rape to the same level of scrutiny as the three other Claremont victims. Lisa was not to be forgotten.

The pair also concentrated on the known crime scenes that should have been rich in physical evidence – the disposal sites of Jane Rimmer and Ciara Glennon. The tiny but crucial forensic samples recovered from those widely separated sites, and from the bodies themselves at the post-mortems, must show something. Every contact leaves a trace.

Within two weeks, they had their eyes opened wide. Their painstaking policy of going right back to original sources discovered serious errors in how crime-scene data had been entered into the records.

Evidence collected early in the investigation had been reviewed many times, but original reporting mistakes had been set in stone when reviewers simply cut and pasted old errors into their new reports.

Once they had discovered the ongoing errors, a startling notion hit the two men. What if these mistakes meant a vital piece of forensic evidence had been missed? One that cracked the case?

That brought excitement, but also trepidation. Big police forces are no different from any other political beast, bureaucracies where reputations are jealously protected and promotions coveted. This Claremont investigation had been going for fourteen years. Some police colleagues would be far from pleased if they were shown to have been barking up the wrong tree all that time.

As the two sergeants toiled on for long days and into the nights, they kept their project secret, afraid that the Lance Williams/Peter Weygers hard-liners on the force would interfere with their open-minded approach.

Each of the 4000 crime-scene samples had to be audited and tracked anew, right from origin and back to one of the laboratories, PathWest or the ChemCentre. To do this, the two sergeants enlisted the help of scientists and scene-of-crime officers.

Special Crime's task was not made any easier by changes in the property-tracking software over the decade to a totally new and totally incompatible computer system. During the decade, removalists had also twice shifted the priceless crime-scene material, first to one then to another storage area.

As the pair ploughed on, that first blank piece of paper grew and grew into twenty volumes, 1.5 million words, all footnoted and annotated, listing and cross-checking every skerrick of detail about the Claremont cases' forensic samples. This status document was to become the sergeants' Bible.

They uncovered more errors. Then, within a month of starting, their work had led to a stunning breakthrough.

They found some crucial samples that had never been tested at all. The significance of this discovery hit them like a sledgehammer: it meant the crime scenes were not forensically barren, as the victims' grief-wracked parents had been told just months earlier.

The pair was hit by an adrenaline rush that saw them staying back in the office working far into the nights, unpaid.

They found that, at the post-mortem examinations of Jane Rimmer and Ciara Glennon, the victims' fingernails had been

Scuff marks among the gravestones where the sexual assault of 'Lisa' took place at Karrakatta Cemetery on February 12, 1995. (Supreme Court of Western Australia via AAP)

The washing line that bound Lisa hand and foot, tied into a complex handcuff-knot that tightened when resisted. (WA Police/Supreme Court of Western Australia)

Sarah's friend Jasmine Glatz, dressed as Sarah was when last seen. She is re-enacting Sarah's last call for a television film screened to prompt information from the public. (Michelle Stanley/Post Newspapers)

The 1902 Continental Hotel, where Jane Rimmer was last seen on June 9, 1996. It is now called The Claremont. (Bret Christian/Post Newspapers)

Jane Rimmer shares a joke with Mystery Man outside the Continental Hotel just after midnight. This image from CCTV footage was her last confirmed sighting. Police were criticised for withholding the image from general release for twelve years. (Supreme Court of Western Australia)

Homicide Detective Sergeant Vicky Smith points towards the body of Jane Rimmer inside a 'cavern' formed by dense scrub beside Woolcoot Road, Wellard, on August 3, 1996. (WA Police/ Supreme Court of Western Australia)

Jane's Guess watch, found the day she was murdered, and the Telstra knife found the day her body was discovered. (Watch: Supreme Court of Western Australia via AAP; knife: WA Police/Supreme Court of Western Australia)

Winter arum lilies grow at the base of the makeshift cross erected by police where Jane Rimmer's body was found. Police had ordered the clearing of dense scrub as they searched for hidden clues. (Michelle Stanley/ Post Newspapers)

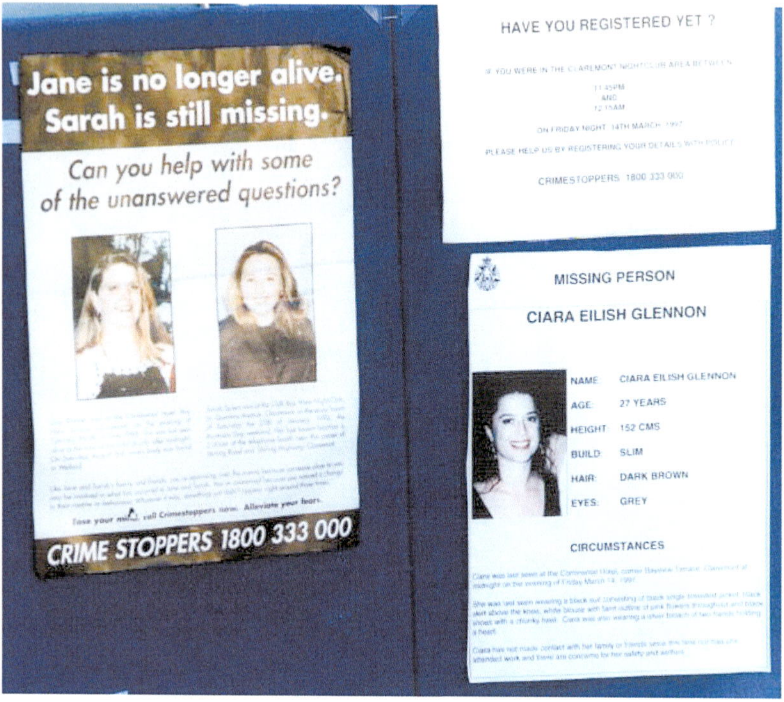

Missing person posters of victims Jane Rimmer (left), Sarah Spiers and Ciara Glennon on a police noticeboard. Ciara was last seen March 15, 1997. The poster of Ciara shows an older photo, taken before her year-long backpacking trip. A more recent photo showed a strikingly different Ciara, with tanned skin and sun-bleached blonde hair. (Michelle Stanley/Post Newspapers)

Robert Hemelaar, officer in charge of police forensics, uses a measuring stick to gauge the height from which tree branches were torn above Ciara Glennon's gravesite. (WA Police/Supreme Court of Western Australia)

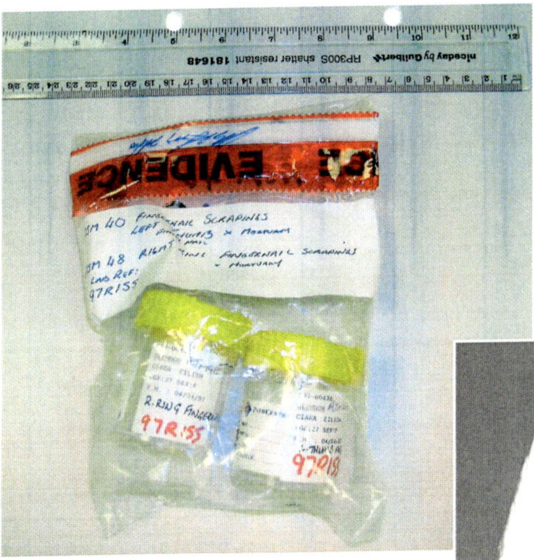

The crucial thumbnail sample AJM 40 (left), retrieved from Ciara Glennon. (WA Police/ Supreme Court of Western Australia)

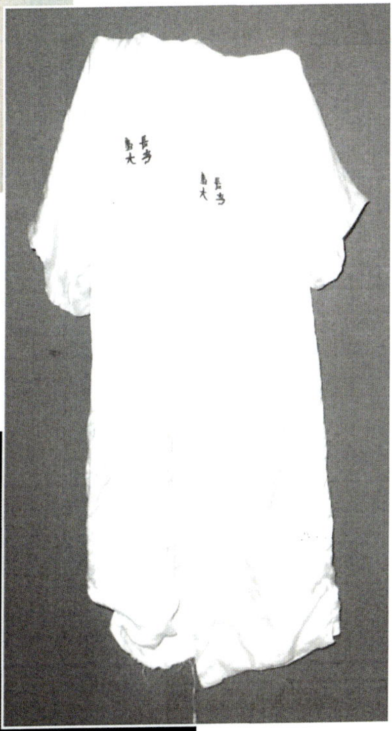

Though it's hard to tell from this grainy photo, black cranes adorn this peach-coloured silk kimono that lay hidden in police storage, its re-discovery the key that unlocked the serial killer case. (Supreme Court of Western Australia via AAP)

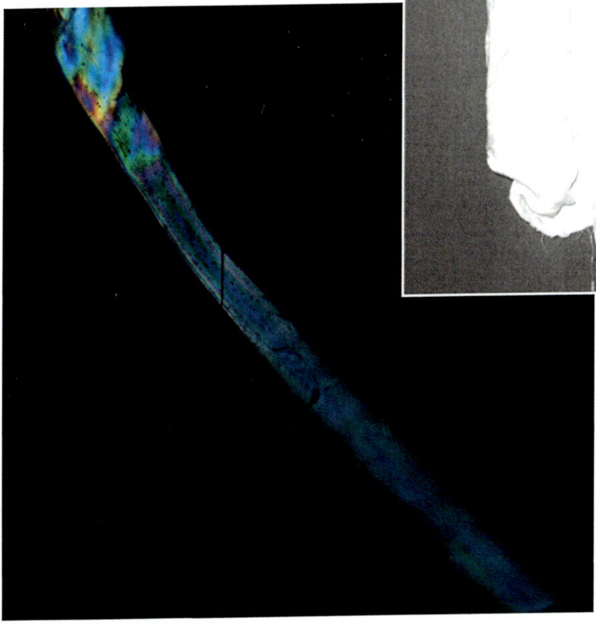

A greatly magnified blue fibre recovered from a Claremont murder victim's body, helping to link the murders of Jane Rimmer and Ciara Glennon. (WA Police/ Supreme Court of Western Australia)

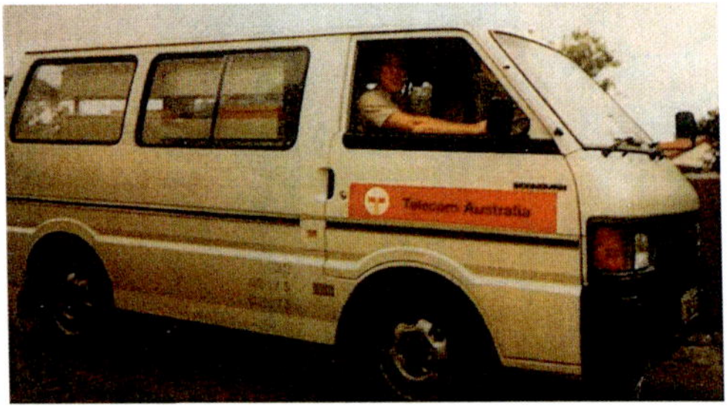

In police custody … The Holden station wagon (left) was driven by the accused man, Bradley Robert Edwards, at the time of the murders of Jane Rimmer and Ciara Glennon. (Below left) A Telecom Mitsubishi van typical of those issued to field technicians at the time of the abduction and rape of Lisa. The driver of this exemplar vehicle was not accused of any crime. (WA Police/Supreme Court of Western Australia)

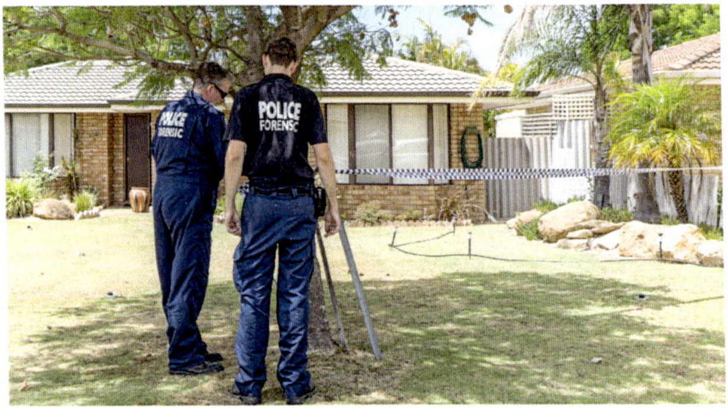

Police forensic officers in December 2016 prepare to enter the house Edwards bought in Fountain Way, Huntingdale, with his first wife, where the couple later took in a lodger. (Kelly Pilgrim-Byrne/Examiner Newspapers)

Court drawing of Bradley Robert Edwards at a final directions hearing before the trial for the murders of Sarah Spiers, Jane Rimmer and Ciara Glennon. The trial began on November 25, 2019. (Anne Barnetson)

Supreme Court Justice Stephen Hall delivers his verdict and reasons for his decisions on September 24, 2020. The judge heard the cases for and against the three wilful murders without a jury. (Supreme Court of Western Australia)

The crowd waiting outside the court applauds prosecutor Carmel Barbagallo and her team as they leave the court after the verdict. (Billie Fairclough/ Post Newspapers)

'The Claremont killings struck at the heart of our way of life,' Police Commissioner Chris Dawson said outside the Supreme Court shortly after the verdict. (Paul McGovern/Post Newspapers)

The impromptu shrine of flowers and heart-wrenching cards left on the steps of the Claremont Hotel within hours of the Supreme Court verdict. (Paul McGovern/Post Newspapers)

cut off and stored, each in separate yellow-top containers. But sometimes, the nail from one finger had been cut off in three pieces and parts sent for testing. The remaining parts of the same nail had been left behind, creating samples and sub-samples that still sometimes carried identical filing codes. All needed to be tracked and reidentified. What was hidden in these untested samples?

Testing fingernails of attack victims has literally pointed the finger at many a violent culprit. A lot of women fight back, and when they do, scratching or gouging an attacker can drag vital fragments of DNA out of his flesh, fragments caught under the victim's fingernails.

Sergeants Stanbury and Paton revisited PathWest and the ChemCentre where exhibits had been stored, the very laboratories David Barclay had criticised for being in separate buildings. The samples had needed to be transported across town from one lab to the other for different tests, carried out in a detective-free vacuum, as David Barclay had reported. They still were.

At the PathWest lab, the sergeants discovered that none of the three clippings from Ciara's right middle finger had been tested at all, with the exception of one piece that may have been sent to New Zealand for advanced testing, without result.

These anomalies prompted them to look further afield.

This search turned up an enlarged colour photograph of Ciara Glennon's left thumb and ring finger. It showed that her left thumbnail had been badly torn, part of it missing. 'You could see she put up a hell of a fight,' one of the men remarked. The officers noticed red dots on the thumb where the nail had been.

It was clear to them that Ciara had ripped off her left thumbnail while trying desperately to protect herself from her much taller and more powerful attacker, before this man stabbed her right arm and cut her throat. In the process, Ciara may well have scoured some material from the skin of her murderer onto the bed of her thumbnail. If so, where was it? Those red dots must mean something.

The two sergeants went looking. The forensic log showed the left thumbnail sample had been 'seized' on April 3, 1997 at Ciara's post-mortem. It was labelled AJM 40.

They traced AJM 40 and found the sealed yellow-top jar inside a PathWest refrigerator. It had never been opened, or tested.

They stared through the Perspex jar at the tiny scrapings inside, the sample that had, back in 1997, been eyeballed by a PathWest scientist who had noted that the contents were unsuitable for testing. There was no nail present, just traces that were half-liquid, half-solid. It had been eyeballed again in 2003 by the same scientist, by that time promoted to team leader, and recorded on the file as 'Debris only. Not suitable for analysis'.

Re-running the video of Ciara's post-mortem, the two Special Crime sergeants clearly saw the morgue technician in close-up, scraping the left thumbnail sample into the yellow-top. He was using a huge pair of scissors, and could be heard on the video soundtrack complaining about the problem he was having finding some thumbnail to cut.

The implications were huge. If the gunk in AJM 40 contained the killer's DNA, it would not only provide an unbreakable link to him, it would, once and for all, rule in or out Lance Williams, Steven Ross, Peter Weygers and many other men on the books. These were the targets at whom so many police resources had been thrown, and who had suffered so much as a result.

There was no point trying to keep this shattering discovery secret from other officers.

Chris Dawson, the deputy commissioner in charge of Serious Crime, was briefed at a meeting the same day that sergeants Paton and Stanbury had recovered AJM 40, August 23, 2008.

'He asked that they be tested as a matter of urgency,' Paton said. 'We explained we didn't have the testing technology in Australia.'

Police hierarchy authorised another $3 million to be spent on forensic tests in Britain. Six days after the meeting, Jim Stanbury met Laurence (Laurie) Webb, PathWest's senior forensic biologist, at Perth airport and boarded the long flight for London. They clutched their precious samples in the aircraft cabin. As well as material from two nails from each of Ciara's hands, the pair carried hair and fibres from the crime scenes, plus a sperm cell fraction and other cells found on Lisa. Not forgotten were the usual suspects – reference DNA samples for them were included in the travellers' hand luggage. The packages, which also contained samples from other unrelated murder mysteries, never left their sight. The two men even took turns to stand guard as the other went to the bathroom at the Singapore stopover. They continued this vigilance right up until their precious cargo was signed for at the Forensic Science Service (FSS) laboratory in Lambeth.

The two sergeants had been very keen to have this work overseen by Dr Jonathan Whitaker, principal forensic scientist at FSS and the father of low-copy-number DNA testing. They had read his damning evidence for the prosecution at the 2005 trial of Bradley John Murdoch for the outback murder of British Kombi-van traveller, Peter Falconio. Murdoch was convicted, his conviction surviving all appeals.

Dr Whitaker said it was clear that violence was involved in breaking Ciara's thumbnail, and that she may have scratched DNA-rich skin or blood from her attacker as a final act of defiance.

'Force promotes transfer,' he said. He decided the two untested scrapings from Ciara's left thumb and middle finger nails be combined as one. Two untested samples from her right hand were combined for a second, separate test.

FSS assigned the DNA analysis to its Specialist Case Review Unit in Birmingham. There, in a high-tech laboratory building called Trident Court, a bright, experienced forensic scientist, Andrew Talbot, was given the job of preparing the samples for DNA extraction.

In early December 2008, working in sterile conditions, Andrew Talbot unscrewed the yellow top of AJM 40 for the first time since it had been sealed in the Perth morgue in April 1997. He scraped out the tiny amount of gunk with a wet cotton bud and repeated the process with the same bud in jar AJM 42, from Ciara's left middle finger. Then he started the complex process of cracking open cells to liberate DNA.

He used the low-copy-number test devised by Dr Whitaker and colleagues. It is sixty-four times more sensitive than standard DNA testing. The process involved adding chemicals, spinning on the centrifuge and baking in an oven. Hours later, there was enough DNA extract to put through the analyser, which produced a printed-out graph of its conclusions.

What Andrew Talbot read from that graph forever changed the Claremont serial killings investigation.

For the first time, after the barrage of tests on samples that had returned only the DNA profiles of the victims, Talbot could say immediately 'there is more than one person present'. He could clearly see two, full, ten-point sets of peaks on the electropherogram he held. One set belonged to Ciara, the other to an unknown male.

When he tested the mixed samples from Ciara's right hand, they yielded only Ciara's own DNA.

By this time, Laurie Webb and Jim Stanbury had returned home with no news, chewing their own fingernails. While they waited, the lab in the UK, under the watchful gaze of Dr Whitaker, retested the samples and rechecked the results.

28
Medical Error

Lance Williams was the culprit, or at least that was what many police and most in the community still believed, while others harboured deep suspicions about Peter Weygers.

Williams felt suffocated and was in a 'terrible state', said his mother Norma. He had missed work and taken to his bed since learning that police had withheld the CCTV footage of Jane Rimmer from the public for twelve years, all the while following and badgering him. It was easy to see that Williams was not Mystery Man caught on film.

Early in November 2008, it came as a surprise to viewers of Channel 9's evening television news bulletin to learn that detectives had effectively told Lance Williams that they had lost interest in him as a suspect in the Claremont case.

What had changed so dramatically?

All senior police would say publicly was that Williams remained a priority person of interest. The media pounced. It reported this new label as a downgrade of Macro's previous description 'prime suspect'.

The *Post* called Williams' father Jim, who said that the head of Special Crime had visited Jim and his wife Norma to relieve their anxiety. Detective Sergeant Jim Stanbury had told them Lance was 'out of the picture'.

'I feel relieved and vindicated,' said Jim Williams. 'It confirms what we said all along is true.'

Ten years of surveillance had left the family socially isolated and had 'an incredible, devastating effect on us all. My wife thought people were staring at her – she stopped coming to Rotary fundraising events with me. They searched our home, pulled everything out and dug up the patio.'

Lance Williams suffered from debilitating depression, while the health of both his parents had suffered badly, with Jim enduring a stroke.

The family had co-operated with police at every turn, he said, but police had continued to tail the couple.

'They suspected Lance was in the boot when we went to family gatherings.

'We gave all the information to David Caporn when he first came around ten years ago. Another officer, John Brandham, came to us and said, "We think he's the Claremont serial killer."

'Then we gave the information to the officers again. Now we have given it a third time.

'Stanbury came to us and said, "You won't be hearing any more from us. I don't believe Lance was the culprit but don't quote me on that."

'These police working on it now seem to be doing a much better job.'

Lance's father still worried about the latest police statement. 'It seems they are putting that [priority person of interest] wording in so he can't claim compensation.'

Peter Weygers was outraged. 'What about me? When are they going to publicly exonerate me as well?' He said he and his partner were living in fear and terror, and he was suffering from post-traumatic stress disorder.

He added that he believed the treatment he had received was payback for his work in Civil Liberties. He and Vicki had also been socially isolated since the public search of his home in 2004. They no longer ate out, after other diners at a restaurant in Dalkeith near his home had pointed at him and whispered 'serial killer'.

Weygers was still working in his barren Education Department outpost, being paid $120,000 a year but not allowed to have contact with children. His previously full professional and personal life had evaporated.

Members of the new Special Crime Squad knew that, as well as no physical evidence connecting him, Weygers was twenty-five year too old to match the profile provided by Caldwell and Minisini. According to them, the serial killer would have been aged between twenty-four and forty at the time of the murders.

Steven Ross was now considered wholly implausible as a murderer. He continued to drive his cab and live on meat pies and Red Bull, a diet that would later cost him a limb through diabetes.

Unexpectedly, Lance Williams found an ally in high places. John Quigley, a fiery member of state parliament, stood in the Legislative Assembly on November 27, 2008, to give David Caporn both barrels.

Quigley, who in 2017 became the state's Labor attorney-general, had been heavily involved in Andrew Mallard's case as instructing lawyer for his successful High Court appeal. He now connected aspects of the Mallard and Claremont murder investigations under parliamentary privilege.

'Lance is no longer the principal suspect in the Macro investigation. How could this be?' he asked. He alleged the existence of a rogue police element where 'allegation equals conviction and destruction of families'.

'It is no coincidence that the principal investigating officer of that [Claremont] case is the person who locked up Mallard: Caporn.

'The police absolutely convicted Lance in the pages of *The West Australian*. They could not convict him in court so they convicted him in the media.

'A decade later it has come out that the police do not believe he is the prime suspect. It is absolutely shameful. The police had all of Perth believing that Lance was the murderer. They destroyed [Lance's] life just as they destroyed Mallard's life.'

Caporn responded that he had never publicly named Lance Williams.

To the public, it was evident that something dramatic must have happened to have cleared Lance Williams, at least in the eyes of members of the Special Crime Squad.

Special Crime had recently brought Williams in for another interview, and were far more satisfied with his answers than had been Dr Saathoff and the raft of other profilers consulted at great expense. It was Dr Saathoff who made his damning, influential remarks about Williams' capability to commit serial murder. The profiler reinforced this view on another Perth visit in 2007.

Lance Williams in no way presented the long list of characteristics that the profilers said the serial killer would exhibit when caught.

There remained his suspicious driving around Claremont, which certainly warranted careful police attention. But as the detailed trawl of trace evidence by sergeants Jim Stanbury and George Paton showed, not a shred of physical evidence existed to connect Williams to the crimes. Clearly, a lot of blood had been spilled at the murder scenes. Exhaustive tests of Williams' clothes, homes, workplace and car showed neither a faint sign of any material transfer nor clean-up.

What of the secret but damning forensic evidence that connected the fire poker missing from the suspect's beachside flat with the skull fractures that had evidently stunned Ciara Glennon?

In 2008, Jim Stanbury made contact with the previous owner of Lance Williams' flat. She had long since moved interstate, but clearly recalled that she had agreed to leave Williams the fireside set as part of the deal, when he had bought her flat in the 1990s. For reasons unknown, the removalists had packed and transported to Queensland some of the four fireside tools, including the poker, but left others. The poker had turned up with the previous owner's other belongings on the other side of Australia – hence why it was missing from Cottesloe. It had never been in Lance Williams' possession, a fact now discovered by basic detective work.

So what caused the skull fractures identified by forensic pathologist Dr Karin Margolius in Ciara's 1997 post-mortem?

By the time the Claremont cases were turned over to the Special Crime Squad in 2005, Dr Margolius had become ill with terminal cancer. In 2009, the year before she died, Jim Stanbury spent three days with her, reviewing all the video footage of the post-mortems, still photos, file notes and reports, compressing them into an invaluable sworn statement that, years later, was read out in court. Dr Margolius repeated her depressed fracture finding.

It was not until 2013 that the mystery was unravelled, which had so excited Macro for fifteen years.

'Oh my God, it's a Wormian bone,' exclaimed Alanah Buck.

This forensic anthropologist and medical scientist, along with forensic pathologist Dr Clive Cooke, had immediately identified Ciara's 'head injury' as a naturally occurring physical anomaly. Unusual but not rare, Wormian or sutural bones are extra pieces of bone that can create uneven joining points as a baby's skull fuses shortly after birth.

'I didn't believe it at first,' Dr Cooke said. The blow-to-the-head 'evidence' against Lance Williams instantly evaporated.

Only one autopsy had been performed on Ciara Glennon's body. Despite the crucial importance of their work and the high esteem in which they are held, forensic pathologists are not infallible. Professor David Barclay recognised this, saying in 2006 it was essential that two separate, independent autopsies be conducted.

Autopsy errors with dire consequences are more common than most people might realise. In one celebrated Texan case, the pathologist identified charred human remains, recovered from a crashed and burned car, as a white male in his early twenties.

The pathologist even detected a possible piece of penis. In fact, Clayton Wayne Daniels, aged twenty-three, had faked his own death to collect insurance. Daniels had visited a cemetery and robbed a grave, then placed the body of an eighty-one-year-old woman in his driver's seat, before torching his deliberately crashed car.

At Jane Rimmer's autopsy, the possible tying of one of her wrists had also been missed. It was a clue that, if explored at the time, may have identified a binding fantasy held by her murderer. This could have provided an early clue that perhaps connected Jane Rimmer's abduction to that of Lisa to Karrakatta Cemetery.

29
Hit

Back in London, through December 2008, the Forensic Science Service team had completed their retesting of promising samples from Australia. Dr Jonathan Whitaker reviewed the work and came up with a reportable conclusion: the complete DNA profile of a male had been found under Ciara's thumbnail.

When his email reached Jim Stanbury late on Monday, January 9, 2009, excitement ran high. Special Crime Squad members could hardly believe their eyes. It was the first genuine forensic breakthrough in thirteen years. The probe that had unlocked this vital clue had been launched just four months earlier from a standing start.

The world outside was to know nothing, but naturally Special Crime rapidly conveyed word to the top strata of police management. It was met with excitement but some trepidation, in full knowledge of all that had gone before.

Laurie Webb received the profile at PathWest the next day, Tuesday, and set about looking for possible matches among reference samples from the Claremont cases.

His first tests compared the British lab results with DNA taken from Lance Williams and Peter Weygers. The results came as a shock to some detectives, a severe blow to their long-held certainties.

No matches.

Finally, after all the attention and resources police had

poured into these two men over almost a dozen years, they were eliminated from contention by two laboratory tests.

Higher authorities in the police decided not to share this news with the public, or the two previously suspected men. To clear them publicly was too dangerous at this crucial stage, they believed.

Such was the intense public interest in the Claremont cases that, if Williams and Weygers were told they had been conclusively eliminated, the two men would no doubt jubilantly share such startling information, bringing their public suffering to an end.

Police hierarchy worried that, if they did, the populace would quickly work out that police had somehow got hold of the real killer's DNA profile.

If the culprit knew that police had his DNA, who knows what he would do? He could cover up evidence, create false alibis, dispose of his trophies, flee overseas – he could even kill himself before arrest, in which case justice would not take its course and Sarah Spiers' remains could never be located.

The official line in the media was that Lance Williams remained a priority person of interest. But police interest now waned – they took the secret slap-on tracker off his car and no longer referred to Williams as the 'prime suspect'. Yet for Williams, Weygers and Ross, apologies came there none.

One officer remarked that, without this DNA breakthrough, police would still be monitoring Lance Williams' parents' house by video camera and also tracking his car.

Back at PathWest, Laurie Webb's next test in January, 2009, would prove pivotal. He ran the result Andrew Talbot had obtained at Trident Court against a 'sperm cell fraction'.

It was the sample kept from the graveyard attack on Lisa, which Webb had identified on the then-new DNA testing kit Profiler Plus in 1999. Because the new result from Britain came from a profile mixed with Ciara's DNA, the comparison was a slow process.

Bingo. The profile from Britain matched Unknown Male 4, Lisa's attacker. Here was absolute proof that, in her last defiant act, Ciara had scraped off DNA belonging to her attacker. And she had left it for the living to prove, way in the future, that this same man had attacked Lisa in the graveyard two years before Ciara had encountered her killer.

At 8 a.m. on the morning of Friday, January 16, four days after the email arrived from Dr Whitaker, a phone rang at the Special Crime Squad office in Adelaide Terrace. Jim Stanbury took the call, hearing the voice of Laurie Webb, his travel companion from the previous year.

'I have one word for you,' Webb said. Then he uttered that word: Lisa's surname.

It was as if the atmosphere in the Special Crime office had been charged with high-voltage electricity. The current flashed to superiors across town at Curtin House, where Macro had once been headquartered.

Officers in the information loop knew, from that instant, everything had changed. In Lisa, the detectives knew they had a living, breathing, highly intelligent, together witness, a survivor who had interacted with the Claremont serial killer. She had seen him and his vehicle, heard him speak, smelt him and could describe how he worked, his MO.

Most significantly, they had this man's full DNA profile.

Find that rapist and you find the Claremont serial killer. From that point, the Claremont serial killings investigation was coded Special Crime Squad Operation 01/2009, in honour of the month that the breakthrough was welcomed.

Here was final proof that all the hours and tens of millions of dollars spent going after a former mayor, a shy and polite public servant, and a taxi driver, was for nought. Nor was the murderer some random cabbie who had driven off into the night with his fares, murder in his mind, given Lisa's impression of being thrust into a van.

All attention turned to nabbing the real culprit. Senior police were convinced they would have an arrest and a man in custody for the serial killings within weeks, once they had compared the Unknown Male 4 DNA profile with other suspects' DNA on file. Meetings were held to discuss how to break the news of an arrest to the media.

Surely, after all the work in collecting DNA samples from among 9000 men of interest, men interviewed in the Macro years, plus 2100 taxi drivers and forensic tests on their 900 cars, the killer's DNA profile would be found somewhere on the Western Australian police database. It would be a relatively simple matter to run the cross-matching software, get a hit, look up the killer's name and address, then drive around to knock on his door, or raid his home.

But all attempts at a match ended in crushing disappointment. They made no hits.

Maybe the killer had moved interstate, where he had committed more crimes and had been caught, then had his DNA-tested there so that his profile and name was with an interstate police force?

No national database existed at that time, so Western Australian police emailed every other state's databases to see if 'their' killer's profile was on file. Attempts at interstate matches had been made several times since 1999, but police held hope that the culprit had been picked up for another crime in the intervening years.

No dice. Another dead end.

It now seemed certain that all four crimes, including that against Lisa, were connected. The probability had always existed that the three murder victims had climbed willingly into their killer's car. But once the link to Lisa was made, there was proof that Unknown Male 4 possessed other decidedly unpleasant traits.

Most detectives had not believed the three Claremont murders were the work of a blitz attacker. Instead, they believed the culprit was a taxi driver or authority figure, such as a police officer. Indeed, many police officers had been thoroughly investigated.

Now, at last, they had another MO.

From the moment of the DNA match, detectives faced a whole new scenario: a blitz attacker, a professional snatch-and-grabber who planned everything right down to his murder kit of gag, bag for placing over the head, cord to tie hands and feet, and professional handcuff knots that tightened more and more as his victim pulled against them.

They were looking for a highly organised, prepared offender, cold and ruthless, without empathy; a man whose cunning, confidence and skill had clearly grown with years of practice.

*

Special Crime, with its shrunken team, now drew massive attention from within the police force. An old Macro hand and more senior officer, Paul Coombes, was brought in to lead it, replacing Detective Senior Sergeant Gary Nicolau, who was then the officer in charge. A superintendent, Coombes outranked detective sergeants on the squad.

He was alert to the sightings of suspicious Telstra vehicles around Claremont, especially conscious of the Schramm team's urgings to carry out a full investigation. He flew a kite: a mass DNA screening of Telstra staff who had after-hours access to work cars. After much discussion, this kite was grounded. Such a plan would involve hundreds of technicians, other staff and many former employees. News of it would certainly leak out. It would have had the same effect as announcing to the public that police now secretly held the culprit's DNA profile.

Urgently, Special Crime officers began another full cold-case review of the attack on Lisa.

Way back in mid-1996, Lisa had gone public with her certainty, her reasoned arguments as to why she believed her attacker was the same man responsible for the disappearances of Jane Rimmer and Sarah Spiers. She had said it all, just a day after Jane had been announced as missing. Lisa, then almost a lone voice, appeared to be right.

Special Crime now assembled all possible information about the rape case, which had been investigated initially for six weeks by Claremont CIB and again, a year later, when Sarah Spiers vanished. Her case was again reopened by the new Sexual Assault Squad, the week after the abduction of Jane Rimmer in mid-1996, while Schramm had trawled through it in 2004. Special Crime had reviewed it once again in 2007 on the Schramm team's recommendation.

Now there was to be another urgent reinvestigation. In February 2009, detectives reinterviewed the witnesses from 1995, including the two officers from 79 Division, the rapid-response team. They had initially attended Lisa at Hollywood Hospital then driven her to Rowe Park and the cemetery. She had pointed out the crime scene among the tombstones, and her shoes, shorts and underpants were recovered from there.

Huge efforts were now put into solving that crime, efforts that ideally should have swung into action when the attacks on Lisa had first occurred. Some detectives were keen to go public with a photo of the unusual handcuff knot the rapist had used, in the hope that somebody would recognise it. But the final decision was that this avenue might lead nowhere, because the rapist might not always have bound his victims or partners.

Jim Stanbury flew back to the UK to take fingerprints and a written statement from the schoolgirl who had lived opposite Rowe Park. Now a woman, she recounted how she had found Lisa's sister's driver's licence, which Lisa had used to gain entry to Club Bayview on that fateful night. This card could have yielded the offender's fingerprint if found in time, but for police, it was still necessary to confirm every link in the chain of evidence for future court purposes.

That trip was one of many Stanbury took to Britain to deliver samples, brief the scientists and clarify the interpretation of evidence. He was soon the go-to man when local police needed DNA expertise.

All up, more than 130 persons of interest had now been investigated and their DNA tested for the Karrakatta crimes. Significantly, their names had been found on Lisa's case file but the individuals had never been investigated by Macro, so convinced was the squad that the same offender was not responsible for all four Claremont crimes. Intriguingly, some of these persons of interest on Lisa's file were Telstra workers. But this new investigation went nowhere.

On advice from a psychologist, some detectives turned their minds to the big pool of soldiers, men who were highly trained in snatch-and-grab techniques, men who lived and worked in Swanbourne, just a few minutes' drive from the centre of Claremont. Special Air Service Regiment (SAS) members are trained in abduction techniques, including placing a black bag over the heads of targets and trussing them using handcuff knots. But how to penetrate the security force field around this highly mobile, highly secretive elite squad and its off-limits compound on Swanbourne beach?

SAS men were trained to use black bags, whereas the fibres recovered from Lisa's hair revealed her attacker had used a cream-coloured calico bag.

The knot was also a problem. There exists an 'official' SAS handcuff knot, but it has around 200 variations, and many people who are not soldiers learn how to tie them. Even SAS soldiers devise their own versions.

Chris Dawson, a deputy police commissioner, travelled to Canberra to front the SAS commander. The reply he received was half-helpful: if the Western Australian police came up with a suspect, the SAS would produce him. The army was not interested in a fishing expedition, such as subjecting troops to a mass DNA screening.

The killer would have to be tracked down the hard way. With twelve officers now in the Special Crime Squad, Jim Stanbury was sent to New Zealand to retrieve samples and continue to document the chain of evidence. He and George Paton flew to the FBI in the USA to do the same for the hair, fibre and soil samples that had been retrieved from the clothing of Ciara Glennon.

They travelled the length and breadth of the USA to confirm and document each link in the exhibits' chain of custody – a top priority should the case ever come to court.

Then began the long task of reviewing wads of old reports and following up those men who had been named in them. Thousands of those named had to be elevated to persons of interest (POIs) after originally being written off as NFIN – no further inquiry needed.

Strong information was found on the files, which had not been followed up when the reports had been made, emphasising the corrosive effects of belief perseverance about Lance Williams, Peter Weygers and Steven Ross.

Among the neglected reports was one from a citizen who had come across a cache of pornography, plus rope tied in unusual knots, in the bush near where the murderer had left Ciara Glennon's body.

Another report was from a woman who had told police that her then-boyfriend had come home on the night of one of the murders with blood all over his clothes. Police had written this off, too, without further inquiry.

Each person of interest now had to be tracked down, interviewed about their alibis for long-forgotten nights fifteen years earlier, swabbed for DNA and eliminated, then the results tabulated.

It was assumed that every person who had been nominated as a suspect or who had otherwise fallen under suspicion had been DNA-tested but, just to be sure, the Special Crime Squad assembled a list of all those who did not have an alibi. They found 1100 on the files, but by no means had all of them been DNA-tested for whatever reason. Then the list kept growing until it reached 1600. Almost twenty men were police officers, and others were overseas, out of reach in practical terms. About a hundred who had not been swabbed were taxi drivers, many of them elderly. Some officers believed chasing down the older men was a waste of time, given what was known about the ages of active serial killers.

In these files, too, this new squad found many glitches. Some tick boxes had been incorrectly filled in during data entry, this list growing when the squad discovered another hundred persons of interest who had no alibis. If they had no alibis, why had they not been interviewed and DNA-tested?

Whenever a man on this expanded list refused to let an officer stick a cotton bud inside his mouth and scrape it around to obtain a DNA sample, suspicion naturally piqued.

There was one peculiar way to check the DNA of an unwilling suspect, and police swung this into action. Squads were sent out on amazing operations to test these suspects without their knowledge. Cops give this trick the name 'by-chance sampling', the only legal way to obtain traces of DNA without alerting the subjects.

Plainclothes police followed their targets through public places until they discarded something that might harbour their DNA, such as a cigarette butt, drink can or used tissue. Undercover officers, UCOs, were reduced to scavenging from café tables, gutters and rubbish bins for that vital clue, which might lead them straight to the Claremont serial killer.

At huge expense in time and resources, squads of UCOs were despatched all over Australia to follow high-priority suspects into cafés and pubs in the hope of retrieving a by-chance sample. Especially difficult were suspects living in rural areas, where a group of strangers driving hire cars into outback towns stuck out like sore thumbs. But the UCOs persisted and got their men, or at least their DNA samples. In total, 16,000 men were DNA-tested in an operation that took an incredible three years, a determined but disheartening slog with no result.

It remained an article of faith that the serial murderer would be somewhere in the case file, and quite probably had already been interviewed. For inspiration, detectives looked to high-profile precedents.

Peter Sutcliffe, the Yorkshire Ripper, and Sydney backpacker serial murderer Ivan Milat had both been on police files, but had been missed during the extensive trawls of suspects.

Naturally, fears grew that a local officer had interviewed and similarly missed the Claremont killer. But it was not necessarily so. Around the world there are cases of serial killers who, when caught, were found not to have been on the police radar during the investigation.

Could this guy, like Sutcliffe and Milat, be buried somewhere in their files? If so, how had he escaped detection for so long? And why had he stopped killing, if he had?

Earlier media statements by police officers had suggested that the killings had stopped because the murderer was under police surveillance. But this was now known to be untrue. The worry was that the real killer might only have pressed the pause button.

*

The behaviour of serial killers and how to stop them was the subject of an animated expert discussion at a conference held just across the Swan River from police headquarters in March 2012. The conference had been organised by a new group called Justice WA, which was spawned by a series of failed police cases and prosecutions. But the front-line justice workers who would have been most interested – police and prosecutors – declined to attend, although they had been invited.

One of the star speakers at the conference was Dr Thomas Müller, the forensic psychologist who, nine years earlier, had spoken at a conference in Fremantle.

Back then, Dr Müller had unpacked the life and crimes of charming, persuasive journalist Jack Unterweger, who had murdered eleven women in four countries.

Unterweger was good-looking and intelligent, fitting easily into society. In his career as a television news reporter, he had occasionally been assigned to compile news reports on his own crimes.

Dr Müller is fond of quoting American author John Steinbeck: 'There are some among us who live in rooms we can never enter.'

The place to look for clues, he said, is not in the demeanour of the suspect, as had so excited Macro in its pursuit of Lance Williams. 'The best camouflage of evil people is the arrogance of the person who thinks they know what evil people look like,' Dr Müller told the 2012 conference. 'You are not looking for someone whose fingernails drag on the ground.'

He explained where truth is to be found about the motivation of unknown killers, who most often reveal sexual motivation and craving for power: 'Just give me the crime scene.'

Of backpacker serial murder Ivan Milat, Dr Müller said, 'The decisions he makes tell me a lot about his personality.'

Milat had treated the men and women he murdered in the forest differently.

'Ivan Milat had a sexual need that was served by an extreme non-sexual act. The crime scenes were full of clues of power and control and indicated a man who had no power in his life.'

Dr Müller also provided insight into what makes men – and it is most often men, who are usually highly intelligent, ordinary-looking and appear to be in stable relationships with steady jobs – become serial killers in the first place.

At the root of serial offenders was fantasy, according to Dr Müller. He'd learned from exhaustive interviews with criminals, including a man who kept prisoner and continuously raped his own daughter, and a real-life cannibal, that these criminals' minds have taken refuge in a fantasy world, sometimes in infancy but typically between the ages of four and eight.

Fantasy enables a child to mentally escape something bad in their real world. A child experiencing trauma takes refuge within their own mind. The tragedy is that this is happening at the same time the child is in the process of finding their self-identity. They may be enduring family violence to themselves or their mothers, or both, to be bewildered by sexual abuse, or be victims of bullying.

'Children abused or laughed [at] at school find that fantasy gives them power,' Dr Müller said.

This sanctuary of a child's imagination can morph during puberty into a whole new dimension, his body flooding with hormones in his early teens. The survival fantasy now develops sexual overtones.

In notorious cases not raised at the conference, Ted Bundy and legions of other serial killers exhibited in adulthood the narcissism of a toddler, along with a two-year-old's feelings of invincibility. These anomalies morphed into a need to sexually dominate. When Bundy's fantasy was challenged, he took it out on the individual making the challenge. Bundy's superior intelligence meant he could arrange his mind into compartments and outwardly act normally, deceiving and charming his way through everyday life. When caught, nobody showed more surprise than those closest to him.

Bundy cut a swathe through the USA in the 1970s, committing at least thirty-six murders and possibly more than one hundred.

While he was on death row, a dark family secret emerged: it was discovered that he had been raised in a household dominated by an abusive and sadistic grandfather, a violent racist bigot. He kicked dogs, swung cats by the tail and hoarded pornography, his magazines discovered and devoured by toddler Ted.

A paradox exists among some serial killers who, as boys, had witnessed their fathers or stepfathers being violent to their mothers and had bravely stepped in as protectors, as serial killer Eric Edgar Cooke had done as a child.

It might be expected that, when such boys reach puberty, they become fiercely protective of women. But in rare cases, quite the reverse can occur – their need for power and control manifests in violence against women; they sexually and violently act out the behaviour they observed in their fathers or other males in their mothers' lives.

Ted Bundy admitted receiving gratification from the act of killing itself, always separating himself from the act by his internal fantasy structure. 'It couldn't be me. It's not me. I was innocent.'

The transition from aberrant childhood fantasy at puberty can begin to show externally in the early teens by fetishes and exhibitionism – stealing underwear, masturbating in public, then in rare cases progressing to rape and killing.

For this reason, 'flashers' are no longer treated by police as poor, sad losers, or worse, as jokes. Serial killers in their twenties are usually found to have been sexual exhibitionists in their teens, progressing to being rapists or to have attempted rape.

Dr Müller told the conference that seventy-five per cent of sex crimes showed no sperm or DNA.

'In a normal person, a sexual need is met by a sexual act,' he said, echoing the words of David Barclay as the Schramm team wrapped up its review in 2004.

'With deviant criminal sexuality, a non-sexual need is met by a sexual act. Or a sexual need is met by a non-sexual act, such as an extreme fetish that degrades the victim.'

There need not be an obvious human victim. Robin Napper, the former British detective superintendent who specialised in serious sexual offenders, said that police trying to catch arsonists take footage of crowds that gather to watch burning buildings. They look for signs of a man in the crowd having a sexual experience, ejaculating while watching the flames, his excitement stimulated by the smoke, frantic fire crews, rescues and gasping crowds.

Serial killers are capable of living lives of deception by an ability to compartmentalise their lives, explained former FBI agent Brad Garrett.

'They can commit murders, go back home, make breakfast for their kids, take them to school, kiss the wife goodbye, go to work, go to bowling, go out socially, and then go back out the next night and do it again,' Garrett said. 'Serial killers love to live in plain sight. They can even have conversations [about the serial killings] with neighbours. In their mind, it's another power thing.'

30

Blue Graphite

Late on a Tuesday night in 2009, David Cohen, the *Post*'s Claremont and police reporter, called his editor from Claremont train station.

'I have to tell you this in case I die,' said Cohen, who was not remotely in danger of dying, but merely travelling home from a meeting of the Claremont Council. 'After the council meeting, the mayor told me that the Claremont murder cases were about to be cracked.'

He'd just learned that in the excitement that had buzzed through senior police ranks after the DNA discoveries in 2008 and 2009, the Minister for Police had confided in Colin Barnett, the state's premier and local member of parliament for the Claremont area. The state's leader was warned to expect an early announcement on the crimes that had so shattered him and his home turf. Police were sure they were about to identify the killer, but the public knew nothing of the new evidence.

The *Post*'s editor made enquiries with Special Crime, only to be met with a flat denial. But as the months and years clicked over, other cracks began appearing in the wall of secrecy. It was clear something had changed. Men were telling the paper that a new wave of interviews was afoot – they had recently been questioned by detectives about their alibis on the nights of the Claremont abductions all those years ago. Some of these men had previously been questioned while others had not. Detectives wanted them to provide DNA samples, whether or not they originally had co-operated with the police in the 1990s.

Police were also intensifying efforts to track the source of the washing line that the rapist had used to bind Lisa, after discovering that the cord had been impregnated with dyes used in screen-printing.

In the mid-1990s, an academic had owned a screen-printing business in Stirling Highway, Claremont, opposite the spot where Ciara Glennon was last seen, and very close to the abduction point of Sarah Spiers. Special Crime Squad detectives had recently quizzed her about who had access to her premises and about whether any screen-printing components or cord she used as clothesline, left at the rear of the premises, had gone missing. She was one of several other professional screen-printers police located, their previous employees' names all checked against the police database.

Special Crime Squad boss K.C. Prins denied that new forensic or other evidence had come to light, despite the secret DNA breakthrough.

Then out of the blue sprang another vital clue. In 2011, the ChemCentre moved premises from East Perth to Bentley, near Curtin University, where the lab was still kept separate from PathWest, against the recommendation of David Barclay. Removalists shifted samples collected from the Claremont cases to the new premises.

Jim Stanbury, still working his way through the Schramm recommendations, visited Dr Karin Margolius at PathWest, asking for the paperwork on Jane's hair.

Dr Margolius produced a receipt, showing it had been received by Robert Hansson at the ChemCentre in 1996. He took officers straight to a fridge in the Toxicology section, not the Trace section, where it was previously thought to have headed back in 1996. Dr Margolius evidently thought the hair needed testing for traces of a stupefying drug that might have been administered to Jane.

The morning before her death, Jane had visited the hairdresser near her home in Shenton Park. There was a good chance that any fibres her tresses had collected after that appointment would include some transferred to her from her murder scene. The police located a 'billy-bucket' in the fridge, sealed with evidence tape. Inside was the long blonde hair cut from Jane Rimmer's head at her autopsy, the day after her body was recovered in July, 1996. Intermingled in this hair was a gold mine of different fibres. In 2012, ChemCentre scientists led by Rees Powell carefully extracted from it twenty foreign grey-blue strands of fibre, among others.

Both Jane and Ciara had long, lustrous hair, their crowning glories forensic treasure troves, especially when fibres retrieved from each mass of hair were compared to each other. The hundreds of fibres scientists picked from these tresses, and from Ciara's T-shirt, became as important as the DNA matches. The list was eventually narrowed down to ninety-eight significant fibres, grey, grey-blue and navy blue. But what was their source?

Powell and fellow scientists had an inkling that the grey-blue fibres came from the upholstery of a car, but which car? The scientists left their pristine lab and visited oily car-wrecking yards. They began crawling through the carcasses of 124 crashed or partly dismantled old vehicles built in the mid-1980s to the 1990s. They cut slices from the seats, carpets and door upholstery, then took them back to the lab. There they created a special indexing computer program that would eventually grow to a library of reference samples containing more than 10,000 different fibres.

Then came a stunning breakthrough from all this meticulous work: the grey-blue fibres matched those from the seats of a Holden Commodore VS Series 1 vehicle. This was the precise make and model of station wagon that the Burger Boys had described in Stirling Highway, Claremont, the night Ciara disappeared. With priceless help from staff at the General

Motors-Holden factory in Melbourne, detectives established that this upholstery suite was named Blue Graphite, fabric unique to that model Holden. There was, however, no way of identifying from the upholstery the paint colour of the car it had come from, nor whether it was a sedan or station wagon. But, clearly, the killer had driven that model Holden.

Three fibres found in Ciara's hair matched the seats of the Holden, the section that passengers sit and lean on. Seven of Ciara's fibres matched that same car model's carpet. Had her head been in contact with the car's floor?

A different carpet then made an appearance, another breakthrough. More delving showed that one fibre from Jane's hair matched carpet made especially for the cargo areas of the station wagon versions of the same model Holden. Jane had apparently been in the boot of a Holden VS Series 1 station wagon.

The scientists then turned their eyes to another set of fibres. These were navy blue and not from the interior material of a car. One was recovered from Jane's hair and forty-four from Ciara, including eleven that the FBI had scraped off her T-shirt in 1999. They were not threads but particles, almost invisible to the naked eye, woven to form threads, evidently shed from clothing.

Bingo. All the navy fibres matched each other in dye colour and structure when magnified and examined using high-tech light processes.

Stunningly, these navy fibres also matched two blue fibres found on Lisa's shorts. Here was a very high chance that a person wearing the same clothing had been in contact with all three women.

Maddeningly, no source was known for the navy blue fibres. Where did they come from? How had so many navy fibres initially clung to Ciara's hair and T-shirt? Detectives speculated that they had first been deposited from the clothing of someone sitting on the seat of a Holden. Ciara had been dragged across that same seat the night she died, they believed.

Naturally, police attention now shifted in high gear to owners of white Holden VS Series 1 station wagons. There had been a concentrated search for just such a car after the Burger Boy interviews in 1997, but this was shelved when Lance Williams came on the scene. He had no access to a Holden station wagon.

Only seventy-six such white wagons had been sold privately in the state, but 660 had been sold as fleet or company vehicles. Police traced the private owners, giving special attention to cross-checking their names against the long list of persons of interest on their files. None matched.

Company and fleet vehicles that had been used by multiple drivers were much more difficult to pin to a particular driver at the crucial times.

At Telstra, some managers and technicians drove home in the same cars every night. But if their usual car was off the road, they also picked up pool cars, almost at random, to drive home. Telstra said scant records existed of who was driving a particular pool car on a particular night.

Tragically, no compatible computer program existed to cross-match the government vehicle registers with the 70,000 vehicle number plates recorded by secret cameras around Claremont at relevant times, number plates that had been laboriously entered manually into a database back in the 1990s. Had details of a white company or government-owned Holden Commodore station wagon appeared in such a cross-check, police might just have been able to track down the driver. But it was not to be.

Who was behind the wheel? The detectives did not know, but at last they had a lot of hard information about him – his DNA profile, a description from Lisa, the make and model of the third car he was known to have driven for his crimes, and possibly the first and second – a Telecom Mitsubishi L300 van described by Hollywood Hospital security man Wayne

Wookey, and a white Toyota Camry station wagon, a vehicle also issued to Telecom and Telstra technicians. Then there was a possible link with screen-printing. But how to join all the dots? What was the origin of that bonanza of navy blue fibres?

It had been three years since police had linked two of the Claremont crimes by DNA. They finally accepted that, contrary to all early expectations, it was frustratingly clear that the Claremont killer was nowhere in their massive case file.

So Claremont was not to be a rerun of the Yorkshire Ripper and Ivan Milat cases. Their man was out there somewhere, but he had neither been nominated to police by the public, traced by detective work, interviewed nor DNA-tested. How to find him, even with the benefit all this new, hard information?

Then someone in Special Crime mentioned the name of a bad man from afar: Richard Ramirez.

31

Supra

Richard Ramirez, a burglar, rapist and serial killer, had terrorised residents of greater Los Angeles and San Francisco in their homes, in 1984 and 1985. He had used a wide variety of weapons, including guns, knives, a machete, tyre lever and a hammer, and was labelled the Night Stalker.

As a teenager, his criminal career had begun to manifest in peeping Tom incidents, his adolescent sexual fantasies then escalating to violence and rape, a horrific series of home invasions, then domestic sexual assaults and murders that involved binding.

He died in jail of medical causes in 2013, while awaiting execution for thirteen murders. That same year, Special Crime began to ponder whether the life story of the man they were hunting might mirror that of Ramirez.

Could the Claremont killer, now known to have carried out at least one planned blitz attack, have developed his criminal career while travelling a similar, ugly path? Had he committed any earlier crimes? If so, while carrying them out, could he have left clues that might direct police to match a name to the DNA profile they now held?

Special Crime decided the Night Stalker theory needed to be thoroughly explored, with much heavier emphasis than before on any apprenticeship pattern building up to serial killings.

Police Deputy Commissioner Chris Dawson convened a meeting with the Special Crime Squad in February 2013 to kick around new ideas on how to tackle serious unsolved crimes, including the Claremont series. He asked for and welcomed ideas for fresh approaches. Jim Stanbury jumped in, suggesting that he now believed the Claremont case was less Ivan Milat and Yorkshire Ripper, and more Richard Ramirez.

He said it was clear from the Ramiraz example that the Claremont killer must have had a long, earlier career of sexually motivated crimes before wreaking havoc in central Claremont. Stanbury had been at Special Crime when the technique of re-examining old, stored forensic evidence from crime scenes had solved the Pamela Lawrence jewellery shop murder, and had also unearthed the Claremont killer's DNA. So there existed a strong possibility that the key Claremont evidence was already in police possession but also lay hidden, buried in police warehouses.

Among those vast shelves of storage bins might have been a crucial sample, seized by police after a more minor sex crime committed at a younger age by the Claremont serial killer. At the time of the earlier crime, there may have been watertight witness or confession evidence leading to his conviction. This meant that, way back then, there had been no need to analyse crime-scene samples scientifically.

What if detectives could now look backwards and prove a previously undetected forensic link between an earlier crime and the Claremont homicides? This work could deliver to Special Crime the name and police record of its most wanted man.

A new project searching along these lines would need to reinvent, in a determined way, the 'precursor crime' inquiries that started but fizzled out in 2000, as had another attempt in 2006, Project Quantum.

Chris Dawson listened intently and gave the green light. The police service labelled it Project Supra. Dawson committed to expanding, setting up and funding two teams of officers to split the work. Special Crime would make a complete, methodical trawl of records of all historic serious crimes with sexual overtones, especially those that had been committed in a five-kilometre radius of Claremont between 1980 and 2002. It would send these pre-2002 cases, such as burglary and rape, to a new, second squad called the Physical Materials Management Team. Special Crime would itself reinvestigate possible linked crimes committed post-2002.

Both squads would have full access to the police exhibit storage warehouse and be able to pull all the physical evidence from the earlier crimes. This job was to sift and test the stored items to see whether they could find any forensic links to each other, with special emphasis on criminals showing escalating levels of planning and brutality.

Results would then be cross-checked with forensic samples recovered from the Claremont victims' persons and crime scenes, whether they be fibres, hairs, fingerprints or DNA.

Supra's mission energised these two teams with focus and a fresh sense of purpose.

Police and forensic scientists could bring attention to detail to their tasks, which was missing in the bad old days, a quantum leap from the pre-David Barclay/Malcolm Boots era. At a warehouse called the Property Receival and Exhibit Storage Section, or PRESS, in suburban Belmont, a secure, sterile room dubbed the 'clean room' was set aside for the exclusive use of the fifteen to twenty Special Crime and Physical Materials staff. They retrieved storage bins from the shelves; opened individual exhibit bags; examined, checked and photographed the evidence seals; then did the same with the inner bags and opened those. Contents were minutely examined by squad members wearing disposable booties, overalls, masks and caps. They worked on cleaned surfaces covered by fresh brown paper, every action recorded by CCTV cameras.

Special Crime continued to collect and plough their way through all the old records of sexually motivated crimes in the

Claremont area and surrounding suburbs – flashers, perverts, home invaders, attempted abductions, sexual assaults – whether a vehicle was noted at the time or not.

Supra detectives soon discovered that the list of reports of such crimes around Claremont was remarkably long, running to thirty-nine offences dating from 1987, when Claremont became party town, until 1996. Details of the crimes committed around Claremont are sickening – flashers and masturbators; young women being followed then jumped, groped, sexually abused and sometimes raped; or attempts made to abduct them in vehicles.

A large number of lone women leaving Claremont on foot had been attacked after partying at Club Bayview or the Continental Hotel, their attackers often following them before pouncing at a spot where their crimes would likely go unobserved. They survived after fighting back, breaking free and escaping.

Detectives now travelled to London to interview the victim of the 1987 attack in Rowe Park, where the victim had escaped after biting her attacker's penis.

The investigators noted a chilling similarity in the descriptions of some of the attackers, after allowing for variations caused by darkness and the sheer terror experienced by victims.

Supra whittled the list down to twenty-three offences that were possibly linked – a frightening prospect considering the number of parents who had watched their daughters disappear into the Claremont night, praying they would return safely home. Most of the police reports had been handled at the time by the local CIB, these crimes not publicised by police. To have done so would have warned of a predator or predators preying on the Claremont area after midnight. Young women continued to wander off into the night in blissful ignorance.

At that time, no apparent police operation was mounted to try to trap the predatory offender or offenders. Claremont's was the same CIB office where some of its detectives had been so scathingly excoriated for their conduct in the late 1980s and early 1990s by Commissioner Geoffrey Kennedy in his 2004 Police Royal Commission report.

The Physical Materials Management Team examined evidence collected at the scenes of these earlier crimes, identifying samples and sending them to the labs for testing or retesting. But it was striking problems. Even in the early 1990s, Western Australian police had been aware of DNA sampling for only a short time. Historic cold cases now being probed reached back into the time before the landmark English case of child-murderer Colin Pitchfork, convicted in 1987 – the first time in the world a criminal had been jailed on DNA evidence. Back then, DNA samples had to be dried before they were stored, and it was not unknown for a drying sample to be knocked onto the floor from a suburban detective's messy desk.

Despite the problems, Supra members found many old crime-scene samples were well preserved. They could very likely harbour unknown traces of the DNA of serious offenders, secreted like time bombs for decades in those almost-forgotten storage bins.

The squad was counting on finding human detritus such as blood, saliva, sweat or semen. Or an offender's hair or clothing fibre may have clung to victims' clothing, or been collected and stored by examining doctors or police forensic officers. Everything depended on the diligence of the original investigators.

Chris Dawson had ensured that both Supra and the Physical Materials Management Team had all the resources needed, enabling members to work relatively quickly through their lists. The Physical Materials squad, which later changed its name to the State Crime Operations Team, the child of Supra, ate up its work. Post-2002, unsolved cases that Special Crime concluded were not related to the Claremont killer were also handed to the Physical Materials squad.

After it had finished ploughing through pending Claremont tasks, this squad used its experience to cast a wider net to include all unsolved sex offences in the state – a decision that was later to prove crucial in cracking the Claremont mysteries.

Thus, the jig was finally up for a number of surprised criminals, who had thought they had got away with it for decades. Traumatised victims who had been raped in their homes, still living in fear of their attackers returning, suddenly felt their burden lift. Startled rapists and other offenders got a knock on the door, while others were taken into custody on arrival at airports as their passports triggered the immigration alarm system.

Supra finally followed the visiting Schramm team's urgings from 2004 to check whether the Claremont series was connected to the disappearance of seventeen-year-old Hayley Dodd. This work, Operation Vestigo, led directly to the arrest and ultimate conviction of a man for Hayley's murder. At the time of writing, an appeal against conviction has yet to be determined.

Supra in 2013 also embarked on another person of interest review, this time concentrating on its list of twenty-three Telstra employees who had access to the telco's vehicles in the mid-1990s. This had also been urged by the external Schramm review back in 2004. These Telstra workers were now asked about their alibis for the relevant times and given forms to fill in that included the questions: Are you the serial killer? Do you know who the serial killer is? There was no result. DNA tests of these men returned no hits.

Crushingly, what had looked like promising avenues of investigation appeared to be bringing Supra no closer to the Claremont serial killer.

*

By December 2014, Special Crime appeared to have exhausted its forensic options. It ran another flag up the mast, involving the public again. Among a population still eager to help solve these monstrous crimes, maybe some citizens out there were unaware that information they harboured was relevant. Maybe they could recall it, their memories triggered by the release of secret information police now held.

Some members of the Special Crime Squad were keen to roll the dice, go public, and take the good citizens of the state into their confidence. They called it the overt strategy. They knew the population wanted to help solve a case that was now twenty years old. The overt tactic had flushed out a key witness who led to the capture of Ivan Milat for the backpacker serial killings in NSW after an eight-month investigation.

A series of meetings – brainstorming sessions, they called them – were held over six months from late 2014. Senior police invited consultants from accounting firm KPMG, who sat with assistant commissioners, commanders and high-ranking public servants.

It was argued that, if the public was provided with accurate and substantial information, good information from the public would flow back to police. This was always true. There would be no repeats of the thousands of time-wasting rubbish calls, such as those nominating men who washed their cars or behaved oddly, calls that had plagued police and wasted thousands of hours in the original investigations.

Police had shared their relatively new information only with the parents of the victims, who were sworn to secrecy.

Not a soul in the general population had an inkling of the massive effort still being expended on the Claremont cases, nor that the Karrakatta rapist had been proved to be the same man who had murdered Ciara Glennon. Nor did they know about the strange connection to screen-printing ink clinging to the washing line he used to tie up Lisa, the handcuff knot her attacker used or the underpants he left years after the murders on Ciara's grave at Karrakatta.

Nobody knew the killer had quite possibly abducted one of his victims in a Mitsubishi van, another in a Toyota Camry station wagon, then two more victims in a white Holden Commodore VS Series 1 station wagon. Police knew, but were not saying, that during the years women were being abducted from Claremont, drivers of such a Holden or other vehicle had been involved in at least six other interactions with young women late at night in the Claremont and Cottesloe areas, with each report mentioning a Telecom or Telstra connection.

What if there had been more? What else had people seen out there? Had someone escaped a car and its driver but not reported the event? If so, could they describe the driver, or was any physical evidence left behind? Did anyone out there know or work with the likely driver of such a car? There could be no answers to these questions unless the police were upfront with the public.

But after six months of deliberation, the most senior police decided to say nothing. They would not be showing their confidence in the public. So why weren't we told?

There is no clear answer. Maybe nobody wanted to make a decision that might have led to the killer destroying trophies, fleeing or committing suicide. Maybe releasing detailed evidence had legal implications that would surface if the culprit was eventually caught and brought to trial.

Or maybe, lingering among some police was the nagging fear that police had already investigated the killer and had written him off as NFIN – no further inquiry needed. A major embarrassment. And what if members of the public again reacted badly when they discovered that vital, helpful information had been withheld, as had happened when the Mystery Man images of the last sighting of Jane Rimmer were finally made public? Would it be too damaging for the police force?

A minority of police officers held the suspicion that the culprit was an SAS soldier, who by now could be anywhere in the world. Nobody would have a clue about his identity, and the chances of finding him were remote in the extreme.

If he wasn't a soldier, maybe the civilian killer had fled long ago and was living overseas. At that time, seventeen known persons of interest were still outstanding, out of the country and out of reach.

Perhaps the culprit had died.

If any of these scenarios were true, there existed only a minuscule hope of the murders ever being solved, let alone finding the body of Sarah Spiers.

Chris Dawson had left the local police in 2014 for a promotion as chief executive of the Australian Crime Commission. As 2015 dragged on, a feeling of defeatism began to grip those in charge of resourcing the various police squads, and in charge of allocating the officers and money required to push ahead with the Claremont investigation.

This pessimism was not shared by most Special Crime detectives, who believed they were working on a viable, live inquiry with many forensic opportunities. Among these officers, levels of enthusiasm varied for putting in endless hours of more work on what some regarded as a lost cause. Most officers were still acutely aware of the strong public desire to see the killer locked up. Parents, relatives and friends of the victims even more so. But at and near the top, the will had waned.

Experienced Special Crime staff were being moved out in the first half of 2015. No new lines of inquiry were being pursued. The work on trying to trace the Holden Commodore station wagon and its driver had been halted.

Detectives who had worked so hard for so long were stunned to learn of a direction to cease investigation and finalise the Claremont cases, to box them up to be sent to the coroner for an inquest. The coroner would formally seek to establish causes of death and whether there was evidence of who may be responsible. It was a signal that the long investigation had run out of suspects, leads, ideas and enthusiasm, an admission of defeat. The end of the line. The twenty-year long inquiry was being shut down.

32
Jackhammer

The dying embers of the Claremont investigation were badly in need of a splash of flammable liquid.

Early on the morning of Friday, October 16, 2015, the *Post*'s editor's phone beeped. It was 6:40 a.m. Kim Jordan, the director of ABC News for Western Australia, had been walking his dog in Subiaco when he saw the *Post* newspaper being delivered. Using his mobile phone, he had snapped a photo of its front page, sending the image to his police reporter Graeme Powell. Attached to the image were instructions to broadcast a story in the ABC's 7 a.m. radio bulletin, based on the *Post* report. Powell got the job done. As other radio stations and news websites picked up the report and sprayed it to a startled audience, Jordan called back. 'Welcome to the six-minute news cycle.'

The *Post*'s large headline read: 'Claremont breakthrough: Fourth serial killer victim.'

The text went on: 'The forensic link shows that the man who abducted a woman from a Claremont street late at night and sexually assaulted her at Karrakatta Cemetery in 1995 is the same man who murdered Ciara Glennon.'

Television news reporters filed reports for the evening bulletins from the cemetery and crossed live to Bay View Terrace, outside the Claremont Hotel, previously the Continental. Crucially, police did not deny the accuracy of the *Post*'s report – in fact, their carefully worded press statement, saying that such publicity might have been detrimental to the investigation, tended to confirm it.

Police Commissioner Karl O'Callaghan said: 'I'd like to be the commissioner that presides over the solution of it because it's been around for a long time.'

The report was repeated multiple times locally and nationally, again proving that the intensity of public interest in the Claremont crimes had never diminished. That weekend edition of *The Australian* newspaper carried a prominent report by the paper's Perth bureau chief, Paige Taylor, who took the long view: 'Perth's long-held belief that the Claremont serial killer left no useful clues has been sensationally shattered by the revelation a taskforce is working to catch a rapist it already has linked to one of the three murders.'

Reaction was exactly what some police would have expected had they made such detail public – they got fresh, good-quality information. Most members of the public were stunned to learn that the murderer was not Lance Williams or Peter Weygers.

New witnesses, women, came forward with new reports that told not just of being approached in Claremont and nearby suburbs, but also of escaping after having been abducted. They had then been in their teens or early twenties, and were now in their late thirties or early forties, many with children of their own. They hoped their fresh information would help catch the real killer.

One woman told of being drunk as a teenager and abducted from outside the Cottesloe Hotel in 1989. A man had driven her to an abandoned drive-in theatre where he had tried to rape her. She managed to escape, but the man had stalked her and caught her again. She had had to summon all her resources to escape from his car a second time.

She had never reported the incident to police, or told her mother, fearing she would be in trouble for being drunk. Her friends had convinced her to call the *Post*. Her contacts were passed to police, with her permission. They opened an investigation and took statements.

Another woman told the *Post* how she had been lured into a car in the darkened car park opposite Club Bayview in the early hours. A man had asked her to help him find his car keys by getting into the back of his white Holden Commodore. Her brother then emerged from the shadows and took her from the car.

This mirrored other attacks in the same car park. Again, with her permission, the woman's information was passed to Special Crime.

The *Post* became aware of other new reports, some that had been made directly to police. How many, police did not say, but Special Crime was very interested in this flood of possible precursor crimes by the Claremont serial killer. A common theme of the new reports was that the women thought they had fallen foul of random creeps in isolated incidents. They had not made a connection to the serial killings because they firmly believed police knew Lance Williams or Peter Weygers was that killer, and that the cops were watching Williams.

The intensity of public interest still shown in the case and the desire for it to be resolved startled some senior police, who were now getting additional pressure from the families of the Claremont victims. The decision to bundle up the case and refer it to the state's coroner, in effect making it a dormant investigation, was quietly dropped. Fresh faces were recruited to Special Crime and inquiries revived with a vengeance.

Revelations kept coming to an agog public: 'Two new clues to serial killer' read the *Post*'s headline on December 5. For the first time, the paper made its readers aware of details of the Holden Commodore station wagon police had been looking for, and the dye-impregnated cord. These details were again repeated in other media – newspapers, online news sites, and radio and television broadcasts – and even more public information was delivered to police.

Special Crime now needed to plough through this new information. Statements were taken; a beefed-up team of detectives travelled interstate to track down nominated men and to recheck their vast files of information. By then, an astonishing total of 16,500 persons of interest had been checked and swabbed. It seemed to some as if every man in the country would need to be DNA-tested to catch the Claremont killer.

*

Towards the end of 2015, Commissioner O'Callaghan quietly ramped up the resources of the State Crime Operations Team (State Ops). State Ops was learning on the job and refining its techniques. Yet any link between less-serious historic Claremont crimes and the serial murders remained out of reach. State Ops was having some great wins, but it had also exhausted its trawl of relevant, historic crimes in and around Claremont, details of which Special Crime had sent its brother squad.

Towards the end of 2016, State Ops members decided to take another look at the leftovers – old, unsolved crimes committed far from the urban village of Claremont.

State Ops went to PRESS (Property Receival and Exhibit Storage Section) to delve into a long-ago sealed storage tub marked Operation Jackhammer. When they opened it, they found a trove of old evidence: boxes and bags from the 1980s. In the clean room, they were surprised to unearth a series of old records of unsolved cases, misfiled under the name Peter Joseph 'Jack' van Tongeren. It turned out to be a goldmine.

Jack van Tongeren, a name familiar to West Australians in the 1980s, was a man who had struck terror into Perth's Asian population, especially those who owned restaurants. Born in 1947, Van Tongeren was a violent neo-Nazi leading a gang of white supremacists. They operated mostly in Perth's southeastern suburbs, the Gosnells-Huntingdale area.

In 1989, van Tongeren began a thirteen-year jail sentence for theft and arson, after robbing and firebombing restaurants owned by Asian people. The thefts were aimed at raising funds to run his Australian Nationalist Movement, a terror organisation warning Asians to stay away from Australia.

State Crime Ops detectives found a series of crime files had been incorrectly put in the Jackhammer box, perhaps by someone who had wrongly linked other crimes in the southeastern suburbs to those committed nearby by van Tongeren and his crew. In the box were the records of a series of unsolved thefts and sexually motivated break-ins around the neighbouring suburbs of Huntingdale and Southern River, close to an hour's drive from Claremont. Householders had reported weird break-ins and burglaries in a one-kilometre radius around Gay Street, where semi-rural holdings were being cut up for inexpensive house-and-land packages as part of Perth's fast-growing urban sprawl.

A strong theme of perversion was clear from the householders' reports of home invasions and sightings of the offender. Women's underwear had been stolen from clotheslines and bedrooms. Frequent sightings were reported of a tall prowler wearing women's nightwear and underwear, one of a man wearing women's underpants on his head.

Fifteen sex crimes had been committed in the area in the previous two years, ABC News reported in 1988. One of these stood out. The intruder had left bindings at the scene. It was unusual for rapists to arrive equipped with restraints – more usually, they assaulted their victims or threatened them with knives.

This standout crime was a home invasion at Huntingdale on February 15, 1988. The offender had entered through an unlocked back door at about 2 a.m. and unplugged the house phone. His eighteen-year-old victim was sleeping on her stomach, her arms under her pillow. She felt a man's calloused hand over her mouth. Assuming the man was her boyfriend with whom she had just spent Valentine's Day, and not wanting to wake her parents, she said, 'It's okay, I won't scream.'

She wriggled and stroked his face, saying, 'I love you.'

Then she realised the man had stubble on his face. Her boyfriend was shaven.

'I dug my fingernail as hard as I could into his cheek,' she said.

The man lifted off. His victim braced, thinking he was about to hit her, but she turned to see a figure wearing a long-sleeved nightie, similar to one worn by her mother, standing near the door. He was as tall as the door frame.

'I turned and started hammering on the wall, screaming for my dad,' she said.

The intruder fled, leaving behind black knotted stockings and a piece of cloth as the teen's parents burst in. Her father plugged in the phone and called police.

In his haste to escape, the man had bumped into a clothes-horse and dropped something else, a garment he had stolen from a nearby home's clothesline days earlier. It was a distinctive, well-worn cream silk kimono, featuring a pair of black cranes standing out from red foliage, onto which the offender had ejaculated.

The kimono had not been DNA-tested by police at the time – this attack had occurred just one year after that first -ever conviction based on DNA evidence.

By November 2016, DNA matching was a routine tool. At PRESS, detectives and forensic staff carefully recorded everything laid out on the brown-paper-covered bench in the clean room, repackaged the kimono and sent it to the lab for DNA-testing. From the dried semen still on the kimono, scientists extracted a DNA profile. When they ran it through the database on December 1, the result stunned everybody.

Jackpot!

DNA from the kimono's semen stain matched the profile of the DNA found both on Lisa and under Ciara Glennon's left thumbnail. This was the DNA profile previously filed as

Unknown Male 4. A match for the Claremont serial killer's profile at last.

The wave of excitement being surfed by State Crime Ops and Special Crime quickly crashed. The home invasion and attack on the sleeping teen had never been solved, nor had any of the other sexually charged crimes committed nearby.

In the same week as the kimono home invasion, police at the local station had received a cluster of strange reports from residents, who described a tall, lanky man who appeared to be very fit terrorising Huntingdale.

'The man is so brazen, he sometimes stands on the road wearing a nightie, waving to women to look out of their windows,' reported the evening *Daily News* on February 17, 1988.

The paper said he was the kimono attacker and labelled him the Huntingdale weirdo. Police called him the Southside Rapist. The paper interviewed a girl who lived on Huntingdale Road who said her father had chased the man, who leapt a fence wearing a nightie.

Police formed a special taskforce to catch him, months later calling a press conference to display the kimono and ask for its owner to contact them. Twelve people came forward with information, adding to the list of reports already held on the cluster of sexually motivated thefts of underwear from clotheslines. People detailed a man wearing women's nightwear in the street, including the sighting of the tall man wearing woman's underpants over his head. There were also peeping Tom incidents, house break-ins and stranger attacks on women.

On offer was a $50,000 reward, because detectives wrongly thought the kimono crime was linked to the brutal murder of thirty-year-old Victoria Clark in her home the previous September. At the time, detectives said that Victoria's murderer was likely to be the Southside Rapist, who was wanted for sixteen major sex crimes in the Huntingdale-Southern River area in two years.

They then said that the investigation had been complicated by a second prowler operating in the area, as well as an intruder, possibly a third man, who had struck the previous weekend. A twenty-five-year-old woman had woken up to find a man standing beside her bed with an iron bar. When she screamed, the man pulled her out of bed, kicked her in the stomach and ran out the back door.

The kimono crime and others police thought were connected to the Southside Rapist remained unsolved. That file was marked 'offender not identified'; the kimono was boxed up, stored in the Jackhammer tub, and forgotten for twenty-eight years.

This meant police had no offender to match to the kimono, which held a clear identifier of one man, the man police now knew to be the same individual who had attacked both Lisa and Ciara Glennon.

Forensic supervisor Colin Beck delved back into the Jackhammer box. He found even more misplaced files, containing details of a series of other break-ins and burglaries in Gay Street, a feeder road connecting Huntingdale with Southern River and surrounding streets. The team trawled the home invasion details and compiled a list.

In one Gay Street burglary file, State Ops found four fingerprint lifts that had been taken from a sliding door of a Huntingdale house, the scene of a burglary. Three of them did not match any print from any other unsolved burglary in the area.

With mounting excitement, the detectives ran these prints through the national automated fingerprint database.

Jackpot, again.

They were identical to prints police had taken from a man in 1990, two years after the kimono crime, and five years before Lisa was abducted. These Gay Street prints matched the prints taken from a man arrested after police rushed to the scene of a reported daylight assault at Hollywood Hospital, in a suburb next to Claremont.

Those prints belonged to a young Telecom technician, who was charged with assaulting a forty-year-old palliative care grief counsellor on May 7, 1990. The tech had been assigned by his employer to repair the hospital's PABX telephone exchange close to her office.

At about two in the afternoon, as the patients slept, the man saw Wendy Davis sitting at her desk, writing in an isolated anteroom lockable from the inside.

'It felt like a very safe place to be,' she said.

The technician asked her for directions to the toilets, then disappeared inside the bathroom, there noticing that the room could be locked from the inside. He returned and asked Davis if he could retrieve a dropped pen.

Without warning, he pounced on Davis from behind, gagging her with a cloth he pushed into her mouth with his right hand, his left arm around her. She was terrified, in fear for her life. 'I honestly thought I was going to die,' she said.

Her attacker was tall, strongly built, and had come prepared. He had cable ties in his pocket.

Pinning her arms, he began dragging the unfortunate woman backwards towards the toilet, still seated on her wheeled swivel chair. As this blitz attack continued, the man said nothing. Almost at the toilets, Davis dug a shoe into the carpet, spun around in the chair, now facing the man, then kicked him in the shin as hard as she could. 'I was fighting for my life.'

The attacker lifted the distressed woman bodily off her chair, which fell over. Then he let her go.

As suddenly as the attack started, it stopped, the two people staring at each other. The man uttered, 'I'm sorry, I'm sorry, I'm sorry,' to his petrified and bewildered victim. She fled down a nearby corridor, having lost one shoe, her cardigan half off. She found a doctor, who called a hospital security guard. The brazen attacker was held until police arrived, while the social worker was treated in a nursing station for bruising and contusions to her neck.

The man told the security guard that he had intended to drag the woman into the toilets.

He was hauled before the court, where the magistrate was told that the offender was frustrated at not being able to fix the phones, and had felt hurt and betrayed after an argument with his live-in partner the night before. While the two of them had been discussing marriage, his partner confessed to having had sex with a previous boyfriend during the couple's relationship. He had felt pressured about setting a wedding date, and said his fiancée was a big spender. The technician pleaded guilty to the hospital assault.

The opinions of a psychologist and a psychiatrist who examined him for pre-sentence reports agreed – the guilty man was 'emotionally constricted' and had a strong need to feel secure in close relationships. He was, they said, deeply distressed by his fiancée's admissions, despite having forgiven her at the time.

His self-esteem was fragile. 'When wrong is done to him, when his relationships are under pressure, he represses his emotions then he takes it out on someone he doesn't know,' another court was to be told almost thirty years later.

The magistrate who heard the 1990 assault charge took everything into account and put the young man on probation for two years. He not only kept his job with Telecom after assaulting one of its clients, but two years later he was promoted and received a pay rise.

An odd feature of the case was that. while police had charged this man with common assault, the magistrate ordered him to take part in a sex offender's treatment programme for eight months – odd because he had not been charged with aggravated assault, abduction, deprivation of liberty nor attempted sexual assault. He pleaded guilty to the most minor assault charge on the list.

This relatively lowly charge was the reason this Hollywood attack had been missed in Supra's recent trawl of sex crimes committed around Claremont. Claremont CIB had been called in to investigate the Hollywood assault four years before the case of the abduction and rape of Lisa had been handed to them. The Hollywood victim's husband was a police officer, who dealt directly with the Claremont officers. Detectives did not interview or take a statement from the traumatised hospital grief counsellor, though she was spoken to by uniformed officers who arrived first.

The incident never made it to the pages of the local newspaper, the *Post*, despite the fact that in the same year the local police had passed on details of far less serious offences to its reporters.

Because the attacker had quickly pleaded guilty, there was no need to sample his DNA, but the routine arrest process meant that the offender was required to ink his fingers and press them on a police fingerprint card. The Claremont serial killer's incredible run of good luck was about to run out.

Twenty-six years after they had been left on the sliding door of a Huntingdale house, Special Ops detectives ran a digitised copy of those prints through their database, and got a hit. A perfect match to the prints of the man who had jumped the hospital worker.

Police pulled the Hollywood attack record of the owner of those fingerprints and saw what had eluded them for so long. Now, at last, they had a name: Bradley Robert Edwards.

33

Sprite

Near the end of November 2016, in extreme secrecy, two police squads were closing in on the Claremont serial killer. No word could be allowed to leak out that might alert their prey before all the necessary evidence could be gathered and an arrest made. The less said in public about the Claremont killings at this time, the better.

But life does not always go as planned. Damned coincidence reared its head again.

Re-entering the narrative at this point, like an unwanted party guest, was Peter Weygers, who had been appearing and re-appearing in this story for almost twenty-one years. For him, the Claremont stigma had not gone away. Nasty incidents kept bringing it to the top of his mind. Just that same month, November 2016, young men in a passing car had spotted him on a footpath, leaned out the windows and shouted, 'Claremont serial killer!'

On Thursday, November 17, 2016, Weygers had been briefly visiting his Irwin Road house in Embleton, once owned by taxi driver Steven Ross, when he saw cameras on tripods trained on the house. Then he spotted a figure familiar to him from media images. It was the Commissioner of Police, Karl O'Callaghan. Weygers, then aged seventy-two, immediately jumped to conclusions, his post-traumatic stress symptoms kicking in.

'It made me tremble in fear,' he said. 'Either he was coming to apologise for the police leading people to believe I was the Claremont serial killer, or he was going to arrest me on camera for it.'

A senior police officer, who evidently did not recognise Weygers, saw him staring. He approached the former suspect in a friendly way and asked him if he would like to be introduced to Dr O'Callaghan.

'I couldn't miss the opportunity – I walked over and called the commissioner Dirty Harry. I said you have labelled me a murderer and terrified my wife and her child and totally destroyed my life.'

This was not an official police visit, however; it had nothing to do with Peter Weygers – it turned out that a media crew happened to choose that spot for a publicity shoot to illustrate a newspaper report on neglected children.

This encounter made unwelcome headlines at this most delicate point in the investigation. Understandably, the commissioner declined to comment to the media. To the relief of the detectives hot on the trail of their prey, secrecy held.

*

By the middle of the next month, Special Crime and State Ops were confident in the name they had put to their elusive DNA sample. Their file showed Bradley Robert Edwards had just turned forty-eight, on December 7, 2016. He had been born eleven months before Ciara Glennon.

Detectives also learned that, as a teenager, he had lived in his family home with his parents, a younger brother and younger sister in Gay Street, Huntingdale. That house had then been on a large semi-rural family property, the land since subdivided and now occupied by multiple newer houses. It was located in the middle of the area where so many property invasions and sexually charged crimes had been committed in the 1980s, when Edwards was a teen.

Edwards was born in the Wheatbelt town of Merredin, three hours east of Perth; his father Bruce was a roaming rural telephone exchange installer for Telecom. Until Bradley was eight years old, he lived in a caravan with his father Bruce, mother Kaye and younger brother.

'It was a bit tough with four of us living in the caravan,' he said.

A sister was born after the family started renting on the outskirts of Perth before buying the Gay Street property. By then, Bruce had switched to selling real estate, after twenty-five years at Telecom.

Bradley attended high school until Year 12 his schoolmates nicknaming him Bogsy.

Later asked about his upbringing, he replied, 'Dunno … I don't know what you want me to say.' He said his relationship with his mother was very close.

At age fifteen, Edwards had a teenage romance: 'just kissing, no sexual contact'. His girlfriend dumped Bradley for an older boy, he said. He had no more girlfriends until he met his first wife.

He was bullied at school for wearing glasses, which he said contributed to his self-perceived unattractiveness to women. For a period in his twenties, he replaced the glasses with contact lenses.

After graduating from Gosnells Senior High School, Edwards followed his father's career, taking an apprenticeship as a telephone technician with government-owned Telecom. He formed friendships at apprentice school that proved to be fleeting.

In 1988, in his words, he 'stole' his best friend's girlfriend. The couple moved in together but, by 1990, the relationship was under strain, climaxing in the Hollywood attack on a stranger.

They married in 1991, the year after he was convicted on a charge of common assault and handed two years probabtion, but kept his job.

The pair bought a house in Huntingdale in 1994. In the middle of that year, Edwards connected his computer to the dial-up internet and found an all-consuming pastime, spending every evening and night online in the third bedroom. The marriage was deteriorating.

On Februray 12, 1995, Edwards abducted and raped Lisa at Karrakatta.

In late 1995, the couple took in a lodger, whom Edwards' wife had met when the tradesman did some work at her employer's city office.

'They started sleeping together, she got pregnant and she left,' Edwards said.

He had caught the pair kissing, in January 1996. 'If she hadn't been sleeping with another guy, we could patch things up and have a family together,' Edwards said.

Early in the morning of January 27, 1996, Sarah was abducted and murdered.

In May or June 1996, his estranged wife announced she was pregnant with the lodger's child.

In early June that year, Jane Rimmer was abducted and murdered.

Later that year, he had a non-sexual friendship with a young woman he had met in Cottesloe. Then he had a 'just sexual' relationship with an older woman he'd met at a party when they were both drunk.

'She wanted to take it a little bit further – I wasn't sure I wanted to be in a long-term relationship with a woman old enough to be my mum.

'It was a month or so before I met my current wife.'

Ciara was murdered two weeks before Edwards met his second wife, who had a three-year-old daughter.

Edwards met the woman who would become his second wife while on a work call to a city law firm on April 1, 1997. Lightning had knocked out the firm's phones. At the time, a frantic search was still underway for Ciara Glennon, who had been murdered eighteen days earlier, her lonely body still undiscovered off Pipidinny Road.

Edwards married his second wife in December 2000. They bought a cheap house at Kewdale near Perth Airport, but with bills and the mortgage payment, they struggled to make ends meet, his wife's parents needing to drop around food for the small family.

Edwards became something of a community hero at his stepdaughter's Kewdale Little Athletics club, winning awards for his volunteer work. This quiet, friendly volunteer had stayed on as chairman and website administrator even after his stepdaughter had left school.

His second wife had a connection with the far-away western suburbs, where the Claremont murders had happened. Her parents had owned a restaurant there between 1985 and 1994.

Remarkably, Ciara Glennon had worked at the same restaurant as a waitress while studying law at the University of Western Australia in 1988. A girlfriend recalls that, on five or six occasions, she picked up Ciara at the back of the restaurant late at night after her shift ended and drove both of them to Club Bayview, Ciara changing out of her waitressing clothes in the car. 'She was a party girl – she loved having fun.' The owner's son, Edwards' brother-in-law, fancied Ciara, she said.

On July 4, 2014, Edwards' second wife moved out, leaving her daughter living in the house with Edwards. Edwards described her as a powerful woman, saying later he continued to love both his first and second wives.

By 2016, Edwards was a Telstra operations manager, whose work was highly regarded. He was entrusted to work with large corporate clients, such as mining companies and government departments, including police stations.

*

Edwards was a name that appeared nowhere in the room full of files and computer systems, the mountain of information accumulated by Macro and Special Crime over more than twenty years. The name Bradley Robert Edwards had never surfaced in the vast investigation of the 16,500 men who had come under suspicion. Edwards had never been interviewed nor swabbed for DNA in connection with the Claremont murders, nor in any other case. This was not a rerun of the Yorkshire Ripper, the killer who had been interviewed by police a number of times before he was caught.

In late 2016, detectives tracked down and interviewed Wendy Davis, the victim of Edwards' historic Hollywood Hospital attack, then living in Tasmania. She had harboured anger for decades, because the charge against her attacker did not reflect the seriousness of the trauma she had suffered. What could these police possibly want?

'They said only that they were investigating old crimes. Everything came back to me. I was in shock – I kept getting flashbacks, reliving every detail.'

She became even angrier and more upset several days later, when detectives told her they believed that, in 1990, she had been an early victim of the Claremont serial killer, the ethereal night-stalker, the elusive phantom, the werewolf who had cursed Claremont. He had all but got away with this bizarre hospital crime and with others, free to roam the streets in his work vehicle, wreaking havoc. She had never recovered from the original assault on that terrible afternoon. Her fresh thoughts about what might have happened brought her to floods of tears.

'It came back to me in the context of rape and serial murders,' she said. 'It caused me a great deal of distress. I had just buried the whole thing until then.' She felt her initial retreat into silence had been misread by people around her as a calm acceptance of what had happened to her – an interpretation that was far from the truth.

'I felt completely powerless. When my husband had told me, back in 1990, that Edwards was only being charged with common assault, and would probably not lose his job, that's when I lost it. I became quite hysterical, something I have never done. I was devastated, absolutely devastated to hear that. I was in total shock and distress.'

Worse was to come.

A few days after the attack, still in deep shock, her husband drove her to a meeting, which she remembers taking place in a police station in Claremont.

'A Telecom manager was there, who actually apologised to me and advocated very strongly for Bradley Edwards. He said he was a good worker and he wouldn't want him to lose his job. [Edwards] had agreed to counselling. He said he had been having relationship problems.

'I was absolutely astounded. I said, "Look, I've been injured – I had to go to a doctor." I said people don't attack people because they are having relationship problems. I was furious.

'But they weren't listening to what I was saying. Nobody was listening. They were advocating very strongly for him. I was really distressed and really angry.

'After that, I handed in my notice for the job I loved. I couldn't go back there. I was devastated.'

At first, she was angry with Telecom, but now she was also extremely upset with the police. When she asked police in 2016 why Edwards had not faced far more serious charges, they replied that there was not enough evidence, she said.

History could have been different.

*

When the cops pulled Edwards' driving record, any doubts they might have held evaporated. Edwards had been pinged for traffic offences twice by police in Stirling Highway, Claremont, at night, in 1996 and 1997, while driving a white Holden Commodore VS Series 1 station wagon. It had to be him, but they needed absolute proof.

Police trawled through Department of Transport records to track the fate of the twenty-one-year-old Holden Commodore station wagon that Edwards had been driving for Telstra from 1996 until 1998.

After Telstra sold it in 2000, it had passed through several owners, records showing it had been registered for the previous ten years to a nurseryman who lived in rural Chidlow, an hour east of Perth. Fortunately, this old farm workhorse had not been wrecked in a crash, stolen, burnt, nor dismantled after dying of old age. It was still registered and going strong. The police went to the farm, watched and waited. Then they saw something about that car that startled them.

Jackpot, again.

The wheel trims on this Holden were not of the usual design fitted to that VS Series 1 model. They were the wrong hubcaps, but identical to those with teardrop-shaped cut-outs described by one of the Burger Boys, who had watched Ciara Glennon interact with that car's driver in Stirling Highway.

Would DNA taken directly from Edwards' body match that recovered from the kimono and from the two Claremont crimes, on Lisa and Ciara, which were committed in 1995 and 1997?

Police needed to obtain a current DNA sample from Edwards himself, without him knowing. A plan was hatched to try to get a by-chance sample. After a glitch or two, the UCOs were set on Edwards.

They had early luck. Edwards was on leave on Monday, December 19, and took in a movie with his stepdaughter. Unknown to him, the UCOs had followed him into the theatre. They were ecstatic when they saw Edwards buy a bottle of Sprite lemonade. Waiting outside, they saw their target take a last swig from the bottle and drop it in a bin. As soon as they had the chance, the UCOs recovered the discarded bottle, sealed it in an evidence bag and sent it for urgent DNA analysis.

Jackpot, once again.

The Sprite bottle's DNA sample matched the profile gleaned from semen recovered from Lisa, from the scraping taken from Ciara Glennon's thumbnail bed, and from the colourful kimono. Loop closed.

34
Bogeyman

At 7:30 a.m. on Thursday, December 22, 2016, black-clad, masked and heavily armed Tactical Response Group (TRG) police burst through the back and front doors of an ordinary single-level suburban house at 344 Acton Avenue, Kewdale, on the fringe of an industrial area. The house had been bought by a married couple in 2000 for $135,000. A white Telstra Holden station wagon was parked beside it. Inside the vehicle was a toolbox, containing two Telstra knives.

Alone inside the house was Bradley Robert Edwards. The forty-eight-year-old had already been at his computer to post a remark on a fan website for the West Coast Eagles, the Australian Rules football team he had membership with.

TRG cops caught him in his front hallway. 'They threw me to the floor,' Edwards said, and handcuffed his hands behind his back.

Waiting outside until the TRG had secured the house was a contingent from the Cold Case Homicide Squad, led by its boss, senior sergeant Joe Marrapodi.

He read Edwards his rights as the prisoner sat on the carpet, leaning on a door frame, surrounded by a mess of boxes and belongings. Edwards said he wanted to call his parents, but that right was suspended until police made further inquiries.

Marrapodi told Edwards he was being arrested under suspicion for the murders of Sarah Spiers, Jane Rimmer and Ciara Glennon; for the abduction and rape at Karrakatta Cemetery; and for the kimono-connected attack at

Huntingdale. Then the sergeant named that victim, whose family Edwards had known in his youth.

'Who?' retorted Edwards. 'What the fuck? Why me? Why are you picking on me? Why are you choosing me? You've got to be joking.'

Joe Marrapodi had his own list of questions.

He and his officers were especially interested in finding the handbags belonging to Jane Rimmer and Ciara Glennon, and their contents, Jane's clothes, and Ciara's shoes and jacket, complete with her Claddagh brooch, all still missing.

It was not known what was missing from Sarah Spiers, but of particular interest was her sunflower key ring.

The cop produced a search warrant and let it flutter to the knees of the handcuffed Edwards, and asked him if there was anything in the house that did not belong to him and his family.

'No. Why me? I'm innocent,' he repeated.

Asked who lived in the house, Edwards said only himself and his stepdaughter. The mess in the hall belonged his wife, who had moved out two-and-a-half years earlier.

Soon after 8 a.m., shocked neighbours saw police lead Edwards to a police car, his hands on his head, dressed in a red T-shirt and blue shorts.

An hour later, a young adult woman arrived. After speaking with police, she left with them in a car.

Forensic officers swarmed through the house, which they described as a hoarder's mess. They set up a tent in the backyard and began the painstaking task of sifting through the lot, finding no items missing from the murder victims.

In Edwards' computer room, they discovered a box of women's underwear with holes cut out where the genitals would be, along with traces of Edwards' DNA. They also found plastic lunch bags containing Edwards' semen. Edwards' wife later told police that her husband had dressed in women's underwear and masturbated into sandwich bags. Other items seized included homemade sex toys and women's and girls' hair ties.

All computers and electronic devices were seized. Remarkably, a horribly sadistic pornographic movie based on the crimes of American rapist and serial killer Richard Ramirez, who had prompted Special Crimes' focus on precursor crimes, was found on the computer. The sexual violence in *Forced Entry* was so realistic that it was panned even by the USA's *Adult Industry News* as 'a very disturbing borderline snuff film', the magazine writing that it was 'promoting violence and/or making, or trying to make, rape look sexy'.

Records detected on the drives showed the graphic story of the abduction and rape of a victim named Chloe, a story that Edwards had written or modified, then decorated with pornographic images.

Edwards kept eight different Facebook accounts running, on which he called himself Bogeyman 1 through to Bogeyman 8. He said he used them for playing computer games.

The Cold Case squad drove Edwards to their office. On video, in an interview room, Joe Marrapodi told him that, if he did not consent to a DNA test, the police would obtain one forcibly using a court order. He complied.

Edwards denied that he had been to Claremont, except to fix the phones at a bank in 2009, more than a decade after the murders.

During the interview, which on-and-off spanned fourteen hours, he gave the impression of being inadequate and inept in his relationships with men and women, recounting how friendships with people of both genders had fizzled out.

His evident low self-esteem brought to mind the words of the profilers, who said the killer, when found, would have no power in his life. FBI profiler and sexual homicide expert Joël Kohout, part of the external Schramm team, had said in 2004: 'Killing gives him a sense of control, a huge sense of real power.'

Edwards told detectives that the family struggled to make ends meet. Marrapodi was interested in why the family was struggling, when Edwards was taking home about $800 a week. Mortgage payments were $225 a week.

'Were you doing anything else with the money?' he asked.

Edwards said his wife had stopped her part-time job, and they had medical insurance and school fees to pay.

'We were not on the bones of our arses,' Edwards said.

He said his wife became suspicious of the time he spent online, snooping on his different email addresses. Police still searching the Kewdale house discovered that she had been suspicious of something else – frequent unexplained cash withdrawals from automatic teller machines (ATMs) in the 1990s.

At Acton Avenue, they had found an exercise book with a charging rhino on the cover. Bank statements had been carefully copied in Edwards' wife's handwriting, dating back to the times of the murders. On the list were two cash withdrawals of $300 each from an ATM in central Claremont, a few doors from Club Bayview, dated between the murders of Jane and Ciara.

Edwards denied to the two detectives that he had any reason to drive around Claremont in the mid-1990s, and that he knew anything about the two sexual assaults and three murders. He said he had not been to Karrakatta Cemetery until the new century.

'I don't remember going there in 1995,' he said. 'I've never been there late at night or early morning. I don't know where Rowe Park is.'

Shown a photograph of Lisa, he said he was not aware of the sexual assault on a teen in the cemetery. Shown aerial photographs, he repeated that he had never been to Rowe Park.

He denied any knowledge of the Huntingdale assault, or either going to or knowing Woolcoot or Pipidinny roads.

'I don't know how many other ways I can say no,' he said.

While awaiting the results of his DNA test, Edwards lay down on the interview room floor. Offered food, he asked for 'a chocolate bar or something'.

'Brace yourself, Bradley,' said Joe Marrapodi, when the interview resumed, with Edwards, Marrapodi and Detective Sergeant Aaron Capes seated at a round table.

Marrapodi was holding a piece of paper that contained the results of that day's DNA tests. They compared Edwards' DNA profiles with those extracted from the kimono, Lisa and Ciara.

'They've come back to us that it's a positive match.'

'Yeah, I understand, but how could it be?' Edwards covered his face with both hands and appeared to cry. 'I didn't do any of this, I …' He coughed.

Detective Marrapodi asked Edwards if he had raped Lisa at Karrakatta. 'The DNA came from your semen, Bradley. What happened?'

'It wasn't me – I wish I could explain it. … I don't know what happened. I wasn't there. How can I explain it? You're assuming I've done it.'

The detective opened a folder and pulled out a photo of Ciara Glennon. 'Do you know who this person is? What happened?'

'No.'

'Are you sure?' Marrapodi asked. He read out her name, age, time, place and date of her murder, and said the male DNA profile recovered from her belonged to Edwards. 'What happened, Bradley?'

'I don't know. I wish I …'

'Your daughter said your most prized virtue is your honesty. This is your chance to show that she is right.'

'I am being honest.'

'Are you a person who takes responsibility for his actions?'

'Yes, I am.'

'Now is the time to accept responsibility.'

'I would accept responsibility for stuff I've done, not to what I haven't done.'

'Explain to me exactly what happened.'

'It's the second time you've asked. I don't know how to explain it properly. I don't know what happened in relation to all this stuff. I wish I knew.'

Marrapodi asked a similar set of questions in relation to the Huntingdale indecent assault, showing Edwards the kimono and saying to him that it contained 'your DNA and no one else's. Have you worn it?'

'I haven't seen it before.'

'She was attacked in her bedroom, Bradley.'

'I didn't do it. I don't know what it is or where it's from. How can it be? I can see you can't believe me.'

'Is there a reason why you don't know?'

'Because it wasn't me. If it wasn't me, then how would I know what happened? I don't know how else to explain it.'

In the last part of the interviews shown in court, Edwards says: 'I'm trying to think about it … everything is going around in my head. I just can't think straight at the moment.'

Twenty-one hours after his arrest, Edwards was charged with the abduction of Lisa from Rowe Park in Claremont on February 12, 1995, plus two counts of sexual penetration without consent at Karrakatta on the same date. He was also charged with breaking into the Huntingdale home twenty-eight years earlier, and with indecently assaulting the sleeping eighteen-year-old woman. Then he was charged with the wilful murders of Jane Rimmer and Ciara Glennon.

*

While the Kewdale raid was underway, other police had swooped on the plant nursery in Chidlow, where they served a warrant on the startled and innocent owner of the white Holden station wagon. He watched officers seize his car and truck it away, destined for the Police Forensic Facility in Midland. There, a painstaking, thorough testing and recovery of samples took place, a process that ultimately involved a bolt-by-bolt dismantling of its interior over three days.

It was about to give up its secrets.

Under special lighting, the ghostly outline of the distinctive Telstra logo could be seen on a front door. It was a logo described by some of the living witnesses who came forward to tell of being offered lifts in the streets of Claremont and Cottesloe in the mid-1990s. Some had mistaken a Telstra car for a taxi.

A puzzle remained. If the station wagon the Burger Boys and all the other witnesses had seen on Stirling Highway the night Ciara vanished was Edwards' Telstra vehicle, why had no witness mentioned Telstra logos?

The answer, said the prosecution, could be that they were looking elsewhere and did not see the small decals, or because Telstra had issued magnetic blanks to cover the signs when cars were working in the areas covered by rival telco companies.

Police established this vehicle had been built in March 1996 and was allocated to Edwards in April, three months after Sarah vanished and two months before Jane was abducted.

Over the following days and into 2017, officers dismantled seats and doors, and collected more than one hundred samples, including plant matter, paint scrapings and swabs for blood.

Pay dirt would have been the discovery of traces of blood or other biological material from Jane or Ciara. It was not to be. Twenty years had passed.

What if there had been transfer of material in the opposite direction, from the interior of the car to the victims?

Police already knew that the long hair of Jane Rimmer and Ciara Glennon had produced a goldmine of fibres. They had matched many of them to the Blue Graphite upholstery, seats, floor carpet and cargo area carpet of a Holden VS Series 1 station wagon.

The car's upholstery used four distinctly dyed polyester, polypropylene and rayon threads. Custom-made to Holden's exacting specifications, they were unique, with the dyes and materials certified by Holden before production was allowed to begin.

Scientists now could, and did, make direct comparisons between that car's fibres and those recovered from Jane and Ciara. Using microscopes, electronic instruments and cameras, ChemCentre scientists concluded that the fibres were perfect matches.

What of the dozens of matching navy blue clothing fibres found on Lisa's shorts, Jane's hair, Ciara's hair and T-shirt? Since 2012, scientists had known that these fibres had come from a common source, but they did not know what this source was. If that source could be found, it would likely link one offender to the crimes against Lisa, Jane and Ciara.

*

Just hours after Edwards was charged, Karl O'Callaghan held a crowded press conference at police headquarters in Perth, flanked by his command team. It was 8:30 a.m. on Friday, December 23, 2016.

Detectives had warned the victims' families to brace themselves for news of the impending breakthrough. The trust between the families and police was such that the officers knew there was no chance that word of their discovery would be leaked in advance.

'This has already been the biggest and most complex investigation in WA Police history,' Dr O'Callaghan said. 'The commitment of the WA Police and its officers has never wavered. We never give up.'

In fact, they *had* all but given up for a time, halting the investigation in 2015 and beginning to wrap up the case to hand to the coroner for an inquest.

O'Callaghan then paid tribute to the stoicism of the families of the victims and the strength shown by Lisa and her family.

The media coverage that followed the charges reached nationwide saturation. The Christmas Eve edition of *The West Australian* devoted its first sixteen pages to the story.

An hour after the police commissioner's announcement, in court, magistrate Evan Shackleton asked Bradley Robert Edwards if that was his correct name and whether he understood the charges against him, which were not read out. Edwards simply said, 'Yes.'

No charges related to Sarah Spiers were laid at that time.

Post reporter David Cohen described the accused man as tall, wearing a red collared shirt with black trim, his dark hair parted on the right. Cohen said Edwards appeared calm when the charges were mentioned. Edwards was remanded in custody, to spend his first Christmas in jail.

*

Don Spiers released an anguished statement, which spoke of the pain the revival of the case had caused. Time had not healed his family's grief.

'Words are inadequate to describe our personal loss and heartbreak. We retain confidence in the Macro Investigation Team to solve this case.'

He later told of the 'unbelievable anxiety' and uncertainty the family was suffering in its search for closure following the arrest, while Sarah's case remained unresolved. There was still no clue to where Sarah was.

Loss of his 'bubbly and energetic' daughter haunted him every day. 'Our lives have been absolute hell, and not knowing what happened to Sarah is worse than the worst possible news about her. Every time the phone rings, we wonder if it's her.

'I just keep working and working, because sure as hell when I sat around, I really started to suffer. I did break down with chronic depression.'

He pleaded on television's Nine News for information about where she now lay. 'Give us back our Sarah.'

Denis Glennon described his feelings on hearing the news as 'raw and bittersweet'.

Jenni Rimmer, Jane's mother, said the new developments were a blessing, while Jane's sister Lee told how moved she was by outpourings of sympathy from strangers.

'After I was on TV, so many people – three in a row when I was in the city – came up to me and said, "You're Lee Rimmer, aren't you? We're so glad for you. Can I give you a hug?"

'And they do. They say, "I just want you to know that the whole community is behind you."'

Jock Barker, then Claremont's mayor for seven years, said a lot of weight had been lifted from people's minds. After the murders, he had worried about his daughters being out on the town at night, even if they just went to buy takeaway food. 'It's tainted Claremont,' he said.

Other reactions were physical. With two decades of pent-up grief, fear and dread, people had burst into tears, shivered or felt ill.

'I broke out in goosebumps, even though I was not directly involved,' said one Club Bayview veteran.

It was a sombre Christmas for the young men and women who had partied in Claremont in the mid-1990s. Many, now with families of their own, had just returned from interstate or overseas to their parents only to be hit with this stark reminder of their haunted youth, to relive how their carefree lives had been wrecked when young women began disappearing from among them twenty years earlier.

'Rest in power, women of Claremont' read notes on two of the many bouquets of flowers now wired to the wrought-iron veranda railings of the Claremont Hotel that Christmas weekend. A spontaneous shrine had sprung up, pinned with touching notes at the spot where some of the victims had last partied.

'May justice prevail for the families. Thank you WAPOL [Western Australian Police] for your ongoing pursuit of justice' read another.

Another listed the victims' names of 'these lovely young women'.

'Forever young, never forgotten.'

35
Satan

Police had a busy Christmas. As well as searching Edwards' Kewdale home, they raided the house in Fountain Way, Huntingdale, which Edwards and his then wife had owned at the time of the Claremont murders. Forensic officers stripped the carpets, dug up the backyard and lifted a concrete slab. After ten hours, nothing of interest was found.

Police also executed search warrants on Edwards' parents' homes. One was a few streets from Fountain Way, and was the house where Edwards had stayed after his marriage had disintegrated, while another was where his parents had moved, an hour to the south at Madora Bay.

On September 17, 2018, the Western Australian Supreme Court suppressed the names of a number of potential witnesses in the pending case, including Edwards' partners and stepdaughter.

David Caporn, who had left the police force in 2009, gave an interview on Christmas Day. He said hardly a day had gone by that he did not think of the families of the victims. Replying to John Quigley's criticism that he had run a 'dud' investigation by focusing on the wrong suspect, he said Macro had conducted a massive investigation for eighteen months, starting after the disappearance of Jane Rimmer, before Lance Williams came on its radar. He said police had to rely on information known at the time. The only way police could eliminate suspects was by alibi.

*

As news of the arrest spread, Glenys Newport notified Crime Stoppers about a crime she had witnessed in 1985 by the Baron Way footbridge, which crossed the Southern River near Huntingdale. Then a pregnant twenty-five-year-old, she had been out walking with her toddler, Michelle, at 4:35 p.m. on Tuesday, September 24. They were crossing the bridge when a teenager on a bicycle appeared beside them.

'He rode past us, then rode down the embankment at the side of the bridge, put down his bike and looked back at me and masturbated,' Newport said. 'He looked me in the eye – he was doing it to me.'

The pair rushed home and Newport called Gosnells police. She described a youth in his mid-teens with dark hair parted on the right side, wearing glasses. She had had a good look at his right profile, an image that burned into her memory. She was to retrieve this memory thirty-two years later.

'The police back then were very interested – they said other people had reported the same teenager, but that they had been unable to catch him.'

The offence had remained unsolved. Edwards would have been aged sixteen.

Newport told detectives she had recognised Bradley Edwards from photographs as the teenager she had seen masturbating. Police retrieved her report of the incident and, in January 2017, two detectives visited Newport's home in Canning Vale for a another interview.

No charges were laid.

Living up to the many profiles of serial killers hiding in plain sight as ordinary citizens, Bradley Edwards had drawn praise from local members of parliament, both state and federal, who publicly lauded his voluntary community work. In 2013, Eric Ripper, his state member of parliament, awarded Edwards a ten-year service medal for his Little Athletics work, inviting his constituent for drinks at his electorate office to say thanks.

In October 2008, when DNA was first being identified from samples extracted from under Ciara Glennon's thumbnail, Edwards was being fêted by his local member of federal parliament, Liberal Steve Irons.

'Bradley Edwards heads up a fantastic committee and a hardworking group of volunteers,' Irons said in a speech. 'As we know, without volunteers, sporting clubs and competitions like this would not exist.'

His friends at Little Athletics confirmed that he had been a hardworking volunteer, but said his arrest had made them embarrassed that they knew him.

One fellow volunteer said she too was embarrassed because she had had no inkling that Edwards could have harboured evil secrets as he went about his everyday life.

Well after the murders, in 2007, Edwards even played football on the same team – the Central Crocs Masters – as one of the Special Crime detectives hunting him. Edwards' teammates, who were grateful for his work managing the club's website, said he liked a beer, once to the point of vomiting violently in a paddock and banging his head on his car's wheel during a club function.

The phone technician who had prowled Claremont in his work car was described by friends and workmates as good-looking and personable. 'He was outgoing and had a quirky sense of humour – he could have got any girl he wanted,' one of his workmates said of him.

Another said: 'I would have put these crimes on a hell of a lot of blokes before him. He would have easily fitted into the Claremont scene.'

State and federal members of parliament declared themselves deeply shocked.

None of this would have come as a surprise to prolific American serial killer Ted Bundy, who described himself as 'just a normal individual'. 'We want to be able to say we can identify these dangerous people,' he confided to journalist Stephen Michaud. 'The really scary thing is, we can't identify them. People don't realise that there are potential killers among them.

'How could anyone live in a society where people they liked, loved, lived with, worked with, admired could next day turn out to be the most demonic people imaginable?'

As the stunning news of an arrest began to sink in, and Edwards was identified from his court appearance, hundreds of pieces of new information flooded into police.

Some of the calls were from Edwards' horrified ex-girlfriends, whom police quizzed over the arrested man's sexual habits. They learned that he had an exceptionally thin penis.

Police were determined to follow up every call. They formed two separate squads with a total of 115 officers – even more than had been assigned at the peak of the Claremont murders in the 1990s.

These squads operated independently. One had the job of documenting every second of Edwards' life. The other had the mammoth task of continuing the work of Special Crime and State Operations, documenting all crimes, prior and subsequent to the Claremont murders, with a view to correlating them or not to Edwards' life.

Detectives called and visited Edwards' work colleagues, past and present. The picture they built was of man with a quirky sense of humour, a man who also liked to discuss the topic of the Claremont murders.

Telstra colleagues were asked about this habit of Edwards, and especially about the work cars they drove in the 1990s – how they were allocated and how such details were recorded.

What they learned prompted them to put out an alert for a specific vehicle, a 1992 Toyota Camry station wagon, a model that some technicians drove in the mid-1990s. They wanted to forensically examine this car, a vehicle with square headlights like those described by a witness in Stirling Road at the instant Sarah Spiers vanished off the street in 1996. Camry-like tail-lights had also been described by the witness who had investigated the screams near the Mosman Park phone box the same night. Police asked to see the old car in any condition, but were out of luck.

In Hakea Prison's remand section, Edwards was a curiosity, including among friends and family visiting other prisoners. One reported that Edwards had several regular visitors, including a young woman in her twenties and a young man, plus another female visitor at other times.

His younger brother emailed *The West Australian* newspaper, vehemently protesting his sibling's innocence. He wrote that the whole family was united in their support for Edwards.

*

So many people wanted to catch a glimpse of Edwards that, at his second Magistrates Court appearance on January 25, 2017, held in a large courtroom, Court 2, of the historic Supreme Court, extra security officers were enlisted to guard the entrances of the jarrah-panelled venue.

Crowded into the well of the court were twenty-six reporters, with detectives sitting at the back. Upstairs, in the public gallery, were seated thirty members of the public. A familiar face was present – it was former taxi driver Steven Ross, riding his mobility scooter into the lift and up into the gallery, his left leg having been surgically removed in 2015.

After some discussion with the prosecutor Carmel Barbagallo about the time needed for Edwards to instruct his lawyer, the hearing was over in a minute.

Outside, the *Post*'s editor caught up with former brothel madam Linda Watson, who had been in the public gallery to look at Edwards. She was convinced he had been a client in 1994 and 1995.

'It's made me sick in the stomach,' she said. 'I'm sure it was him. When I saw him on the screen, the hairs on my arms stood up. His face is different but you never forget the eyes – piercing, cold eyes but a nice personality. He came and had coffee with me in my office upstairs. He was not violent – quite the opposite, polite and calm, a gentleman.' He was not an 'ugly mug', the label working girls pin on aggressive clients.

Edwards had a new barrister for his third court appearance in Court 6 on March 29. Steven Ross was forced to wait outside in the autumn sunshine, handing out copies of newspaper clippings and regaling television camera operators with his version of the abduction of Sarah Spiers.

Gigabytes of electronic documents began to be sent to Edwards' lawyers. 'We cannot just back it up in a truck and give it to the defence lawyers,' said Amanda Forrester, Director of Public Prosecutions. It had to be catalogued, redacted of sensitive material, scanned and managed. Such 'disclosure' took years, as it turned out.

A public impatient to see Edwards face details of his charges in court was disappointed. Many did not understand that, before a trial could start, everything uncovered in thirty years of police investigations, plus the post-arrest trawl, all had to be delivered to and read by the small defence team. Defence experts had to probe crucial forensic evidence and perhaps retest it, then send their results back to the Office of the DPP.

The state's army of lawyers and paralegals formed the Macro prosecution team, who worked closely with detectives. As they tackled the mammoth job of preparing for trial, they took over an entire office floor.

The state government gave prosecutors an extra $1.8 million to run the state's most complex criminal case ever. Analysing thirty years of evidence, and assembling an army of potential witnesses, was an enormous task. That sum would not be enough.

Charges for the murder of Sarah Spiers were added to the list against Edwards on February 22, 2018.

At the first opportunity, on July 25, 2018, Edwards pleaded not guilty to all nine charges. This number was later reduced to eight, when charges relating to the Huntingdale attack were consolidated.

Edwards' first preliminary appearance in person, rather than his image on a video screen from the remand section of Hakea Prison, was always going to heighten the frisson.

On Thursday, February 14, 2019, a capacity crowd, including surviving victims and their families, had packed Court 2 of the 1903 Supreme Court building next to the Swan River. The accused man had barely sat down when a woman's strident voice from above split the gravity of the moment.

'Edwards, you'll burn in hell with Satan. Go to hell, you Satan. You are a dog, Edwards, a dog, evil, Satan. Burn in hell.'

The judge barely turned a hair as security hustled out the woman, about the same age as Edwards, into the February sunshine.

After calm was restored, the court was told that the Macro prosecution team was assembling 580 potential witnesses. People across Australia and the world received summonses the year before, telling them to prepare to travel to court in Perth or appear by video link at dates to be advised.

Both the prosecution and defence said they would work to try to whittle the list down. Barbagallo said the trial would begin with evidence about Edwards' background, before proceeding chronologically.

More drama followed at Edwards' next scheduled appearance, Monday, February 18. Everyone filed into the same court, but this time the central character was a no-show. Edwards had been taken to hospital that morning, Justice

Stephen Hall announced. Every accused has the right to face his accusers, so the judge had no option but to postpone until the next day to see if the patient was fit to appear. He was.

Now, for the first time, Edwards looked hesitant and uncertain, his blank fixed expression broken by rare grimaces.

A small wad of cotton wool in his right ear was a clue to his changed demeanour. It was the leftover sign of an injury he received the day before, preparing for court in the showers at Hakea Prison. While Edwards wasn't saying anything, the wound was self-inflicted, the result of stabbing a pencil into his ear.

With two days of unrelenting horror stretching ahead, Bradley Robert Edwards looked wobbly and uncertain as he climbed from the holding cells into the dock at the Supreme Court. Gone were the tie and purposeful stride of last week. Once seated in the dock, he displayed no emotion as, for the first time, the packed courtroom heard what police had discovered in their top-secret trawl of Edwards' life, and their investigations into rapes and murders in the western suburbs. Things were about to get very personal.

*

In pre-trial hearings starting in March 2019, state prosecutor Carmel Barbagallo struck trouble when she tried to link the murders with the pornography and mutilated women's underwear seized by detectives in their police raid on Edwards' home.

'The state says that the plethora of material seized shows [Edwards] had or has an obsessive sexual interest in the abduction, imprisonment, forcible rape of women in violent and degrading circumstances,' Barbagallo said.

Edwards had accessed 3942 pornographic websites, most of them rape-themed or concerning bondage, discipline and sado-masochism (BDSM), she said.

Edwards' lawyer Paul Yovich responded that only ten or twelve per cent of the sites appeared to be extreme.

After watching the 2002 extreme pornographic movie *Forced Entry*, which Barbagallo described as 'violent, shocking and disturbing', on March 19, 2019, Justice Hall ruled it out of the main trial. Yovich had objected that the pornography was not relevant and was prejudicial towards his client.

Barbagallo described the seized electronic copies of 'stories' accessed, contributed to or modified by Edwards, which contained detailed incidents of violence, restraint and taking sexual advantage of women affected by alcohol and drugs, as well as using blackmail to overcome resistance.

One of the many stories was a 'sexually sick' and 'violent, erotic' work, titled 'Chloe', with its writer as the narrator, the prosecutor said.

Barbagallo said the 'Chloe' story mentioned 'meticulous planning, abduction, blitz attack, cloth inserted into the mouth of the victim, use of handcuffs, hood and driving them around for some time.

'We say there are strikingly similar features in that story to the Karrakatta offences,' she said. 'It cannot be a coincidence.'

Justice Hall also ruled out on March 19 the 'Chloe' story, which Edwards had contributed to, modified and illustrated with pornographic images.

'It is not suggested that any of the pornography depicts any of the victims,' the judge said. He said he could not accept that a person with such an interest is more likely to commit the crimes alleged. The 'Chloe' story would be relevant if it identified the offender in the cases before him, but it was not relevant to the facts at issue.

'Another [story] had a male driving around at 2 a.m. abducting visibly drunk nineteen-year-olds,' Barbagallo said.

This too was ruled out of evidence by the judge. Barbagallo had said that the semen-stained and mutilated women's underwear found in Edwards' house showed a continuation of a 'garment fetish', stretching back to when Edwards was not yet aged fourteen. An alleged teasing remark by his younger brother about Bradley keeping a 'stash of chicks' undies' in his bedroom was excluded by the judge on August 9, 2019. Along with the material found on Edwards' computer on the day of his arrest, the underwear and homemade sex toys were also excluded from evidence, with the judge 'instructing himself' to ignore them.

36
Marriages

A month before the main trial started, there was another big courtroom surprise.

At his first opportunity in July 2018, Edwards had, in a ringing voice, pleaded not guilty to nine charges involving five women, these alleged crimes spread across nine years.

On October 20, 2019, during a scheduled pre-trial hearing, Justice Hall asked Edwards to stand in the dock while the now eight indictments were read to him.

The first charge was that he had broken into the house of the Huntingdale teen at night on February 15, 1988, the kimono attack, with intent to commit an offence. The judge asked him how he pleaded.

Edwards' answer was so quiet and so unexpected that some doubted whether they had heard him correctly.

'Guilty,' he answered.

He had denied this and all the other charges from the moment of his arrest, almost three years earlier. His distressed victim was present to hear his admission to that horrifying crime three decades before.

To the charge that he had unlawfully deprived the teen of her personal liberty, Edwards gave the same reply.

The same happened with the charges regarding Lisa. Edwards admitted that he had unlawfully detained her on February 12, 1995, at Claremont and at Karrakatta on the same date, and that he twice sexually penetrated her without consent, on each occasion causing her bodily harm, acts 'likely to substantially degrade or humiliate'.

Lisa was in court to hear Edwards say, at last, 'Guilty.'

Five admissions that day.

What would he say to the three murder charges? All on the media benches held their breaths, as did the families of the murder victims behind them in the gallery.

'Not guilty,' he said, three times.

There would be a trial, after all.

*

On November 1, 2018, Justice Michael Corboy had ruled that Edwards' trial would be decided by a single judge, not a jury. Both Edwards and the prosecution had requested a 'judge alone' trial.

'The case has both engrossed and distressed members of the public like no other,' state prosecutor Carmel Barbagallo had said, in making her application.

'Graphic and disturbing' post-mortem photos could prejudice some jury members, Justice Corboy had said, while giving his reasons why Edwards' charges should be heard without a jury. Complex technical evidence would also be difficult for some jurors to digest, he said. Saturation media coverage, which rested on the assumption that the murders were committed by one person, 'the Claremont serial killer', would be hard for some civilians to shake. Sympathy and grief for the victims' families, and the desire to see a resolution for them, could also weigh on jurors.

A criminal trial is a search for the truth. For such a complex case – three murder trials in one – the 'judge only' set-up appeared to assist this search. Justice Stephen Hall, the presiding judge, was an active participant, interrupting lawyers mid-flight, something no jury foreman would dare. He probed both sides, questioning, seeking clarifications, starting conversations and dredging long-ago witness testimony from his prodigious memory.

Sometimes, he delved into the thought processes he would follow, on separate days quoting obscure reasoning principles such as 'Occam's razor' and the 'Texas sharpshooter fallacy'.

The pre-trial hearings were held in the timber-lined Federation-era Supreme Court 2, with the main trial shifting to the biggest courtroom in the modern District Court building, on the seventh floor. This became a workplace, an intimate space, a second home. Lisa and the Huntingdale victim had formed friendships, as had Denis Glennon, his daughter Denise and Don Spiers, plus other family members who, on most days, sat among the detectives on one side of the public gallery.

Trevor Rimmer had died in 2008. His widow Jenni was in court in a wheelchair during the first week of the main trial to eyeball the man she believed had murdered her daughter Jane. She had suffered a stroke many years after Jane's death. Her surviving children, Lee and Adam, also came to watch and listen.

Edwards' ageing parents, Bruce and Kaye, sat across the aisle, often holding hands. Each day they made the long rail journey to court and back from Halls Head, well past the end of the southern train line.

Behind them, ordinary citizens had come to see justice done, sometimes so many that the 'Court Full' sign went up. In front of them were two rows of seats for reporters, which were packed on peak days. Then three long rows of bar tables, with Cold Case Homicide Squad police at the back and banks of lawyers in front. On the left-hand end of the front row was the state prosecutor, Carmel Barbagallo, calm, methodical and quick-witted, with two assistants to her right. On the opposite end was Paul Yovich, Edwards' lead defence lawyer. Pleasant when cross-examining witnesses, and extremely sharp of mind, this was a man who did not let one detail escape unexplored. He was assisted by Genevieve Cleary.

To everyone's right, except the judge and his associates, sat the accused man, Sphinx-like.

Often, a pen in his left hand could be seen moving furiously over a foolscap pad. Otherwise, he stared ahead from the elevated dock, his mouth downturned. Edwards never once looked at the corner inhabited by the victims, family members and their shadows, the Cold Case cops.

During especially excruciating passages of evidence, Edwards rested his right cheek in the palm of his right hand, sometimes slumping, his expression hidden from the no-nonsense, whip-smart judge, who would occasionally glance towards the dock from his elevated desk.

Once or twice, Edwards allowed himself a smile, such as when his old Telstra friend Paul Luff took the stand.

On at least two other occasions, that impassive Edwards face cracked. He had his own monitor, so he could watch the detailed photo and video court exhibits. The most gruesome were hidden from the view of the families, public and media, but not from the judge, lawyers and Edwards. The first time an image of Jane's decomposing body flicked up in front of Edwards, he allowed himself a smirk, then caught his expression. This happened once more when another unimaginable image was shown a few days later.

*

The trial proper started on November 25, 2019. From the witness box came the harrowing first-hand accounts of Edwards' surviving victims, bravely facing their attacker in court, their evidence heard between December 3 and 9, 2019.

Wendy Davis, her memories still raw, travelled from Tasmania to front Edwards in court, even though there was no case to be proved, because he had pleaded guilty to the attack on her at Hollywood Hospital thirty-one years before.

'A hand came around my face with a cloth on it,' she recalled. 'It pressed me back.' It was the moment she thought she was going to die.

When Edwards had shoved the cloth into her mouth, she had stopped breathing, fearing there was a chemical on the fabric. Then, realising she could breathe, she started to fight.

'I began to really struggle,' she said.

She apologised to the court for appearing to give 'garbled' evidence, saying she became distressed when reliving the experience.

The attack was 'the strangest thing. All of a sudden, it just kind of stopped. Edwards apologised profusely.'

Edwards' charmed life with Telstra was demonstrated by another witness, Tony Vomero, the telco's global payroll manager. He said he had searched Edwards' personal file back to the 1980s, but could find no note of the Hollywood Hospital charge and conviction.

Edwards refused to look at the Huntingdale victim as she described the attack, telling how, when she was eighteen, she awoke at 2 a.m. to feel him straddling her. Edwards was then aged twenty.

'I thought my boyfriend had come back – I said, "It's okay, I won't scream."'

But then she felt a 'calloused hand, a working hand,' stuff a piece of fabric into her mouth. She shook her head and managed to push it partly out.

She went to stroke what she thought was her boyfriend's cheek. 'I felt stubble and [my boyfriend] had shaved that day. So I dug my fingernails as hard as I could into his cheek.'

Trembling at one point, she told how Edwards released the pressure and got off her. She could see he was wearing a white, long-sleeved cotton nightie. The teen hammered on the wall dividing her bedroom from that of her parents, shouting, 'Dad, dad, dad!' The man disappeared, dropping a silk kimono.

Both women were still visibly shaken, angry and extremely upset by being blitz-attacked, fear lingering for up to thirty-two years until they finally faced their demon. Their evidence jangled the nerves of all the spectators in the courtroom, especially those of the parents, siblings, relatives and friends of the victims sitting at the back.

There was relief on the media benches when Barbagallo said that Lisa's four statements to police spoke for themselves. She would not make the witnesss relive that terrifying night twenty-five years ago, in front of a room full of people.

Her words from 1995 and 1996 were read into the record with stunning power. Lisa sat stoically in the courtroom's public gallery, surrounded by supporters and other surviving victims.

She heard how her sister had picked her up from a work function to party in Mosman Park and Northbridge before ending up at Club Bayview. As she walked towards her friend's house, head down and arms folded, the unseen man jumped her from behind in dimly lit Rowe Park.

'I kept my eyes shut – I thought it would be better if he thought I didn't see him.'

Edwards listened from the dock, not looking at Lisa, his face immobile, sometimes rested on his right hand.

'He didn't speak at all. I felt a lot of pain,' she said of her ordeal in the cemetery. 'I thought at the end of it all he was going to kill me.

'I was in a state of shock. I remember repeating, "Oh my God, I can't believe this is happening." It was very painful.'

After the sexual assaults, the man 'chucked me in some scrub', returning five minutes later to lift her again and drop her in more dense bushes.

After she had run towards Hollywood Hospital, she called her father.

'I said, "I've been raped."'

Her statement read in court ended with these words: 'I didn't want him to do these things to me. I didn't know any way I could stop him.'

Chilling also were the stories of 'damsels in distress', other random, innocent young women who had accepted lifts in Cottesloe and Claremont from a lone, dark-haired driver of a Telstra vehicle. These women shuddered in the witness box to think how narrowly they might have escaped the fate that befell Lisa, Sarah, Jane and Ciara.

Before a magistrate sentenced Edwards for the Hollywood Hospital attack, two clinical psychologists interviewed him for pre-sentence reports. Both now gave evidence in court. Lyn Millet said Edwards had felt very ashamed of his actions, but could not say why he had done it.

Edwards said he was stressed because his girlfriend had admitted to a fling with one of his friends. He had few close friends. His girlfriend was trying to pressure him into marriage and they had been arguing a lot over money. She was a prolific spender.

'He tends to control his emotions and tries to suppress his anger as he feels he has a bad temper,' said this report.

In the week leading up to the attack, 'nothing was going right for me,' he told another psychologist, Paul McEvoy.

At the start of the trial, Barbagallo outlined that she would expand on the theme identified by the two psychologists. The prosecution would demonstrate a pattern of 'emotional turmoil' and feelings of rejection, which spiked just before each crime against a stranger, including the rapes and three murders.

'When wrong is done to him, when his relationships are under pressure, he represses his emotions then he takes it out on someone he doesn't know,' the prosecutor said.

In video-link evidence given over two days on November 27 and 28, 2019, Edwards' first wife said that, in 1990, she had asked Edwards if marriage was on the cards.

'He seemed to be a little upset about it, then I got upset,' she said. She went to her bedroom, Edwards following, but she would not let him in, she told the court.

The following day, Edwards could not pick her up from work because of 'the Hollywood Hospital incident'.

Laid out were the couple's courtship; arguments; marriage; buying of a house, cars, pet dogs and a horse; their work and social lives; and their break-up around the times of the first two Claremont disappearances. During this evidence, Edwards looked ahead or closed his eyes.

They had married in 1991 and bought a house near Huntingdale. Edwards had owned a computer from mid-1994. He would come home from work each day, shower and change, then disappear into the third bedroom. The couple would eat dinner, then Edwards would return to his computer, and his wife would go to bed alone. She had seen him at his computer at 3 a.m., she said in evidence.

'He wasn't interested, he wasn't present in the marriage,' she told the court. 'It slowly deteriorated.'

She said that, in 1994 and 1995, Edwards did not discuss their relationship issues, even when she was losing interest in him.

The early morning abduction and rape of Lisa in February 1995 occurred when the married couple was moving apart emotionally. Edwards' wife invited a tradesman she had become friendly with at work, and his children, to see a horse that the Edwards kept on an agistment property. To thank her, the man took her to dinner at an Italian restaurant. Then the Edwards rented a spare room in their house to the tradesman for $100 a week.

Edwards had caught her hugging and kissing their lodger while she was sitting on the end of his bed, she said.

This lodger, who Edwards told detectives Joe Marropodi and Aaron Capes had fathered his wife's child, also gave evidence. He and Edwards had developed a friendship, joining a softball team together. The man told how, early on some Sunday mornings while Edwards was asleep, Edwards' wife would come into his bed where they would have sex. In January 1996, the month Sarah Spiers disappeared, Edwards caught his wife on the lodger's bed at the Huntingdale house. The two were amused by photos of Edwards' wife in a wet T-shirt competition.

'We were laughing and she kissed me or I kissed her on the lips,' the lodger told the judge. 'It was a mutual thing. It just happened. At the same time the door opened – Bradley opened the door and put his head in.

'Bradley didn't say anything. He just walked off, and [his wife] went after him. I could hear they were having an argument in their room.

'I panicked. I started getting my stuff together. I'd crossed the boundaries – I thought I'd better get out of here.

'She came back and I asked her, what's happening? She said, "Don't worry."

'I said, "I'm going." I said, "I'm not staying another night with that thing in his room." I just feared for my life.

'I said, "I've got to go." She said, "Well, Bradley doesn't want you to go."

'I said, "If he doesn't want me to go, he'd come and tell me himself," which he did do.

'He came into my room and said, "I don't want you to go." He was crying. I was crying, she was crying.

'It prompted me to stay a couple more weeks.'

Edwards kept a baseball bat and rifle under his bed, the lodger said after the trial.

Edwards' wife soon moved out to live with her parents. Later, Edwards dropped in unannounced to the parents' house, staying for a 'civil' dinner for four with no reference to the married couples' relationship issues. At dinner, Edwards invited his wife out to see fireworks. She did not go. This was the night Sarah Spiers was abducted and murdered, Australia Day, January 26, Barbagallo alleged.

When Edwards' first wife gave evidence on 27 November, she remembered refusing the fireworks invitation, but not the date. A newspaper clipping advertised Australia Day fireworks in the district on the same night that Sarah disappeared.

Edwards listened to the evidence from the dock with his eyes closed as his first wife described their life together.

Weeks afterwards, the wife and lodger rented a house together. Edwards called the man, threatening to kill him, the lodger told the court. 'I said, "You know where I live, you've got my address." That's the last I ever heard of him.'

Edwards had appeared upset and depressed and began drinking heavily, said Paul Luff, Edwards' friend and workmate. He recalled asking Edwards' parents to check on him.

'You're not going to top yourself or anything like that?' Luff asked him.

'Nah, mate, I'm all right. I'm going to get through this,' Edwards replied.

As part of the alleged pattern, Edwards suffered more 'emotional turmoil' in the days before Jane Rimmer was murdered in June that same year, 1996. Edwards' estranged wife called him to say she was pregnant to the lodger. She did not want Edwards to hear the news from anyone else. She and Edwards had spent one night together after their split.

She recounted their conversation in court: 'He asked if the baby was his. I said it was not his – he made no response I can remember.' She said Edwards accepted the news and did not seem upset. 'We were always civil,' she said. The baby was born in December.

Just two weeks before Edwards had met his second wife, Ciara was murdered, on March 15, 1997. At that time, Edwards had been confronted with the debris of the messy and humiliating failure of his first marriage. Contracts were being exchanged for the sale of the former couple's house. He had also had another break-up.

The women from the two relationships Edwards had between the murders of Jane and Ciara took the stand.

'I never felt I got below the surface,' the woman he had met at the Ocean Beach Hotel told the court. They had no sexual contact, she said, maybe a kiss.

Edwards' Telstra vehicle, a Holden station wagon, was kept meticulously clean, she said.

The older woman recalled her break-up with Edwards, apparently just weeks before Ciara Glennon was abducted and murdered.

Right at the end of the trial, Barbagallo abandoned her 'emotional turmoil' line of argument. She did not explain why, but when Edwards' lawyer, Paul Yovich, asked Edwards' ex-partners to dredge their memories from twenty-three years earlier, their hazy recollections of dates, times and various incidents appeared to make it hard to correlate the timelines.

*

Edwards had met his second 'lightning strike' wife on April 1, 1997. He courted her at her workplace, a law firm. 'I thought it was an April Fool's joke,' she told the court on November 28, 2019.

The frantic search for Ciara was still underway, her body not discovered until April 3.

On April 2, the sale of the Huntingdale house had settled.

Edwards' job kept him at the law firm for a few days. The employee agreed to meet him if he bought her roses. Two dozen red roses later, they met for their first date, at McDonald's. His future wife brought along her toddler daughter. They were a package deal, she told the court.

Edwards arrived in a white station wagon with Telstra logos on the doors. He was wearing long trousers and a short-sleeved shirt with the Telstra insignia.

'We fell in love pretty quickly, I guess,' she said.

The woman, aged fifty-four at the time she gave evidence, said Edwards had confided to her that, when he had learned of his first wife's infidelity just before the Hollywood Hospital attack, the news had greatly upset him.

The couple was on a date in June 1997 when Edwards stopped the car outside a high school and announced he had a criminal record.

'He said his first wife cheated on him when they were going out. He couldn't handle it and he had a brain-snap. When they were girlfriend and boyfriend, she cheated on him – he couldn't cope with it.

'He cried and everything. I felt so sorry for him because it was all like, "woe is me," and I even cried with him.'

'He said it was just an assault and he minimised it. I heard the severity of it only–' Her sentence was cut off by lawyers at that point.

The new couple became engaged in mid-2000 and married in December that year. They had not lived together or spent the night together before marriage. Since his first marriage split, Edwards had lived at his parents' Huntingdale home. His parents had another home on the coast south of Perth.

A pattern of suspicion grew inside the house the couple had bought together at 344 Acton Avenue, Kewdale, during financially tough years of marriage.

'I was just – I was sick and tired of all the lies that–' Edwards' second wife started to tell the judge, but was again cut off. She appeared keen to elaborate, but the rules of evidence did not allow it. Defence lawyer Paul Yovich asked her not to 'editorialise'.

'I left him on July 4, 2015. My daughter remained living at the house,' she said, her voice cracking with emotion.

Her exercise book with the charging rhino on the cover and careful notations inside it was produced in court. In her handwriting was a list of transactions she had copied in mid-

2014, from Bankwest statements dating back to July 1996, at the time Jane Rimmer's body still lay undiscovered.

Barbagallo: 'When did you make those notes?'

Witness: 'Well, the relationship was really starting to escalate and I … feared for my life. I wanted … I–' She was cut off again. 'I was terrified when I was writing this … I was scared stiff.'

The Bankwest statements showed ATM transactions between 1996 and 2000, but the statements for the three months before Ciara Glennon was abducted in March 1997 were missing. The originals had disappeared from the bank's electronic archive.

In his videoed police interview, Edwards had denied being familiar with or driving around Claremont late at night and in the early mornings in the mid-1990s.

The statement copies showed two withdrawals, each of $300, from the Bankwest ATM in central Bay View Terrace, a few doors from Club Bayview, on December 5 and December 13, 1996.

Barbagallo later told the judge that Edwards' admissions about Lisa's abduction from Claremont and the central Claremont bank transactions meant he had lied to police.

He had also clearly lied to detectives Marrapodi and Capes when he vehemently denied the kimono and graveyard attacks on teenaged women, because he had admitted to those crimes three years after the interview.

He had expressed the same surprise, denial and bewilderment at those accusations as he had about the three murders, Barbagallo said.

On the day of his arrest, Edwards was recorded by police telling 'a plethora of lies, outrageous, blatant lies'. Telling lies did not make a person a murderer, Justice Hall chimed in.

Edwards lied about what he was doing the Friday night Ciara was murdered, the prosecution alleged.

'What the hell? You were supposed to be here on Friday night,' friend and fellow Telstra technician Murray Cook said to Edwards when he finally arrived at the Cook family's south coast holiday house at 11 a.m. on Saturday, March 15, 1997.

Cook and his wife Brigita had waited for Edwards until ten or eleven that night, after he had accepted their invitation to stay over.

Edwards had arrived in a white Telstra station wagon the next day.

'He said, "I was trying to reconcile with my wife,"' Cook said in evidence. When asked how it went, Edwards shook his head, Cook said.

Barbagallo said these, too, were lies. No such make-up attempt had occurred – his first wife was then living with another man and the couple's three-month-old baby.

By coincidence, the two technician friends, Edwards and Cook, had seen each other about five hours after Sarah had disappeared, just after 2 a.m. on Saturday, February 27, 1996.

Brigita Cook said that Edwards lived in the neighbouring suburb to her family. Edwards had arrived at their house so the two men could travel to work together for an urgent overtime job at government offices in West Perth. Before the pair left at about 7:20 a.m. in Cook's car, Edwards had offered to fix the couple's air conditioner. Edwards did not finish work until 9:45 p.m. that night. The bus-stop staring incident by a man in a Telstra car had occurred in Claremont in the early hours of the next morning, a Sunday.

While detectives had spent years since Edwards' arrest piecing together Edwards' movements in the 1990s and afterwards, they were unable to find alibis for Edwards at the times of the murders.

37
First-hand

From among the 200 witnesses who were eventually summonsed to court, those in the galleries heard the profound, indelible effects they suffered.

Tammy van Raalte-Evans cried in the witness box as she relived the moment when, as she picked giant lilies in Wollcoot Road, Jane's small bare foot accidentally touched the back of her own leg. She was in tears as she recalled her first sight of Jane's body 'laying on her tummy' under the bush. She told how she had refused to leave Jane alone while her husband rushed to summon police.

Jane's older sister, Lee, sitting in the courtroom's public gallery, cried along with Tammy.

Vivid images from that day had also never left Jonathan Adams, the first detective on the scene. As he gave evidence on January 6 and 7, six years after retiring as a police inspector, it was clear that, among all the gruesome sights he had seen as officer in charge of Kwinana detectives, this day had stood out.

'Once you see a body in the bush like that, it never leaves you. I can recall it as clearly as yesterday,' he told the court twenty-three years later.

Jason Atkinson, the twenty-three-year-old plasterer whose morning search for cannabis plants had led him to stumble across Ciara Glennon in a grove of grass trees, also became emotional in court as he relived that hot autumn morning.

Reeling back in horror, he had run and driven to call police, he told the court on December 17. Detective Sergeant Charlie

Carver and Detective Senior Constable Edward Besson were diverted to the scene from another job.

'He was distressed, he was in shock,' was how then acting Detective Sergeant Carver, officer in charge of Joondalup detectives, described Atkinson's reaction. 'He pointed – he said, "I don't want to go anywhere near it."'

Detective Besson, who never went closer than fifteen feet to Ciara, was also permanently scarred: 'I could see a deceased female person, her hair and black clothing. Her hair was a blonde colour and her short black skirt appeared to be pulled up.

'I noticed that particular sight and smell. I'll never forget it – I can still visualise it now. It so affected me in the way I saw it and I was shocked by it, and haven't forgotten it in twenty-odd years.'

A seemingly endless stream of workers took the witness stand to relive their tasks from the 1990s. Their jobs were to take care of the results of the worst that humanity can offer. They were police officers from junior ranks to senior detectives, forensic officers, pathologists, photographers, video operators, and undertakers contracted to remove bodies from the sites of sudden deaths. Now they were confronted again with those indelible moments through scene-of-crime video close-ups, plus colour photographs.

*

Edwards and his defence lawyers did not have to prove a thing. That burden fell to the prosecution side. Edwards was innocent unless proven guilty beyond reasonable doubt. The state's case against him was circumstantial: nobody had witnessed the murders, there were no admissions, only denials. In Sarah's case, no body had been recovered.

The tenacious prosecutor was determined to stick to her propensity argument that linked all six crimes, three of them now admitted by Edwards.

She was to weave the six crimes together to help her ascend her most difficult mountain. This was an attempt to prove to the judge that Edwards had murdered eighteen-year-old Sarah Spiers. No body meant no connecting physical evidence – no hair, no fibre, no clothing, no jewellery, no sunflower key ring, no weapon, no DNA. How to link her death to Edwards?

She argued that his admissions to the 1988 kimono and 1995 Karrakatta crimes made it more likely that Edwards was the kind of person who would abduct and murder three other young women.

As the trial wore on, Yovich was relentless in forcing the prosecution to prove each element of its DNA and fibre evidence, a process that took the court four long months, from early January to early May 2020.

He clearly recognised that the dormant DNA fingernail sample tested back in 2008 was the evidence most dangerous to his client's case. But, he indicated, it could also be Edwards' get-out-of-jail-free card.

Yovich said that, if Justice Hall ruled that Edwards' DNA did not get under Ciara's fingernails via a fight with Edwards, the judge could not find his client guilty of any of the murder charges. 'The rest of the evidence taken at its highest wouldn't get you there,' he said.

His broad tactic was to suggest the possibility of two types of contamination: contamination of the memory of the witnesses over time, and contamination of microscopic samples somewhere in the chain of DNA and fibre evidence – from crime scene to methods of transport to inside the laboratories themselves.

Did everyone wear protective clothing? Not usually. Protective clothing protocols had yet to be established. Awareness of the possibilities of DNA and fibre transfer was very low. What make and model of car did they drive? Any Holdens? How close did they get to the bodies? Weeks of cross-examination were dedicated to questions like these.

Yovich had a big hurdle to leap. Why was the full male DNA profile scraped from Ciara's left thumbnail bed an exact match to Edwards' DNA, if Edwards was not Ciara's murderer?

The state had failed to prove Edwards was the Claremont serial killer, he said, suggesting the DNA sample did not get Edwards' profile on it because Ciara had gouged it from him, but that it got there via contamination.

He pointed out that Edwards' DNA was already somewhere in the PathWest lab after being collected from Lisa at the Sexual Assault Referral Centre in Subiaco, more than two years before samples from Ciara's body were brought in that April day in 1997.

Through his cross-examination of scientific witnesses, Yovich raised the possibility that the yellow-top containers holding samples AJM 40 and AJM 42 had somehow been contaminated by the sperm-cell sample recovered from Lisa.

He did such a good job of raising doubts that, towards the end of February 2020, some headlines had readers believing that the prosecution case had collapsed because of DNA contamination in the PathWest lab.

The DNA of four PathWest scientists had been found on samples tested at the lab. DNA from another case was found on twig samples collected from Jane Rimmer's gravesite.

PathWest scientists admitted ten cases of contamination in 17,000 tests.

Maybe Edwards had done the first three attacks but not the last three, people began to say. Yovich said there was no proof that Ciara had torn her left thumbnail as a result of a fight with her attacker. She may have broken it during her long day at work in the city lawyers' office, or in the front bar of the Continental Hotel.

Justice Hall pointed out that there was other evidence Ciara had suffered defence injuries, which pointed to a violent struggle. Ciara had tried to defend herself from an attack with a knife. Ciara's right forearm received two cuts to the bone, Barbagallo said.

Ciara had died shortly afterwards, and mummification of her hand had preserved the foreign DNA. It was a compelling scenario, the prosecutor said.

The LCN (low-copy-number) tests in Birmingham had discovered two, full ten-point profiles of Edwards and Ciara. They were in the combined samples from two of Ciara's nails from her left hand, the most important fingernails in the state's history.

Yovich suggested contamination events at the PathWest lab had made it possible for Edwards' DNA to have entered the jar containing the tiny left-hand nail scrapings.

Barbagallo called this a desperate theory. The fingernails told the opposite story, she said. 'This is that Bradley Robert Edwards abducted Ciara Glennon, that she physically fought for her life.'

The prosecution's big gun, Dr Jonathan Whitaker, took the stand. He was the international DNA expert who had been in charge of the LCN tests at Trident Court, Birmingham, in 2008.

He told the judge that Ciara's broken nail was evidence of violence, and that she may have scraped skin or blood from her attacker while confronting him in a boxer stance. 'Force promotes transfer,' Dr Whitaker said.

Dr Whitaker had travelled from Britain to give evidence. As the state's DNA expert, he was able to give summaries and opinions while the other experts were restricted to the facts.

Months of careful defence challenge to the provenance of the state's DNA evidence seemed to melt away under Dr Whitaker's measured, cautious and precise delivery, backed by a lifetime of expertise.

He said a series of unlikely events would have had to occur in an unlikely combination for the lab contamination scenario Yovich had put forward.

The sample taken from Lisa at the Subiaco sexual assault survivor's clinic on the day of her rape back in 1995 had contained both Lisa's and Edwards' DNA. If the cemetery sample had contaminated Ciara's thumbnail sample, when tested at Trident Court it would have shown three profiles – those of Ciara, Edwards and Lisa. But Ciara's thumbnail sample from 1997 contained only Edwards' plus Ciara's DNA. Lisa's DNA was absent from the Trident Court tests.

'I don't accept that there would be any way for [Lisa's] DNA to have disappeared from the [thumbnail] swab,' Dr Whitaker told the judge.

The expert also said it was 'extremely unlikely' that Edwards' DNA had lingered loose in the lab for fourteen months, surviving thousands of bleach-cleaning cycles then contaminating nothing but one crucial jar: the one containing Ciara's sample. And the contaminated sample was from a man who had admitted he 'captured, restrained and raped' the teenager, and just happened to concern an almost identical abduction from the streets of Claremont.

'Entirely implausible, extraordinarily unlikely,' said Barbagallo.

Dr Whitaker concluded that, when Edwards' DNA was discovered in 2008 mixed with Ciara's, analysis showed that both these DNA profiles had degraded at the same rate over time.

This strongly suggested that both samples had been exposed to the same environmental conditions: in the open at Pipidinny Road, in storage at the lab and in transport to England, Dr Whitaker said. They had travelled the same journey together over eleven years. One part of the sample was not a random bit of DNA that had somehow survived separately in the lab for fourteen months.

After Dr Whitaker's evidence, the Macro detectives present and the prosecutors were in a buoyant mood. An ABC reporter sitting next to the *Post* editor turned and said: 'That was devastating to the defence case. They've got him.'

In the end, the answers to these questions were in the hands of the judge, who demonstrated his extraordinary background knowledge of DNA, occasionally asking his own highly technical questions of expert witnesses. Who knew what he would decide?

*

When the COVID-19 crisis collided with court on March 25, four months into the trial, the courtroom saw another side of Edwards as he waited in prison for the court to convene for an urgent hearing. He was visible on a silent video link from Casuarina Prison, laughing, joking and gesticulating to someone just off camera, an animated Edwards doing most of the talking. Despite COVID-19, the trial continued uninterrupted but with a sanitised witness box, more witnesses giving evidence by video, and a near-empty public gallery.

Another discernible mood-shift could be seen in the teams of prosecution lawyers and Cold Case Homicide Squad officers, six weeks before the 'closing addresses' by lawyers from both sides.

In the witness box in the last week of April 2020 was the ChemCentre forensic scientist Reece Powell, who was brilliant with the intricacies of complex fibre evidence. He had worked on the Claremont case for nine years, originally identifying the Blue Graphite fibres that came from a Holden Commodore. The courtroom screens lit up with his magnified images of glowing, beautifully coloured fibres. The dry, scientific descriptions of the way critical fibres matched each other seemed to be the convincing evidence that the prosecution was anticipating. The judge was paying rapt attention.

If Justice Stephen Hall was to accept Powell's evidence of these ninety-eight tiny fragments, then a Telstra technician driving a Telstra car was likely to have been at the scenes of the rape of Lisa and the murders of Jane and Ciara. Was that technician Edwards? He had already admitted he was the Karrakatta culprit.

Edwards had looked uncomfortable a year earlier, when he learned in a pre-trial court hearing that fellow Telstra technician, Jeffrey Cohen, had hoarded his Telstra-issued blue shorts and trousers.for more than twenty years The man in the dock, who up until then had been staring fixedly at the judge, suddenly found his own black shoes more interesting. Police had picked up the clothes from Cohen's home in April 2019, two months before the trial was originally due to start. Now the scientists had a way to directly compare and match the mystery navy fibres found on Lisa, Jane and Ciara with something specific: actual trousers and shorts made from the unique Telstra navy fabric and dyes. They matched perfectly, Powell said.

A shock of curled, blonde-reddish hair separated from Ciara's head suddenly appeared on the court screens. Ciara's father Denis and sister Denise looked on.

The clump of 200 hairs had been cut at both ends by Ciara's murderer, evidently with two passes of a sharp knife, as he cut her throat. This lock of hair was discovered at Ciara's bush grave, pristine, sitting on her shoulder.

The lopped-off hair was of critical importance to convicting Edwards, Barbagallo said, because it contained two navy blue fibres that matched Cohen's Telstra uniform exactly.

Because the lock had been immediately collected, sealed in a sample jar and recorded in Pipidinny Road in 1997, and the yellow-top jar was never opened until 2018, there was no way the charge of contamination could be levelled against those two fibres.

Reece Powell's nine days in the witness box starkly revealed how important Cohen's old pants had become.

The unique Telstra navy fibres discovered at three crime scenes were common to three women – Lisa, Jane and Ciara –

plus the Holden car driven at the time by Edwards, plus Jeffrey Cohen's hoarded Telstra pants.

Powell said the combination of other fibres found in Jane and Ciara's hair could all have originated only from a Holden Commodore VS Series 1 with the Blue Graphite upholstery set.

Paul Yovich questioned whether random fibres were picked up by both Jane and Ciara before they were murdered. Both had been at the Continental Hotel on their last nights of life. Ciara had thrown her jacket on the floor, and a man had picked it up, tied it around his waist then given it back to her.

This question was one of many answered by the state's fibre expert, Dr Ray Palmer, another world expert called to provide his opinions. He gave video-evidence from Britain in three night-sittings of the court.

It was the last days of April 2020 in the all-but-deserted COVID-quiet city and court building, where bored security guards were eager for case details as the reporters walked through their scanners. This trial was the only show in town.

Dr Palmer had given evidence in famous cases such the Sussex Strangler, who killed five sex workers.

The fibre expert had identified fibres from two bodies that had been in a river for weeks. Jane went undiscovered for fifty-five days, Ciara for nineteen.

Dr Palmer was critical. Video footage showed debris from Jane's hair shaken onto the morgue floor. A lock of her hair was shampooed and the contents not filtered but discarded. Dr Palmer watched people running their hands through the hair of each woman 'with no real consideration of what they're disturbing or what may be lost by doing that'.

He had studied the work of Rees Powell and his team, saying the fibres on the women were indistinguishable from companion fibres found in the car.

'What we have to ask ourselves is what are the chances of finding these specific combinations of fibres … it's a bit like the winning numbers in the lottery,' he said. 'It is highly unlikely they got there by chance.'

Western Australian forensic scientists could not produce such results, Dr Palmer asserted, unless Jane and Ciara had been inside the Edwards' Holden.

Answering questions from Justice Stephen Hall, however, Dr Palmer said it was 'equally likely' that the combination of Telstra navy fibres and fibres from the car could have come from an identical vehicle of the same make and model owned by Telstra. They could also have come from an identical privately owned car driven by a Telstra employee.

Dr Palmer disagreed that the two women could have acquired the common fibres while socialising at the Continental, because of the elapsed time between the two murders.

'That scenario begs credibility,' Dr Palmer said.

If the judge was to accept the DNA and fibre evidence, it was all over for Edwards. In that event, he had to be Jane's and Ciara's murderer. That killer was a Telstra technician, wearing Telstra clothing, driving a Telstra vehicle around Claremont, trying to pick up possibly ten women, and succeeding in murdering three.

Justice Hall signalled that he might consider the 'near miss' young women who had seen Telstra vehicles in the context of the Texan sharpshooter fallacy – a tendency to see unverified patterns.

Ciara's silent evidence carried the most weight. She had scratched this man in one final, desperate act of defiance. The fear she felt that moment is heartbreaking to imagine, but still she gave her survival a red-hot go.

That act nailed Edwards, if the DNA sample, locked in a yellow-top jar at Ciara's autopsy in 1997 and first opened inside the British lab in 2008, remained uncontaminated by the detritus from Edwards' ugly graveyard crimes.

38

Climax

In her closing address, beginning June 9, Carmel Barbagallo said that sex was the driving force for all of Edwards' attacks, including that on the hospital worker. He had a sexual fetish, she said. Edwards had first scoped out the toilets as a hiding place, then acted normally until he could jump the woman from behind and drag her out of sight. He had told a hospital security guard that was his intention.

'He was calculated, methodical and predatory,' the prosecutor said.

The kimono and cemetery attacks had obvious sexual motives, she said. In addition, Jane had been found naked, while Ciara's skirt was torn and pulled up to her waist. Clothing, handbags and shoes had been taken as trophies after the 1996 and 1997 murders. No trace of them was ever found by police.

During Barbagallo's closing address, the prosecution alleged for the first time that Edwards had intended to murder the apparently unconscious Lisa, who may have been able to identify him after he took the bag off her head. Edwards had thrown her twice into bushes because he had been spooked by lights from the car of a cemetery security guard, who had given evidence at the trial, the prosecutor said.

Lisa had played dead, waiting until she could no longer hear Edwards' van before running for help, wearing only her top, her hands tied tightly behind her.

Rather than flee the scene, Edwards had driven off but lurked in the area; a white Telecom van had been spotted nearby by Lisa and hospital security man Wayne Wookey.

'He was coming back for her,' Barbagallo said.

Barbagallo said the assault on Lisa showed a 'fetishistic' sexual propensity that ultimately led to the murders of Sarah, Jane and Ciara. His propensity to attack women who were strangers to him, including in Claremont, was beyond question, she told the judge.

She argued that the judge could boost the likelihood of Edwards' guilt for the murder of Sarah, in the absence of connecting forensic evidence, if he found Edwards guilty of the last two murders and added them to the three crimes Edwards had already admitted.

Justice Hall said the alleged tendency of Edwards to pick up young women and attack them, however strong, will not be enough on its own to prove Sarah's case beyond reasonable doubt. 'There must be something else,' he said.

That something else was provided by Mosman Park witness Wayne Stewart, Barbagallo said. He was one of four people who heard 'blood-curdling screams' within forty-five minutes of Sarah being abducted.

She reminded the court that Stewart, a qualified motor mechanic, described the partial wrap-around concave tail-lights as belonging to a light-coloured station wagon like those of the Toyota Corolla he connected to the screams.

Barbagallo said Edwards, at the time, had been issued with a white Toyota Camry station wagon with similar tail-lights.

The experiences of women who had encountered a roaming Telstra driver made it likely that Sarah had climbed willingly into Edwards' car, and was offered a lift to Mosman Park, the prosecutor said.

It was not reasonable, she said, that more than one culprit was responsible. All three victims were young, of slight build, last seen looking for taxis on the outskirts of Claremont's CBD and had disappeared within a fourteen-month period.

Edwards, she argued, was a liar, a figure who lay in wait in the dark side streets of Cottesloe and Claremont, a sexually motivated attacker.

Justice Hall asked Barbagallo whether she was suggesting that Sarah had told the driver her destination was Mosman Park, which would explain what happened next.

Once there, Edwards did something that caused Sarah to scream, later murdering her by unknown means and disposing of her body in an unknown location, the prosecutor said.

Barbagallo said Edwards was selective. He did not abduct every woman he picked up. The Telstra driver had taken survivors of other incidents towards their destinations. It was reasonable to suppose he was playing for time to calculate whether his passenger was a suitable victim.

'There must have been a point in time when that scenario turns him into making a decision that this is a girl he is going to subdue, abduct and murder.'

In his closing address, Yovich posited that different attackers were involved in the first three crimes versus the last three, the murders. He said there were holes in Wayne Stewart's witness evidence, descriptions of the vehicle that could not be ignored.

The state's case was that Stewart saw a white Toyota Camry station wagon identical to the Telstra car Edwards was driving that night. He heard female screams that he connected to the vehicle, saw two figures near it and heard two car doors slam.

According to Yovich, holes in Stewart's description of the vehicle made it impossible to link the car to Edwards. Justice Hall could not be asked to fix up the evidence to make it fit the state's case, he said. 'He [Stewart] can't even say if the screams were associated with the car.'

'Clear differences in behaviour' existed between the three attacks Edwards had admitted to and the three murders he denied, Yovich said in his client's defence. Edwards had abducted but not murdered Lisa.

'If he had wanted to kill her, she would be dead,' Yovich said.

The three women who were blitz-attacked all lived to tell the tale. The three who had apparently got into vehicles voluntarily were murdered.

'The murders are fundamentally different,' Yovich said. The lack of evidence of sexual assault also weakens the murder accusations against his client, he argued.

Pathologist Martin Blooms had given evidence saying that, because of the length of time the two murder victims' bodies went undiscovered, he was unable to say whether or not sexual assault had occurred.

Yovich disputed that the three murders were sexually motivated, as the Karrakatta abduction clearly was. That Edwards was the type of person who was likely to have committed all six crimes, the propensity case, was weakened because of the absence of evidence of sexual interference in the three murder victims.

*

During the trial, the editor of the *Post* did what no court reporter should do – speculated in print on the evidence mid-trial, even though this argument had not been raised in court. There was no jury to influence and judges are immune from outside influence.

In a front-page report published December 21, 2019, he wrote that Sarah, Jane and Ciara may have been victims of a sexually motivated attack, which was not completed because all three women screamed. Of the other three, two had been gagged and the other played dead.

On the last day of the trial, the judge pointed out that Edwards had removed Lisa's gag from her mouth during his attack, but that Lisa did not take the opportunity to scream.

Justice Hall suggested the killer of Sarah, Jane and Ciara may have treated them differently to Lisa, because they responded to him in different ways. He said differences in responses of victims could affect the weight he gave to the propensity evidence.

*

The evidence phase of the trial had wrapped up on May 6, 2020, nearly six months after the trial had begun.

In her closing statement, Carmel Barbagallo transported Court 7.2 back in time twenty-five years, to the still-vivid era when Claremont was gripped by fear.

'The greatest terror created by these offences was due to the great unknown,' she told a hushed court, calling it 'the enigma of the dark'.

The normal behaviour of young women socialising in the safe, affluent suburb of Claremont met with an abnormal force that abducted, terrorised and attacked young women walking alone, wilfully murdering three of them, the state prosecutor said.

'Bradley Robert Edwards is the Claremont serial killer,' were Barbagallo's final words in summing up her case, near the end of a trial spanning seven months. Both a summer and winter solstice came and went during the trial. Edwards, sitting stolidly in the dock between two guards, had marked his fifty-first birthday there on December 7, 2019, two weeks after the fight to save him from a lifetime behind bars began.

The evidence the state presented was formidable proof, Barbagallo said. It established the truth about what had happened.

Justice Hall told Edwards to stand in the dock. He asked the accused man if he wished to give evidence on his own behalf, a question usually answered via lawyers. The judge said that, because of the importance of the case, he wanted to hear the answer directly from Edwards.

'No,' Edwards replied. His decision to say nothing was expected. If he was to give evidence, he would expose himself to intense cross-examination. He did not have to prove anything.

Edwards' immovable expression changed when Yovich attacked the state's case over three days, beginning on June 22. His client sat up straight, looking interested and engaged.

Paul Yovich offered no witnesses for the defence, no scientific experts and no alibi evidence, although the possibility of an alibi had been raised months before the trial proper. Yovich said that his client was at a disadvantage, having been arrested so long after Ciara's murder; he was unable to remember what he was doing that night to provide an alibi. Yovich did not suggest anyone else who might have committed the crimes, but disputed that the case against his client had been proved beyond reasonable doubt.

Edwards' defence was that it simply was not him. He says he didn't do it, Yovich had told a preliminary hearing.

Suddenly, on the afternoon of Thursday, June 25, 2020, it was all over. Justice Hall adjourned the court for three months. Before this judge lay the mammoth task of deciding the guilt or innocence of the accused man on each murder charge, and justifying each step of his reasoning in writing. That is a burden juries do not carry. In fact, by law, juries are forbidden from disclosing what went on in the jury room.

*

A person on the prosecution side had told the *Post* that the size of the case and list of potential prosecution witnesses was so huge, the list had to be reduced to the central issues. 'There is only so much evidence we can present.' That had left unexplored puzzles.

The trial ended without discovering whether police believed the teenage Baron Way Bridge masturbator, reported to police by Glenys Newport in 1985, was connected to the accused man, then aged sixteen. The incident had happened near Huntingdale, one of many similar reports, police told Newport. That young offender was tall, dark-haired and wore glasses.

There was a series of reported prowling and home invasions by a man wearing women's sleepwear, including underpants on his head, about the time of the Huntingdale attack in the 1980s, the judge had said.

What of Ciara's underpants found on her gravestone three years after her death?

A cryptic mention of the bizarre incident was made in court, but any inclusion of it in the case was shut down immediately by an objection from prosecution lawyer Bradley Hollingsworth. 'It is highly irrelevant,' he had said.

A New Zealand scientist had confirmed that Ciara's DNA and possible male DNA were detected on the handed-in garment in 2003, in what looked like hot leads in the serial killings case.

So who put them on Ciara's gravestone and why? An underwear fetishist? An over-confident murderer? Both? Police concluded they had been left on the grave by Ciara's murderer, but this did not gel with what they knew about the movements of Lance Williams, on whom they were fixated at that time.

*

Some trial moments linger in memory, not all of them headline-grabbing. During the long days of evidence, a vignette from seemingly routine evidence suddenly jolts the courtroom to attention.

Court 7.2 froze when a colour photograph of Ciara's badly blood-stained T-shirt suddenly appeared on the big monitor screens. It had been white, ringed with pink flowers.

Sleep specialist Jack Philpott gave evidence on December 3, 2019. He had examined Edwards at Sir Charles Gairdiner Hospital for sleep apnoea early in 1997, a short time before the murder of Ciara that March. Edwards told Dr Philpott that he had separated from his wife eleven months earlier and had been drinking about a bottle of spirits a week.

The doctor had weighed in his patient at 92 kilograms. He was 185.5 centimetres tall.

'Those poor girls' was a remark often overheard on the streets of Claremont in the frought years after the mid-1990s.

Those poor girls indeed. Sarah was just 160 centimetres, Jane was 170 centimetres, and Ciara was 45 kilograms and 152 centimetres tall.

39

Judgment Day

In 4 a.m. darkness, a jumble of citizens anxious to see justice done thronged the entrance of 500 Hay Street, Perth, in a line that zigzagged around the disabled access ramp then up Irwin Street. Doors would not open until 8:30 a.m. on this long-anticipated day – Thursday, September 24, 2020.

At 9:16 a.m., inside Court 7.2, two raps on the judge's door heralded the arrival of Justice Stephen Hall.

At the back of the courtroom, one side of the public gallery was packed with the survivors of Edwards' crimes, plus relatives of the murder victims and their Cold Case Murder Squad shadows. Chris Dawson, now the commissioner of police, took his seat among them. Bruce and Kaye, Edwards' grim-faced parents, sat holding hands on the opposite side of the gallery.

Their son was brought in, wearing a dark jacket over his checked shirt and tie, dark trousers and, incongruously, thongs on his otherwise bare feet. He sat stony-faced as usual, staring straight ahead, never looking at the corner of pain or at his parents.

The judge wasted no time in starting a short summary of his massive 619-page judgment.

'This is a trial like no other. This is a trial like every other. These apparently irreconcilable statements are both true.

'The events in question occurred more than twenty years ago but have haunted the memory of many people and troubled the public conscience.' The disappearances of three young women 'inspired a real and pervasive sense of fear', he said. But the fundamental principles that apply to every criminal trial apply to this one, he added. The accused is presumed innocent. The State bore the onus of proof beyond reasonable doubt.

Forensic evidence was strongest in respect to Ciara Glennon, the judge said. There was some in the case of Jane Rimmer, but none for Sarah Spiers.

Similarities existed in the disappearances of Jane and Ciara – their age and appearance, their connection to Claremont nightlife, the locations of their bodies and how those bodies were left. Both had fibres from a VS Holden Commodore car used by a Telstra employee.

'Those similarities establish beyond reasonable doubt that the same person killed both Ms Rimmer and Ms Glennon,' Justice Hall said.

'The DNA evidence was critical to the prosecution case. I am satisfied that the evidence establishes beyond reasonable doubt that the DNA of the accused was under the nails of Ms Glennon's left hand, and that it got there in the course of a violent struggle that occurred some time shortly before her death.'

He said he relied on Lisa's case, but not the Huntingdale or Hollywood Hospital attacks, to establish that Edwards had a tendency to violently abduct and attack young women from the Claremont area. Those first two attacks were too dissimilar from the abductions, he said.

The judge's words that followed caused Edwards to look more animated than he ever had before in that courtroom. He shook his head three or four times, as Justice Hall announced he was satisfied beyond reasonable doubt that Edwards was the killer of Jane and Ciara, and that he had intended to kill them.

The judge said that, after driving Jane to Wellard, Jane was able to scream but Edwards had attacked her with a knife or sharp object. She tried to fight him off but Edwards caused fatal injuries to her neck. He removed her clothing and concealed her body, taking or concealing her clothes.

That attack was sexually motivated, the judge said.

Ciara was walking home when Edwards, again driving his work vehicle, used it to drive her from the area. How he managed to get her into his car is not known, the judge said.

At some point, there was a violent struggle in which Ciara scratched or clawed DNA from Edwards, who again had a knife or sharp object. In trying to fend off Edwards, Ciara received defensive injuries to her arm. With intent to kill, Edwards had caused one or more fatal injuries to her neck. Given the blood-soak patterns, this probably occurred at Eglinton, where Edwards concealed her body.

Turning to the case of Sarah Spiers, Justice Hall said there were some similarities with Jane and Ciara. All were young women abducted and killed after nights out in Claremont over a fourteen-month period.

But the similarities in Sarah's case were far fewer and more general. Inconsistencies in the Mosman Park scream evidence and the differences to Lisa's case left only the evidence that showed an offender's pattern of behaviour, the propensity evidence, to connect Jane's murder to the other two murders. It was not enough.

Don and Carol Spiers, sitting in the front row of the public gallery, looked puzzled, then ashen-faced. Grief at their inability to bury their daughter, to finally farewell her, was hammered home by the judge's next words:

'The propensity evidence makes it more likely that [Edwards] was the killer of Ms Spiers, but it cannot prove it beyond reasonable doubt in the absence of any other evidence as to the identity of her killer.'

Justice Hall told Edwards to stand while he formally pronounced his verdicts. Edwards now looked in the direction of the judge.

To the wilful murder of Sarah Spiers, not guilty.

To the wilful murder of Jane Rimmer, guilty. Edwards' head dropped for an instant, his chin almost on his chest.

To the wilful murder of Ciara Glennon, guilty.

The courtroom was deathly quiet. Loud cheering erupted inside Court 7.1 at the other end of the corridor, where overflow members of the public were watching proceedings on monitors.

The judge told Edwards he would be sentenced on Christmas Eve, or the day before. An application for a 'Never to be released' order was being considered, chimed in prosecutor Carmel Barbagallo.

The judge ordered the guilty man to be taken away.

Guards ushered Edwards towards the doorway behind him. As he turned, his expression blank, he could see his parents but did not appear to acknowledge them.

Barbagallo strode to the back of the court and hugged Don and Carol Spiers. Lisa stood, her eyes glistening with tears.

Chris Dawson went up and down the lines, talking to and comforting survivors and the Spiers, Glennon and Rimmer family members.

A massive media contingent and others waited outside at the court steps. Carmel Barbagallo and her team were greeted with applause.

To one side of the courthouse, at the base of a steep driveway, Edwards flip-flopped his way into the white prison van for his journey back to Casuarina Prison, which would be his home for a very long time, possibly for the rest of his life.

*

News spread across the city, the country and the world. Within hours of the verdicts, a second spontaneous shrine to the murdered young women sprang up on the steps of the COVID-closed Claremont Hotel, formerly the Continental.

One mourner jammed a bunch of roses into the handle of the corner door that Ciara had last exited. Jon Sainken arrived to add the fourteenth bouquet to a growing line of flowers below.

By Sunday, the number of floral tributes had grown to ninety-two.

Clutching flowers, Dr Sainken sobbed on the steps of the hotel as he welcomed Edwards' conviction, then spilled out twenty-five years of pent-up emotion for the 'ghastly' events that pervaded Claremont.

'We always felt terribly bad about it. This series of events ruined many lives, and ours were only a small portion of that and the effect it had – on families, friends, relatives, schoolmates. These were beautiful girls. It should never have happened.'

He lamented that the not-guilty verdict for Sarah's murder greatly reduced the chances of an 'extremely cruel' murderer giving up the location of Sarah's body, if he was her killer.

'I don't think Bradley Edwards is capable of humanity. Either because he's a brute – but I actually think he's probably suppressed the memory of what he's done and doesn't know himself. But that's not an excuse, it's a horrible thing, and cowardly.'

He said all of Claremont had grieved alongside the families, 'but we couldn't provide any useful solace. What could you say or do that would make anybody any easier?

'Certainly, we as the operators of the venues couldn't – you know, we felt bad about it. We knew that we didn't bear responsibility but we were still associated.'

*

With time to digest it, Justice Hall's long, clearly argued judgment offered few surprises given the way his verdicts fell.

He refuted the possibility that the crucial DNA sample had been contaminated.

He devoted more than one hundred pages to analysis of those arguments, with Dr Jonathan Whitaker emerging as a central witness in the trial.

'His evidence was clear, cogent and compelling,' the judge said. 'The methodology he used was well explained.

'The only rational explanation for the presence of the DNA at that time is that it was deposited under the nails of Ms Glennon as she fought against her attacker shortly before her death.'

The judge also accepted the fibre evidence that pointed to a Telstra technician habitually driving a VS Holden Commodore, evidence that linked Ciara's death to Jane's, but did not directly point to Edwards. It is clear that, without the DNA found under Ciara's nails, Edwards would not have been convicted.

Strengthening the Ciara–Jane link was the Burger Boys, childhood friends and truck drivers who came within seconds of witnessing the moment of Ciara's abduction, and whose evidence, the judge said, was convincing and reliable. Troy Bond and Brandon Gray had described Ciara and the white Holden station wagon in detail, and the events that had unfolded in front of them as they sat at the bus stop. It was likely Ciara was taken from the area in the car they saw, the judge said.

But no such strong witness evidence to the abduction of Sarah was available to add to the propensity evidence provided by Edwards' proven murder of Jane and Ciara.

Mosman Park witnesses who heard 'blood-curdling' screams after Sarah was abducted, or saw a car like the one issued to Edwards at the time, did not present a consistent picture, the judge said.

Carmel Barbagallo had said local mechanic Wayne Stewart was critical to identifying Edwards as Sarah's murderer. The judge said Stewart's description of the station wagon he saw was not enough to support the conclusion that it was Edwards' car. The car and screams might be unrelated, the judge said. The car parked near the phone booth, and the sounds of two car doors closing could have had an innocent explanation. The scream evidence of the various witnesses 'does not point clearly to Ms Spiers being the source of the screams'.

It was impossible to say how Sarah was abducted and killed, given the available evidence, the judge said.

However, the propensity evidence made it more likely that Edwards was Sarah's killer, in the absence of any other evidence of her killer's identity. Propensity evidence included the Rowe Park and cemetery crimes against Lisa, which had features in common to the murder counts, the judge said. They were planned, not a momentary lapse of judgment, with Edwards equipping himself with a hood, gag and cord; selecting an evidently vulnerable young, Caucasian victim unknown to him; and the attack continuing over an extended period.

But Justice Hall shot down the relevance of the parade of women who, walking from Claremont and Cottesloe venues as teens or twenty-somethings, had seen or been offered early morning lifts in vehicles, many with Telstra markings. He said it was impossible to conclude whether the drivers were all the same man, let alone whether that man was Edwards. This was because of the effects of alcohol, the darkness, the lack of distinctive features of the drivers, the brevity of the encounters and the loss of memory over time, along with other factors.

Simply because all the sightings were in the same area did not connect them to the three murders, he said.

'Beguiling' was how Justice Hall described the amazing coincidence of an open Telstra knife being found by horse riders in Woolcoot Road on the same day Jane's body was discovered, along with Edwards' connection to Telstra.

However, the judge said, there was no evidence that the knife was the murder weapon used on Jane. It was possible that it had been left by another Telstra employee and impossible for the judge to conclude that it had been dropped by Edwards.

His judgment invited speculation about information the public may have volunteered to police, had Macro shared the news of the discovery of the Telstra knife, even if it was unconnected to the crime. The same applied to witnesses sighting or being offered lifts around Claremont late at night by a man cruising in a Telstra vehicle.

*

'The Claremont killings struck at the heart of our way of life stretching back almost a quarter of a century,' Chris Dawson said on the steps of the court an hour after the verdict. Police would never give up trying to find Sarah's body or her killer. 'Sarah and her family deserve justice.'

The morning after the verdict, Denis Glennon fronted the cameras, paying tribute to Ciara's 'great courage and spirit'. Although Ciara's family was not permitted to view her body because 'her wounds and injuries were too gruesome,' he had read the autopsy report and viewed photographs of his daughter's neck wounds.

'For twenty-three years, I have lived with those images,' Denis Glennon said.

His special trust-based relationship with the Western Australian police force 'permitted me to enter their world. They allowed me to assist wherever I believed I could and answered requests for information, no matter how hard to bear,' he said.

The force was willing to break with orthodoxy and explore new avenues for answers. He had no criticism for police, including for their honest mistakes.

But there were countless heartbreaking setbacks, he said, most triggered by dramatic headlines and subjective media reports containing selective information, reports that inflicted needless suffering on his family. Other journalists displayed acumen and wisdom, producing sensitive, balanced reports, he added.

In contrast, that same day, Peter Weygers called for a formal inquiry into the police investigation. It had ruined three lives – those of Lance William, Steven Ross and his own, he said. 'It brings me to tears when I think about what they did to us so publicly.'

He blamed his own health problems and those of Lance Williams on their pursuit by police. Williams was a good citizen, a quiet hard-working public servant, looking out for the welfare of young women walking home from Claremont. He had delivered the decoy policewoman safely to her destination.

'If Lance had picked up Ciara Glennon that night, she would still be alive,' Weygers said.

Ciara's father preferred to speak about his daughter's tenacity. He recalled that, in 1997, while Ciara was missing, he appealed to the public through tears for help in finding her.

'I said, because of the way she was brought up, she would fight for her life. Little did I know how prophetic those words would be. But as she fought to save her life, she could not save herself.'

Edwards took Ciara's life, but she took something from him, something that enabled Chris Dawson to stand outside the court that had just convicted Edwards and pronounce: 'Bradley Edwards can now be called for what he is: a brutal rapist and murderer.'

40
Unforgiven

Before he learned his punishment, Bradley Edwards sweated in his cell for three months at Casuarina Prison, just six kilometres from where he had disposed of Jane Rimmer's body.

He was being housed in the protective custody section of the jail, and had been there since, in a fit of despair, he had stabbed himself in the ear with a pencil just before a preliminary court appearance back in February 2019. Life in 'protection', which restricted contact with fellow prisoners, was even more unpleasant than in the general jail. Each day, a guard escorted Edwards from his cell to a yard where he would pace in solitude.

As he counted down the days to when he would discover his fate, he knew he did not face execution. Western Australia had belatedly abolished the death penalty in 1984, the last Australian state to do so. The next, rarely used nuclear option was to lock up Edwards and throw away the key – a life sentence without parole, and without hope.

Early in the morning of Wednesday, December 23, 2020, exactly four years since Edwards' dramatic arrest in 2016, the big white prison van left for the long trip to the District Court holding cells.

Soon he was confronted across a few metres of courtroom by the hard stare of the woman he had last spoken to twenty-five years earlier, when he had spat the words 'shut up' at the then terrified seventeen-year-old stranger. That was just after he had thrown her to the ground in Rowe Park, Claremont, and bundled her into a vehicle for that vile encounter at

Karrakatta Cemetery, which she described that morning twenty-five years later as 'the worst night of my life'.

But now in court, everyone present felt the power balance shift. Lisa visibly regained her strength.

She directly addressed her tormentor: 'I will leave this behind ... and finally go and live my life ...

'I will live, and you won't.

'As one of the victims of your crimes, I hope you are treated as well in prison as you have treated us.'

Edwards stared back impassively.

His parents, Bruce and Kaye Edwards, holding hands in the public gallery to his left, looked ashen-faced. At times during the trial, they could be heard sighing in disbelief as witnesses gave evidence against their son. It was only when, in a video interview with police, Edwards said, 'I just want to go to sleep and for all this to have been a bad dream,' that Kaye buried her head in her hands and wept along with her son weeping on the video replay.

Now parents and son together endured Lisa reading her searing victim impact statement aloud from the witness box, free at last to speak her truth in public.

She spoke up, she said, not just for herself, but to honour Edwards' victims who could no longer speak for themselves.

'I will find joy knowing you are to be locked behind bars, without freedom, without choice, suffering for the rest of your life inside your own crippled mind,' she growled at Edwards.

Lisa provided to the hushed courtroom a glimpse into how that summer night back in 1995 had permeated her entire adult life.

'You don't ever recover from sexual assault; it is a life sentence … It was a night of so much terror and so much pain, it is hard to know where to begin.'

She said she had struggled to sleep and eat, lost clumps of hair and endured twenty-five years of paralysing anxiety. 'I'll never be able to truly convey the impact of being captured and deprived of my liberty.'

Bound, gagged and hooded, thrust into the back of Edwards' Telecom van, she had known instantly that she was in very real danger. 'By the time I was in his vehicle, I was picturing my own gravesite … Then I actually had to survive.'

Afterwards, learning how to trust people again was an Everest to climb, always made worse by the pain she saw etched on the faces of her family and friends. 'So much is taken from you so quickly … your dignity, your security … my home … If you actually want to know what it feels like to experience all of this pain, your Honour, it is lonely – deep, gut-wrenching loneliness that literally no-one else can understand because your experience is solitary.'

Claremont was all she knew – it was where she had worked four part-time jobs, shopped, socialised, learned to drive and lived with her family. '[Claremont] was my complete childhood. It was where I felt safe,' she said. 'After that night it all [became] different … Sexual assault makes you feel like not only are you unsafe but you also don't belong like you did before … Until you learn to fight again.'

That fight was made more difficult because of the need to relive that night repeatedly in multiple police interviews and statements for the court. She spoke of having to suffer through medical tests, the interrogation, the legal meetings and Edwards' harrowing trial.

Adding to her trauma was her discovery years after her attack in 1995 that her assailant had gone on to commit murders. Lisa recalled that, during the trial, she had to endure listening to the judge and a lawyer coolly speculate on whether Bradley had intended to murder her that long-ago night.

All this she had to suffer because Edwards was too gutless to own up, she said.

Yet in spite of the crime and its legacy, she told Edwards that she had made a choice that her ordeals would not define her. 'It is not the measure of who I am,' she said.

She had faced a choice between letting the event control her, or choosing to spend each day fighting to get her life back, as she had done. She learned she could survive and thrive. 'There is a power to that,' she said.

She relished her victory over Edwards, noting that she and her family never spoke the perpetrator's name. 'We used to refer to him as "the monster"; however, since his capture I have realised he is not a monster at all, rather the definition of a coward. He preyed on weak and vulnerable women … How pathetic.'

Understandably, she could not find it in herself to forgive Edwards. 'Far more resolved people than I will find the courage and foresight to forgive … I have the utmost respect for that kind of bravery and compassion. I, however, will never offer forgiveness and I am completely at peace with that.'

She resolved to finally put the horrific events of that night behind her. 'The … pain, for me, can stop now … I will leave this courtroom and finally go and live my life without you in it. I will live it joyously, respectfully and gratefully for myself, my family and for the lives that were lost.'

*

Another brave witness took the courtroom back to another terrible night, this time in Huntingdale in 1988, when Edwards broke into the bedroom of a sleeping eighteen-year-old acquaintance. The unshaven Edwards had left his DNA on a stolen kimono, the clue that twenty-eight years later sealed his fate by linking him to his crimes against Lisa and Ciara.

This witness revealed she had lived with a lifelong abhorrence of men's facial hair after Edwards had straddled her in bed, attempting to gag her.

Like Lisa, she held back tears at times, while reading her statement to an aghast courtroom. 'I'm okay when I'm awake – it's when I'm asleep that I'm scared. Every night of my life I fall asleep with the fear someone might attack me, and I've been that way for twenty-eight years. Then there are the dreams.'

In those dreams she would be trying to get away, but found she was always breathless and trapped. Upon waking, she'd look frantically to see if her attacker was still there.

She has never been able to sleep alone in her house since the offence.

Her dreams changed when Edwards was arrested in 2016, and she could finally put a face to her attacker. 'Bradley Robert Edwards features as the villain of my nightmares and I can't make it stop,' she said. 'This trial has exposed one of the worst moments of my life to the whole world. I now go weeks without speaking to my friends and family … I feel like I have a label on my forehead with "Huntingdale Victim" tattooed there.'

She still hates to be touched and has never been able to embrace her children and her husband affectionately. The anxiety and panic attacks had also transmitted to her children, causing intergenerational trauma.

The worst day of the trial, she said, was the second-last one of the prosecution's case, during which Edwards' post-arrest interview was played. On video, a photograph of her childhood bedroom was placed before Edwards by Detective Sergeant Joe Marrapodi – the man who arrested Edwards and was a constant presence at his trial. She felt Edwards was invading her bedroom all over again.

'I wanted to scream, "Stop, Joe, stop – don't let him in there."'

'At times it has made me feel guilty for being alive, and guilty for not helping police stop Edwards.'

*

Who really was this man, the source of such misery? The doting stepfather, the accomplished technician, the Little Athletics coach and awarded community volunteer?

'Not an evil genius,' said Lisa. Edwards had 'slipped through the cracks because he is so unremarkable'.

But that is not the full story.

Much is known about the minds of multiple killers because their extensive jailhouse interviews with psychiatrists are usually made public.

But Edwards, while admitting to being a rapist, continues to deny he is a murderer. He refused to submit to psychological interviews for this trial, depriving Justice Stephen Hall of psychological reports to consider when sentencing.

Only occasional signs of his evil subterranean life burst through his calm surface.

State prosecutor Carmel Barbagallo described him to the judge this way: 'A socially awkward teenager with a fetish for wearing – and stealing – women's underwear, which, as he grew older, evolved into an obsessive sexual interest in the abduction, imprisonment and forcible rape of women.'

Insights into Edwards were caught by surviving victims. They revealed a big man who went to water when his slight female victims fought back – until the first night he armed himself.

He leapt off the sleeping Huntingdale teen when she awoke and called her father for help.

At Hollywood Hospital, two years later, he relaxed his grip on Wendy Davis when she lashed out hard with her foot, kicking Edwards in the leg, causing Wendy to fall backwards.

'He was just standing there silent. I saw a lost, blank look in his dark, molten eyes,' she wrote in her book, *Don't Make a Fuss,* about her attack by Edwards and its devastating aftermath. She thought he was crying.

She wrote that Edwards had at the time admitted his intention to abduct her, but he did not face that charge. '"The system" valued a man's career and wellbeing over a woman's right to safety,' she said.

She believes that, had she made a fuss, the courts might have dealt more harshly with Edwards at the time, but he 'went unchecked, and he was able to go on to become the Claremont serial killer'.

*

By the end of his sentencing hearing, Bradley Robert Edwards would have had to have been delusional to expect mercy from the judge, who had sat through his trial and absorbed those gut-wrenching victim impact statements.

A published poet, Justice Hall chose his words carefully when he addressed Edwards, facing him directly.

He called Edwards 'pitiless and remorseless'.

He said that when Edwards had attacked Jane Rimmer with a sharp weapon in 1996, he had intended to kill her. Jane's large and gaping wound to the neck and shoulder was evidence she had tried to defend herself. 'She screamed, but you were not deterred, and killed her. She died fighting for her life.'

He remarked on Edwards' attempt to hide his terrible deed. 'You made an effort to conceal Ms Rimmer's body to ensure any connection with you [and this crime] would not be discovered. Her family had to suffer the ordeal of not knowing what happened to her.'

He cited evidence of premeditation. 'You went to that area [Claremont] knowing there was likely to be vulnerable and intoxicated young women. [Jane's] vulnerability must have been obvious to you; indeed, it must have been what attracted you.

'I am satisfied that the killing was sexually motivated,' he said, citing Jane's age, gender, her absence of clothing when her body was discovered, and Edwards' prior history.

He said Edwards had also intended to kill Ciara Glennon when he'd attacked her in 1997. Ciara had also fought for her life, managing to scratch and gouge Edwards' skin. 'Whatever method was used, you were able to subdue her,' the judge said.

He pointed out that Edwards' life of crime began with the Huntingdale home invasion. 'Your behaviour in 1988 was not a youthful aberration. You cannot be considered a man of prior good character.'

He noted that, during the trial, Edwards had appeared stoic. 'You maintained a calm demeanour throughout the trial. This ability to dissimulate ... may explain how you went on to lead such an overtly unremarkable life. Under the cover of ordinariness, you were committing a series of increasingly serious offences.'

Turning to the murder victims' families, who Justice Hall noted had attended most of the trial, the judge called the circumstances 'an unspeakable tragedy'.

He told the Glennon family that he understood why they did not want to make a victim impact statement. It did not mean they were any less devastated by what Edwards had done. 'No parent wants to outlive their children. Every detail of the life of your beloved child was examined and reported on. Take the cherished memories of your child back to a quiet and private place.'

Turning back to Edwards, the judge spelled out some of the wreckage his murders had caused.

'They were both young women with family and friends who loved them,' he said. 'They had much to live for, such as successful careers, marriage and children of their own. You robbed them of their lives, their hopes, their dreams and the dreams of others for them. When seen as a whole, [the offences] show you were a dangerous predator who sought out vulnerable young women for your own personal gratification. Your actions were premeditated, executed with pitiless determination; [you were] remorseless in the pain and suffering you caused.'

The judge weighed up the options the law permitted him when setting sentences, comparing these cases to other sickening murders where non-parole sentences had been handed out. Edwards' crimes were not extreme enough for a life sentence without parole, he said.

Justice Hall sentenced Edwards to four years for the Huntingdale home invasion and two deprivation of liberty offences, plus twelve years for each of the rape offences, to which Edwards had eventually pleaded guilty. The judge said he deserved little discount for his late guilty pleas, because they appeared to be tactical moves to show the court he was 'a rapist, not a murderer'.

For the murders of Jane Rimmer and Ciara Glennon, Edwards was sentenced to a life term for each offence, with forty years to be served before being eligible for parole. All sentences would be served at the same time, not added together as often happens in the US.

Having already served four years in jail since his arrest, Bradley Robert Edwards, then aged fifty-two, will rot in jail at least until the age of eighty-eight.

Loud applause erupted from the victims' families, Edwards' survivors and their supporters as they absorbed this news.

'There is a high likelihood that you die in prison. You have had the undeserved benefit of your liberty for many years,' Edwards heard the judge say before being taken back to jail, with a glance towards his parents as he left the dock.

After everyone had filed outside, Police Commissioner Chris Dawson told the waiting media pack that Edwards was 'evil'. He added that the police would never stop until they had brought Sarah Spiers' killer to justice.

As the Rimmer and Glennon families left the courtroom steps for the last time, Dawson reported that they had told him they believed Edwards had received a just sentence, before adding, 'But it will never replace their loved ones.'

Edwards did not lodge an appeal against his conviction or sentence, the state-funded Legal Aid Commission having, on December 1, 2020, refused him further legal aid to conduct an appeal.

Afterword

One disturbing police theory, not aired in court, was that Edwards toyed with his victims, that he played cat and mouse.

Edwards' strange behaviour at the cemetery supports this. He removed Lisa's gag and twice dumped her in the bushes, then stood back, the first time appearing to leave.

Jane and Ciara were restrained in some way in the car. Hog-tied, just as Lisa had been? One of Jane's wrists showed binding marks. Did Edwards take his victims to remote places, untie their wrists to see how they would react, knowing he would physically dominate them, this time armed with a knife?

Both young women suffered defence wounds to their forearms.

Ciara was killed where she fell, thirty metres from where a car could be parked. Did she escape, running into the dark scrub, to be chased and eventually caught by Edwards, Ciara turning to face him and fight? This repellent scenario could only be confirmed or denied by Edwards himself.

While he continues to deny the charges, we will probably never know.

*

Two men deeply affected by Edwards' crimes died after he was arrested, but before he went on trial.

Steven Ross, who had developed diabetes in his forties, was due for one of his many doctors' appointments at 9 a.m. on Friday, September 15, 2017. One leg had been amputated; his remaining foot, also affected by diabetes, needed dressing. Frequent visits to hospital saw fluid drained from his lungs, and he complained that his eyesight had become so bad he could not read his street directory, although he continued to load and drive his taxi truck, balancing on his artificial leg.

He lived alone and continued to stress about the non-release of his taxi records for the night Sarah Spiers vanished, convinced he would eventually be blamed and be unable to prove his innocence. Ross was a frequent visitor to the editor at the *Post*, usually after appointments at the nearby hospital. He appeared desperately lonely, and often obsessed about coming under more police attention.

On this day, Ross had arranged to help Peter Weygers move furniture. When his always-punctual driver did not turn up, Weygers contacted Ross's doctor. He learned that Steven Ross had died that morning, aged sixty.

His neighbours in Ramsdale Street, Doubleview, said Ross had walked out of his home unit as usual at about 6:30 a.m., climbing into his truck parked in his driveway. Soon afterwards, a man walking past noticed Steven slumped with his head on the steering wheel. The good Samaritan tried unsuccessfully to revive the driver while neighbours called an ambulance.

Despite his cavalier front, Steven Ross had felt the sting of suspicion deeply, the trauma of street take-downs by police, and the false accusations by detectives that he was homosexual and a catcher of girls for Peter Weygers.

He was a hardworking man, desperate to connect with members of his fractured family, a simple soul who took pride in his taxi career, bewildered that, after he offered police his help, he was rewarded by being named a person of interest.

Steven Geoffrey Ross was cremated at Karrakatta Cemetery.

*

Just months before Ross died, police had announced that they planned to stop using the term 'person of interest', instead substituting the description 'suspect' for all suspects.

Confusion brought on by the poorly defined terms 'person of interest' and 'suspect' had caused much aggravation among Macro and Special Crime Squad detectives. It even affected the priority that investigators allocated avenues of investigation, and affected how the public saw people who had come to the attention of police. Lance Williams appeared to morph almost casually from a person of interest into a suspect and back again in police statements to the media. As Peter Weygers had so tartly pointed out many years earlier, however, the public did not make any distinction.

Lance Williams, that long-suffering suspect, died five months after Ross. In February 2018, a government office worker, who had worked with Williams, called radio 6PR presenter Simon Beaumont to break the news.

By the time their son had fallen ill, Jim and Norma Williams had moved from Eric Street. They were shocked by the rapid decline in his health.

'He had bowel cancer and had been suffering for quite a while,' Norma told the *Post*'s David Cohen.

Williams overcame his reluctance to see a doctor and was immediately admitted to hospital. The cancer had spread to his liver. 'He looked to be in terrible pain,' Norma said.

Lance Kenneth Williams died of a massive heart attack at 5:57 a.m. on Friday, February 2, 2018, aged sixty, like Steven Ross. His remains were interred in the garden of remembrance at Karrakatta Cemetery.

Williams had worked for the Main Roads Department for about thirty years, quitting work because of ill health the previous November. 'His passing away was his retirement,' mourned Norma.

For many years, he stayed at home from the end of each working week on Friday night until he went to work again on Monday morning. 'He was always good-natured, quiet and introverted,' said Norma.

Peter Weygers, wearing his psychology researcher's hat, was convinced that intense police scrutiny was a big contributor to Lance Williams' death through post-traumatic stress disorder.

'All the world's experts on PTSD say it doesn't just affect the mind, it takes its toll on the body, too,' said Weygers. It's obviously taken its toll on poor old Lance's body and it's taken its toll on mine.'

More recent research indicates that physical symptoms appear ten years after the first bout of PTSD.

'The body keeps the score,' Weygers said.

Weygers himself had suffered a heart attack while under surveillance, then underwent three emergency heart surgeries. Neither Williams nor Weygers received apologies nor compensation for the trauma they suffered.

Norma, however, disagreed with Weygers' assessment. She said that she did not think the constant and obvious police surveillance had contributed to her son's death. Lance Williams had said, on several occasions, that police had a job to do and he was prepared to co-operate because he had not murdered anyone.

Jim Williams had not forgotten the family's encounters with detectives. One name stuck in his mind. 'The softest part of David Caporn was his teeth,' he told David Cohen in 2018.

By the time of Lance William's death, John Quigley, the lawyer who had been central in the fight to exonerate Andrew Mallard, had been appointed the state's attorney-general. While in opposition, he was adamant that Lance Williams should be compensated after revelations that DNA tests had cleared him. At the time of writing, compensation is yet to come.

*

Four men had collaborated on identifying Edwards' DNA under Ciara's thumbnail: Dr Jonathan Whitaker, Andrew Talbot, George Paton and Jim Stanbury. After the British government closed the Forensic Science Service in 2012, Dr Whitaker became a private consultant and his international scientific reputation continues to grow. Andrew Talbot, the scientist who extracted Edwards' DNA at the Trident Court lab, became a postman in far north Scotland. Special Crime Squad's George Paton is a senior sergeant at the State Operations Command Centre. His co-worker Jim Stanbury is a detective senior sergeant in charge of a suburban detectives' office. Both visited the murder trial after they had given evidence, to closely observe Edwards.

Wendy Davis left the state and divorced five years after Edwards attacked her at Hollywood Hospital. She was writing a book about her interaction with Edwards, the effect of it, and on her life and her experience with the criminal justice system. 'Without a doubt it impacted my life, but it did not define me,' she said. 'With some validation from the Western Australian judicial system and some counselling, I am starting to let it all go.'

Three days after she told her story on television, Wendy received a call from a senior lawyer at Telstra, who told her an apology was being sent.

'Telstra's response at the time let you down and we are very sorry for that,' said Alex Badenoch, the telco's group executive for transformation, communications and people.

'It is clear that we didn't respond in the way we should have or would today,' she said, noting Telstra's anguish about what one of its employees had done.

'We recognise the enormous harm and grief that many people have experienced due to the dreadful acts committed by Bradley Edwards.'

Telstra said the time that had passed since the 1990s made it difficult to locate information and understand why certain decision were made at that time.

Ms Davis said that, because Edwards suffered no real-life consequences such as jail or loss of job for his attack on her, he had considered himself bulletproof, going on to commit more serious crimes.

'This is only the beginning of the aftermath,' she said.

After David Caporn resigned from the police in 2009, he took a job with the Fire and Emergency Services Authority as the Executive Director of Community Development. He is now Manager, Compliance and Emergency Liaison and Manager, COVID-19 Business Continuity at the City of Rockingham, south of Perth. After the Edwards verdict, he told the author: 'It's been a good result.'

He said there were good reasons for the focus on Lance Williams.

'None of the public knew about Lance Williams' deviant behaviour. That is what led to him becoming the key focus.

'If, with what we knew, with all the information we had, you did not put a significant effort into this person, you would be derelict in your duty.

'If he had turned out to be the offender, you would be open to criticism.

'Telstra was one of our top ten lines of inquiry, and Macro passed all details it had collected to the Schramm review.

'We were all over the [Lisa] abduction.'

The vast number of low-quality tips, such as nominations of people washing cars, 'came out of the profilers', he said.

'In hindsight, it would have been a good idea to put more information out to the public now we know what we know.

'Identifying vehicles is a subjective thing. It can go wrong. These things can get locked in and cause problems if wrong. People might know who the murderer was but not come forward because he did not have a Holden Commodore. That mistake was made in other cases.'

He said the questionnaire to Weygers was before he was in charge, and the focus on Weygers and Ross was afterwards.

'I can't beat myself up for what I should or shouldn't have done. Edwards was not caught for seven years after they had his DNA profile.

'In the days I was on the task force, the only thing you had to eliminate people was by alibi.'

He said he had worked closely with Denis Glennon. 'I had a lot of time for him and still do.

'I have huge respect for Don Spiers, the way he went about things, how he held himself together. Don has had no answers – it just breaks your heart.'

Chris Dawson, who was appointed Police Commissioner in 2017, was announced as the next Governor of Western Australia on April 4, 2022. He was due to take office in July 2022 after forty-six years of police service, a career he had launched as a seventeen-year-old.

*

Unexpectedly, after publication of the first edition of this book, the enduring enigma of the unidentified man seen on security vision sharing a joke with Jane Rimmer outside the Continental Hotel was solved by Mystery Man himself.

He revealed that when police belatedly released the security vision to the public, twelve years after Jane's death, he recognised himself immediately.

He told the author he had attended the neighbourhood primary school with Jane and her siblings, and he knew Jane and her family well. Recalling the night he spotted Jane outside the hotel, he said that, until then, he had not seen her for many years.

'I was surprised to see her all grown up and out and about,' he said. 'I've walked up to her and said: "Little Jane Rimmer – what are you doing here?"'

He cannot remember her exact reply, nor did he see which direction she walked after she had reacted by laughing. It's likely he was the last person to speak with her before she disappeared.

By the time the security tape was released, Mystery Man's life was filled with personal drama. He also felt unable to deal with the possibility of being accused of involvement in Jane's murder.

He told nobody he was the man in the video until he contacted the author in 2022 after reading this book.

Notes and Sources

Preface

Serial killer Eric Edgar Cooke's life and crimes: *Presumed Guilty: When Cops Get It Wrong and Courts Seal the Deal*, Bret Christian, Hardie Grant Books, 2013.
A businessman weeps: 'Public pain', *Post*, March 22, 1997.

1: Graveyard

Kings Park rapist: 'Special unit hunts Kings park rapist', *Post*, March 13, 1990. Three women walking or jogging in the park were blindfolded and tied up before being sexually assaulted.
SARC doctor: Evidence of Dr Jill Amanda Barnard at trial, State of Western Australia v Bradley Robert Edwards, Supreme Court of Western Australia, January 13, 2020.
Dead-end in Lisa attack investigation: 'No response to rape reports', *Post*, February 21, 1995.
Subiaco assault: 'Bystanders watch as girls are attacked', *Post*, March 7, 1995.
Woman stalked near Eric Street: 'Nightclub patron stalked', *Post*, April 18, 1995.
Home invader rapist: 'Girl (4) sees mother raped', *Post*, September 12, 1995.
Telco vehicle sightings: Detailed in a Supreme Court ruling to admit propensity evidence: State of Western Australia v Bradley Robert Edwards, Supreme Court of Western Australia, delivered March 20, 2019, and by witness evidence at the trial during the week December 3–6, 2019.
First-hand accounts: Evidence to State of Western Australia v Bradley Robert Edwards, Supreme Court of Western Australia, December 2019.
Hollywood Hospital: Hollywood reappears in this story. In the 1920s, it was the name real estate developer Cyril Dudley gave to the pig and poultry farms he was subdividing for housing, naming his

estate after the Californian original in the hope that some glamour would rub off. A large military repatriation hospital built in the district adopted the Hollywood name, which has been retained to this day by the upmarket private hospital now on the site. Hollywood High School occupied a corner next to the cemetery.
Notes on Karrakatta: 'Katta' is the local indigenous name for a hilltop. 'Karra' is close to three words that mean spider, orchid or red-tailed black cockatoo; 'karak' is the cry and Aboriginal name of that cockatoo.

2: Sarah

False hope of Sarah in a taxi: 'Sarah got into taxi with man', *Post*, February 6, 1996.
Responsible Sarah: Interview with Sarah Spiers' friend Rebecca Giglia: 'Worried friends join search for Sarah', *The West Australian*, February 1, 1996.
Public response to Sarah's disappearance: In the two weeks after Sarah was abducted, police followed up 307 separate calls to Crime Stoppers. They said publicly that these calls produced no new leads. 'Police tell of bogus taxis', Catherine Fitzpatrick, *The West Australian*, February 10, 1996.
Scream Serials: Evidence to State of Western Australia v Bradley Robert Edwards, Supreme Court of Western Australia, December 2019.
Young women offered lifts in Claremont around the time Sarah Spiers disappeared: 'Club girl tells of kerb crawler', *Post*, February 20, 1996.
'Concern' for Sarah: 'Deep concern for the safety and well-being of Sarah Spiers', press release from Club Bayview, January 31, 1996. 'Call for a safe route home', faxed press release from Dr Jon Sainken, February 2, 1996. 'Club offers reward', press release from Club Bayview, February 8, 1997. The same press release also announced a courtesy bus for patrons who could not find their way home, and pointed out that a free taxi phone operated in the club.
Filmed re-enactment of Sarah Spiers leaving Club Bayview: 'Sara Who?', Nelli Noakes, *Post*, February 13, 1996. Ms Noakes' report of the activity in the street was described as offensive to clubbers and the club by Sophie Gargett, who called for an apology. 'How dare she suggest that any young girl is asking for trouble by the way she dresses,' she wrote. 'All nightclubbers are hedonists, but this does not mean they are unconcerned for their safety'. 'Report "offensive" to clubbers and club', Sophie Gargett, letter to the editor, *Post*, February 20, 1996.

3: Taxi!

Peter Weygers' bus-shelter clean-up: 'Bottom job for the top person', *Post*, March 27, 1990. He later realised that the bus shelter was not in Claremont but in Nedlands, on the other side of the Alfred Road border. 'I would still have cleaned it,' he said.
Steven Ross's personal habits: 'The odd couple: Weygers and the cabbie', Torrance Mendez, *The West Australian*, September 17, 2004.
Woman yanked from cab: 'Woman pulled out of cab', *Post*, February 6, 1996.
Taxi lament: 'Did Sarah leave club by taxi?', Jenny Smithson, letter to the editor, *The West Australian*, February 2, 1996.
Clubbers tell how they get home: 'We take off our shoes and run', *Post*, June 18, 1996.
Ross and his cab trip to the Windsor Hotel with Sarah Spiers: 'I told police about Sarah', *Post*, August 28, 2004. Extra details from interviews with the author, March 13, 2013, March 1, 2016 and October 3, 2016.
Weygers' meeting with Don Spiers: Spiers' visit to Weygers was on March 6, 1996, according to Weygers' diary.
Ross's record: The story behind Ross acquiring a criminal record is a great tragedy in itself. Police had called at the home he owned with his partner, Erica Muller, to arrest him for the serious offence of attempting to pervert the course of justice by falsely claiming a Taxi Control Board officer had lied during a hearing. Erica, a former beauty queen, was bleeding and so sick in bed that she might die. Before Ross left with the police, he had called a doctor to the house, but, unknown to him, the officers had accidentally locked his guard dog in an enclosure that prevented the doctor knocking on the front door.

After ten hours of heavy questioning, Ross says he falsely confessed to the crime so that he could get home to check on Erica's welfare.

'They said, "Sign this and we'll let you go",' he said.

He did and was duly charged. By then, his partner had indeed died in bed of natural causes.

Ross became worried that he would also be charged with her murder, so sought help from the Council for Civil Liberties.

Ross, then aged 34, sobbed when he appeared in court, his lawyer advising him to plead guilty to perverting the course of justice. The magistrate handed him two years' probation. He was never charged with murder.
Ross court appearance and sentencing: 'Driver's tragic bid to clear name', *The West Australian,* December 6, 1991.

4: Party Town

International search: 'Police cast wider net for Sarah', *Post*, March 12, 1996.
Clairvoyants have never solved a crime: 'Murder and Clairvoyants. Well-meaning or malicious clairvoyants can be cruel to the grieving', Bret Christian, *The Skeptic*, Autumn 2004.
Don Spiers on the effects of clairvoyants on Sarah's family: 'Sarah's dad pleads for video bank', *Post*, May 21, 1996.
Don Spiers tells of his fears of predators and being misled by clairvoyants: 'Sarah's dad: My fears came true', *Post*, February 27, 1996. This report pointed out the similarities between Sarah's disappearance and the abduction and rape of a seventeen-year-old at Karrakatta Cemetery the previous February.
Jon Sainken's defence of his club: 'The club, the mayor, the truth and the media,' Dr Jon Sainken, letter to the editor in regards to Club Bayview, *Post*, May 28, 1996.
Club Bayview patron interviews: 'The inside view of life at Club Bay View', Michael Edwards, *Post*, June 22, 1996.
Collapsed hotel patron: 'Lucky survivor', Rodney Thiele, letter to the editor, *Post*, July 6, 1996.
'Women continued to walk alone': *Post*, June 19, 1996.
Assault on Club Bayview patron: 'Woman assaulted near Club Bayview', *Post*, March 12, 1996. The Church Lane attack was in the early hours of Sunday, March 3, 1996. The attacker was described at the time as about twenty-five years of age, of medium to stocky build, Caucasian with olive skin, dark features and dark hair, and wearing a blue shirt and jeans. The case was re-opened after the death of Ciara Glennon, without result. 'That case has never been closed,' acting police inspector Con Calameri said after Ciara Glennon was murdered. 'Police look again at attack in March', *Post*, August 12, 1997.
Four new reports: 'Attacker not identified', *Post*, April 19, 1997.

5: Downward Spiral

Dr Deller on reporting of sexual assault: Interview with author, March 28, 2018. SARC now stands for the Sexual Assault Resource Centre.
Lost video evidence: 'Sarah's dad pleads for video bank', *Post*, May 21, 1996.
Police emphasise Claremont's 'very low crime rate': 'Claremont is safe', *Post*, April 23, 1996.
Dispute over nightclub approval: 'When is a piano bar, cabaret bar, or American bar really a nightclub, and if it is a nightclub, should it have ever been allowed in the middle of Claremont?' began this

Post report headed 'Club Bayview makes its claim' by Nelli Noakes in the May 28, 1996 edition, on the opening hearings of the Local Government Appeals Tribunal on Friday, May 24, 1996. The council argued it had made a mistake when it first approved the club without realising it was a nightclub. The club argued that the council had known all along that it *was* a nightclub.

Further court hearings re Club Bayview: 'Club Bayview … more Hilton than Hannibal's', Nelli Noakes, *Post*, June 4, 1996.

Expansion of Club Bayview: 'All clear on Club Bayview', *Post*, June 22, 1996. In 1995, Club Bayview, owned by Hillgrove Pty Ltd, had the opportunity to acquire more floor space, but in September 1995 the local council had said no. The extra 443 square metres would have allowed it to increase its maximum number of club patrons from 270 to 385, potentially boosting its income.

In arguing against the expansion, the council had delved into the minutes of its old meetings and exhumed the original 1985 approval for Club Bayview. It was for a piano bar to be called 'Geri's of Claremont'. The council said it doubted whether approval had ever been given for a nightclub, only for 'a sophisticated après-theatre, piano bar and coffee house, where young adults and their parents might happen upon one another as the witching hour approaches', according to the original application.

Club Bayview's ten overcrowding charges: None of the first nine charges was against the club's owner, Dr Sainken, personally, but the latest summons was, alleging he had allowed the club to exceed its then permitted number of 270 people by 160.

Just before that case was due before court, ten months after the summons was issued, the Claremont Council issued a new overcrowding charge against club employee John Masel, who had agreed to plead guilty. In exchange, the charge against Dr Sainken was withdrawn. 'Deal over club charge', *Post*, October 25, 1997. Dr Sainken said he had not been in the club at the relevant time. Masel was fined $3000 with $1500 costs.

Club criticised at meeting of electors: 'Electors target Club Bayview', *Post*, April 9, 1996.

Council court action against the Continental Hotel: 'Continental faces music', *Post*, May 28, 1996. It reported on the first hearing of the Liquor Licensing Authority, following the lodging of a formal complaint by the Town of Claremont to enable residents to take their complaints direct to the Authority. 'The Continental Hotel in court', *Post*, June 11, 1996.

Jon Sainken sues for defamation: 'Club man sues Weygers', *Post*, May 14, 1996.

Claremont venues alleged to be associated with anti-social behaviour: 'Club urged to help end assaults', *The West Australian*, March 5, 1996; 'Club's approval under a cloud', *The West Australian*, March 2, 1996. Weygers' call for The Continental and Club Bayview to contribute to cost of extra police patrols, 'Local fears surface again', *The West Australian*, June 11, 1996.
Sainken's claim: The writ claimed defamation by Peter Weygers in comments quoted in three newspaper reports, two television news reports and a radio broadcast about the club and its management following the disappearance of Sarah Spiers.
Jon Sainken's letter to the editor: 'The club, the mayor, the truth and the media', *Post*, May 28, 1996.
Negative public reaction to writ: Peter Dunk's 'Can't we be critical?' and Pip Buxton's 'Give us some peace' letters calling for peace in Claremont, *Post*, May 28, 1996. Jon Sainken's reply, 'The club, the mayor, the truth and the media', *Post*, June 4, 1996.
Weygers applies for the council to pay his legal costs: 'Omodei decides on Weygers' costs', *Post*, June 11, 1996.
Sainken lobbies against public payment of Weygers' legal costs: Dr Jon Sainken's letter headed 'Defamation Writ – Mr Peter Weygers', dated May 14, 1996, addressed to Paul Omodei, MLA, Minister for Local Government, Multicultural and Ethnic Affairs. 'I feel that the views he has chosen to express may be personally or politically motivated rather than the properly expressed view of the council,' he wrote.
Claremont Council ponders Weygers' legal fees: 'Claremont decides on Weygers' costs', *Post*, May 28, 1996.
Real estate agent defends Claremont venues: 'Hats off to club', Mack Hall, letter to the editor, *Post*, June 11, 1996. The published publication date was then several days after printing. The following year, printing was done on the Friday and the editions were dated the Saturday and Sunday.
Sainken's newspaper advertisement: Dr Jon Sainken's 'Hex, Jibes and Red Tape' advertisement was published in the *Post*, dated June 11, 1996, with its logo surrounded by type reading, 'Still open ten years on. Be there or miss out'. It said: 'The tide of community disapproval against the antics of the young is very vocal and fortified by a determined and self-certain morality.' Weygers was later to dispute the accuracy of some of the words in the advertisement as they concerned him: 'Club ad wrong, says Weygers', *Post*, June 18, 1996.

The same edition reported the adjournment of a formal complaint against the Continental Hotel by the Claremont Council health inspector, alleging that the residential amenity was unduly disturbed by noise from patrons, music from the hotel and disorderly conduct by hotel patrons after leaving the premises. 'Conti case postponed', *Post*, June 11, 1996.

6: Jane

Lee Rimmer: Jane's sister was the organiser of Reclaim the Night marches: 'Jane's sister leads march to reclaim Claremont', *Post*, August 30, 1997. The march was held on October 31, 1997. Lee Rimmer had been involved in the Reclaim the Night movement for 10 years before her younger sister was abducted and murdered.
Jane's last hours in Claremont: Evidence to State of Western Australia v Bradley Robert Edwards, Supreme Court of Western Australia, December 2019.
Scream serials from Wellard: Evidence of Kenneth and Judith Mitchell, and Ian and Cheryl Sturcke to State of Western Australia v Bradley Robert Edwards, Supreme Court of Western Australia, December 2019. They were not asked why they took no further action, and did not explain.
The Rimmer parents on Jane: 'Please come home, plead parents', *Post*, June 18, 1996.
Poster campaign: 'Jane Rimmer posters cover the country', *Post*, June 19, 1996.
Birnies: David and Catherine Birnie abducted five women, most of them from streets of suburban Perth over a five-week period in late 1986. They raped and murdered four. The couple was caught when a fifth victim, Kate Moir, aged seventeen, who had been to Claremont's Cagney's Hotel, later re-named The Continental, escaped from their 'house of horrors', only to initially be disbelieved by police. In the hours she spent convincing them of the truth of her story, the murderous couple burnt incriminating evidence and created a cover story. Interview with former policewoman Laura Hancock, September 16, 2018. Hancock believed the escaped victim, 'but I was told it was a bizarre story and to stitch her up for a false report', she told the programme.

Both Birnies were sentenced to life imprisonment. David Birnie killed himself in prison in 2005. Catherine Birnie has been repeatedly denied parole.

7: Unstoppable

Lisa's suspicions: 'Lisa' interview with Ingrid Mansell: 'Fears confirmed: victim', *The West Australian*, June 11, 1996.
Connection of rape to two homicides, etc.: Evidence of Betty Jo Thompson, née Francis, to State of Western Australia v Bradley

Robert Edwards, Supreme Court of Western Australia, December 2019.

Telstra vehicle confusion: Telstra letter to the Bureau of Criminal Intelligence, July 2, 1996, with list of drivers' names: Evidence of Lynda Eldridge, a Telstra business analyst, to State of Western Australia v Bradley Robert Edwards, Supreme Court of Western Australia, December 2019.

Telstra had written back to BCI a year after the logo changeover: 'The vehicle you were looking for had a Telstra logo on the side as distinct from a Telecom logo, and the witness was fairly definite about that.'

It went on to point out that Telstra did not begin branding its vehicles with the new logo until mid-July 1995. 'If a vehicle was sighted in February 1995, I don't think it was possible it could have been a Telstra logo.'

Security guard Wayne Wookey transposed Telecom/Telstra brands: Evidence of Wayne Wookey to State of Western Australia v Bradley Robert Edwards, Supreme Court of Western Australia, December 2019.

Fake taxi: 'Club couple catch bogus taxi', George Williams, *Post*, June 19, 1996.

Forty-five-minute wait for taxi opposite Continental Hotel: 'Patrols, taxis inadequate', Andrew Matthews, letter to the editor, *Post* June 18, 1996. He and his companion eventually gave up waiting.

Claremont safety audit: Town of Claremont night-walks log, listing 49 items, dated June 15–16, 1996. Police praised the mayor's walks and the efforts Claremont made to promote safety. Acting Assistant Commissioner Bob Kucera told Claremont Council's Safety and Security Committee that police could not ask for more than Claremont had provided. 'Police praise crime fight', *Post*, August 3, 1996.

8: Liberties

Weygers served with warrant: 'Weygers: make police justify search warrants', *Post*, April 24, 1990.

Police racial bias: Cradle-to-grave discrimination by police against indigenous Australians, 'Aborigines police victims', *Post*, June 12, 1990. The Council for Civil Liberties made a submission to the Law Reform Commission calling for a reduction in police powers to 'harass'. Weygers on black victimisation, *Post*, June 26, 1990. The correspondence sparked a lively and prolonged public debate.

Police Commissioner Chris Dawson says sorry to Aboriginal people: 'Top cop apology', *The West Australian*, July 12, 2018.

Weygers' scrutiny of police: 'Call for Royal Commission into police', *The West Australian*, August 15, 1989. 'Let's breathalyse police, says Weygers', *Post*, December 31, 1991. 'Police quizzed about shot suspect's gun', *Sunday Times*, January 20, 1991. 'Find the gun', Peter Weygers, letter to the editor, *Sunday Times*, February 3, 1991. 'Weygers lectures booze-bus cops', *Post*, December 19, 1995.
Police hate Weygers' guts: Statement by Steven Ross, September 22, 2004.
Life-changing questionnaire to Peter Weygers: 'Police questions anger Weygers: Did you murder Sarah?', *Post*, July 6, 1996, and author interviews with Weygers.
Police questions for Weygers: Did you murder Sarah Spiers/Jane Rimmer questionnaire, an undated eight-page typed form containing sixteen questions headed INSTRUCTIONS. Weygers said the written question were 'intrusive to my value system'. 'Did you murder Sarah?', Post, July 6, 1996.
Media knowledge of police questions: *The West Australian*'s reporter John Townsend said he could not reveal who tipped him off about homicide detectives allegedly wanting to interview Weygers. He would not say whether or not it was a police officer. 'It was not a malicious source,' he said. 'Police questions anger Weygers', *Post*, July 6, 1996. On August 21, 2019, Townsend told the *Post* editor he could not remember his source but he had diligently sought and published all points of view, including those of Weygers, in his original report.
News report on Weygers: 'Claremont mayor Peter Weygers has refused to be interviewed by homicide detectives investigating the disappearance of nightclubbers Jane Rimmer and Sarah Spiers,' began the report in *The West Australian*, July 6, 1996. The large headline over the report was changed after the first edition from 'Mayor refuses to help Rimmer police' to 'I don't trust probe police, says Weygers' in the second edition. Weygers said afterwards he did not speak to a detective or see the questions until after *The West Australian*'s report was printed.
Wood Royal Commission: Royal Commission into the New South Wales Police Service, 1995 to 1997. It was set up to inquire into whether corruption in the police force was systemic and entrenched. Sensational evidence was provided by surveillance tapes and by 'rollover' officers, who gave evidence against their colleagues.
Irony of Council of Civil Liberties president suffering breach of his civil liberties: 'It's sinister: Weygers', *Post*, July 13, 1996. 'I can only assume I was set up to suffer the worst kind of adverse publicity,' he said. 'Many people would have a motive to falsely smear my reputation. By the time Grant Milner received the questions, *The*

West Australian was on the phone to me implying that I was a suspect. Was it the same person who tipped them off? Had they told me who it was I could quite possibly have told them why that person would want my name smeared. It's totalitarian.'

Police Commander Bob Ibbotson said those given questionnaires were suspects: 'Suspects given surveys', *The West Australian*, July 10, 1996.

Lawyer reaction to questions: John Prior, secretary of the Criminal Lawyers' Association, criticised the two police questionnaires in the article 'Big risks in police questions: lawyer', John Townsend, *The West Australian*, July 9, 1996.

Don Thomson reaction: 'Questionable tactics: Blunt instrument tools of detection come under fire', Victoria Laurie, *The Bulletin*, August 27, 1996. Later, Thomson further annoyed police when he said lie detectors, if assumed to be foolproof, could lead to a guilty person passing unnoticed. Also 'Lie tests advance hunt for killer', Hal Crawford, *The West Australian*, September 18, 1997, which reported that lie detector tests on 58 suspects meant that the noose was tightening on the Claremont serial killer.

Assistant Police Commissioner Bob Kucera's statement clearing Peter Weygers as suspect: 'Claremont a safe place, asserts police chief', *News Chronicle*, August 7, 1996.

Weygers' behaviour with young women: 'The many sides of Peter Weygers', Bret Christian and George Williams, *Post*, September 25, 2004.

Move to censure mayor over 'non-co-operation with police': 'Club ad wrong', *Post*, July 13, 1996. The *Post* reporter at the meeting wrote: 'Mr Weygers silenced all potential critics when the meeting opened by slamming *The West Australian* for inaccurate reporting.' He said he had never refused to help police. The council then unanimously passed a motion of confidence in its mayor.

9: Rooster

Boxer stance: Evidence of Dr Alanah Buck to State of Western Australia v Bradley Robert Edwards, Supreme Court of Western Australia, January 29, 2020.

Keepsake hair: Evidence of Vicky Young to State of Western Australia v Bradley Robert Edwards, Supreme Court of Western Australia, January 13, 2020.

Horrified expert: Evidence of Dr Ray Palmer to State of Western Australia v Bradley Robert Edwards, Supreme Court of Western Australia, April 29, 2020.

Trevor Rimmer on the shock of the discovery of Jane's body: 'Jane's father says he feared the worst', *Post*, August 10, 1996.

Vicious maniac preying on Claremont: 'Maniac feared as crimes list grows', *The West Australian*, August 5, 1996.
Poster and safety campaign: 'Police warn girls', *Post*, September 7, 1996.
Reaction to taxis: 'Missing women: Taxi drivers lose their jobs', *The West Australian*, March 19, 1997. 'Missing women: check on taxis', *The West Australian*, March 20, 1997. 'Taxi drivers demand DNA tests', *The West Australian*, March 21, 1997. 'Taxi logs under scrutiny', *The West Australian*, March 22, 1997.
DNA testing blitz: PathWest filed 9000 DNA reference samples in the course of the twenty-five-year investigation, and conducted 8000 tests on other exhibits. Evidence of PathWest forensic scientist Scott Egan to State of Western Australia v Bradley Robert Edwards, Supreme Court of Western Australia, February 27, 2020.
Jane Rimmer's funeral: 'Hundreds of friends turn out for Jane's funeral', *Post*, August 17, 1996.

10: Ciara

Club Bayview wins its appeal to exist and expand: 'Club Bay View can expand, says Tribunal', *Post*, November 23, 1996. Lawyers for the club told the Local Government Appeals Tribunal that the council knew all along that the premises housed a nightclub, going back ten years earlier when it approved the application. The club's manager, Craig Hutchinson, said the approval was fabulous news for a club that advertises itself as the best neighbourhood bar in Australia. Claremont's CEO Rob Stewart said the detail of the decision vindicated the council's stand and proved its point that antisocial behaviour could be linked to Club Bayview.

The club's lawyer, Wayne Martin QC, suggested such behaviour was unlikely to undermine the moral fabric of society. 'Club told to hire trouble-shooter', *Post* December 28, 1996.
Anti-social behaviour, 11 p.m. to 4 a.m.: 'Urine, abuse, fornication', *Post*, November 30, 1996. In the same edition, the *Post* reported further observations by security guard Paraskevas Hatgivasiliou, hired by Claremont Council to document night activity in central Claremont, in his evidence for the Claremont v Club Bayview Town Planning Appeal Tribunal case. From 11 p.m. on Saturday, November 2, 1996, he listed nine incidents over the next three hours, ranging from young people blocking traffic to urinating and vomiting in shop fronts. The next night he listed another twenty-three incidents. 'What the guard saw on one night in Claremont', *Post*, November 30, 1996.
Claremont's nightspots 'attracting crime': 'Claremont against bigger club crowds' – report of the tribunal hearing, *Post*, December

7, 1996. 'Club to ask court for more bulletin patrons', *Post* January 4, 1997.

Rule proposed for liquor outlets: 'Weygers suggests "10-strike" rule', *Post* November 30, 1996.

Club overcrowding charge: 'Deal over club charge,' Nelli Noakes, *Post*, October 25, 1997.

Liquid accelerant used in fire: 'Club fire "deliberate"', *Post*, March 14, 1995.

Summer sweep of Wellard: 'Police search dried-out bush for murder clues', *Post*, February 22, 1997.

Police ask for 'living witnesses' to come forward: 'Ex-officer questioned in serial killer search', Luke Morfesse, *The West Australian*, July 23, 1997.

Ciara sightings: 'Was it Ciara on the highway?', *Post*, March 22, 1997.

Out-of-date photo of Ciara Glennon used by media: 'Police pin hope on new photograph of Ciara', *The West Australian,* March 20, 1997. 'Photo casts light on search for woman', Natalie O'Brien, *The Australian*, March 21, 1997. 'Contrast in photos no worry: police', *The West Australian,* March 21, 1997.

Denis Glennon statement: 'Weeping father's appeal for help', Jerry Pratley, *The West Australian*, March 19, 1997. 'Father wants cameras', *Post*, March 22, 1997.

Una Glennon appeals for information: 'Police canvass overseas help', *Post*, March 29, 1997.

11: Siege

Bob Falconer issues call for calm: 'Police warn city of serial killer mania', *The Weekend Australian*, March 22–23, 1997.

Public identifying with victims: 'Why we identify with victims', *Sunday Times*, November 17, 1996.

Sense of depression: 'Support police, says Barnett', *Post*, March 22, 1997.

Premier and police minister offer reward for information on Ciara's disappearance: '$20,000 "carrot"', *Post*, March 22, 1997. State Premier Richard Court said the government offered the big reward early because it wanted to act quickly to get information while it was still fresh in people's minds.

Complaint from Margaret Dodd: In 2002, five years after Hayley Dodd disappeared, after much agitation from Margaret Dodd, the reward sum for Hayley was raised to match the Claremont killer reward. 'Hayley Dodd "not important enough"', ABC morning radio, January 31, 2018.

Margaret Dodd took up a petition calling for an inquiry into the police investigation into her daughter's disappearance.
Hayley's disappearance 'written off': 'Hayley case wound up too early, says ex-cop', *The West Australian*, October 26, 2017.
State of siege: 'Highway connection', *Post*, March 22, 1997.
Serial killers' progression to murder: 'Inside the mind of a serial killer', *Post*, March 22, 1997. The other serial killers who prowled the suburbs were Eric Edgar Cooke (eight murders between 1959 and 1963) – see *Presumed Guilty*, Bret Christian, 2013 – and David and Catherine Birnie (four murders in 1986) – see endnote to Chapter 6.
Serial killer rehearsals and call to review earlier crimes: Advice from former FBI serial killer profiler Dick Ault, 'FBI view', *Post*, April 5, 1997. Macro did not appreciate such input. Acting assistant commissioner Bob Ibbotson said the media should not distract the public with the opinions of outsiders who did not have the facts. 'Remarks not a help', *The West Australian,* April 8, 1997.
Women subdued: The size and weight of Edmund Kemper, California's 'co-ed killer', made him impossible to fight off. He stood 2.06 metres tall (6'9") and weighed 133 kilograms (21 stone). During 1972–73, he cruised for young female hitchhikers in California prepared with handcuffs, plastic bags and knives, abducting and murdering six. Psychiatrists theorised his victims were surrogates for the mother he hated. His last two victims were his mother, whom he mutilated, and her best friend. His first murder victims were his maternal grandparents, in 1964.
Profilers announce press conference outside the Continental: 'Video shows Rimmer at road corner', *The West Australian*, April 3, 1997.
Ciara's feistiness: 'Zest, tenacity a fond memory', Torrance Mendez, *The West Australian*, April 4, 1997.
Discovery of Ciara's body: 'A state mourns', *The West Australian*, April 4, 1997. *Post*, April 5, 1997.
Visual assessment of DNA evidence of AJM 40: Evidence of forensic pathologist Aleksander Bagdonavicius to State of Western Australia v Bradley Robert Edwards, Supreme Court of Western Australia, February 7 and 13, 2020.
Denis Glennon says God let him down: 'Grief was exhausting', *Post*, June 28, 1997.

12: Tiny Dancer

Paul Ferguson appeals to friends and work colleagues for information: 'The tell-tale signs', *Post*, April 5, 1997.

Hard times at the Continental: Author interview with Barry Jones, March 5, 2019. 'Claremont scene looks quiet – and safe', *Post*, May 3, 1997. 'Thousands spent on better [hotel] security', *Post*, May 3, 1997.
Drivers under suspicion: 'Angry taxi drivers call for DNA tests', *The West Australian*, March 21, 1997.
Check on taxis: 'Every taxi to be checked', *Post*, March 29, 1997.
Millions lost in taxi fares: 'Cabbies fear killer alert will cut work', Torrance Mendez, *The West Australian*, August 28, 2004, quoting Taxi Council member Hugh McLennan.
Taxi drivers unwilling to service Claremont: 'Taxi drivers avoid Claremont', *Post*, March 22, 1997.
Taxi drivers DNA-tested: 'Every cabbie to be checked', *Post*, March 29, 1997.
Supervised taxi ranks installed: The taxi rank outside Club Bayview was proposed at a Claremont Council meeting as far back as March 1996, a month after Sarah Spiers vanished. 'Phone, taxi rank for Club Bayview', *Post*, March 12, 1996.
Pizza delivery drivers' observations: 'Pizza men tell of drunk women hitching lifts', *Post*, April 12, 1997. The drivers interviewed for the report had approached the newspaper to warn young women of the dangers.
Madness or hope: 'Priest sees compassion', *Post*, April 12, 1997.
Ex-Iona student changes hair colour: 'The search for Ciara', *Post*, March 29, 1997.
Ciara Glennon's funeral: 'Farewell my little friend', *Post*, April 12, 1997.

13: Incendiary

Weygers' mayoral door-knocking campaign: 'Weygers launches his fight for mayor', *Post*, July 27, 1996. 'Weygers gets leave for Spiers doorknock', *Post*, August 31, 1996. 'Weygers gives his sole to Claremont', *Post*, March 15, 1997.
Denis Glennon visits Claremont CEO: 'Ciara's father wants cameras', *Post*, March 22, 1997.
Glennon's questions to Claremont Council: 'Glennon targets Weygers', *Post*, April 26, 1997.
Mayor Weygers and cameras: The *Post* reported in March 1996, between the first and second murders, that Weygers spoke on measures to improve security including the need for more police and security patrols, but that 'he strongly criticised the use of security cameras in the area of the club, claiming they were not effective and breached people's right to privacy'. 'Phone, taxi rank for Club

Bayview', *Post*, March 12, 1996. 'Club tape misses glass jab', *Post*, February 7, 1998.
Broken cameras: 'Claremont fooled, says Weygers', *Post*, May 19, 2001.
Glennon vows to pursue Mayor Weygers and CEO until he receives answers: 'Glennon targets Weygers', letter from Denis Glennon to Town of Claremont, April 18, 1997. 'Glennon questions CEO on Claremont safety', *Post*, May 24, 1997.
Denis Glennon threatens ministerial inquiry: 'Glennon threat to Claremont', *Post*, May 31, 1997. CEO Stewart subsequently said that Glennon was happy with the answers after receiving clarifications.
Peter Olson criticises Weygers on safety: 'Battle of the two Peters', *Post*, April 19, 1997.
Security cameras: Mayor Weygers said in the week after Ciara Glennon disappeared that he was 'in favour of security cameras in the present crisis. They can be removed after the culprit was caught.' 'Ciara's father wants cameras', *Post*, March 22, 1997.
Claremont security camera delays: Security upgrade awaiting Premier: 'Security cameras [in Perth CBD] are failing', *Post*, June 14, 1997. 'Cameras not the cure (police minister)', *The West Australian*, March 2007. 'Electronic eye to watch Claremont', *Post*, August 2, 1997. 'Cameras turned on again', *Post*, October 20, 2001.
Letter from Patrick O'Brien: It was addressed to Claremont CEO Rob Stewart, Mayor Peter Weygers and all Claremont councillors, copied to P. Omodei, Minister for Local Government, April 26, 1997.
Weygers lodges 'undue influence' complaint against Denis Glennon: 'Mayor calls for inquiry – Glennon targets Weygers', *Post*, April 26, 1997. 'Glennon–Weygers probe dropped', *Post*, June 14, 1997. Two statutory declarations sworn by Weygers were sent for legal advice by the Department for Local Government to the Crown Solicitor. Glennon strongly denied the allegations to department investigators. The Crown Solicitor later advised the department to drop this inquiry, saying that in the absence of corroborating evidence for Weygers, it came down to one man's word against another. Glennon was happy with this outcome. Weygers was not.
'Mr Weygers' attack on Ciara Glennon's dad – the last straw?': Letter addressed 'Dear Fellow Resident', signed on letterhead by Jon Sainken M.B., M.Phil., M.R.C.Psych., F.R.A.N.Z.P., 'Specialising in biochemical emotional & trauma-induced disorders of the nervous system'.
Pamphlet in reply: The flyer headed 'Who is Dr Jon Sainken?' was authorised by Rod Thiele of Mount Street, Claremont.

Anti-venue pamphlet: The flyer of May 1997, 'Help stop Continental Hotel and Club Bayview nightclub expanding', was authorised by M. Woods, 365 Stirling Highway, Claremont. It also misspelled Olson's name as 'Olsen'.
Unsigned 'Vote Olsen' pamphlet: The pamphlet, which also misspelled the candidate's name, did not carry the name and address of the person authorising it, as required by law.
'Weygers "put off" Glennon queries': *The West Australian*, May 3, 1997.
Councillor letterbox campaign against Weygers: 'Councillors turn on Weygers,' *Post*, May 3, 1997.
Fearis campaigns against Weygers: 'When fear comes to town', Victoria Laurie, *Good Weekend* magazine, *Sydney Morning Herald*, June 14, 1997. The report said Fearis was campaigning in response to a request from Denis Glennon. A letter from Weygers to Fearis days later, asking the reasons for the campaign, went unanswered.
Weyger's complaint against Sainken: Peter Weygers' undated letter of complaint to David Kerslake, Director, Office of Health Review, with supporting documents, plus letter dated May 5, 1997 to the Australian Medical Association. Letter to the Medical Board of Western Australia, dated May 5, 1997, followed by a statutory declaration dated May 30, 1997, signed by Claremont councillor Richard Hatchett. The Board replied (June 20, 1997) that it appeared Dr Sainken had not breached the Medical Act and that the Board would take no further action.

After a letter of complaint to the Minister for Local Government, May 5, 1997, Minister Paul Omodei replied in a letter dated October 24, 1997, that the legal question as to 'would ordinary decent folk in the community think less of Mr Weygers as a result of [Dr Sainken's] statement were questions only a court could decide', meaning that Weygers or councillor Richard Hatchett would need to institute proceedings if they chose.
Pamphlet blizzard: 'Letterbox war on election eve', Nelli Noakes, *Post*, May 3, 1997.
Clubbers celebrate Peter Weygers' election loss: 'Young people dance as mayor is ousted', *Post*, May 10, 1997. 'Weygers blames nightspot campaign', *Post*, April 2, 2005. 'The fear, the smear is still there and I just have to face it and go on,' he said.
Olson at arm's length from anti-Weygers campaign: '"Sainken didn't tell me," says the new mayor', *Post*, May 10, 1997.
Peter Weygers on his election loss: 'Weygers mud stuck', *Post*, May 10, 1997.

Former mayor as scapegoat: 'I can keep going, says Peter Weygers', *Post*, August 23, 1997.
Cat's head in mailbox: 'Gruesome find in Weygers' letterbox', *Post*, May 17, 1997.

14: Unconventional

Secure Communities Foundation established: 'Help us stop the killings: Lawyer', *Post*, April 5, 1997. 'Friends stake cash for murder hunt', Layla Tucak, *Post* September 5, 1998.
Church Lane blitz attack: 'Police look again at attack in March', *Post*, August 12–13, 1997.
Tracing 1800 Claremont revellers: 'When fear comes to town', Victoria Laurie, *Good Weekend* magazine, *Sydney Morning Herald*, June 14, 1997.
Picnic camera's limited effectiveness: Evidence of Detective Sergeant Justin Geary to State of Western Australia v Bradley Robert Edwards, Supreme Court of Western Australia, December 2019.
Secret video cameras to record car registration numbers: This strategy was suggested by Club Bayview owner Jon Sainken the week after Ciara Glennon was abducted: 'If police had a tape of all car numbers through Claremont after the last [Jane Rimmer] incident, the crimes could have been solved before Ciara went missing,' he said at a fraught Claremont Safety and Security Committee meeting. 'Police nearby when Ciara went', *Post*, March 22, 1997.

Mayor Weygers told the same meeting he was in favour of security cameras 'in the present crisis'.
Profilers: Geographic profiling, developed in Britain, has been proven to be far more effective than the techniques utilised by Macro. 'Mental maps' are utilised by criminals in their patterns of behaviour. Skilfully interpreting these has on many occasions pointed to the home or work range of the killer. The technique has led to actual people being locked up.

Geographic profiler David Canter, from the Centre for Investigative Psychology at the University of Liverpool, probably the world's leading and most successful geographic profiler, was willing to give his services for the Claremont case while he was in Perth presenting a 1998 seminar. Despite local police being well aware of his reputation and presence, he was not asked for help. 'The hunt for a serial killer', *The Age*, May 30, 1998.
Police inundated with tips: 'Flood of Crime Stoppers reports: 10 missing, all found', *Post*, May 10, 1997.

Innocent lives turned upside down by Macro investigation: 'Suspect says police visits made him ill', *Post*, June 29, 1996. 'Murder suspect tells of turmoil', *Post*, August 2, 1997.
Killer trophies: A notorious trophy-keeper was Ivan Milat, the Sydney backpacker serial killer. Police found victims' camping gear and clothing stashed in his house, which helped them convict him of seven murders between 1989 and 1992. He had even presented his girlfriend with a Benetton shirt that he had stolen from victim Caroline Clarke. David and Catherine Birnie, the 1980s Perth serial-killer couple, also had keepsakes of their four victims.

15: Kerb-crawler

Lance William's shrunken social life: 'Murder suspect tells of tests', *Post*, June 12, 1999.
Williams' suicide attempts: Tony Barrass interview: 'Sad life of suspect led to suicide bids', *The West Australian*, May 10, 2001.
Policewoman picked up by Williams: 'Police decoy used in killer hunt sting', Bret Christian, *Post*, February 1, 2003.
Williams detained: 'Serial killer force strikes', *The West Australian*, April 8, 1998.
Williams' home visits: Visiting sex worker's interview with author, February 2019.
Police continue to surveil Williams: 'Macro police break silence', Matt Price, *The Australian*, May 21, 1998. The report said the public servant (Lance Williams) was still a significant person of interest. He was not publicly named in the media until September 1998. *The West Australian* did not publish his name until 2015, though it frequently published Peter Weygers' and Steven Ross's names in 'suspect' context from 1996. Sergeant Tony Potts was quoted as saying, 'He is still a major focus in the investigation. He is a major focus because of his activities. You can read into that whatever you want.' 'Police silent on serial killer rumour', *Post*, June 7, 1998.
'Sunflower' trophies release: 'Macro police break silence,' Matt Price, *The Australian,* May 21, 1998.
Items missing from murder victims: 'Callers respond to Macro appeal', *Post*, May 22, 1998.
Eighty thousand pieces of information: 'Police silent on serial killer rumour', *Post*, June 6, 1998.
'Police stakeout puzzle': Layla Tucak, *Post*, July 4, 1998.
Scout Hall water rates outed police surveillance of Lance Williams: The *Post*'s George Williams (no relation), who was reporting on the meeting, followed up. 'Media watches the watchers,' *Post*, September 5, 1998.

First polygraph tests on taxi drivers etc. detailed: 'New move in killer hunt', *The West Australian*, April 24, 1999.
Polygraph test on Williams: 'Serial killer suspect to take lie test', Luke Morfesse, *The West Australian*, August 29, 1998.
Dr Peter Birrell on polygraph tests: *The Law Report*, ABC Radio, September 8, 1998.
Fallibility of polygraphs: 'Psychopaths can beat lie detector tests', *Post*, September 12, 1998. As with his psychiatric examination, Williams did not demand to have a lawyer present for his lie-detector test.
Leaking of polygraph test results: The sequence of events is documented in 'The Courage of Our Convictions', *Background Briefing*, ABC Radio National, produced by Gerald Tooth, June 25, 2000. The tests took place on the weekend of August 29–30, 1998. The ABC quotes David Caporn as saying the polygraph test was a screening tool; nothing more, nothing less. Local journalists interviewed for the programme said they were encouraged by police to publish the fact that Lance Williams failed the test, in order to put pressure on the suspect. 'Cottesloe man remains more than just a person of interest', Luke Morfesse, *The West Australian*, August 27, 2004.
Front page of *The West Australian*: 'Murder suspect: I am not guilty', *The West Australian*, September 1, 1998.
Lance Williams upgraded from person of interest to suspect: 'Suspect feels the heat – relentlessly', *The West Australian*, September 1, 1998. In the interview, David Caporn praised the FBI's widespread use of lie detectors, saying it was very effective technology.
Tainting of a future trial: 'Lawyers fear publicity a threat to fair jury trial', Grace Meertens, *The West Australian*, September 2, 1998. Police Commissioner Bob Falconer response to these criticisms: 'Police had acted ethically and not orchestrated publicity surrounding Lance Williams. No suspect in any case so serious had previously spoken directly to the media: 'Police defend killer hunt', Charlene Wilson-Clark, *The West Australian*, September 4, 1998.
DPP John McKechnie's lie-detector warning: 'Publicity fears in serial killer case', Grace Meertens, *The West Australian*, September 3, 1998. The same article reported the concerns of Dean Richard Love, Council of Civil Liberties vice-president, who said that 'police should refrain from manipulating the influence of the media'.
DNA tests questioned: 'Weygers questions Macro "bully" tactics', *Post*, September 5, 1998. Lance Williams was neither cleared nor charged after supplying DNA samples. Taxi drivers were 'bullied' to take DNA tests in breach of civil liberties, Weygers said.

Secure Communities Foundation and unconventional tests: 'Friends stake cash for murder hunt,' Layla Tucak, *Post*, September 5, 1998.
Police ninety-eight per cent sure Lance Williams was their man: 'Until proven innocent', *The Bulletin*, September 15, 1998. With the subtitle 'Rush to judgment', it said the lack of a breakthrough had led police and the media to stretch the definition of 'prime suspect'.
Media stakes out police: 'Media watches the watchers', *Post*, September 5, 1998.

16: Primal Person

Caporn replaced Ferguson: Paul Ferguson faced a charge of giving false testimony to an anti-corruption investigator, and was acquitted by a jury. 'ACC charges top cop after raids', *The West Australian*, March 28, 1998.
Lance Williams in or out of the picture: 'Murder suspect tells of tests', *Post*, June 12, 1999.
Telstra details missed from second list: Report of Telstra's operational vehicles dated December 12, 1998, provided by Telstra to Western Australia Police. Evidence of Lynda Eldridge, Telstra business analyst, to State of Western Australia v Bradley Robert Edwards, Supreme Court of Western Australia, December 2019.
No mention of Telstra: Author conversation with Tim Atherton, April 21, 2020.
Superintendent David Caporn promoted: 'Macro chief at peak of career', *The West Australian*, February 13, 1999.
Claude Minisini's killer profile of Williams: 'The Courage of Our Convictions', *Background Briefing*, ABC Radio National, June 25, 2000. 'We did find sufficient behavioural evidence to be able to make some very strong and incisive conclusions.'
Lance Williams speaks: Interview with Channel Seven reporter Alison Fan at his flat in Little Marine Parade, Cottesloe, Australia Day holiday, January 2002. 'A suspect speaks out', *Sunday Times*, February 10, 2002.
Man police believe to be serial killer: 'Leave my son alone', *Sunday Times*, January 31, 1999. The report quoted a Macro Task Force spokesman: 'He still remains the prime suspect – the position hasn't changed.'
***Irish Times* report on Williams:** 'Family deals with its loss as serial killer roams free', *Irish Times*, February 6, 1999. Its reporter recounted how Denis Glennon, during the interview, dialled directly to the head of Macro to clear the path for the journalist to speak with him.

Gary Adshead's off-the-record information about Lance Williams: 'Notes from a crime reporter', *The West Australian*, February 28, 2019.
Editorial on police 'pressure tactics': 'Murder hunt takes misguided risks', *The Australian*, September 7, 1998.
***Bulletin* criticism:** 'Until proven innocent: rush to judgment', Victoria Laurie, *The Bulletin*, September 15, 1998.
Man standing by car as Ciara allegedly walked past side street: Evidence of Karen Mabbott to State of Western Australia v Bradley Robert Edwards, Supreme Court of Western Australia, December 2019. Police had shown her a photo line-up that included Lance Williams. She did not recognise him.

17: Shoot Me

'Murders have us stumped: Falconer': *The West Australian*, June 14, 1999.
Macro shrunk: 'Macro investigation downgraded', *The West Australian*, April 24, 1999. 'The Courage of Our Convictions', *Background Briefing*, ABC Radio National, June 25, 2000.
Crimes unlikely to be solved without breakthrough: 'Claremont killer's trail fades', *Sunday Times*, February 27, 2000. Detective Superintendent David Caporn: 'The further you go from the moment of a crime, the more difficult a conviction becomes.'
Lance Williams on lie tests: 'Murder suspect tells of tests', *Post*, June 12, 1999.
Shoot me: 'He [Lance Williams] was so upset he was at the point of getting the police to "just shoot me"': 'The Courage of Our Convictions', *Background Briefing*, ABC Radio National, June 25, 2000.
The point of DNA testing: 'The Courage of Our Convictions', *Background Briefing*, ABC Radio National, June 25, 2000.
Olson on kids' complacency reigning: 'Young women still walk alone at night', *Post*, April 15, 2000. 'Clubbers unaware of terror that changed Claremont', Paige Taylor, *Post*, January 25, 2003.
Operation Wintergreen: The DNA was confirmed as Ciara Glennon's profile, according to cross-examination of senior forensic pathologist and DNA expert Sally Ann Harbison, who tested the samples in New Zealand in 2004. The prosecution objected to the admission of this evidence as 'highly irrelevant'. State of Western Australia v Bradley Robert Edwards, Supreme Court of Western Australia, February 2020.
Macro's success: 'Task force a life saver', *The West Australian*, January 27, 2001.

Detective Superintendent David Caporn said at his medal ceremony that he had a sense that Macro may have prevented other women becoming victims.

Details of deaths of Claremont victims kept a tight secret: 'Clubbers unaware of terror that changed Claremont', Paige Taylor, *Post*, January 25, 2003.

Forensic review of 2002–04: Prior to conducting DNA testing, PathWest scientists ran only four reference DNA samples: those collected from personal items belonging to Sarah Spiers, Jane Rimmer, Ciara Glennon and that collected from Lance Williams.

DNA in killer prevention: 'Burglars' DNA holds a key, say crime experts', *Post*, March 13, 2003.

Trevor Rimmer on police eggs in one basket: 'Killer still at large', *Sunday Times*, June 8, 2003.

Macro wound down: 'End of the line for Macro?', *Post*, April 24, 2004. *West Australian*, February 14, 2004.

Macro focus on Lance Williams: 'Serial killings review rejected', John Flint, *Sunday Times*, November 9, 2003.

18: Napper

Robin Napper's record: At the National Crime and Operations Faculty, Napper had been part of Operation Enigma, which in three years, 1995 to 1998, had reviewed, and solved, the majority of more than 230 cold-case homicides. Typical was one that Detective Superintendent Napper had chaired at Bramshill House, a full external examination that cracked the baffling murder mystery of Dr Joan Francisco, aged twenty-seven, in 1994. A spot of her killer's blood had been missed during the long police investigation because an officer had innocently folded the victim's T-shirt inside-out after it was 'seized' from the crime scene. Five years after the crime, a young civilian technician in the review room spotted on video the error everybody else had missed. The victim's ex-boyfriend Anthony Diedrick, thirty-nine, whose DNA matched the previously hidden blood spot, was jailed for life when found guilty of the murder, after Napper had left for Australia. 'Family wins fight to jail doctor's killer', *BBC News*, September 29, 1999.

Rita Knight case: The victim lived alone. Her forty-four-year-old lawnmower man Stephen James Boney returned at night as she slept, savagely bashing and sexually assaulting her. After he provided a DNA sample, his certainty of discovery from the DNA sweep led to his going to the local police station to confess to the crime. Boney had previously been sentenced to six years by an Orange Country Court judge for the 1984 sexual assault of a woman in her home, and acquitted by a jury of the rape of another woman in her home in 1981.

NSW cold cases listed as solvable by DNA comparison: Eleven by the 'Campsie rapist', four by the 'Newcastle rapist', two by the 'Galston Gorge rapist', a serious assault in Coffs Harbour, a laneway rape and murder in East Sydney, and four by the 'Central Coast rapist'. Napper won no friends when he pointed out that DNA comparison could have prevented the cold-blooded murder of two police officers in Melbourne. In Sydney in 1995, Donna Anne Hicks was murdered and samples containing her attacker's DNA were retained by police. But this DNA was not linked to serial killer and armed robber Bandali Michael Debs until 2000. In the meantime, Debs had become notorious for the 1998 murders of Victorian police officers Gary Silk and Rodney Miller. Debs was convicted of Donna Hicks' murder in 2011 and is serving four life sentences. His brother revealed that the Debs brothers were tortured as children, including being whipped with copper wire. 'Everyman serial killer Bandali Debs', *Herald Sun* (Melbourne), May 29, 2013.
Murder case to be reopened after 35 years: 'DNA bid to solve Wanda Beach murders', Warren Owens, *The Sunday Telegraph* (Sydney), January 4, 2000.
Mel Hay approach to Napper: 'Serial killings review rejected', *Sunday Times*, November 9, 2003.
Napper not setting out to embarrass Macro: 'Serial killings review rejected' and 'Police under forensic microscope', *Sunday Times*, November 9, 2003.
Claremont case is 'sorted': Napper interview with author, 2017.

19: He Who Waits

Wendy Page: The few Perth people who knew Wendy Page's pedigree were unsurprised at her steely determination to seek and tell the truth. Her father, Lieutenant Colonel Bill Brathwaite, was a legendary World War Two Z-Special Force commando and the founding commanding officer of the Special Air Service Regiment. West Australians are proud of 'their' SAS, the hardest of the hard soldiers, who are based in seaside Swanbourne, a few minutes' drive from the centre of Claremont. Some clues, SAS training and the nearby location of the regiment were to bring their members, too, under intense scrutiny in the hunt for the Claremont serial killer.
Robin Napper's Sutcliffe remarks: 'He Who Waits', *Australian Story*, ABC TV, February 9, 2004.
Pre-emptive strike: Assistant Commissioner Mel Hay's broadcast email pre-emptive strike and David Caporn on the new forensic review, 'Police defend Macro', Luke Morfesse, *The West Australian*, December 3, 2003.

20: Fuming

Liam Bartlett interview with Mel Hay: Morning show, ABC Local Radio, as reported in 'We will fly in experts: police', *Post*, February 14, 2004.

Disgusted Crime Stoppers caller: 'We will fly in experts: police', *Post*, February 14, 2004.

Police focus on getting a confession from a likely looking suspect: 'Napper keen for murder review to start', *Post*, February 21, 2004. Where evidence is lacking, focus on the wrong suspect has led some police to what those in the USA call 'railroading'. British cops call it 'fitting up' or 'framing', and in Australia it's 'loading up'. All around the world, shocking injustices have resulted when police have wrongly guessed a suspect's guilt and have 'loaded him up' with false evidence. See *Presumed Guilty*, Bret Christian, 2013.

Napper on external reviews: 'We will fly in experts: police', *Post*, February 14, 2004. That report ended with a police statement contradicting a front-page report in *The West Australian* that the Claremont deaths could be referred to the Coroner's Court within twelve to eighteen months. Assistant Commissioner Mel Hay said he had told the paper that he did not want to put a timeframe on any reference to the Coroner. Reference to the Coroner is an admission that all leads have been followed and exhausted.

Police push-back against Napper: 'Team points to critic's past: Claremont case review call has detectives fuming', *The West Australian*, February 14, 2004. The report said that criticism of Macro could boost the offender's confidence while it characterised Napper as a used-car salesman.

'Well-meaning outsiders': 'UK forensic expert for Claremont case', *Sunday Times*, February 15, 2004. It reported: 'Mr Napper said he was well aware he had made himself unpopular with a handful of officers and he claimed some had done their best to discredit him.'

Corruption at Claremont CIB office: 'Royal Commission Into Whether There Has Been Corrupt or Criminal Conduct By Any Western Australian Police Officer' final report, January 2004.

'Police lied in court': Also 'Police pick "lucky dip" from stolen goods' and 'Detectives shared cash, tortured suspects', *Post*, March 6, 2004.

Claremont murder investigation may be shelved: 'End of the line for Macro?', *Post*, April 24, 2004.

'If there's no evidence then we really have to move on': Commissioner Barry Matthews quoted in report 'Claremont killings taskforce may be disbanded', *The West Australian*, April 23, 2004.

21: Raids

Further raid on Lance Williams' flat and his parents' home: 'Mother's plea for peace', *Post*, April 24, 2004.
Weygers' public swipe at police: 'A parallel culture of corruption in the force', *Freedom Today*, Issue 18, April 2003.
Gary Narkle a sexual predator and psychopath: Justice Michael O'Sullivan's sentencing comments, 'Sex monster jailed for life', David Darragh, *The West Australian*, August 3, 2002.
Education minister Alan Carpenter accuses Weygers of making 'outrageous, ridiculous, disgraceful remarks': 'Carpenter in bitter attack on Weygers', *The West Australian*, April 28, 2004. 'Narkle defence horrific: Carpenter', *ninemsn.com.au*, April 29, 2004. 'Narkle branded a sex monster in Parliament', *The West Australian*, May 19, 2004.
Senior politician accuses Weygers of victim-blaming: Letter from John Day, Liberal Shadow Minister for Education, to Paul Albert, Director General, Department of Education and Training. It mirrored the words of an editorial in *The West Australian* on April 27, 2004: 'Freed Narkle a failure of legal system'. Day's letter was dated April 2004, but the day of the month was redacted by the department when released under Freedom of Information laws. In his reply on May 21, 2004, Education Minister Alan Carpenter said advice was being sought from the State Solicitor's Office with respect to comments made by Peter Weygers to the media. Weygers challenged the accuracy of some of the media reporting of his alleged statements. Day declined to withdraw his complaint after the Director of Public Prosecutions withdrew the charges against Narkle. 'Liberal MP sparked Weygers inquiry', *Post*, May 20, 2006.
Peter Weygers suspended from contact with children: 'Weygers faces sex complaints', *The West Australian*, April 27, 2004.
Weygers cleared of complaints, seniority re-instated: 'Weygers gets his job back', *Post*, November 17, 2012.
Narkle's record: Application to have Narkle declared a dangerous sexual offender, State of Western Australia v Narkle, Supreme Court of Western Australia, November 2019.
Vicki and Matthyas: The mother and son begged the author not to reveal their surnames, both saying they had been permanently traumatised by their experiences with police, media and the public. Matthyas eventually moved to a secret address.
Irwin Road search warrant details: Copy of search warrant executed on August 25, 2004. It noted that inquiries were to be directed to Detective Sergeant Crane.

Macro raid on house in Irwin Road: 'I told police about Sarah', Bret Christian, *Post*, August 28, 2004. 'Psychic link to Macro', Bret Christian, *Post*, September 11, 2004. Author interviews with Peter Weygers in 2004 and Matthyas in 2017.
Irwin Road raid reasons: 'New lead on Claremont killer sparks raid', *The West Australian*, August 26, 2004. See also 'New clues led to raid by police', *ninemsn.com.au*, August 27, 2004.
New information ... an important development in the eight-year-old case, quoting Police Commissioner Karl O'Callaghan: 'Break in Claremont killings', Paige Taylor, *The Australian*, August 27, 2004.
Holden or Ford?: When in 2008 a television company made a re-enactment of Ciara's last known sighting, the Holden wagon used in the shoot was blurred in an attempt to mask its make and model. Conspiracy theorists believed this left open the possibility that Steven Ross was involved.
Breakthrough items seized from Ross's two vehicles: 'Items of interest', *ABC News,* September 9, 2004.
Forensic examination of Steven Ross's two vehicles yielded items of interest: 'Psychic link to Macro', Bret Christian, *Post,* September 11, 2004.
Vigilantes: 'Psychic link to Macro', Bret Christian, *Post*, September 11, 2004.
Police intelligence: 'New clues led to raid by police', *ninemsn.com.au*, August 27, 2004. 'I told police about Sarah', Bret Christian, *Post*, August 28, 2004.

22: Circus

Ross account: Conversations with author and contents of his statuary declaration. 'Taxi man refused to give DNA', Luke Morfesse, *The West Australian*, August 27, 2004. But the police commissioner dashed Williams' hopes that the focus on Ross and Weygers let him off the hook. Asked if Williams was still the prime suspect, Commissioner Karl O'Callaghan said, 'That is still the case. We haven't changed that.' *Herald Sun*, September 24, 2004.
Police grill Ross: 'I'm being framed for murder', Paige Taylor and Amanda Banks, *The Australian,* September 23, 2004. 'Urban myth email fans Claremont killings fears', Amanda Banks, *The Australian*, September 27, 2004.
Grant Milner's account: Interview with author, September 2004.
Weygers' change of mind on DNA sampling: Weygers said police refused to say whether or not they had any DNA with which to

make a comparison. 'Police forced DNA sample', Bret Christian, *Post*, September 19, 2009.

Forced DNA sampling: Detective Sergeant Martin Crane's statement on forced DNA sampling under new identification laws reported by Australian Associated Press, September 16, 2004.

'Gross invasion': 'Macro raids Weygers' home', Bret Christian, *Post*, September 18, 2004.

Peter Weygers' forced DNA test and his account of arrest, search of home and Detective Sergeant Martin Crane's response: 'Weygers: It's body banditry', Bret Christian, *Post*, September 25, 2004. 'Police forced DNA sample', Bret Christian, *Post*, September 19, 2009.

Drugs in jails: Council for Civil Liberties members were angry when they learned that one of their senior members had leaked the tip-off to his political associate, the Minister for Police, Michelle Roberts. Weygers felt police might have found references to the drugs evidence when they seized the Civil Liberties computer and looked through Civil Liberties paperwork in the Embleton raid. (Matthyas interview with Bret Christian, 2017.) Years later, Weygers pointed to revelations of severe problems with drugs being smuggled into prisons by prison officers as evidence that confirmed the information from Civil Liberties had been leaked. '"Disturbing network" of corrupt guards, crime gangs smuggle drugs into WA jails: CCC', *WAtoday*, June 26 and 27, 2018. 'Corruption rife in jails', *The West Australian*, October 27–28, 2018.

Police raid on Killara: 'Macro raids Weygers' home', Bret Christian, *Post*, September 18, 2004. Details of the raid and its suggested links to the three Claremont murders were reported on television, radio and print throughout Australia and in many international news outlets, including:

'Claremont killer task force raids home of civil libertarian; Weygers forced to give DNA,' Luke Morfesse, *The West Australian*, September 17, 2004. It was published on that newspaper's front page and prominently in *The Australian*: 'Civil rights chief tested in killer hunt', Amanda Banks, September 17, 2004. Martin Crane was quoted in *The West Australian*'s September 17 report as saying: 'Mr Weygers is a person of interest in this investigation. It is a murder investigation that's unsolved after eight years.' The report said that Weygers had recently been driving the seized deregistered taxi used by a taxi driver who had had Sarah Spiers in his car the night before she disappeared.

See also 'Ex-mayor forced to give DNA sample', *The Advertiser* (Adelaide), September 16, 2004, and *The Sunday Mail* (Queensland),

September 17, 2004. 'Weygers "outraged" by police treatment', *ninemsn.com.au*, September 18, 2004. 'Ex-mayor called dead girl's dad', *The Courier-Mail* (Brisbane) and *The Advertiser* (Adelaide), September 17, 2004.

Police scrutiny on Ross: 'Taxi driver denies link to killings', *The Australian*, September 22, 2004. 'Cabbie denies link to Claremont killings', *The Sunday Mail* (Queensland) and *news.com.au*, September 23, 2004, and *Herald Sun* (Melbourne), September 24, 2004.

Police tackle rumours: 'Urban myth email fans Claremont killings fears', Amanda Banks, *The Australian*, September 27, 2004.

23: Psychic

'Claremont killer task force raids home of civil libertarian' and 'Weygers forced to give DNA': Luke Morfesse, *The West Australian*, September 17, 2004.

Weygers 'fled country': 'Weygers out of sight, may be out of country', *The West Australian*, September 20, 2004. 'Former mayor may have fled', *The Australian*, September 19, 2004, *The Advertiser* (Adelaide) and *The Courier-Mail* (Brisbane), September 20, 2004, and *news.com.au*, September 29, 2004. 'Weygers may have left country', *Sunday Times*, September 20, 2004. 'Weygers just laying low, says lawyer', *Herald Sun* (Melbourne), September 20, 2004. 'Weygers still in Perth: lawyers', Luke Eliot, *The West Australian*, September 21, 2004. He denied he was avoiding authorities and any involvement in the murders. 'Weygers in Perth says lawyer', *Perth Sunday Times* and *New Zealand Herald*, September 21, 2004.

Weygers profile: 'The many sides of Peter Weygers', Bret Christian and George Williams, *Post*, September 25, 2004.

'Closing in on a killer': Robert Wainwright', *Sydney Morning Herald*, September 25, 2004. Details were taken from that same weekend's *Post*.

'Lynch mob': Detlef Ullrich, letter to the editor, *The West Australian*, September 1, 2004.

Publicity about police raid on the house of an innocent man: The British High Court found against police and the BBC under Britain's privacy laws for identifying singer Cliff Richard in a search of his house. He, too, was not charged and was handed a big damages award. 'Cliff Richard wins £210,000 in damages over BBC privacy case', *The Guardian*, July 18, 2018. Weygers was advised that Western Australian law would not allow him to successfully sue.

Suicide pressure: 'Macro raids Weygers' home', *Post*, Bret Christian, September 18, 2004. 'Serial killer stress "may drive me to suicide"', Paige Taylor and Amanda Banks, *The Australian*, September 25–26, 2004. 'Weygers' suicide pressure', *Sunday Times*, September 26, 2004.

'Please keep up your articles connecting Peter Weygers and the taxi driver with the Claremont serial killings': Email to *Post*, September 2, 2004.
Psychic's advertisement: *The Vincent Times*, May 1996.
Broadcast email: Sent from the psychic woman to Minister for Education, Alan Carpenter, and leader of the opposition, Colin Barnett, on April 27, 2004. 'I believe all the information I am providing and all the allegations I am making against Peter Weygers are true and can be verified,' she wrote.
'No grudge': 'I'm not the loony trying to do things to him, I have no grudge against him other than to want a mass murderer off the streets,' the psychic woman wrote in an email to the author, September 8, 2004.
***Post* interview with psychic woman:** She claimed when interviewed that it was possible to impersonate her email address, even impersonating the author's own to demonstrate how it could be done. She said she was entitled to her opinions on Weygers.
Email accusing Weygers of murder: Allegations and a copy of the statement she made to police and the Education Department were sent to the author in a series of emails in 2004, dated September 6 and 8. Included was the suggestion that a taxi driver had abducted the women and delivered them to Weygers. The emails stated among other things: 'He's been allowed to get away with murder', 'someone has to stop him before there are other victims', 'at least the public should be aware of the animal that he is', and 'I have done it all through letters and phone calls to police after Jane went and again after I heard a third girl was missing'.

After publication of her allegations in the *Post* on September 11, 2004, the woman emailed the author that day to say it was a 'good article … now maybe something will get done'. On the day of the raid on Weygers' house Killara (September 16, 2004), she wrote, 'Are they finally onto him?'

She said her April 27, 2004 email sent to the Education Minister and leader of the opposition 'finally resulted in me being interviewed by the police Child Abuse Unit and an Education Department investigator'. These concerned allegations were separate to the Claremont murders, and later discredited.

'I had been contacting police since Jane Rimmer went missing,' she wrote in July 2007.

In an email to a third party (September 7, 2008) she claimed to have money, power, influence and powerful friends. On July 27, 2007, she wrote: 'I actually take credit for being the one who first drew attention to Weygers'. She also claimed credit for first describing Steven Ross as Weygers' delivery man.

In an email to the author, headed 'Weygers and Ross', September 17, 2004, she said: 'How dumb is this guy? How dumb are our cops? I believe that Ciara Glennon would be alive if police had done something when I first reported Weygers for his dealings with the underage student. I believe that the fact that my constant calls to Crime Stoppers & Macro & even my letter to Barry Matthews [Commissioner of Police] were not followed up & no-one ever contacted me for a statement about "Sally" (until about three months ago). Or about the girl in Claremont in the mid '90s or about my belief that Weygers was connected to the three missing or murdered girls … I knew him fairly closely when I was so close to Sally, especially when I was living with her. I think if he knows he's caught he will kill himself.'

Another email, headed 'New info', sent on the same date, said she had been contacted by the Education Department, who said she had told him about Weygers and Sally. Email to author, August 13, 2005: 'I am certain of my own first-hand psychic experiences, which I don't understand and can't explain, nor should I have to. I have had visitations from the dead, and that I know the details behind at least one major unsolved Perth crime because I spent a sleepless night talking to one of the victims.'

In a letter to the *Post*, 2008: 'I hope people like Bret Christian can learn tolerance for things that are above their level of understanding.'

'Explain that to the Glennon family': This comment was made on the Rodney Olsen blog, September 26, 2004. 'Some of us have been giving police & politicians information about him since there were only TWO Claremont victims, so explain that to the Glennon family, when Weygers is finally convicted,' she wrote.

Interview with a psychic: 'Why I was in the serial killer frame', *Post*, September 13, 2008.

Multiple names used by psychic: 'Psychic obsessed with Weygers', *Post*, October 10, 2008.

Martin Crane: Tip not from the psychic woman: 'Psychic link to Macro', *Post*, September 11, 2004.

Necessity to eliminate all persons of interest: Australian Associated Press, September 23, 2004.

Woman's 'intimate knowledge' of Weygers: 'Psychic link to Macro', *Post*, September 11, 2004. 'I see things,' the psychic said. 'You can't explain what people feel or see.'

Dangers of police and media working too closely together: 'Police are chasing the wrong people', *Post*, October 2, 2004.

'I'm being framed': Interview with author and written statement by Steven Ross, September 22, 2004.
Police want a taxi driver charged: 'I'm being framed for murder: cabbie', Paige Taylor and Amanda Banks, *The Australian*, September 23, 2004.
Police pressure Steven Ross: 'Police pressure "suspect" cabbie', Paige Taylor, *The Australian*, October 12, 2004. The report says police had been visiting Ross almost every morning since October 4, urging him to confess to being a 'delivery man' for the crimes and offering a lighter sentence for a confession.
Claremont Council raided: 'Documents seized from Claremont', *Post*, October 2, 2004. 'Police raid council in Claremont case', *news.com.au*, September 29, 2004, and *The Courier-Mail* (Brisbane), September 30, 2004.
Police seize their own documents: Post Newspapers P/Ls Freedom of Information Act 1992 Complaint – Town of Claremont, fourteen-page determination by D.A. Wookey, A/Information Commissioner, October 21, 2005. 'Why Macro raided Claremont Council', *Post*, October 29, 2005. Macro said that disclosure could allow the criminal to destroy evidence or create a false alibi.

24: Fresh Eyes

'Last roll of the dice in hunt for serial killer': Paige Taylor, *Weekend Australian*, November 6–7, 2004. 'Hopes rest with Claremont review', *The West Australian*, November 8, 2004.
Schramm review team visits Claremont: 'Murders under new microscope', Bret Christian, *Post*, November 13, 2004.
Predatory crimes: 'Team treads where murderer stalked', *Post*, November 20, 2004.
Non-threatening vehicle: 'New leads to Claremont killer', *Post*, December 11, 2004.
Julie Cutler's car within easy walking distance of Lance Williams' home: In June 2018, a reward of $250,000 was offered in the Julie Cutler case – an identical figure to that offered after Ciara Glennon was found murdered in 1997. The Cutler case was reopened by the Cold Case Homicide Squad in 2018, with a forensic dig at South Cottesloe Beach and a fresh appeal to the public. No arrest was made. The squad said then that Julie Cutler's disappearance had no connection with the Claremont murders. The renewed interest brought forward new information. 'Bouncer "admitted" murder', *Post*, December 1, 2018.
Margaret Dodd's anger at reward: Peter Weygers' diary note, 1999.

Wrongful convictions overturned by DNA and other scientific evidence: Since the US Innocence Project began examining false convictions using only DNA evidence in 1989, 367 people wrongfully convicted of serious crimes, including rape and murder, were exonerated as of May 2020. To 2018, the real perpetrators had gone on to commit forty-eight additional crimes, including twenty-five murders and fourteen rapes.
The British Criminal Cases Review Commission, set up in 1997 in response to a series of high-profile wrongful murder convictions, has had the courts hear 657 appeals to August 2019. Of these, 441 appeals succeeded.
Forensic samples the key: 'New leads to Claremont killer', *Post*, December 11, 2004. 'Murder team sifts new links', Bret Christian, *Post*, September 3, 2005.
David Barclay's and Malcolm Boots' takes in the review: 'New leads to Claremont killer', *Post*, December 11, 2004.
Pessimistic view cases would be solved: *The West Australian* said Police Commissioner Bob Falconer had indicated that the Claremont investigation would have to be disbanded and sent off to the Coroner for an inquest, signalling the end of the line after exhausting all leads. 'Bid to find Claremont killer gets more cops', *The West Australian*, September 1, 2005. 'Police focus back on serial killer', *The West Australian*, September 2, 2005.
Fibres overlooked: 'New leads to Claremont killer', Bret Christian, *Post*, December 11, 2004.
Macro marking its own homework: 'Serial killer inquiry gets thumbs-up by reviewers', Luke Morfesse and Torrance Mendez, *The West Australian*, December 3, 2004. This report predicted that the Schramm panel would find few faults with the eight-year inquiry.

It confirmed itself the next day under the headline 'Panel puts Weygers in the clear', *The West Australian*, December 4, 2004. Confusingly, despite the headline, it quoted Paul Schramm as saying 'there is justification to support that focus [on Lance Williams, Peter Weygers and Steven Ross]'.

In the words of the Macro Independent Review Panel media release, dated December 3, 2004: 'The panel has looked at all major persons of interest and, having done so, we agree that the work done by police on those individuals has been justified, Supt Schramm said.'
Lisa link: The *Post* also again made the Karrakatta connection in a front-page report: 'Falconio case echoes teenager's rape ordeal', Bret Christian, *Post*, December 21, 2005.
Barclay's detective work: Barclay told the author of a British crime scene where police had concluded the murderer had carried his victim

to a site above a lovers' lane car park, to sloping ground below an elevated golf course. Professor Barclay went to the scene in person. He knew immediately the detectives must be wrong – murderers carried bodies a maximum of twenty-five metres. He concluded the body must have been dropped from above, so he drove up to the entrance of the golf course and found that the gate padlock had been cut. Then he microscopically matched tool marks on the padlock with a pair of bolt-cutters found in a suspect's home. The owner of the bolt-cutters was convicted.

Scientists working in isolation: 'Police are making changes: crime expert', *Post*, September 9, 2006.

First public knowledge of 'Secret Annexure': 'Murder team sifts new links', Bret Christian, *Post*, September 3, 2005.

25: Special Crime

Steven Ross detained again: 'Macro hauls in taxi man', *Post*, December 29, 2004. 'I was on the way to a job and they arrested me last Thursday,' he confided. 'Cab driver: Police have proof I did not abduct Sarah Spiers', Steven Ross, letter to the editor, *Post*, June 4, 2016.

Macro disbanded: 'New squad takes over Macro case,' Luke Morfesse, *The West Australian*, September 2, 2005.

Election-losing serial killer slogan: 'Weygers seeks mayor's chair', *Post*, April 2, 2005.

Missing fibres, Dawson comment: 'Murder team sifts new links', *Post*, September 3, 2005.

Return of Barclay and birth of the Special Crime Squad: 'Murder team sifts new links', *Post*, September 3, 2005. 'Special Crime Squad's Anthony Lee looks ahead', *The West Australian*, January 21, 2006.

Barclay advises Special Crime Squad: 'David Barclay working as advisor in cold case Special Crime Squad', *Post*, July 29, 2006.

Andrew Mallard wins High Court appeal: Mallard v The Queen, High Court of Australia, November 2005.

Remarkable coincidences have led to wrongful convictions: John Button was at the scene of a fatal car-versus-pedestrian crash involving his fiancée, seconds after serial killer Eric Edgar Cooke had departed. Victim Rosemary Anderson, aged seventeen, and Button, aged nineteen, had had an argument; his car was damaged and her blood was on his car. Appeal judges originally sneered at defence claims as 'the miracle' and said that such coincidences 'beggared belief'. But it was true. Police had charged and a jury had convicted the wrong man. Appeal decision: Button v The Queen, High Court of Australia, February 2002. For more on the subject of coincidence, see *Presumed Guilty*, Bret Christian, 2013.

Andrews Mallard's release in 2006: He was still not off the hook. Director of Public Prosecutions Robert Cock added that Mallard remained the prime suspect for the murder, and if more evidence emerged, he could still be prosecuted.

Rochford's unusual weapon: It was fashioned from a length of broom handle and a steel collar that had retained weights on a weightlifter's barbell. Police lost it after Rochford's trial for the murder of Brigitta Dickens, and did not find it until 2013, when it was conclusively matched to the wounds in Pamela Lawrence's skull. David Weber, *ABC News*, September 11, 2015.

Corruption and Crime Commission hearings: Its Mallard report had the not-so-succinct title: 'Report on the inquiry into alleged misconduct by public officers in connection with the investigation of the murders of Mrs Pamela Lawrence, the prosecution and appeals of Mr Andrew Mark Mallard and other related matters', delivered October 7, 2008.

Barclay's evidence in Mallard CCC review: 'Expert raps Mallard police', *Post*, November 24, 2007.

Prosecutor Bates fined: The police report that prosecutor Ken Bates failed to disclose to the court would have alerted the jury that Pamela Lawrence's injuries had not been consistent with the spanner Mallard had sketched for police during his interrogation when asked to speculate about the murder weapon, according to the CCC report.

David Caporn, appointed to Macro in 1996, Mal Shervill and three other officers were stood down on full pay to have the opportunity to respond to the CCC's allegations and its recommendations that the police commissioner take disciplinary action against the two assistant commissioners.

Mallard's fate: Andrew Mallard was awarded $3.25 million in compensation in 2008. He had served twelve years in jail for a crime he did not commit. The compensation was classified as an ex gratia or 'act of grace' payment, described by the state's then attorney-general, Christian Porter, as a gift. Mallard was able to travel the world without working. He was crossing Sunset Boulevard, California, in the early hours of April 18, 2019, when he was struck and killed by the car of a hit-run driver.

26: Smear

'Civil liberties chief interviewed as part of Rayney murder inquiry': Phillipa Perry and Sean Cowan, *The West Australian*, January 12, 2008.

Weygers questioned over Rayney murder: 'Calls smeared Weygers', Bret Christian, *Post*, February 2, 2008. When the detectives asked Weygers to provide a DNA sample and fingerprints, he reminded them that they already had a sample, which had been taken from him forcibly in 2004. If they had had Rayney's killer's DNA, they would have compared samples before visiting him, he believed.
Twelve-year delay in releasing footage: Police Commissioner Karl O'Callaghan joined the public chorus demanding explanation as to why the footage had been withheld from public view. 'Senior police grilled over video', *The West Australian*, August 19, 2008. The decision was criticised by Jenni Rimmer; the leader of the opposition, Colin Barnett; Lance Williams' mother; and, later, the state's premier. 'Mum queries tactics', *Sunday Times*, August 17, 2008.
Mystery man was not Lance Williams: 'Let's hope it's not another costly bungle', Colleen Egan, *Sunday Times*, August 17, 2008. The writer asked whether the video had not been shown publicly because its subject looked nothing like the prime suspect.
Burger Boys describe Holden station wagon: 'Murder suspect drove Holden wagon', *Post*, August 30, 2008. The report quoted Major Crime Detective Superintendent Jeff Byleveld as saying it was not clear whether or not the wagon was a taxi, and that witness accounts of it could not be confirmed.
Collie murder: Twelve-year-old Lisa Mott disappeared from the main street of Collie in 1980. A man in a yellow panel van was sighted nearby. Serial killer David Birnie was in the area at the time and drove a yellow panel van. That mystery remains unsolved.
Vehicle blurred in Claremont re-enactment: 'Murder doco cleared me, says cab driver', *Post*, September 6, 2008. Steven Ross pointed out his car at the time was a Ford Falcon station wagon, not a Holden. His car was registered and fully identified as a taxi at the time Ciara vanished.

27: Breakthrough

Exhibits trail: In 2002 and 2003, the Western Australian Police transitioned from its Property Tracing System (PTS) to a new electronic case management system called the Incident Management System (IMS). The Special Crime Squad used a third system called Viper. Exhibits stored from old cases were first trucked from police headquarters to a storage warehouse in Midland, east of Perth, and then to another warehouse in suburban Belmont.
Sergeant Paton on testing: Evidence of Senior Sergeant George Paton to State of Western Australia v Bradley Robert Edwards, Supreme Court of Western Australia, March 23, 2020.

Force promotes transfer: Evidence of Dr Jonathan Whitaker to State of Western Australia v Bradley Robert Edwards, Supreme Court of Western Australia, March 9, 2020.
Sensitive testing: Low-copy-number (LCN) DNA profiling was developed in 1999 in response to the infamous case of James Hanratty, hanged in Britain in 1962 for a 1961 lovers' lane rape and gunshot murder. A long campaign to prove Hanratty was innocent of the crime came undone when LCN proved his semen was on the rape victim's underpants, still held in police storage.

Dr Whitaker had travelled to Darwin in 2005 to give crucial LCN evidence at the trial of Bradley John Murdoch, who was convicted of the abduction and murder of British backpacker Peter Falconio on a deserted road in the Northern Territory in 2001. Dr Whitaker had identified Murdoch's DNA, mainly from small traces trapped in adhesive tape Murdoch wrapped around the cable ties used to tie up Falconio's girlfriend, Joanna Lees, and from Murdoch's blood on Joanna's T-shirt.

Whitaker is also an expert in familial DNA searching, using computer databases to test criminals' DNA and find their possible relatives, a technique that detectives on the Claremont case also used.

28: Medical Error

Williams in a 'terrible state': 'Claremont police ruined our lives: suspect's mum', Ronan O'Connell, *The West Australian*, August 20, 2008.
Jim Williams interview: 'Cleared suspect won't sue', Bret Christian, *Post*, November 29, 2008.
Weygers too old: The average age for serial killers to begin murder is 27.5 years. (Data from a survey of 399 serial killers, quoted in *Serial Murderers and Their Victims*, Eric Hickley, Wadsworth Publishing, 1997.) Eric Edgar Cooke, the serial killer who prowled Claremont and surrounding suburbs in the late 1950s and early 1960s, committed his first attempted murder when he was aged twenty-seven years and six months.

The age anomaly and the publicity did not stop most citizens believing in the guilt of Williams and Weygers. They went on believing it for many more years.
John Quigley's speech: Parliamentary attack on the identification of Lance Williams as suspect, Legislative Assembly, Hansard, November 27, 2008.
Caporn's response: Report on persons adversely referred to in the Legislative Assembly, Procedure and Privileges Committee Report No. 3, presented to the Legislative Assembly on March 12, 2009.

Saathoff on Rayney case: During his 2007 visit, Dr Saathoff's advice was also enlisted by the lead detectives investigating the murder of Corryn Rayney, a case where the lead detective had publicly named her husband, barrister Lloyd Rayney, as the prime and only suspect three years prior to his arrest. Police notes of the 2007 meeting with Dr Saathoff, presented at Lloyd Rayney's 2012 trial that emphatically found him not guilty, read: 'meeting with Dr Saathoff cemented our thoughts and perception of person of interest Lloyd Rayney, and also firming the house at Como [the Rayney family home] as the place Corryn was killed'. In acquitting Rayney, Justice Brian Martin and later the Court of Appeal found there was no evidence for either assertion. State of Western Australia v Lloyd Patrick Rayney, Supreme Court of Western Australia, November 1, 2012.

Lloyd Rayney sued for defamation and was awarded damages and compensation for economic losses. The defamation trial judge, Supreme Court Justice John Chaney, was especially critical of those police officers giving evidence in court ten years after the murder, saying these police had continued to express opinions about Rayney's guilt despite two court acquittals. Justice Chaney found that police had 'formed a prejudicial view' of Rayney and there were not reasonable grounds to suspect him of killing his wife.

Rayney lodged an appeal against the amount of economic losses, originally claiming a total of $11 million. Rayney v State of Western Australia, Supreme Court of Western Australia, December 2017. In February 2018, the state paid Rayney $2.62 million for damages and economic losses, plus his legal costs.

Wormian bones: Evidence of Drs Alanah Buck and Clive Cooke to State of Western Australia v Bradley Robert Edwards, Supreme Court of Western Australia, late January 2020. Dr Buck said in evidence that the skulls of many people in the courtroom that day would show that feature.

Professor Barclay says two autopsies are essential: 'Police are making changes: crime expert', *Post*, September 9, 2006.

Grave robber: In 2005, Clayton Daniels was sentenced to thirty years for insurance fraud, arson and desecration of a cemetery. *Playing Dead, True Tales of Fake Suicides*, Wendy Lewis, Five Mile Press, 2014.

Autopsy errors: 'Eight years of hell to bring killer to justice', *The Australian*, January 13–14, 2018. A 2009 autopsy on the body of Lainie Coldwell, who died in Charleville, Queensland, concluded that her death was due to a fall from a ladder. When the case was reopened, two specialist forensic pathologists said death was more likely to have been caused by a blow to the head. A household iron was the suspected murder weapon. Coldwell's husband was convicted of his wife's murder.

Dr Margolius's opinion was also questioned by two international pathologists in the notorious Western Australian case in which three men were jailed for killing Phillip Walsham, aged nineteen, by throwing him off a freeway overpass. Dr Margolius's courtroom evidence was that Walsham's injuries were consistent with a fall from the overpass. Contrary opinions presented to an appeal were that Walsham was a pedestrian struck by a hit-and-run vehicle, because he had two distinct sets of injuries, said to be from contact with the vehicle and then the road. The three men were acquitted on appeal on other evidence. 'What really happened to poor Phillip Walsham?', Bret Christian, *Post*, July 14, 2007.

Over the border in South Australia, Henry Keogh spent twenty years in jail after he was wrongfully convicted of the drowning murder of his fiancée, Anna-Jane Cheney, in 1994, partly on the evidence of Dr Colin Manock, who conducted the only autopsy on the deceased woman. Keogh's conviction was overturned in 2014 after a successful appeal at which Dr Manock's evidence was disputed by two other pathologists. Keogh was released, and a scheduled retrial did not proceed. Keogh received $2.5 million in compensation. Networked Knowledge and Flinders University Miscarriage of Justice Program, *ABC News*, July 2, 2018.

29: Hit

Serial killers who paused then killed again: Fred and Rosemary West, Britain's notorious House of Horrors rapists and serial murderers, waited long periods between their twelve known murders, stretching from 1967 to 1987, in one period pausing for nine years.
Bundy's record: Theodore 'Ted' Bundy (1946–89) eventually admitted to more than thirty sexually motivated murders, which included instances of necrophilia, of young women across seven US states between 1974 and 1978. *The Stranger Beside Me: The Shocking Inside Story of Serial Killer Ted Bundy*, Ann Rule, Gallery Books, 2009. *Conversations with a Killer: The Ted Bundy Tapes*, Netflix International, 2019.
Müller on serial killers: Dr Thomas Müller at the International Justice Conference, Perth, March 9–11, 2012.
Napper on arsonists: Robin Napper interview with author, May 15, 2018.
Garrett on serial killers: *ABC News* (USA), April 27, 2018. Brad Garrett was speaking after the arrest in California of an ex-police officer charged with being the Golden State Killer. Joseph James DeAngelo, 72, was accused of committing twelve murders, at least

fifty sadistic rapes and multiple home burglaries in the 1970s and 1980s. He pleaded guilty in July 2020 and was sentenced to life in jail without parole.

30: Blue Graphite

Premier Barnett on serial killer tip: 'I don't precisely remember but the Minister for Police often told me things.' Author interview with Colin Barnett, 2018.

Screen-printing clue and renewed search for source of cord: 'Serial killer squad in printer probe', Bret Christian, *Post*, April 14, 2011.

Fibres in Jane Rimmer's and Ciara Glennon's hair: International fibre expert Dr Ray Palmer later gave evidence that the fibres discovered were only remnants of those that would have originally been in the victims' hair. Typically, eighty per cent of fibres would have been lost in the first two hours, he said. The length of time Jane's body had lain undiscovered could account for a discrepancy in the fibre populations, with far fewer fibres found in her hair than in Ciara's. Evidence of Dr Palmer to State of Western Australia v Bradley Robert Edwards, Supreme Court of Western Australia, April 30, 2020.

31: Supra

Supra process: In order to separate Supra team members from other police work, exclusive passes to the clean room were issued to Special Crime Squad members – they had their own parking area and entrance.

Corruption at Claremont CIB office: 'Royal Commission Into Whether There Has Been Corrupt or Criminal Conduct By Any Western Australian Police Officer' final report, January 2004.

Unrelated cold cases solved: The trawl through old sex cases locked up a surprised Air Asia pilot for the rape of a young woman sleeping in her bed in suburban Perth. He had been arrested in the USA for attacking a woman in a university toilet cubicle, then paroled. He was DNA-tested when he breached parole by ejaculating on the hair of a woman in a library at another American university. His DNA went on the USA national database. After State Operations from Western Australia sent crime-scene DNA worldwide and got a hit, the pilot was arrested for the Western Australian rape when he landed his aircraft at Sydney airport.

Truck driver Darren Atkinson was also trapped by Supra's work: 'Brutal Perth rapist Darren Robert Atkinson has jail term reduced', *Daily Telegraph*, August 17, 2017.

32: Jackhammer

Breakthrough report: 'Fourth serial killer victim', Bret Christian, *Post*, October 17, 2015.

Report by Paige Taylor: 'Serial killer cold-case breakthrough', Paige Taylor, *The Australian,* October 17–18, 2015.

Attempted rape of drunk young woman: 'Kidnapped teen in Claremont attack', Bret Christian, *Post,* November 14, 2015.

Car and handcuff cord details: 'Two new clues to serial killer', Bret Christian, *Post* December 5, 2015.

Coerced into car: 'Teen lured into Claremont car', Bret Christian, *Post,* December 22, 2015.

Jack van Tongeren: After his release in 2002, he was charged in 2003 for yet more alleged arson plots and firearms offences. During his trial on these charges, he collapsed in court. He ended up confined to a wheelchair and was eventually moved interstate.

Huntingdale home invasion: The attack on the sleeping teenager was reported at the time. Police had called a media conference because they believed the same man could have been responsible for the murder of Victoria Clark in her home. *ABC News*, February 16, 1988. 'Kimono clue may solve brutal killing', Cyril Ayris, *The West Australian*, February 16, 1988.

Victoria Clark's murder was reported in September 1987. In 1998, David Troy Masters was charged with her murder and pleaded guilty. He had previously been convicted of murdering Fiona Carty.

Stolen silk kimono: 'Nightie rapist stalks suburb,' Bill Power, *Daily News*, February 17, 1988. The report stated that a tall, lanky man who wears women's nighties and was extremely fit was terrorising Huntingdale, 'so brazen he sometimes stands on the road in a nightie waving at women looking out of their windows'. He collected women's nightwear and underwear from clotheslines and from the owners' bedrooms, the report said.

Southside crimes: *ABC News* broadcast two reports on the Southside Rapist, plus a report on the home invasion titled 'Kimono Assault', broadcast on February 16, 1988. The summary reads: 'Attempted assault on young girl in Huntingdale home. Offender escapes but drops distinctive kimono at scene, crime is handed to taskforce investigating murder of Vicki Clark.'

Attack on Hollywood Hospital grief counsellor: Evidence of Wendy Davis to State of Western Australia v Bradley Robert Edwards, December 3, 2019, and Wendy Davis interview with author, September 2, 2020.

Reported crimes around the time of the Hollywood Hospital assault: In one issue of the *Post* that year, September 4, 1990, the paper reported five counts of indecent assault on young boys in local parks, and other local crimes including wilful exposure, thefts and burglaries.

A man was arrested and charged with five counts of indecent assault on women around Claremont 'Arrest in lake assault cases', *Post*, September 18, 1990. The same edition reported a rapidly rising crime rate in Claremont and Cottesloe. 'Crime rate soars to 10 a day,' *Post*, September 18, 1990.

33: Sprite

Shouting 'killer' from cars: This November 2016 incident occurred outside one of the many rental properties Weygers owned, this one in Armstrong Road in the suburb of Wilson.

Weygers' tale of woe spilled out when the *Post* interviewed him over the Irwin Road incident. Such incidents had driven him and Vicki to lead an isolated life, spending much of their spare time together tending to the investment houses or collecting household goods for charity.

'The police and press publicly lynched me,' Weygers said at the time. 'I've gone from being a mayor who was welcomed into Claremont homes while out doorknocking, even at ten at night, to being a serial killer scapegoat, based on what? "Reasonable suspicion"? Reasonable suspicion is no more than a hunch. You can't ruin someone's life on a hunch. But they did. Now I have no other life.'

He said he had decided against joining his old classmates for the fifty-fifth-year reunion of his final year at Christ Church Grammar School, a year from which many graduates had gone on to glittering careers. 'I'm not going. Nobody will talk to me. No one stood up for me, and now I guess they are embarrassed. They are too scared. I've endured the silence of the good people.'

Weygers calls O'Callaghan 'Dirty Harry': 'Dirty Harry' Callahan is the fictional San Francisco police officer who street-executed criminals in a series of 1970s and 1980s movies starring Clint Eastwood.

According to Weygers, Dr O'Callaghan replied that he recalled the raid on an Irwin Road house, but said the Major Crime Squad had been responsible for that investigation.

O'Callaghan said he did not wish to comment on the encounter. The publicity shot was to illustrate a report 'Lost kid to baby killer', on the front page of *The West Australian*, November 19–20, 2016.

'Weygers confronts O'Callaghan', Bret Christian *Post*, November 26, 2016. 'You ruined my life: Ex-POI in Claremont serial killing

confronts WA top cop', *WAtoday*, November 25, 2016. 'Weygers calls top cop "Dirty Harry"', *Perth Now*, November 25, 2016.
Ciara's restaurant job: Friend's conversation with author, 2017.

34: Bogeyman

West Coast Eagles blog posting: 'Man behind the mystery,' John Flint, *Sunday Times*, January 1, 2017.
Film reviews: *Forced Entry* is a pornographic film, described by Rccarts Movies Erotica as 'a disturbing piece of hardcore, made by and for some very disturbed people'. *Adult Industry News* called it 'a borderline snuff film'. Prosecutor Carmel Barbagallo called it in court 'pornography that is extreme, neither beige nor vanilla'. 'Edwards challenges porn at murder trial', Bret Christian, *Post*, February 16, 2019.
Fibres unique to Holden Commodore VS: Evidence of former senior Holden engineer Craig Porritt to State of Western Australia v Bradley Robert Edwards, Supreme Court of Western Australia, April 2, 2020.
Matches of fibres: Evidence of ChemCentre scientist Rees Powell to State of Western Australia v Bradley Robert Edwards, Supreme Court of Western Australia, mid-April 2020.
Car seized: 'Fibre tests key to trial', David Cohen, *Post*, February 2, 2019.
Don Spiers' interview on Edwards' arrest: Nine News (Perth), January 20, 2017.
Claremont's reaction to Edwards' arrest: 'Emotions erupt after arrest', *Post*, December 31, 2016.

35: Satan

David Caporn's post-Edwards-arrest interview: 'Ex-cop defends serial killer probe', *The West Australian*, December 26, 2016.
Bradley Edwards' volunteer work fêted: 'Man behind the mystery', John Flint, *Sunday Times*, January 1, 2017.
Suspect played on the same football team as Special Crime detective: 'Hiding in plain sight,' John Flint, *Sunday Times*, November 24, 2019.
Suspect vomiting from too much beer: Central Crocs unofficial newsletter, undated.
Bundy confides to Michaud: *Conversations with a Killer: The Ted Bundy Tapes*, Netflix International, 2019.
Bradley Edwards innocent: 'He's my brother & he's no killer', *The West Australian*, March 2–3, 2019.
Search for Toyota with square headlights: 'Hunt for car and Sarah continues', David Cohen, *Post*, February 24, 2018.

Edwards in jail: Hakea Prison visitor conversation with author, 2017.
Ross at Edwards' court appearance: In July 2015, staff at a Perth hospital contacted detectives about a patient who was doing a lot of talking, a man who seemed to know too much about the movements of Sarah Spiers at around the time she had disappeared. Two detectives visited the man – taxi driver Steven Ross – in hospital and, for the first time, according to him, took a real interest in the man who he said had got into his taxi with the passenger he believed had been Sarah Spiers.

Ross was recovering from having his left leg amputated, and he had had a heart attack while in hospital. He would never again drive a taxi.

'I first offered them this information twenty years ago,' he said then. 'Fortunately, I have an alibi for the night she disappeared, the night after she got into my cab. But I can't prove it because the police won't give me my radio call computer records for that night.'

Ross was to offer further information about his alleged taxi passenger 'Sarah Spiers' in a letter published in the *Post*, May 26, 2016.

36: Marriages

Murder indictments: The murder indictments read: 'On or about 27 January 1996 at Claremont and elsewhere, Bradley Robert Edwards wilfully murdered Sarah Jane Spiers.

'On or about 9 June 1996 at Claremont and elsewhere, Bradley Robert Edwards wilfully murdered Jane Louise Rimmer.

'On or about 15 March 1997 at Claremont and elsewhere, Bradley Robert Edwards wilfully murdered Ciara Eilish Glennon.'
'Judge alone' trial decision: Justice Michael Corboy, State of Western Australia v Bradley Robert Edwards, Supreme Court of Western Australia, heard and decided November 1, 2018, published April 30, 2019.
Reasoning principles: Occam's razor says, roughly, the correct answer is the one requiring the least number of assumptions. The Texas sharpshooter fallacy warns against the human tendency to see patterns where none exist: a cowboy takes hundreds of random shots at a barn, then paints a target around the tightest group of bullet holes.
Witness testimony: Former wives and lovers of Edwards, as well as surviving victims and others, have no names in this story because of strict suppression orders made by the judge.

37: First-hand

Propensity argument: The introduction of propensity evidence flowed directly from the Gary Narkle case that had brought a barrage of adverse publicity onto the head of Peter Weygers.

The 2005 changes 'all arose out of the Gary Narkle case where the complainant had declined to give evidence', said Jim McGinty, the state attorney-general who introduced the changes. Interview with author, July 21, 2020.

DNA protocols in the 1990s: Most police officers at the time would have been amazed to learn what invisibly lurked on the skin, hair and clothing of the Claremont victims – in their hair and person: a total of 4501 items, including DNA.

It had been eight years since the Colin Pitchfork case in England. He was convicted in 1988 for the murders of two fifteen-year-old girls in 1983 and 1986, the first ever on DNA evidence. DNA was routinely being used in the state for identification in the 1990s.

Contamination headlines: 'Huge DNA blow to prosecution case', 'The seven DNA errors that could derail the trial', and 'Claremont DNA farce: How SEVEN blunders at lab could derail trial of the century', *The West Australian*, February 27, 28 and 29, 2020.

38: Climax

Car puzzle: One of the three young men, Mark Laidman, who saw Sarah leaning on a bollard in Stirling Road, Claremont, had looked back at the car believed to have picked her up. He said it looked like the Mazda 808 owned by his friend. Mazda 808s and Toyota Camrys have identical square headlights.

Impossible to determine sexual attack: Evidence of retired PathWest scientist Martin Blooms to State of Western Australia v Bradley Robert Edwards, Supreme Court of Western Australia, February 4, 2020. Analysing material recovered from them 'doesn't help me one way or another', he said in evidence.

Scream theory: 'Case could hinge on screams', *Post*, December 21, 2019.

The victims who had escaped from Ted Bundy had all fought and screamed.

Underpants DNA: Document tendered during cross-examination of New Zealand DNA expert SallyAnn Harbison, State of Western Australia v Bradley Robert Edwards, Supreme Court of Western Australia, early February 2020.

40: Unforgiven

'He was just standing there silent': *Don't Make a Fuss: It's only the Claremont Serial Killer* by Wendy Davis © 2022 Fremantle Press. In her book, Davis writes that society had conspired to deter women, including her, from 'making a fuss', in cases such as the attack on her by Edwards.

Afterword

Death of Lance Williams: Interview with Lance Williams' parents, Jim and Norma Williams: 'No apology for life wreck', David Cohen, *Post*, February 10, 2018.
Jim Williams: Jim did not live to see Edwards convicted. He died suddenly two years before the verdict.
No compensation for Lance Williams: 'Compo call for cleared suspect', Grant Taylor, *The West Australian*, October 19, 2015. In Western Australia, the law entitles compensation from police only if it is proved they acted maliciously towards the claimant. Awards in other circumstances are ex gratia, any award and the amount depending entirely on the grace and favour of politicians.

Acknowledgments

Just as it takes a village to raise a child, it took a village to nurture this tome.

Well over 200 real people are named in *Stalking Claremont*, many of who will never forget the things they should never have had to face.

Special thanks to Jenni, Trevor and Lee Rimmer, Denis Glennon and Don Spiers for their forthright insights.

I'm eternally grateful to the talented, dogged Post Newspapers staff, past and present, whose work I plundered – George Williams, Kathryn Shine, Nelli Noakes, Paige Taylor, Jen Cunniffe, Layla Tucak, David Cohen and Hugo Timms, plus photographers Michelle Stanley, Paul McGovern and Belinda 'Billie' Fairclough. My thanks also to the army of reporters on other publications, electronic and print, who have covered this story over the past twenty-five years and produced so much fine work.

Special thanks are due to the sources, official and non-official, who filled in the puzzling but crucial gaps in public knowledge that previously existed in the Claremont investigation.

Along this journey, 'book friends' offered fresh eyes and made invaluable suggestions. Thanks to *Post* sub-editor Lesley Zampatti, and journalists Kim Christian and Bonnie Christian.

Bruce Burke, my lawyer, mentor and friend, was as insightful as ever.

Jude McGee, publisher at HarperCollins Australia, had the foresight to conceive this book years ago, then steered it to publication with a shrewd, steady hand. Her talented and ever-patient colleague Rachel Dennis, senior editor, made crucial suggestions, knocked off the rough edges and made it all cogent.

Finally, thanks, love and apologies to my long-suffering family, especially Jane, who once again stoically endured life as a book widow.